SOUTH CAROLINA NEWSPAPERS

Compiled and edited by

JOHN HAMMOND MOORE

Published by the
UNIVERSITY OF SOUTH CAROLINA PRESS

In cooperation with the
THOMAS COOPER LIBRARY

Columbia, South Carolina

COPYRIGHT © UNIVERSITY OF SOUTH CAROLINA 1988

Published in Columbia, South Carolina by the
University of south Carolina Press

Manufactured in the United States of America

LIBRARY OF CONGRESS
Library of Congress Cataloging-in-Publication Data

Moore, John Hammond.
     South Carolina newspapers / compiled and edited by John Hammond Moore.
        p.   cm.
     Bibliography: p.
     Includes index.
     ISBN 0-87249-567-1
        1. American newspapers—South Carolina—Bibliography—Union lists.
     2. South Carolina—Periodicals—Bibliography—Union lists.
     3. Catalogs, Union—South Carolina.   I. Title.
     Z6952.S7M66 1988
     [PN4897. S63]
     015.757035—dc 19   88-4779
                                                                              CIP

CONTENTS

FOREWORD

Were it not for the cooperation of scores of librarians, editors, and publishers throughout the state of South Carolina, the conscientious effort of Cynthia K. Waters and David Lowder (who prepared this material for the University of South Carolina Press), and the persistence and faith of a handful of individuals, among them, Kenneth E. Toombs, Elizabeth Ann Lange, Augustus T. Graydon, Jr., and Betty E. Callaham, you would not hold this book in your hands. The goals of the South Carolina Newspaper Project that produced this volume were three in number: a capsule history of each and every newspaper published in this state during the past two-and-one-half centuries (1732-1987), a guide to the location of files of those publications, if any exist, and a summary listing of out-of-state and foreign newspaper collections to be found in libraries and museums in the Palmetto State. I hope these objectives have been achieved.

J. H. M.

PREFACE

The story of efforts to develop a comprehensive guide to the files of newspapers held within the state of South Carolina is almost as complex as the drift toward separate political status in December 1860. And, at times, it seemed as if the outcome might be similar. Nevertheless--both with and without and *despite* federal cooperation--that goal has been realized.

In 1975 the National Endowment for the Humanities (NEH) launched a program to revise and update Winifred Gregory's well-known newspaper bibliography, a scheme spearheaded by the Organization of American Historians (OAH) and the Library of Congress. This led to various regional meetings, including one held at the University of South Carolina on April 4, 1977, attended by local historians, librarians, and other interested individuals, as well as the director of the newly-formed National Newspaper Project and the acting microfilm coordinator of the Library of Congress. Still more sessions followed from time to time, and three years later in June 1980 an NEH official said South Carolina soon would get funding for the first phase of its newspaper project. However, the following month yet another NEH spokesman indicated that guidelines for state grants were incomplete and any decision concerning awards would have to await publication of a newspaper cataloging manual then being prepared by the Library of Congress.

Meanwhile, inspired by the vision conjured up by Washington officialdom and frustrated by concomitant delays, Dr. Perry Ashley of the University of South Carolina's College of Journalism began compiling a county-by-county listing of all of the newspapers ever published in the Palmetto State. With the aid of students, over a four-year period, he put together a 668-page reference book or "checklist" of South Carolina newspapers through two-and-one-half centuries. This work, completed in the fall of 1980, obviously was an important step forward and went far toward demonstrating this state's deep commitment to the undertaking proposed by the Endowment five years earlier.

In 1981 the first edition of the long-awaited cataloging manual (since that time revised and much enlarged) finally appeared. Its purpose was to detail how to prepare information on individual newspapers for entry into the CONSER data base. The CONSER (Conversion of Serials) Program is a cooperative effort to construct a body of information utilizing OCLC in Dublin, Ohio. In August of the following year NEH grants enabled six so-called national depositories to begin work on their holdings, and three months later NEH invited individual states to apply for planning grants, the initial step leading to an in-depth analysis of newspaper files.

South Carolina's application for a planning grant was at first rejected and then, after changes were made to overcome NEH objections, approved. (It might be noted that the original OAH-Library of Congress request for funds in 1974, although much larger, had to jump through similar hoops.) With approval, Kenneth E. Toombs, who was leading the struggle to launch this research effort, asked Dr. John Hammond Moore to oversee the planning stage. Toombs, director of libraries for the University of South Carolina, also assembled a sixteen-member advisory committee to assist in obtaining support state-wide.

This group, representing a varied spectrum of interests, included Davy-Jo Ridge, associate director of University of South Carolina libraries and Elizabeth Ann Lange, assistant director for technical services; State Librarian Betty E. Callaham; John H. Landrum, director of reader services for the South Carolina State Library; Dr. Allen Stokes, director of the South Caroliniana Library; Dr. Walter B. Edgar, director of the Institute for Southern Studies; Dr. Perry Ashley of the College of Journalism; State Archivist Charles E. Lee; Dr. Reid Montgomery, director of the South Carolina Press Association; Paul Dove, president of the South Carolina Library Association; Augustus T. Graydon, Jr., executive secretary of the State-Record Foundation; Dr. Robert King of the University of South Carolina Press; Dr. Leland Cox, executive secretary of the South Carolina Committee on the Humanities; Catherine E. Sadler of the Charleston Library Society; Gene Waddell, director of the South Carolina Historical Society; and William D. Workman, Jr., veteran newsman, writer, and editor.

At last it seemed that something might happen. During the fall of 1983, Moore, who compiled and edited a guide to research materials in this state published by the University of South Carolina Press in 1967, proceeded to anaylze the scope of the proposed undertaking. He also generated interest in the newspaper project throughout the state, a campaign that culminated in a gathering of over one hundred and fifty individuals from all parts of South Carolina in Columbia in December of that year.

In succeeding weeks the results of all of this planning and coordination were forwarded to NEH. Close upon the heels of this information followed an official application for funds to begin work on the South Carolina Newspaper Project. Several months later this application was turned down and, unlike earlier decisions from Washington, was not reversed. Virtually all other states seeking funds for phase two enjoyed a similar fate during the spring of 1984. Admittedly, the National Endowment made it patently clear that a planning grant carried with it no assurance of further funding. Yet, at the same time, NEH officials insisted that planning *must* provide proof of widespread local interest in the proposal being put forth, thus raising not unreasonable expectations among rank-and-file individuals.

In any case, it left those at the state level with mixed feelings as they tried to explain the situation to friends and associates.

In the midst of this pall of disappointment, Kenneth Toombs and Elizabeth Ann Lange made a fateful decision: the work of previous months, even years, somehow had to be salvaged. In effect, they decided to return to the OAH-Library of Congress plan of the early 1970s--an updating and expansion of the South Carolina section of Gregory's compendium, minus the CONSER requirements that had been grafted onto that original proposal. Subsequent consultation with several members of the advisory committee indicated resolve to proceed, even without NEH assistance. And, by the late summer of 1984 the pieces of a workable arrangement began to fall into place. With funds gathered from various sources-- notably the Thomas Cooper Library, the South Caroliniana Society, the South Carolina State Library, and the State-Record Foundation--it seemed possible that Dr. Moore could begin work on the South Carolina Newspaper Project, at least for twelve months.

As these plans were taking shape, this unfolding saga took an unforeseen and most unlikely turn. On August 14, 1984, State Librarian Betty Callaham attended a United Way meeting held at the governor's mansion in Columbia. During that session she was approached by Jim Walker, head of public relations for the South Carolina Highway Department, who was searching for someone to write a history of that vital state agency. Walker and his associates, looking forward to the seventieth birthday of their department in 1987, hoped to have the work completed so as to mark the occasion in proper fashion. Callaham, aware that Moore had published material on a variety of subjects, immediately saw the possibility of joining newspapers to highways in a manner mutually beneficial to all concerned.

In time, pertinent details were worked out and a three-year schedule devised for the research and writing of *both* projects--a guide to newspapers in the state of South Carolina and a history of the Highway Department. Thus to the long list of those who have contributed to the publication of this volume must be added (strangely, but with sincere appreciation) the South Carolina Department of Highways and Public Transportation. And, although few university libraries are engaged in the business of overseeing publishing ventures, the Thomas Cooper Library now has at least two of them to its credit.

Compilation of a guide to newspapers involves long hours of research, a keen eye, and careful attention to detail. Those engaged in such pursuits must decide what they are looking for, where it most likely will be found (if indeed it can be found), and how to express succinctly the results of their search. A handful of books provide clues to newspapers published in South Carolina over the past two-and-one-half centuries. Among these are the twin volumes of Clarence Brigham covering American newspapers from earliest times to 1820 and the work of Winifred Gregory, which continues the story to 1936. Two annual publications, commercial directories produced by Rowell (1869-1908) and Ayer (1880 to the present under a variety of titles), furnish still more grist for the mill, although both often ignore small-town weeklies and tend to carry titles long after they have ceased to exist. To this foursome must be added the "checklist" of Professor Ashley and his journalism students, which, although based to some extent upon Brigham, Gregory, Rowell, and Ayer, benefits from considerable on-the-spot digging.

Early in this process one must decide which publications actually are newspapers and which are not, for an admixture of journals, magazines, periodicals, or whatever one wishes to call them is inevitable. Ayer, for example, makes no clear distinction, simply lumping everything together under the headings of state and community. The American Library Association's Glossary (1983) defines a newspaper as "a serial issued at stated, frequent intervals (usually daily, weekly, or semi-weekly) containing news, opinions, advertisements, and other items of current, often local, interest." This certainly is straight-to-the-point and conforms to widely-held views. On the other hand, the long-awaited cataloging manual designed for what is now known as the United States Newspaper Project presents a definition that rambles on for five pages through headings and sub-headings resplendent with qualifying phrases and ends up raising many more questions than it answers.

The basic problem seems to be that most authorities tend to regard a newspaper as a somewhat static entity, while, in fact, title, content, format, frequency of appearance, virtually any and all aspects of a publication may change at the whim of editor, publisher, or printer. What looks like a newspaper one week may have a magazine-type cover the next. Interestingly, Brigham, whose research set very high standards, handled this problem most deftly, often pointing out that a publication he chose to cite actually was a magazine and even might so designate itself. But, since that "magazine" contained current news, in his opinion, it had earned a niche in his survey of newspapers.

In addition to the chameleon-like nature of some newspapers, until the advent of microfilm their size also has baffled even the most experienced librarians. Big, bulky, hard to handle, and seemingly impossible to catalog as one would a book, bound volumes of newspapers often were pushed aside and largely ignored. Some libraries have developed individual guides to their newspapers, others have not. And, since no one can determine the boundary line between newspapers, journals, and magazines with precise accuracy, "fringe" publications still can be found in different categories in different libraries, that is, the same title may be a newspaper in one place and a periodical in another.

A case in point would be the Southern Christian Advocate, a Methodist weekly established in Charleston in 1837 and still going strong. During the past 150 years the Advocate, as it is now called, also has been published from time to time in Columbia, Greenville, Orangeburg, Spartanburg, and Anderson, as well as in Augusta and Macon, Georgia. Moving frequently, much like the hard-working clergymen described in its columns, at the outset the Southern Christian Advocate differed little from any other four-page newspaper of the 1830s. And, while much of the reading matter was religious *and Methodist*, an issue might contain political gossip, obituaries, health and gardening tips, and vital information such as Charleston prices current and cotton market quotations. Over the years, however, this weekly has been transformed from what might be called a semi-newspaper into a slick-paper magazine. As a result, the South Caroliniana Library classifies the Advocate as both newspaper and periodical.

The Ware Shoals Life of a later era, published in the Greenwood County town of Ware Shoals from 1922 to 1984, presents a somewhat different dilemma. Issued weekly for over four decades, this publication was both a community newspaper and the house organ of the the Riegel Corporation, which was, in fact, long the community itself. In this instance, those seeking back files at the South Caroliniana Library will find the Ware Shoals Life classified as a periodical, not a newspaper.

Both of these publications--as well as numerous others designed primarily for a religious, industrial, business, or professional audience--are included in this guide *if* they also furnish some news of interest to the public at large.

NOT INCLUDED ARE THE FOLLOWING:

1. Weeklies, bi-weeklies, etc. issued by schools, colleges, and universities, as well as by groups associated with academic institutions such as alumni and sports organizations.

2. Publications sponsored by professional societies, fraternal organizations, and veterans groups.

3. So-called shoppers or "flyers" consisting for the most part of advertising material.

These items are excluded largely because they do not contain information of a general nature, that is, true news. However, some shopping guides, notably those that have sprung up in Chesterfield County, Florence, and the Myrtle Beach-Georgetown area since 1980, have taken on many of the earmarks of community newspapers and therefore are included. Any printed matter provided for the members of a group or club by its very nature is not intended for public consumption. College and university newspapers, on the other hand, present a dilemma of sorts. The University of South Carolina's <u>Gamecock</u>, for example, often comments on current events, yet it is intended primarily for a special, not general, audience. Also, unlike a true daily or weekly, an academic newspaper has an erratic schedule, appearing only when classes are in session, and thus provides disjointed, even inconsistent coverage. One consolation for researchers interested in such items is the fact that they do not have to look far to find out if back files exist, a problem often faced when dealing with more conventional press. In most instances the library, archives, or alumni office of the school in question can furnish a ready answer.

And a few more cautionary notes. If files of a newspaper no longer exist, it frequently is impossible to ascertain its precise title. Ayer and other sources often cite short-lived weeklies in a cavalier fashion, ignoring the name of the community even if part of the title. For example, a weekly listed in Ayer (1899) under the town of Prosperity as the <u>News</u> may well have bore on its masthead the proud words "Prosperity News," but until stray copies are dug out of some attic or closet no one can be sure. Secondly, random copies of well-established dailies such as the <u>State</u> and the <u>News and Courier</u>, publications known to be available on microfilm in numerous depositories, are not listed in the pages that follow. And, finally, the question of strict continuity can be baffling indeed. Many 19th century South Carolina weeklies did not publish during the last week of each year, the Yuletide-New Year's season. Others, such as the <u>Pendleton Messenger</u>, which rounded out a volume each February, provided customers with 52 issues and then stopped, even if the calendar rhythm would seem to require still one more. Instead, publishers of that well-known journal took a week's vacation and began another volume on the anniversary of their paper's founding.

Actual compilation of this guide was done in the following manner. All of the facts known about a newspaper were assembled on 5 x 8 cards. This information included data such as when a paper started and when it ceased (something often difficult to ascertain), frequency of issue, key personnel, files known to exist, location and nature of those files (original or microform), and predecessors and successors of the paper in question, if applicable. Since the South Caroliniana Library at the University of South Carolina has the state's largest newspaper collection, those holdings comprised a base from which to work and with which to compare information gathered from other sources.

Once the newspaper history of a county was virtually complete, the data was typed up and sent to the county librarian for review and comment. At the same time, Moore began traveling about the state calling at newspaper offices, museums, and libraries to verify, correct, and update this growing body of information. Much of 1985 was spent "on the road" working on newspapers, while 1986 was given over to the Highway Department. During the latter period, two very able graduate students from the Institute for Southern Studies at the University of South Carolina re-checked material that had been gathered. Wendy Satin concentrated upon original newspaper files at the South Caroliniana Library, while Steve Hranilovich poured over hundreds of microfilm reels.

In addition to the exclusion of various types of publications, several other ground rules were laid down.

1. Individual entries would be organized alphabetically by place of publication under county headings, with any introductory "the" in a title eliminated.

2. Abbreviations would be kept to an absolute minimum, thus curtailing endless page flipping often demanded by bibliographic manuals.

3. Efforts would be made to summarize *incomplete* files in a truly helpful manner, something more than the ever-frustrating single parentheses or phrases such as "scattered issues" or "scattered issues wanting."

4. Whenever possible, the essential volume-issue number data found in most newspaper files would be reproduced from a precise copy, usually the earliest one located.

5. Original files of an individual title, if such existed, would be cited before microform copies held by a depository.

The material condensed in each title entry needs little explanation. It includes information such as publication schedule, political preference (if known), date when paper began and perhaps ceased, its relationship to other newspapers, the names of key personnel, and the location and form of any known files. Since political ties tend to change over the decades, that tag sometimes has little real significance. Frequency of issue, however, presents certain difficulties. Everyone realizes that weeklies may grow into semi-weeklies (twice a week), tri-weeklies (three times a week), and even dailies. And a reverse pattern, although less common, may occur.

Through past decades, especially during the 19th century, some daily papers in larger communities such as Charleston and Columbia devised a somewhat more complex publication schedule. In addition to a daily edition (usually Monday through Saturday), the <u>Charleston Courier</u>, for example, at times published weekly and tri-weekly papers. Weeklies of this sort, often bearing slogans such as "for the country," might or might not have a masthead title related to their parent company.

And tri-weeklies, at first only the inside pages of standard, four-page dailies, sometimes had no masthead at all.

The practice of one newspaper producing daily, tri-weekly, semi-weekly, and weekly editions continued on into the early 20th century and, in time, took new forms. The State, for example, offered a semi-weekly subscription to the eve of World War II. This was, however, somewhat different. Those interested received the regular Tuesday and Friday daily papers together with occasional "farm supplements." During the same decades, Greenwood's Index-Journal tried to hold on to rural readers with a so-called tri-weekly, the Monday-Wednesday-Friday copies of the daily paper. Although these truncated subscriptions obviously cost less, they must have left readers wondering what happened on Tuesday, Thursday, and Saturday and played havoc with any "continued" story.

In any case, it should be noted that *true* variant editions of daily papers usually are listed separately, especially if files of those weeklies, semi-weeklies, or tri-weeklies are known to exist. However, if a newspaper merely altered its publishing schedule from time to time, offered readers two or three out of six daily papers each week, or issued regional editions of its daily paper (a practice that has become common in recent years), those changes are noted within a single entry.

Organization of entries by county and then by cities and towns within each county--a geographical approach spurned by OCLC's introductory eight-volume report of June 1985 in favor of a strictly alphabetical "Union List"--produced some unexpected results. Not only did this regional scheme reveal links between seemingly unrelated publications, it also provided insight into local economic conditions. Publishers in Cheraw, Greenwood, and Darlington, for example, had reason to believe c. 1900 that their cities could support daily newspapers. Although such hopes turned out to be either premature or misguided, these records nevertheless tell a poignant story. The same could be said of short-lived weeklies in Donalds, Wagener, Midway, Lamar, Ridgeway, and scores of other little crossroads settlements that dot the South Carolina countryside.

Perhaps yet another ingredient common to any bibliography of this sort should be noted. Files of newspapers, much like some newspapers themselves, are far from static. As the result of a change in management or a spate of general housecleaning, copies stacked in the back room of a print shop in 1985 may not be there a few years later. The greatest on-going change, however, undoubtedly is the trend from original to microfilm files. Two decades ago virtually every county library had several hundred pounds of old newspapers stashed away somewhere. Today those collections probably have been replaced by a few microfilm reels--or soon will be. And the same phenomenon is evident at the college and university level. This means, of course, that researchers expecting to find original copies at a depository may discover when they get there that only microfilm is available.

The pages that follow clearly are not what they could have been with the assistance of federal funds. They do, however, possess certain virtures. Included in this mass of information is much of the detail that will be needed when and if a newspaper cataloging program is developed in South Carolina. Also, this compendium provides a handy guide to titles for which, at the moment, no files are known to exist. An open invitation to prove the compiler wrong, such entries may, in fact, spur efforts to assemble and preserve still more newspapers in libraries and museums throughout South Carolina. But most important of all, while other states procrastinate or await action at the federal level, here is a useful bibliographic tool in hand, one, with all of its shortcomings, ready to be used.

ABBREVIATIONS AND SYMBOLS

Apr — April. All months are indicated by the first three letters--Jan, Feb, Mar, etc.

Arndt — Karl R. J. Arndt and May E. Olson, The German Language Press of the Americas (3 vols., Munich, 1973).

Ayer — N. W. Ayer & Son's Directory of Newspapers and Periodicals (Philadelphia, 1880-1982). Annual publication except in 1893/4 when two years combined. Title varies, absorbed Rowell's directory in 1910. Now Gale Directory of Publications (Detroit).

Behling — Charles F. Behling, "South Carolina Negro Newspapers: Their History, Content, and Reception," (M.A. thesis, University of South Carolina, 1964).

Brigham — Clarence S. Brigham, History and Bibliography of American Newspapers, 1690-1820 (2 vols., Worcester, 1947).

CL — County Library, the central public depository for each of forty-six counties in South Carolina.

CLS — Charleston Library Society, Charleston 29401.

Ellen — John Calhoun Ellen, Jr., "Political Newspapers of the Piedmont Carolinas in the 1850s," (Ph.D. dissertation, University of South Carolina, 1958).

Fri — Friday. Days of the week are identified by the first three letters--Sun, Mon, Tue, etc.

Gregory — Winifred Gregory, American Newspapers, 1821-1936 (New York, 1937).

King — William L. King, The Newspaper Press of Charleston, S. C. (Charleston, 1872).

mfm — microfilm.

mp	microprint.
NFK	no files known to exist.
no	number of an individual issue.
North	S. N. D. North, <u>History and Present Condition of the Newspaper and Periodical Press of the United States</u> (Washington, 1884).
orig	original copy or copies...used only when a depository holds identical original and microform files.
Rowell	<u>Rowell's American Newspaper Directory</u> (New York, 1869-1908). Title varies, absorbed by Ayer in 1910.
SC	South Carolina.
SCL	South Caroliniana Library, University of South Carolina, Columbia 29208.
Tindall	George Brown Tindall, <u>South Carolina Negroes, 1877-1900</u> (Columbia, 1952).
USC	Thomas Cooper Library, University of South Carolina, Columbia 29208. All other college-university libraries are identified by key word in name of the institution [Clemson, Winthrop, Coker], unless short form would tend to create confusion [Columbia College, Newberry College, College of Charleston].
vol	volume of a newspaper.
Woody	Robert H. Woody, <u>Republican Newspapers of South Carolina</u> (Charlottesville, 1936).
( )	incomplete file, less than 100 issues, usually accompanied by a number estimating extent of coverage for years cited within parentheses.
(( ))	incomplete file, more than 100 issues, usually accompanied by a number estimating extent of coverage for years cited within double parentheses.
+	file currently being added to.

=   wherever description is based upon an extant copy, an equal sign relates date of issue to volume and numerical sequence...Nov 3, 1972 = vol 4, no 5.

SAMPLE ENTRIES WITH EXPLANATION

CAROLINA AFRO-WEEKLY   weekly, black publication--established 1969, ceased c. 1974. Nov 3, 1972 = vol 4, no 5, James A. Whetstone (editor), Carolina Afro-Publishing Company. Mazie B. Ferguson also associated with paper. *Files: SCL (Sep 1973-Mar 1974) 17; Winthrop Nov 3, 1972.*

> This black weekly apparently existed for about five years. South Caroliniana Library has 17 issues dating from September 1973 to March 1974; Winthrop, one issue. No microfilm files are known to exist. Description is based upon copy held by Winthrop--November 3, 1972.

DAILY RECORD   daily--established 1897, continued by the Columbia Record Apr 4, 1913. May 28, 1897 = vol 1, no 29, George R. Koester (manager). Paul M. Brice, H. A. Whitman, and James A. Hoyt also associated with paper. *Files: Columbia Record and Richland CL mfm Jan 1909-Apr 1912, Jul 1912-Apr 1913; SCL ((1897-1910) 300, mfm (1898-1905) 23, Jan 1909-Apr 1912, Jul 1912-Apr 1913).*

> This well-known afternoon daily, established in 1897, changed its name to the Columbia Record on April 4, 1913. Description is based upon issue of May 28, 1897. The Columbia Record and Richland County Library have microfilm files from January 1909-April 1913, except for May-June 1912. The South Caroliniana Library has the same microfilm files, plus some 300 original issues dating from 1897 to 1910 and 23 microfilm copies dating from 1898 to 1905. Note that (a) depositories are listed alphabetically, (b) identical files are combined as a single entry item and separated by a semi-colon from those found in other depositories, and (c) original files precede microfilm holdings whenever both are held by a single depository.

STAR-REPORTER   weekly, independent--established 1963. May 7, 1964 = vol 1, no 29, Harold C. Booker, Jr. (editor and publisher). Cited by Ayer 1966 + . *Files: SCL May 7, 1964, ((1970 +)); Star-Reporter 1963 + .*

> This independent weekly, established in 1963, was first cited by Ayer in 1966 and continues to be listed by that annual directory. Description is based upon issue of May 7, 1964. South Caroliniana Library has one copy for 1964 and an incomplete but growing file of 100 or more issues dating from 1970 to the present. The Star-

Reporter, which apparently has not been microfilmed, has files from 1963 to the present at its offices.

CLOVER REVIEW weekly--established 1901, ceased c. 1902. Cited once by Ayer (1902): Lewis B. Gwin Company (publisher). *NFK*

The only information available on this weekly is found in Ayer's directory for the year 1902. No files are known to exist.

PIONEER AND SOUTH-CAROLINA WHIG weekly--continues Pioneer and Commercial Register Jul 1829. Jul 4, 1829 = vol 1, no 1 (new series). Paper ceased c. 1831. *Files: Library of Congress (1829-1831) 12. Apparently no SC files.*

This weekly continues another paper bearing a similar name in July 1829; however, a new number sequence was instituted at that time. Description is based upon an issue held by the Library of Congress, where a dozen copies may be consulted. Whenever random issues of South Carolina newspapers are to be found *only* outside of the state, then at least one depository holding files is cited.

CAROLINA TELEGRAPH weekly--established 1816, ceased c. 1817. Dec 13, 1816 = vol 1, no 49, David P. Hillhouse (publisher). William Cline also associated with paper. *Files: SCL orig & mfm Dec 13, 1816, Jan 3, 1817.*

The South Caroliniana Library holds two original issues of this short-lived weekly that also are available in microfilm form. Note that the abbreviation "orig" appears only when a depository holds identical original and microform files.

A NOTE ON SOUTH CAROLINA
DEPOSITORIES

County libraries, almost without exception located at county seats throughout the state, frequently can provide original or microfilm files of local newspapers. The largest of these facilties, as well as libraries associated with colleges and universities, often hold microfilm copies of both in-state and out-of-state dailies. Depositories of special significance for researchers include Columbia's Benedict College, the Charleston Library Society, Clemson University, and two libraries at the University of South Carolina.

Benedict College has some 300 reels of black-oriented newspapers and related materials from the New York Public Library's Schomberg Collection. The Charleston Library Society, a private institution, holds a substantial file of regional newspapers from 1732 to the present, together with some early 19th century Georgetown weeklies and several volumes of Greenville newspapers (c. 1850-1890) found nowhere else. It should be noted, perhaps, that all pre-1830 publications listed by Brigham and Gregory as being housed at the College of Charleston have been transferred to the Charleston Library Society.

In addition to standard in-state and out-of-state files, Clemson University can boast of a truly unique collection of contemporary weeklies highlighting the nullification crisis of the early 1830s. The state's largest concentration of newspaper records is found in Columbia at the University of South Carolina, with South Carolina weeklies and dailies located in the historic South Caroliniana Library and non-South Carolina materials available a couple of blocks away at the Thomas Cooper Library. The South Caroliniana Library, it should be emphasized, has instituted an on-going, cooperative program with various editors and publishers to commit original files to microfilm.

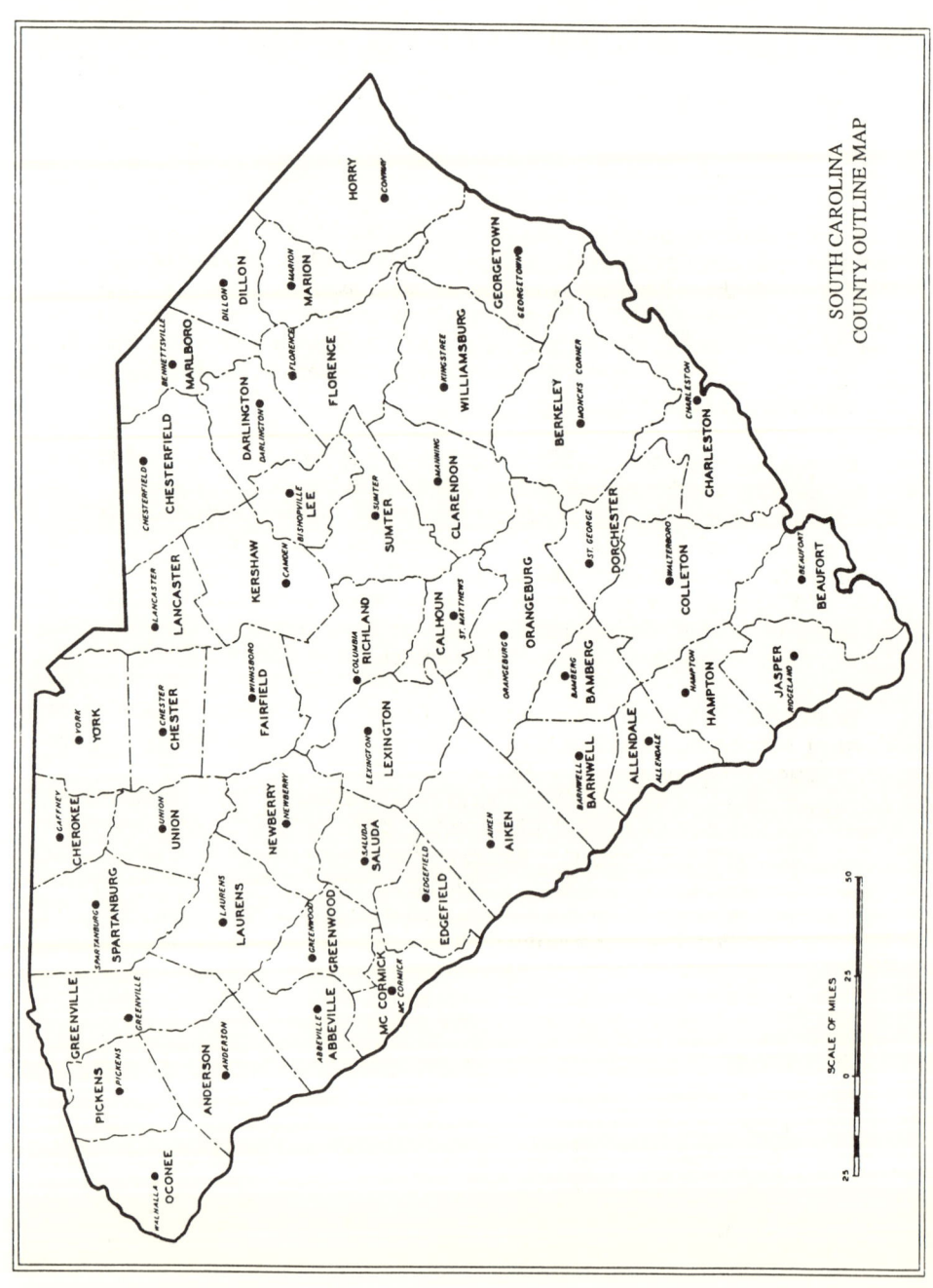

SOUTH CAROLINA
COUNTY OUTLINE MAP

SCALE OF MILES

ABBEVILLE COUNTY

The first settlers of this region were eight Presbyterian families who moved south from Pennyslvania. The county, however, takes its name from Abbeville, France, home of yet another pioneer, John de la Howe, a Huguenot doctor. It was organized in 1798 when old Ninety Six District was split into five parts.

ABBEVILLE

ABBEVILLE BANNER   weekly--continues the Banner on Mar 3, 1847, merged with the Abbeville Press on Oct 1, 1869, continued by the Abbeville Press and Banner. Mar 3, 1847 = vol 4, no 1, Charles Henry Allen (editor and proprietor). Paper not published during the Civil War. Henry S. Kerr, Francis W. Selleck, William C. Davis, William A. Lee, John L. Logan, James Hollingsworth, Thomas B. Crews, James S. Cothran, and William W. Farrow also associated with paper. Note: Mfm reel of Abbeville Press contains final issue of the Abbeville Banner (Sep 20, 1869 = vol 25, no 47, W. W. Farrow, editor). This is apparently the only post-Civil War issue in existence. *Files: Erskine orig & mfm ((1847-1860)) 250; Lander mfm Feb 23, 1848; SCL mfm ((1847-1860)) 250.*

ABBEVILLE BULLETIN   weekly--interim publication Jul-Aug 1865. A single sheet produced by Hugh Wilson, editor of the Abbeville Press before and after the Civil War. Only six issues published. Aug 10, 1865 = vol 1, no 3. On Sep 7, 1865 Wilson's Abbeville Press resumed publication after a break of unknown duration. *Files: Erskine orig & mfm Aug 10-31, 1865; SCL mfm Aug 10-31, 1865.*

ABBEVILLE MEDIUM   weekly, semi-weekly--established Nov 22, 1871. In 1917 became semi-weekly and in 1923 was continued by the Evening Medium (daily except Sun). Nov 22, 1871 = vol 1, no 1, Robert R. Hemphill (editor), Hemphill & Company (proprietors). Others associated with paper include James C. Hemphill, Mary I. Hemphill, Grace C. Hemphill, and E. C. Horton. *Files: Erskine and Lander mfm (1878-1909) 90; SCL Nov 22, 1871-Oct 1, 1879, Jan 8, 1885-Jan 10, 1889, Jan 4, 1894-Dec 26, 1907, mfm (1878-1909) 90.*

ABBEVILLE MESSENGER   weekly, Democrat--established 1884, ceased c. 1888. Nov 9, 1886 = vol 3, no 6, M. L. Bonham, Jr., and James S. Perrin (editors and proprietors). May have been Saluda Argus [Greenwood] c. 1882-1884. *Files: SCL (Oct 1886-Jun 1887) 18; Erskine, Lander, and SCL mfm (Oct 1886-Jun 1887) 18.*

ABBEVILLE PRESS   weekly--created Nov 9, 1860 when the Independent Press changed its name to the Abbeville Press, which merged with the Abbeville Banner on Oct 1, 1869, continued by the Abbeville Press and Banner. Nov 9, 1860 = vol 8, no 28, William A. Lee and Hugh Wilson (editors). Both men subsequently entered military service, leaving paper with William A. Wilson, a former owner. Some issues published during the Civil War, but impossible to say how many. Oct 7, 1863 = vol 12, no 22,

Sep 7, 1865 = vol 13, no 21. William A. Lee and Hugh Wilson resumed operations on Sep 7, 1865 and four years later purchased the Abbeville Banner. *Files: Erskine orig & mfm ((1860-1869)) 265; Lander mfm Mar 9, 1866; SCL Mar 9, 1866, mfm ((1860-1869)) 265.*

ABBEVILLE PRESS AND BANNER weekly, semi-weekly, tri-weekly--created by the merger of the Abbeville Press and Abbeville Banner on Oct 1, 1869, merged with the Evening Medium in 1925, continued by the Press and Banner and Abbeville Medium. Originally a weekly, paper became semi-weekly in 1917, tri-weekly in 1920. Oct 1, 1869 = vol 17, no 23, William A. Lee and Hugh Wilson (editors and publishers). Sometimes issued as Press and Banner. Hugh Wilson, Jr., W. C. Benet, H. T. Wardlaw, W. W. and W. R. Bradley, W. T. Walker, and William P. Greene also associated with paper. *Files: Erskine orig & mfm 1869-1897, 1899-1910, 1912, 1914-1925; Lander mfm (1873-1914) 40; SCL mfm 1869-1897, 1899-1910, 1912, 1914-1925.*

ABBEVILLE REPUBLICAN weekly--established by B. W. Reynolds in 1873, but Woody says only three issues published. *NFK*

ABBEVILLE WHIG AND SOUTHERN NULLIFIER weekly, pro-nullification--established 1831, ceased c. 1833. Jan 17, 1833 = vol 2, no 8, Samuel Townes (editor), John Taggart (publisher). According to Townes family papers at SCL, Townes moved to Marion, Alabama, in 1834 to edit the Mercury. See Harry L. Watson, "Early Newspapers of Abbeville District, 1812-1834," Proceedings, SC Historical Association (1940), pp. 18-35. *Files: Clemson Jan 17, Feb 28, Mar 28, Apr 18, 25, 1833.*

BANNER weekly--established Apr 24, 1844, became the Abbeville Banner on Mar 3, 1847. Feb 18, 1846 = vol 2, no 51, Charles H. Allen (editor), Allen and Kerr (publishers). *Files: Erskine orig & mfm Feb 18, Apr 1-Jul 22, Aug 5-Nov 11, Dec 15, 1846, Feb 24, 1847; Lander mfm Aug 12, 1846; SCL Aug 12, 1846, mfm Feb 18, Apr 1-Jul 22, Aug 5-Nov 11, Dec 15, 1846, Feb 24, 1847.*

CHRISTIAN'S QUIVER weekly, Methodist--established 1899, ceased c. 1901. Cited in Ayer 1899 thru 1901: D. H. Johnson (editor and publisher). *NFK*

EVENING MEDIUM daily c. 1923-1925--title of Abbeville Medium after becoming daily, ceased when merged with Abbeville Press and Banner in 1925. See Abbeville Medium and Press and Banner and Abbeville Medium. *Files: Erskine and Lander mfm Aug 18, 20, 1924; SCL orig & mfm Aug 18, 20, 1924.*

INDEPENDENT PRESS weekly--established May 13, 1853 by B. L. Posey, changed name to Abbeville Press in Nov 1860. Jun 3, 1854 = vol 2, no 56, C. C. Puckett and George W. Fant (editors). William A. Lee and William H. Wilson also associated with paper. *Files: Erskine orig & mfm Jun 1854-Nov 1860; Lander mfm (1860) 5; SCL (1860) 6, mfm Jun 1854-Nov 1860.*

JOURNAL OF ENTERPRISE   weekly, black publication c. 1883--according to Tindall, edited by S. H. Jefferson. Not cited by Ayer. *NFK*

PIEDMONT VOICE   weekly, black publication--established 1910, ceased c. 1914. Cited once by Ayer (1914): W. F. Rice (editor and publisher). *NFK*

PRESS AND BANNER.   see the Abbeville Press and Banner.

PRESS AND BANNER AND ABBEVILLE MEDIUM   tri-weekly, semi-weekly, weekly--created Feb 1925 by merger of Abbeville Press and Banner and Abbeville Medium. First joint issue (tri-weekly) Feb 2, 1925 (no vol number), F. D. West (editor). Paper became semi-weekly c. 1926, weekly c. 1939. Lewis Perrin and F. D. West, Jr., also associated with paper. *Files: Erskine orig & mfm 1925 + ; SCL ((1927-1948)) 315, ((1985 +)), mfm 1925-1970.*

SCIMITAR   weekly, semi-monthly--established 1914, ceased c. 1918. Began as Sat weekly, then issued semi-monthly. Jul 11, 1914 = vol 1, no 1. W. P. Beard (editor and publisher) imprisoned for pro-German views in May 1918. *Files: Erskine and Lander mfm (Oct 1914-Jul 1917) 45; SCL orig & mfm (Oct 1914-Jul 1917) 45.*

TRUE AMERICAN   weekly, Republican--according to Woody, this paper was scheduled to begin publication on Sep 1, 1873, T. A. Sullivan (publisher). *NFK*

CALHOUN FALLS

CALHOUN FALLS HERALD   weekly c. 1959--after two or three issues merged with the Calhoun Falls Times, continued by the Times-Herald. *NFK*

CALHOUN FALLS NEWS   weekly--created in 1961 by name change, formerly the Calhoun Falls Times, which was issued briefly as the Times-Herald. Jan 11, 1962 = vol 1, no 32, L. Abner Hall (editor and publisher). According to Hall, title changed to avoid confusion with the Calhoun Times of St. Matthews. *Files: Calhoun Falls News ((1961 +)); Jack Burton [Calhoun Falls] ((1961 +)).*

CALHOUN FALLS TIMES   weekly--established Oct 4, 1946, merged briefly with the Calhoun Falls Herald c. 1959 to form the Times-Herald, continued by the Calhoun Falls News c. 1961. Original publisher was a man named Todd, who soon sold paper to T. M. Tucker. May 21, 1958 = vol 12, no 35, Jack H. and Bertie Brewster (owners and publishers). Roy Ethridge also associated with paper. *Files: Calhoun Falls News ((1951-1961)); Jack Burton [Calhoun Falls] ((1949-1961)); SCL May 21, 1958.*

TIMES-HERALD   weekly--created c. 1959 by merger of the Calhoun Falls Times and the Calhoun Falls Herald. According to Ayer 1961, Roy Ethridge (editor and publisher). Paper continued by the Calhoun Falls News c. 1961. *NFK*

DONALDS

DONALDS PROGRESS   weekly, Democrat--established 1906, ceased c. 1906. Aug 23, 1906 = vol 1, no 1. Listed once in Ayer (1906): Harold C. Booker (editor and publisher). *Files: SCL Aug 23, 1906 (xerox copy).*

DUE WEST

ASSOCIATE REFORMED PRESBYTERIAN   weekly, monthly, religious--established in 1850 as the Erskine Miscellany, continued by the Due West Telescope c. 1851 and the Associate Reformed Presbyterian in 1867. Issued monthly since 1975. Sep 5, 1889 = vol 36, no 30, J. T. Chalmers (editor). J. I. Bonner, R. S. Galloway, R. M. Stevenson, C. B. Williams, and Ebenezer Gettys also associated with paper. *Files: CLS Dec 24, 1891; Erskine 1911 + , mfm 1867-1878, 1884-1913; SCL (1882-1888) 10, mfm (1876-1889) 3. Note: SCL classifies as a periodical after 1890, has incomplete files (1903-1971).*

DUE WEST TELESCOPE   weekly--established 1850 as the Erskine Miscellany, became the Due West Telescope c. 1851, continued by the Associate Reformed Presbyterian in 1867. Apr 18, 1856 = vol 7, no 16, J. I. Bonner (editor and proprietor). *Files: Erskine mfm ((1851-1863)); SCL Oct 10, 1862, mfm (1856-1863) 8.*

DUE WEST WEEKLY   mimeographed community weekly--established 1949, ceased c. 1958. Dec 21, 1949 = vol 1, no 44. *Files: SCL ((Feb 1949-May 1956)) 170.*

ERSKINE MISCELLANY   weekly--established 1850, continued by the Due West Telescope c. 1851. Jun 22, 1850 = vol 1, no 19, J. Oliver Lindsay and J. I. Bonner (publishers). *Files: Erskine (1850-1851) 4, mfm Mar 7, May 23, 1851.*

VILLAGE OBSERVER   weekly--established 1976. Apr 8, 1976 = vol 1, no 1, Mrs. Mildred Davis (editor and publisher). Tunis Romein also associated with paper. *Files: Erskine ((1976 +)).*

LOWNDESVILLE

LOWNDESVILLE ADVERTISER   weekly--established 1888, ceased c. 1889. Feb 14, 1888 = vol 1, no 7, W. S. Martin and J. M. Baker (editors). Baker, an Abbeville County resident, was secretary to United States Senate Democrats during Wilson's administration and ambassador to Siam [Thailand] under Franklin D. Roosevelt. *Files: Erskine orig & mfm Feb 14-Nov 28, 1888; SCL May 16, 1888.*

AIKEN COUNTY

Aiken County was formed in 1871 from parts of Edgefield, Barnwell, Lexington, and Orangeburg counties. It is named for the county seat which honors Irish-born William Aiken (d. 1831), first president of the South Carolina Railroad and father of William Aiken, who served as governor from 1844 to 1846.

AIKEN

AIKEN COUNTY RAMBLER   weekly, independent--established Aug 18, 1977, ceased Jun 9, 1983. Aug 18, 1977 = vol 1, no 1, Kay Lawrence (editor), Rambler Publications, Inc. *Files: Aiken CL Aug 18, 1977-Jun 9, 1983. Index available.*

AIKEN COUNTY REGISTER   weekly, established Nov 1983, ceased Apr 1984. Nov 18, 1983 = vol 1, no 1, Stephen D. Hale (editor), Helen Marine (publisher). *Files: Aiken CL and SCL Nov 18, 1983-Apr 19, 1984.*

AIKEN COURIER-JOURNAL   weekly, Democrat--continues Courier-Journal sometime after Jun 1877. Oct 18, 1877 = vol 3, no 147, new series, vol 7, no 350, old series, John McCray (editor and publisher). McCray began new number system Nov 7, 1874 when he took over Aiken Journal and renamed it Courier-Journal. Merged with Aiken Review c. 1880 to form Journal and Review. Note: Source of "Courier" unclear, unless McCray was honoring the Charleston Daily Courier, which in Apr 1873 merged with the Charleston Daily News to form the News and Courier. *Files: Aiken CL mfm Oct 11, 1877-Feb 14, 1878; SCL orig & mfm Oct 11, 1877-Feb 14, 1878.*

AIKEN JOURNAL   daily (evenings except Sun), tri-weekly, weekly--established 1871, became Courier-Journal Nov 1874. Rowell 1872: John S. Shuck (editor and publisher). Shuck, editor and publisher of Barnwell Journal 1869-1871, claimed at outset that Aiken Journal was the only daily outside of Columbia and Charleston, but by 1874 was weekly, edited and published by Wilmer O. Cammack. Feb 21, 1874 = vol 4, no 158, Wilmer O. Cammack (editor and publisher). John McCray purchased Aiken Journal Oct 1874, published at least one issue citing "Yarcam" as editor (McCray spelled backwards), and on Nov 7, 1874 began Courier-Journal. In an extra edition of Aiken Journal (Oct 28, 1874) "Yarcam" noted gleefully that Cammack was now with the Republican Aiken Tribune..."buzzards of a feather flock together." *Files: SCL (Feb 21-Oct 31, 1874) 28.*

AIKEN JOURNAL   weekly, black publication, c. 1943-1945. According to Behling, published by a man named Brooks. Not cited by Ayer. *NFK*

AIKEN LIFE   weekly, society news--established 1905, ceased c. 1909. Originally published Sat during Jan-Mar season, later expanded to all months except summer. Cited Ayer 1905 thru 1909: Steedman Weatherbee (editor), Aiken Life Publishing Company. Ayer 1912 notes that Weatherbee was editor and publisher of Branchville Journal. *NFK*

AIKEN PRESS   weekly--established 1867, ceased c. 1868. Jul 4, 1867 = vol 1, no 1, R. H. Machen (proprietor), H. D. Machen (publisher). *Files: SCL orig & mfm Jul 4, Aug 15, 1867.*

AIKEN RECORDER   weekly, semi-weekly, Democrat--established 1881, continued by Aiken Sentinel c. 1910. Aug 22, 1882 = vol 1, no 45, Charles E. R. Drayton (editor and publisher). In 1890s became semi-weekly, then weekly, and by 1907 was semi-weekly again. In addition to Drayton, Arthur P. Ford and W. A. McCracken were associated with paper. *Files: Aiken CL and SCL mfm ((1882-1907)) 112.*

AIKEN REVIEW   weekly, Democrat--established 1878, merged with Aiken Courier-Journal c. 1880 to form Journal and Review. Rowell 1879: James Gray Porter (editor and publisher). *NFK*

AIKEN SENTINEL   semi-weekly, weekly--created c. 1910 by purchase of Aiken Recorder. New owners continued number sequence but changed name. Mar 11, 1910 = vol 28, no 33, Robert M. Hitt and Walter E. Duncan (editors), Sentinel Publishing Company. Circa 1913 merged with Horse Creek Valley News to form Sentinel-Valley News. *Files: Aiken CL mfm Mar 11, May 6, 1910; SCL orig & mfm Mar 11, May 6, 1910.*

AIKEN STANDARD   weekly--established May 13, 1915, merged with the South Carolina Gazette [Columbia] in 1930, continued by the Aiken Standard and South Carolina Gazette. May 20, 1915 = vol 1, no 2, Walter E. Duncan (president and editor), Aiken Publishing Company. *Files: Aiken CL and Clemson mfm ((1915-1930)) 775; SCL ((1915-1930)) 700, mfm ((1915-1930)) 775.*

AIKEN STANDARD   On Dec 15, 1969 Aiken Standard and Review changed from morning to afternoon daily and shortened name to Aiken Standard. See Aiken Standard and Review.

AIKEN STANDARD AND REVIEW   semi-weekly, daily--created Nov 22, 1935 by merger of Aiken Standard and South Carolina Gazette and Journal and Review. Originally semi-weekly, became daily Apr 15, 1952 as result of Savannah River Plant construction. Began Sun edition Oct 6, 1985. Nov 26, 1935 = vol 65, no 7, B. J. King (editor and business manager). Jan 3, 1936 (vol 66, no 1) masthead bears these words: "Journal & Review established 1869, Aiken Standard established 1915, South Carolina Gazette established 1925...only newspaper in Aiken County." Title shortened to Aiken Standard Dec 15, 1969. Annie H. King, Albert T. Howell, Donald M. Law, and Samuel A. Cothran also associated with paper. *Files: Aiken CL 1953 + , mfm 1954 + ; Aiken Standard 1970 + ; SCL Oct 1986 + , mfm Nov 1935-Dec 1983.*

AIKEN STANDARD AND SOUTH CAROLINA GAZETTE   weekly, Democrat--created by merger of Aiken Standard and South Carolina Gazette Sep 1930. Oct 3, 1930 = vol 16, no 22, Walter E. Duncan (president and editor), Aiken Publishing

Company. Merged with Journal and Review Nov 1935 to form Aiken Standard and Review. *Files: SCL ((1931-1935)) 110; Aiken CL, Clemson, and SCL mfm ((Oct 1930-Nov 1935)) 125.*

AIKEN TELEGRAPH AND COMMERCIAL ADVERTISER weekly-- established 1835, ceased c. 1836. Jul 8, 1835 = vol 1, no 15, A. Mezick McCaine (editor and publisher). In this issue, McCaine announced that William A. Pritchard, former editor of "Hamburg Galaxy" [Carolina Galaxy and Commercial Advocate] would succeed him. Jun 25, 1836 = vol 2, no 6, edited by Pritchard (also town clerk), has this running head on inside pages: "Aiken Telegraph and Barnwell Advocate." *Files: SCL mfm Jul 8, 1835, Jun 25, 1836.*

AIKEN TIMES weekly, Democrat, pro-Tillman, Farmers' Alliance--established 1892, ceased c. 1905. Ayer 1893/4: J. T. Gantt (editor and publisher). W. W. Williams, L. Bradwell, and Walter E. Duncan also associated with paper. Cited Ayer 1893/4 thru 1904. *Files: SCL May 12, 1897 (fragment, no vol or issue no).*

AIKEN TRIBUNE weekly, Republican--established 1871, ceased c. 1876. Nov 25, 1871 = vol 1, no 1, Henry Sparnick (editor and proprietor). SCL 1873 volume contains this note: "This newspaper was founded and for three years published by a notorious carpetbagger, Henry Sparnick. In 1876 the Hampton regime ran him out of town and the paper ceased publication." Nov 25, 1871 issue states Aiken Tribune is "official paper of the counties of Barnwell and Edgefield." *Files: SCL Nov 25, 1871, Jan-Dec 1873, Jul 11, 1874, mfm 1875.*

COURIER-JOURNAL weekly, Democrat--continuation of Aiken Journal, purchased by John McCray Oct 1874, became Aiken Courier-Journal sometime after Jun 1877. McCray began new number sequence Nov 7, 1874, while continuing old. Source of "Courier" not known, unless McCray was honoring the Charleston Daily Courier, which in Apr 1873 merged with the Charleston Daily News to form the News and Courier. *Files: SCL ((Nov 1874-Jun 1877)) 130.*

HERALD weekly, Republican, black publication--established 1898, ceased c. 1901. Cited Ayer 1900: S. E. Smith (editor), E. Morry (publisher). Ayer 1901: S. E. Smith (editor), J. A. Jones (publisher). Not cited 1902. *NFK.*

JOURNAL AND REVIEW weekly, semi-weekly, Democrat--created by merger of Aiken Courier-Journal and Aiken Review c. 1880. Jan 7, 1880 = vol 9, no 44, F. B. Henderson (proprietor). Became semi-weekly c. 1903. In 1935 merged with Aiken Standard and South Carolina Gazette to form Aiken Standard and Review. In addition to Henderson, M. C. Hammond, L. C. Ligon, W. L. Washburn, S. S. Lamb, James F. Byrnes, A. K. Lorenz, S. H. Byron, and James S. Kerr associated with paper. *Files: Aiken CL mfm ((1885-1935)) 3700; SCL ((1880-1927)) 850, mfm ((1885-1935)) 3700. Note: Original files virtually complete 1880-1885.*

LITTLE OBSERVER   semi-monthly, black publication--established 1891, ceased c. 1894. Cited Ayer 1892: R. L. Hickson (editor and publisher). Ayer 1893/4: R. L. Hickson and T. J. Clark (editors and publishers). Not cited 1895. *NFK*

RESORT LIFE   weekly, during winter season--established 1929, ceased c. 1935. Cited Ayer 1933 thru 1936 as "Resorts Life," Walter E. Duncan (editor and publisher). Evidently produced by Aiken Standard and South Carolina Gazette since Duncan (who died c. 1934) also edited that paper. *NFK*

SENTINEL-VALLEY NEWS   weekly, Democrat--created c. 1913 by merger of Aiken Sentinel and Horse Creek Valley News [Warrenville], ceased c. 1918. First cited Ayer 1914: George R. Webb (editor and publisher). Listed Ayer 1914 thru 1918. Ernest R. Ussery and James E. Webb also associated with paper. *NFK*

SOUTH CAROLINA GAZETTE   weekly--established in 1925 in Columbia, moved to Aiken in 1930 and merged with the Aiken Standard, continued by the Aiken Standard and South Carolina Gazette. See South Carolina Gazette [Columbia].

GRANITEVILLE

GRANITEVILLE NEWS   weekly, independent--established 1899, ceased c. 1903. Cited Ayer 1901 thru 1903. May 17, 1900 = vol 1, no 24, Samuel H. Beard (publisher). *Files: SCL May 17, 1900.*

VALLEY TIMES   weekly--established 1929, ceased c. 1930. Not cited in Ayer. May 23, 1930 = vol 1, no 26, Walter E. Duncan (editor), O. A. Duncan (managing editor). Walter E. Duncan also editor and publisher of Aiken Standard. *Files: SCL May 23, 1930.*

HAMBURG

CAROLINA GALAXY AND COMMERCIAL GAZETTE   weekly--established 1834, ceased c. 1835. Oct 4, 1834 = vol 1, no 1, William H. Pritchard (publisher). Pritchard became editor and publisher of the Aiken Telegraph and Commercial Advertiser Jul 1835. *Files: SCL Oct 4, 1834.*

HAMBURG COURIER   weekly--established Oct 1855, ceased c. 1856. According to Ellen, founded by S. S. Browne, but soon ceased publication. *NFK*

HAMBURG GAZETTE   weekly--established 1823, ceased c. 1825. Jul 23, 1823 = vol 1, no 23, Frederick W. Pleasants (publisher). Charles S. Pleasants also associated with paper. *Files: American Antiquarian Society Jul 23, 1823, Jul 24, 1824. Apparently no copies in SC.*

HAMBURG JOURNAL   weekly, semi-weekly--established 1840, ceased c. 1849. May 9, 1840 = vol 1, no 6, Yarborough and Mullay (editors and publishers). SCL has no complete issues, but does have three, single-sheet supplements dated Jul 23, 1842, Aug 10, 24, 1848. Aug 24, 1848 = vol 9, no 10, Thomas G. Key and Henry D. Wray (proprietors). Since paper not cited by Ellen, presumably ceased before 1850. *Files: Library of Congress Apr 18, May 9, 1840; SCL (1842, 1848) supplements.*

HAMBURG REPUBLICAN   weekly, established 1845, became Republican c. 1850. Apr 24, 1845 = vol 1, no 30, James Cochran (publisher). *Files: SCL Apr 24, 1845.*

REPUBLICAN   weekly, established 1845 as Hamburg Republican, became Republican c. 1850, ceased c. 1853. May 15, 1850 = vol 6, no 34, H. Baird (editor and publisher). Ellen says ceased soon after Jan 1853. *Files: SCL May 15, 1850.*

VALLEY PIONEER   weekly--established 1854, ceased c. 1855. Jan 3, 1855 = vol 1, no 17, James M. Robinson (publisher). Ellen says founded by Robinson Sep 1, 1854 and ceased Sep 15, 1855. *Files: Duke Jan 3, 1855; Erskine mfm Jan 3, 1855.*

LANGLEY

COUNTY INDEPENDENT   see Valley Independent.

VALLEY INDEPENDENT   weekly--established Oct 1, 1960, as "Enterprise." Following a name-the-paper contest became Valley Independent. Nov 9, 1960 = vol 1, no 6, Ben P. Davies, Jr. (editorial writer), first issue bearing name of Valley Independent. By Oct 1961 issued as County Independent. Ceased c. Nov 1961. *Files: Aiken CL (1960-1961) 60.*

NORTH AUGUSTA

GAZETTE   weekly, independent--established 1907, ceased c. 1909. Cited Ayer 1908 and 1909: George F. Evans (editor), Evans and Glover (publishers). *NFK*

NEW ERA   weekly, Democrat--established 1909, ceased c. 1912. Cited Ayer 1910 thru 1912: R. E. Belcher (editor and publisher). *NFK*

NORTH AUGUSTA NEWS   weekly, independent--established 1948, ceased c. 1951. Cited Ayer 1950 and 1951: Margaret Cameron (editor and publisher). *NFK*

NORTH AUGUSTA STAR   see Star.

NORTH AUGUSTA WAY   weekly, non-partisan--established 1939, ceased c. 1945. Cited Ayer 1941 thru 1945: L. B. Eargle (editor and publisher). *NFK*

STAR   weekly, independent--established Sep 2, 1954 as North Augusta Star, now issued as Star. Cited Ayer 1961 to present: Samuel L. Woodring (editor and publisher). *Files: North Augusta Branch Library Dec 1983 + ; SCL (1982-1983) 13, Dec 1984 + ; Star 1954 + .*

VAUCLUSE

CAROLINA TRIBUNE   weekly, Republican, black publication--established 1891, ceased c. 1894. Cited by Ayer 1891 thru 1893/4: A. W. Nicholson (editor), Tribune Publishing Company. Listed in the Afro-American Encyclopaedia (1896) as the "South Carolina Tribune." *NFK*

WAGENER

EDISTO NEWS   weekly, Democrat--established 1911, ceased c. 1918. Cited Ayer 1913 thru 1918. Ayer 1913-1917: Wagener Publishing Company (no editor listed). Ayer 1918: J. Rutledge McGhee (editor), Western Carolina Publishing Company. *NFK*

EDISTO RECORD   weekly--established 1903, ceased c. 1905. Cited Ayer 1904 and 1905: J. W. Cooner, Jr. (editor and publisher). *NFK*

NEWS   weekly, Democrat--established 1893, ceased c. 1896. Cited Ayer 1895 and 1896. Ayer 1895: Wagener Publishing Company (no editor listed). Ayer 1896: Eugene Able (editor), A. G. Baltzegar (publisher). *NFK*

WAGENER EDISTO RECORD   weekly--established 1924, ceased c. 1926. Cited Ayer 1925 and 1926: Thomas C. Weir (editor and publisher). *NFK*

WAGENER WHEEL NEWS   weekly--established Sep 30, 1976, ceased Nov 10, 1977. Published by Kilgus Printing Company [Bamberg]. *Files: Advertizer-Herald [Bamberg] Sep 30, 1976-Nov 10, 1977.*

WARRENVILLE

HORSE CREEK VALLEY NEWS   weekly--established 1901, merged with Aiken Sentinel c. 1913 to form Sentinel-Valley News. Cited Ayer 1903 thru 1916. Ayer 1903-1905: G. B. McCracken (editor), News Publishing Company; Ayer 1906-1909: G. R. Webb (editor), News Publishing Company; Ayer 1910-1916: G. R. Webb (editor and publisher). *NFK*

ALLENDALE COUNTY

Created in 1919 from parts of Hampton and Barnwell counties, Allendale is named for its county seat. That community, once known as "Swallow Savannah," honors the town's first postmaster, Paul H. Allen.

ALLENDALE

ADVANCE   weekly, independent--established 1919, but soon changed name to Tri-County Record. Only cited once in Ayer (1920): Ed. N. Clark (editor), Allendale Printing Company. *NFK*

ALLENDALE COUNTY CITIZEN   weekly--established 1919, merged with Allendale County News Leader in Dec 1981 to form Allendale County Citizen Leader. Eugene B. McSweeney, also publisher of Hampton County Guardian, original publisher. First cited Ayer 1920: Cliff Langford (editor). Tom O'Connor and Robin Denny also associated with paper.   May 29, 1930 = vol 11, no 34, McSweeney (editor and publisher). *Files: Aiken CL mfm (1930-1938) 6; Allendale County Citizen Leader 1976-1981; Allendale CL 1976-1981, mfm Aug 1947-1975; SCL (1930-1958) 8, mfm (1930-1938) 6, Aug 1947-1975.*

ALLENDALE COUNTY CITIZEN LEADER   weekly--created 1981 by merger of Allendale County Citizen and Allendale County News Leader. Dec 2, 1981 = vol 60, no 39, Carol B. Barker (editor), Paul Jones (publisher). Dianna S. Simmons and Art Grimm also associated with paper. *Files: Allendale County Citizen Leader 1981 + ; Allendale CL 1981 + ; SCL ((1985 +)).*

ALLENDALE COUNTY NEWS LEADER   weekly--established 1980, merged with Allendale County Citizen Dec 1981 to form Allendale County Citizen Leader. Feb 13, 1980 = vol 1, no 1, Carol B. Barker (editor), Kilgus Publications [Bamberg]. *Files: Allendale CL Feb 13, Mar 26, 1980.*

ALLENDALE ENTERPRISE   weekly, Democrat--established 1889, ceased c. 1892. Cited Ayer 1890 thru 1892. Ayer 1890: I. L. Tobin (editor), Enterprise Company (publisher). Mar 20, 1891 = vol 2, no 23, T. P. Miller (editor), T. P. Miller & Company (publisher). *Files: SCL Mar 20, 1891.*

ALLENDALE HERALD   weekly--established 1910, ceased c. 1916. Cited Ayer 1911 thru 1916: F. Earle Bradham (publisher). Mar 12, 1914 = vol 4, no 33. *Files: SCL Mar 12, 1914.*

ALLENDALE PEN AND PRESS   weekly--established 1897, ceased c. 1899. Only cited once in Ayer (1899): Corrine Searson (editor), R. P. Searson (publisher). *NFK*

COUNTY NEWS   weekly, independent--established 1943, ceased c. 1969. Cited Ayer 1946 thru 1969. Ayer 1946: Ray B. Edenfield (editor and publisher). Sep 20, 1962 = vol 20, no 43, Evelyn B. Edenfield (publisher). *Files: Allendale CL (1962-1968) 75.*

TRI-COUNTY RECORD   weekly, independent--established 1919 as Advance, ceased c. 1922. Cited Ayer 1921 and 1922: Ed. N. Clarke (editor), Allendale Printing and Publishing Company. *NFK*

FAIRFAX

ADVANCE   weekly--established 1913, ceased c. 1914. Cited once in Ayer (1914): W. Walton (editor and publisher). *NFK*

FAIRFAX CITIZEN   weekly, Democrat--established 1917, ceased c. 1919. Cited Ayer 1918 and 1919. Oct 5, 1917 = vol 1, no 15, Mrs. E. A. McDowell (editor), Eugene B. McSweeney (publisher). This issue says established Jul 6, 1917. *Files: SCL Oct 5, 1917.*

FAIRFAX ENTERPRISE   weekly, Democrat--established 1892, ceased c. 1908. Cited Ayer 1899 thru 1908. Ayer 1899 and 1900: T. P. Miller (editor and publisher). Ayer 1901-1908: Mrs. Virginia D. Young (editor and publisher). Nov 16, 1898 = vol 6, no 50, Miller (editor and publisher). *Files: SCL Nov 16, 1898, Jun 10, 1903, Oct 19, Dec 21, 28, 1904, Dec 20, 1905.*

ANDERSON COUNTY

Created in 1826 when old Pendleton District was divided into two parts, Pickens and Anderson, the latter is named for Virginia-born Robert Anderson (1741-1813). A colonel during the Revolutionary War and then a brigadier-general in the state militia, Anderson also represented both Ninety Six and Pendleton districts in the lower house of the General Assembly.

ANDERSON

ANDERSON APPEAL   weekly--established 1866, ceased c. 1866. May 30, 1866 = vol 1, no 10, W. E. Walters and W. W. Humphreys (editors). *Files: Boston Athenaeum May 30, Jun 13, 1866. Apparently no copies in SC.*

ANDERSON CONSERVATOR   weekly--established 1872, ceased c. 1875 when reportedly sold to Anderson Intelligencer. Cited Rowell 1873 thru 1875. Rowell 1873: William S. Brown (editor), Brown and Haynie (publishers). Rowell 1874: McGill and Langston (editors and publishers). Rowell 1875: E. B. Murray (editor), Murray and McGill (publishers). *NFK*

ANDERSON DAILY INTELLIGENCER   daily except Sun--created in 1914 when semi-weekly Anderson Intelligencer launched daily morning edition, ceased c. 1917. Jan 13, 1914 = vol 1, no 1, William Banks (editor). Cited by Ayer 1915 thru 1917. L. M. Glenn also associated with paper. *Files: Anderson CL and Clemson mfm Jan 13, 1914-Jun 1916; SCL orig & mfm Jan 13, 1914-Jun 1916.*

ANDERSON DAILY MAIL   daily--established Oct 6, 1899, merged with Anderson Independent Sep 30, 1981, continued by Anderson Independent-Mail. Daily Mail originally daily except Mon, by 1906 except Sun, c. 1975 except Sat and Sun. Jan 2, 1900 issue has no vol number, "first year," Advocate Publishing Company. G. P. Browne, original editor and publisher, continued to issue People's Advocate as weekly and semi-weekly edition of Daily Mail until c. 1918. In addition to Browne, A. M. Carpenter, L. M. Glenn, R. Glover Miller, W. E. Hall, J. B. Hall, Henry Womack, John Ginn, and James A. Brown associated with paper. Also issued at times as Daily Mail. From 1932 to 1981 Anderson Daily Mail and Anderson Independent jointly owned. *Files: Anderson CL and SCL mfm 1900-Mar 1918, (1920-1922) 8, 1923-May 1939, May 1945-Mar 1952, Aug 1973-Sep 1981; Anderson Independent-Mail mfm 1972-Sep 1981; Clemson mfm 1900-1904, 1944-1949.*

ANDERSON DAILY TRIBUNE   daily--established as semi-weekly Farmers' Tribune in 1915, on Oct 16, 1917 became Anderson Daily Tribune, and merged with Anderson Independent in 1925 to create Anderson Independent-Tribune. Cited Ayer 1919 thru 1925. Ayer 1919: Victor B. Cheshire (editor), Bivine Cheshire (publisher). Wilton E. Hall, K. P. Cheshire, and Ernest V. Crist also associated with paper. Sometimes published as the Anderson Tribune. *Files: SCL (1920-1924) 7.*

ANDERSON FARMERS' TRIBUNE   semi-weekly--established as Farmers' Tribune in 1915, but soon became Anderson Farmers' Tribune, and in Oct 1917 continued by Anderson Daily Tribune. Dec 21, 1915 = vol 1, no 69 ("Farmers" in small type). Ayer 1918: Victor B. Cheshire (editor), Bivine Cheshire (publisher). *Files: Clemson Jan 7, 1916; SCL Dec 21, 1915, mfm Jul 3, 1917.*

ANDERSON FREE PRESS   weekly--established Aug 28, 1953, ceased c. 1978. Feb 18, 1954 = vol 1, no 26, H. G. Anderson (president), Anderson Free Press, Inc. Cited Ayer 1954 thru 1978. Beth Ann Klosky and Roy Ethridge also associated with paper. *Files: SCL Feb 18, 1954, Jan 19, May 31, Jun 7, 1956.*

ANDERSON GAZETTE   weekly--established Nov 11, 1843, James L. Orr (editor), R. E. Wyatt (publisher). After one year Archibald Todd replaced Orr. According to Ellen, published by Todd and T. H. Russell in 1850. Circa Dec 1854 merged with Southern Rights Advocate to create Gazette and Advocate. Samuel G. Earle, publisher of Anderson Gazette and Gazette and Advocate, apparently sold latter to A. O. Norris & Co., which revived original name and continued number system. May 21, 1861 = vol 17, no 50, A. O. Norris & Co. (proprietors), H. Manly Darlington (publisher), Thomas Hall (editor). Paper ceased c. 1861. *Files: Clemson Jun 21, 1854; SCL (1844-1861) 9; Anderson CL, Clemson, and SCL mfm Nov 11, 1843-Feb 24, 1848.*

ANDERSON INDEPENDENT   semi-weekly, daily--established 1924, merged with Anderson Daily Tribune in 1925 to create Anderson Independent-Tribune. Published under that title (or Anderson Independent and Tribune) until c. 1950 when resumed original name. Merged with Anderson Daily Mail Sep 30, 1981 to create Anderson Independent-Mail. According to Ayer, began as semi-weekly, but soon became daily. Oct 1, 1924 = vol 1, no 73, daily including Sun, Wilton E. Hall (editor). In addition to Hall, L. S. Hembree, Haney Womack, John Ginn, Bill Coats, and Richard Gorrell associated with paper. From 1932 to 1981 Anderson Independent and Anderson Daily Mail jointly owned. *Files: Anderson CL, Clemson, and SCL mfm Oct-Dec 1924, Apr 1929-Sep 1981; Anderson Independent-Mail mfm Jan 1972-Sep 1981.*

ANDERSON INDEPENDENT-MAIL   daily-created Sep 30, 1981 by merger of Anderson Independent and Anderson Daily Mail. Sep 30, 1981 = vol 82, no 365, Richard L. Gorrell (editor), John C. Ginn (publisher). Also publishes weekly Hometowner for Anderson and nearby Georgia communities. Georgia Hometowner (established 1981) has offices in Lavonia, Georgia. East and west editions of Anderson Hometowner bear same number sequence as paper. *Files: Anderson CL, Anderson Independent-Mail, Clemson, and SCL mfm 1981 + .*

ANDERSON INDEPENDENT-TRIBUNE   see Anderson Independent.

ANDERSON INTELLIGENCER   weekly, semi-weekly--established 1860 as weekly, became semi-weekly c. 1907, and on Jan 31, 1914 launched Anderson Daily Intelligencer, which ceased c. 1917. Semi-weekly edition appeared as Anderson Semi-Weekly

Intelligencer c. 1915-1917. Aug 14, 1860 = vol 1, no 1, J. C. C. Featherstone and James A. Hoyt (editors). Others associated with paper include E. B. Murray, J. F. Clinkscales, C. C. Langston, Victor B. Cheshire, Harold C. Booker, Leon B. Green, and William Banks. *Files: Greenville CL Aug 16, 1888; Anderson CL, Clemson, and SCL mfm (1860-1861) 35, (1865) 19, Jun 1866-Aug 1906.*

ANDERSON JOURNAL   weekly--established 1875, ceased c. 1876. Cited Rowell 1876: Belcher and Earle (editors and publishers). *NFK*

ANDERSON JOURNAL   weekly, Independent Democrat--established 1876, ceased c. 1897. Cited Rowell and Ayer 1877 thru 1897. Rowell 1877: A. S. Todd (editor and publisher). A. R. Todd also associated with paper. Aug 22, 1882 = no 343, A. S. and A. R. Todd (publishers). *Files: SCL mfm (1882-1889) 8.*

ANDERSON SEMI-WEEKLY INTELLIGENCER   see Anderson Intelligencer.

ANDERSON TRIBUNE   see Anderson Daily Tribune.

BLEASE'S WEEKLY   weekly--established 1925, ceased c. 1928. Dec 10, 1925 = vol 1, no 1, Senator Cole L. Blease (contributing editor), Anderson Daily Independent (publisher). Cited Ayer 1927 and 1928: Wilton E. Hall (editor and publisher). *Files: SCL mfm (1925-1926) 13.*

DAILY ITEM   daily c. Mar-Apr 1946, soon ceased. *NFK*

DAILY MAIL   see Anderson Daily Mail.

FARMERS' TRIBUNE   see Anderson Farmers' Tribune.

GAZETTE AND ADVOCATE   weekly--created c. 1854 by merger of Anderson Gazette and Southern Rights Advocate, continuing number sequence of Anderson Gazette. May 21, 1856 = vol 13, no 10, Samuel G. Earle (editor), S. G. Earle & Comapny (proprietor). By 1858 being published as Anderson Gazette by A. G. Norris & Company. *Files: SCL mfm May 21, 1856.*

HERALD   weekly, semi-monthly (irregular), black publication--established 1957. Jul 1, 1962 = vol 5, no 16, Davis Lee (publisher). Although based in Anderson, issues highlight events in Charleston, Columbia, Orangeburg, etc. Not cited by Ayer. After 1966 apparently published in Anderson and Orangeburg. See Herald [Orangeburg]. *Files: SCL mfm (1962-1965) 8.*

HIGHLAND SENTINEL   weekly--established in Calhoun [Pickens County] on Sep 4, 1840 = vol 1, no 1, J. P. Reed (editor and proprietor). Paper moved to Anderson on Jan 7, 1842 and ceased in Oct 1843 when sold to James L. Orr, who then started the Anderson Gazette. *Files: Anderson CL, Clemson, and SCL mfm ((Sep 1840-Oct 1843)) 150.*

HOMETOWNER   see Anderson Independent-Mail.

NEWS LEADER   daily--established 1969, ceased c. 1969. Jun 1, 1969 = vol 1, no 1, Robert C. Fort (editor), Roy Ethridge (publisher). Not cited by Ayer. *Files: SCL Jun 1, 1969.*

PEOPLE'S ADVOCATE   weekly, semi-weekly--established 1890 as a Farmers' Alliance weekly, ceased c. 1918. Cited Ayer 1891 thru 1918. Jan 4, 1892 = vol 2, no 10, D. H. Russell (editor), Advocate Publishing Company. In 1899 Advocate Publishing Company launched the Anderson Daily Mail, continuing People's Advocate (sometimes issued as "Weekly Advocate") as weekly edition of Anderson Daily Mail. In Oct 1899, G. P. Browne (publisher). From c. 1908-1918 People's Advocate semi-weekly. A. M. Carpenter also associated with paper. *Files: Aiken CL mfm 1892, 1897; Erskine mfm 1897, 1899-1901, 1904, 1908, Jul-Dec 1909, Jul-Dec 1911, Jan-Jun 1912, 1915; Greenville CL Jun 5, 1897; SCL orig & mfm 1892-1893, 1897, 1899-1901, 1904, 1908, Jul-Dec 1909, Jul-Dec 1911, Jan-Jun 1912, 1915.*

RECORD   semi-weekly, daily--established 1931, ceased c. 1939. Issued semi-weekly to Nov 15, 1934, then daily except Sun. Apr 21, 1931 = vol 1, no 2, Browne Publishing Company. Ayer cites G. Paul Browne as editor. *Files: SCL (1931, 1935) 8; Anderson CL, Clemson, and SCL mfm Apr 17, 1931-Jun 30, 1936.*

SOUTH CAROLINA BAPTIST   weekly-established 1866, ceased Dec 1868 when sold to the Religious Herald [Richmond, Va.]. Apr 20, 1866 = vol 1, no 1, W. E. Walters (editor). Cited by Rowell 1869: Hoyt and Walters (publishers). *Files: Furman and SCL mfm ((Apr 20, 1866-Dec 1868)) 120.*

SOUTHERN CHRISTIAN ADVOCATE   weekly, Methodist--established in Charleston in 1837 and published in various cities, including Anderson, 1915-1918. See Southern Christian Advocate [Columbia].

SOUTHERN RIGHTS ADVOCATE   weekly--according to Ellen, founded by Ibzan J. Rice in Sep 1851, merged with Anderson Gazette c. 1854 to create Gazette and Advocate. Jul 7, 1852 = vol 1, no 10, Ibzan J. Rice (editor and publisher). *Files: American Antiquarian Society Jul 7, 1852; Duke Jul 28, 1852, Feb 1, 1854. Apparently no files in SC.*

TEXTILE HERALD   weekly--established 1940, ceased c. 1944. Cited Ayer 1942 thru 1944. Ayer 1942: O. M. Hays (editor and published). *NFK*

TEXTILE WEEKLY   weekly--established 1927, ceased c. 1931. Cited Ayer 1928 thru 1931. Ayer 1928: H. S. Tilden, C. A. Ashley, Jr., and T. C. McCants (publishers). Clyde W. Epperson also associated with paper. *NFK*

TRUE CAROLINIAN   weekly--established 1856, ceased c. 1858. May 14, 1857 = vol 2, no 15, John V. Moore (editor and proprietor), F. E. Martin (publisher). According to Ellen, paper moved to Pendleton in May 1858; however, no Pendleton files exist. *Files: SCL May 14, 1857.*

WEEKLY ADVOCATE   see People's Advocate.

BELTON

BELTON JOURNAL   weekly--established 1914, ceased c. 1925. Cited Ayer 1915 thru 1925. Ayer 1915: Claude A. Graves (editor and publisher). Jul 6, 1917 = vol 4, no 16, Claude A. Graves (editor and manager). Foy A. Vause and D. W. Hiott, Jr., also associated with paper. *Files: SCL orig & mfm Jul 6, 1917.*

BELTON NEWS   weekly--continues Belton Times c. 1912, ceased c. 1914. Cited by Ayer 1913 and 1914. May 30, 1912 = vol 1, no 16, Francis L. Morrow (editor and publisher). *Files: SCL orig & mfm May 30, 1912.*

BELTON NEWS   weekly--established 1925. Cited Ayer 1933 to present. N. A. Coward (1887-1939), founder. Sep 18, 1941 = vol 16, no 3 (no personnel cited). R. Glenn Coward and B. J. Coward also associated with paper. *Files: Belton News 1925 + , mfm 1925-1936, 1966-1968; SCL (1941-1942) 6, ((1984 +)), mfm (1941-1942) 6.*

BELTON TIMES   weekly--established 1901, ceased c. 1903. Cited Ayer 1903: George E. Clarke (editor and publisher). *NFK*

BELTON TIMES   weekly--established 1903, became Belton News in 1912. Cited Ayer 1905 thru 1912. Ayer 1905: George E. Clarke (editor and publisher). J. Archie Willis and S. Brooks Marshall also associated with paper. *NFK*

HONEA PATH

HONEA PATH CHRONICLE   weekly--established 1894. Ayer 1895: L. Y. Moore (editor and publisher). Jul 4, 1917 = vol 23, no 15, G. E. Moore (publisher). R. L. Crawford, H. H. Watkins, C. H. Culpepper, Fred T. Moore, Fredda M. Gilmer, S. Daniel Branyon, and Patty Drosieko also associated with paper. *Files: Anderson CL mfm Feb 1941-Sep 1945, Nov 1945 + ; Honea Path Chronicle ((1950 +)); SCL Jul 4, 1917, Jul 15, 1932, Apr 3, 1941.*

HONEA PATH PLAINDEALER   weekly--established 1885, ceased c. 1887. Cited Ayer 1885 and 1886. According to Ayer ad (1886), J. B. Watkins (editor). Dec 9, 1886 = vol 2, no 41, Thomas H. Brock (business manager), Plaindealer Company (publisher). *Files: SCL (Dec 1886-Feb 1887) 8.*

HONEA PATH TORPEDO   weekly c. 1890, cited in Abbeville papers. Soon ceased. *NFK*

WEEKLY MESSENGER   weekly--published by T. W. Lomax and D. L. Malone c. 1887. Cited in Abbeville Medium (Oct 16, 1887). *NFK*

PELZER

ENTERPRISE   weekly--established 1905, ceased c. 1908. Cited Ayer 1907 and 1908: George E. Clarke (editor and publisher). *NFK*

HERALD   weekly--established 1897, merged with Sun [Piedmont] c. 1899 to create Sun-Herald [Piedmont]. Cited Ayer 1898 and 1899. Ayer 1898: P. B. Langston (editor), John R. Dortch (publisher). Ayer 1899: John T. West (editor), A. S. Rowell (publisher). *NFK*

PELMONT   weekly--established 1913, ceased c. 1914. Cited once in Ayer (1914): P. W. Smith (editor and publisher). *NFK*

UPLIFTER   weekly--established 1910, merged with Advertiser [Williamston] c. 1911 to create Advertiser and Uplifter. Cited once in Ayer (1911): I. E. Wallace (editor), E. C. Horton (publisher). *NFK*

PENDLETON

MILLER'S WEEKLY MESSENGER   weekly--established Jan 16, 1807 by John Miller & Son. Miller soon died and his son (John Miller) continued paper. Circa 1812 became Pendleton Messenger. *Files: Clemson, Furman, and SCL mfm (Mar 1807-Dec 1808) 81, (Feb 1810-Jan 1811) 43.*

PENDLETON MESSENGER   weekly--established as Miller's Weekly Messenger 1807, title changed to Pendleton Messenger c. 1812. Published in Pendleton until Jun 1858 when, according to Ellen, sold to Anderson True Carolinian. Moved to Hartwell, Ga., c. Jun 1859. May 22, 1813 = vol 7, no 13, John Miller (publisher). *Files: CLS (Jan 1828-Aug 1832) 50; Clemson Jun 17, 1818-May 19, 1819, ((1831-1839)) 272, Feb 3, 1843-Jan 23, 1846, mfm ((1831-1843)) 300; Furman mfm ((1831-1843)) 300; Pickens CL mfm (1816-1823) 6, Feb 1826-Sep 1851; SCL (1816-1823) 6, Feb 1826-Sep 1851, mfm (1813-1814) 40, ((1818-1826)) 310, Feb 1826-Sep 1851; Wofford mfm 1836-1837.*

PENDLETON NEWS   weekly--established 1912, ceased c. 1914. Cited Ayer 1913 and 1914. Ayer 1913: E. A. Trescott (editor), Phillips Printers. Ayer 1914: P. W. Smith (editor), Phillips Printers. *NFK*

RECORD   semi-monthly, black publication c. 1907. Cited Ayer 1907: C. E. Minor (editor and publisher). *NFK*

WILLIAMSTON

ADVERTISER AND UPLIFTER weekly--created c. 1911 by merger of Williamston Advertiser and Uplifter [Pelzer], ceased c. 1914. Cited Ayer 1912 and 1913. Ayer 1912: DeWitt G. Stone (editor and publisher). Ayer 1913: James L. Brown (editor), DeWitt G. Stone (publisher). *NFK*

JOURNAL weekly--established 1955. Cited Ayer 1959 to present. Ayer 1959: Edward Wills (editor and publisher). Jan 1, 1970 = vol 15, no 16, William C. Meade (editor and publisher). *Files: Journal 1955 + ; SCL ((1984 +)).*

NEW ERA weekly--established 1890, ceased c. 1890. Cited once in Ayer (1890): H. M. Wroton (manager), New Era Publishing Company. *NFK*

TEMPERANCE STANDARD weekly--established 1878, according to North ceased Apr 1880. Official organ of the Sons of Temperance and Good Templars of South Carolina. May 2, 1878 = vol 2, no 5, D. H. Witherspoon and F. V. Capers (editors and publishers). Cited Rowell 1879: Lockwood and Donalds (editors and publishers). *Files: SCL May 2, 1878, Aug 7, 1879.*

WILLIAMSTON ADVERTISER weekly--established 1907, merged with Uplifter [Pelzer] c. 1911 to create Advertiser and Uplifter. Cited Ayer 1909 thru 1911: E. C. Horton (editor and publisher). *NFK*

WILLIAMSTON NEWS weekly--established 1900, ceased c. 1906. Cited Ayer 1901 thru 1906. Ayer 1901: R. Brooks Goodgion (editor and publisher). Ayer 1902-1906: George E. Clarke (editor and publisher). *NFK*

WILLIAMSTON NEWS weekly--established 1914, ceased c. 1919. Cited Ayer 1916 thru 1919. Ayer 1916: Allan R. Hawkins (editor), P. W. Smith (publisher). *NFK*

WILLIAMSTONIAN weekly--established 1897, ceased c. 1899. Cited Ayer 1898 and 1899: Frank Lander (editor), Oscar D. Gray (publisher). *NFK*

BAMBERG COUNTY

Separated from Barnwell County in 1897, Bamberg County is named for General Francis Marion Bamberg (1838-1905). Bamberg, a prominent businessman and a Confederate lieutenant, earned the title of "general" as a brigadier-general on the staff of Governor Wade Hampton.

BAMBERG

ADVERTISER   weekly, Democrat--established 1889, became Barnwell County Advertiser [Blackville] c. 1891. Cited Ayer 1889 and 1890: D. H. Witherspoon (editor and publisher). *NFK*

ADVERTIZER   weekly, independent--established 1967, merged with Bamberg Herald 1972 to create Advertizer-Herald. Feb 16, 1967 = vol 1, no 1, Kilgus Printing Company. According to Ayer (1971), Carl L. Kilgus (editor), Betty S. Kilgus (publisher). *Files: Advertizer-Herald 1967-1972.*

ADVERTIZER-HERALD   weekly, independent--created Dec 1972 by merger of Advertizer and Bamberg Herald. Carl and Betty Kilgus founded Advertizer in 1967. When Orangeburg plant where Bamberg Herald was being printed burned in Oct 1972, they acquired that paper. Dec 6, 1972 (vol 6, no 50) was first joint issue, Kilgus Printing Company. *Files: Advertizer-Herald 1972 + ; Bamberg CL and SCL mfm Jan 1973-Dec 1984.*

BAMBERG COUNTY TIMES   weekly, Democrat--established 1888 in Denmark as News by R. W. D. Rowell (publisher), changed name to Times c. 1892 (also published in Denmark), and transferred operations to Bamberg c. 1901, becoming Bamberg County Times. Continued number sequence begun in 1888. May 29, 1902 = vol 14, no 47. First cited Ayer 1902: R. W. D. Rowell (editor and publisher). Rowell (1852-1917) was county superintendent of education in 1902. W. D. Rowell (1880-1935) and R. Clyde Rowell also associated with paper, which ceased c. 1944. *Files: SCL (1902-1938) 29, mfm (1930-1938) 26.*

BAMBERG HERALD   weekly--established 1891, merged with Advertizer Dec 1972 to create Advertizer-Herald. First cited by Ayer 1891: Henry S. Hartzog (editor and publisher). Note: In first three decades paper had no volume or issue numbers. In addition to Hartzog, A. W. Knight, Otis Brabham, R. M. Hitt, R. M. Bruce, Lewis F. Brabham, P. E. Brabham, and Thomas B. Salley associated with paper. *Files: Advertizer-Herald 1910-1911, 1917-1919, 1925-1972; Bamberg CL mfm (1955-1966) 10, Jan 1967-Nov 1972; SCL (1891-1955) 21, mfm (1891-1932) 14, (1955-1966) 10, Jan 1967-Nov 1972.*

CHRONICLE   weekly--established 1880, ceased c. 1884. Cited Ayer 1882 thru 1884. No personnel named. *NFK*

DENMARK

EDISTO NEWS   weekly--established c. 1921, ceased c. 1944. First cited Ayer 1922: Andre R. Wallace (editor), News Publishing Company. May 30, 1930 = vol 10, no 4, E. E. Crowson (editor and publisher). Last cited Ayer 1944. Mrs. A. G. Steadman, J. A. Latimer, and S. B. Allen also associated with paper. *Files: SCL mfm May 23, 30, 1930.*

EDISTO NEWS   weekly, independent--established 1959, ceased c. 1969. Ayer 1960: Jack H. Brewster (editor and publisher). In 1965 Brewster was succeeded by Edgar V. Hightower, Jr., and the following year P. E. Brabham (editor and publisher of the Bamberg Herald) acquired the Edisto News. Probably ceased c. 1969 when Brabham sold Bamberg Herald to Times and Democrat [Orangeburg]. *NFK*

NEWS   weekly, Democrat--established in 1888 when Denmark was "Graham's" in Barnwell County, became Times c. 1891. Cited Ayer 1889 thru 1891: P. E. Rowell (editor), R. W. D. Rowell (publisher). *NFK*

TIMES   weekly, Democrat--created c. 1891 by name change, formerly News. Cited Ayer 1892 thru 1901: R. W. D. Rowell (editor and publisher). Circa 1901 became Bamberg County Times [Bamberg]. *NFK*

MIDWAY

GAZETTE   weekly--established 1896, ceased c. 1897. Cited once Ayer (1897): Walker and Cauthen (editors and publishers). *NFK*

BARNWELL COUNTY

Descended from old Winton and Orangeburgh districts, Barnwell County is named for John Barnwell (1748-1800), a Revolutionary War veteran who later served in the South Carolina Senate and became a brigadier-general in the state militia. Barnwell was organized as a separate entity in 1798. Nevertheless, as late as the 1820s official records continued to refer to this region as "Winton District."

BARNWELL

BARNWELL JOURNAL   weekly, semi-weekly--established 1869, c. 1871 became Barnwell Journal and Ledger and then reverted to former title, ceased c. 1872. Cited Rowell 1870 and again 1872: John S. Shuck (editor and publisher). Issues at the Library of Congress (Jul 24, Nov 27, 1869) indicate paper was published in Blackville at that time. May 18, 1870 = vol 2, no 84, John S. Shuck (publisher). *Files: SCL mfm May 18, 1870.*

BARNWELL JOURNAL AND LEDGER   weekly--established 1869 as Barnwell Journal, issued under this title c. 1871. Cited in Rowell (1871): John S. Shuck (editor and publisher). In 1872 resumed former name and soon ceased publication. *NFK*

BARNWELL PEOPLE   weekly--established 1877 as People, became Barnwell People Aug 14, 1884 = vol 7, no 50, John W. Holmes (editor and proprietor), merged with Barnwell Sentinel in 1925 to create Barnwell People-Sentinel. Holmes (1840-1912) was succeeded by B. P. Davies, who also edited the Barnwell People-Sentinel. *Files: SCL Sep 18, 1924; Barnwell CL and SCL mfm Aug 1884-Aug 1906, Sep 1907-Aug 1911, Jan 1914-May 1925.*

BARNWELL PEOPLE-SENTINEL   weekly--established Jun 1925 by merger of Barnwell People and Barnwell Sentinel. Jun 4, 1925 = vol 48, no 40, B. P. Davies (editor and publisher), first joint issue. B. P. Davies, Jr., R. C. Harris, and William C. Nesbit also associated with paper. *Files: Barnwell CL mfm 1925 + ; Barnwell People-Sentinel 1969 + ; SCL mfm 1925 +.*

BARNWELL RECORDER   see Recorder.

BARNWELL SENTINEL   weekly--established as Palmetto Sentinel in 1852 by E. A. Bronson, became Barnwell Sentinel c. 1859, merged with Barnwell People in 1925 to form Barnwell People-Sentinel. Mar 9, 1861 = vol 9, no 48, Edw. A. Bronson (editor). J. I. Bronson, C. L. Brown, Mrs. J. Bronson, R. B. Cole, W. M. Jones, and K. M. Sims also associated with paper. *Files: SCL (1862-1903) 8, mfm (1861-1914) 13, 1917-1919, 1923.*

NEW SENTINEL   weekly--established 1902, ceased c. 1904. Only editor and publisher was Clarence L. Brown, editor of Barnwell Sentinel in 1898 and again in 1905.

Apparently short-lived rival of better-established <u>Barnwell Sentinel</u>. Oct 1, 1902 = vol 2, no 7, Brown (editor and publisher). *Files: SCL Oct 1, 1902, Jan 24, 1903.*

PALMETTO SENTINEL   weekly--established 1852 by E. A. Bronson, became <u>Barnwell Sentinel</u> c. 1859. Bronson formerly published a newspaper in Camden. According to <u>Barnwell Sentinel</u> (May 11, 1882), paper was established Mar 17, 1852. Oct 30, 1852 = vol 1, no 33, Bronson (proprietor), J. A. Bellinger (editor). *Files: SCL Jun 23 (fragment), Oct 30, 1852.*

PEOPLE   weekly--established Sep 1877, became <u>Barnwell People</u> Aug 14, 1884. Sep 13, 1877 = vol 1, no 2, John W. Holmes (editor). *Files: SCL Feb 9, 1882; Barnwell CL and SCL mfm Sep 1877-Aug 1884.*

RECORDER   weekly, Republican, black publication--established 1893, moved to Columbia c. 1896 where issued as <u>People's Recorder</u>. Cited once in Barnwell by Ayer (1895): Samuel H. Nix (publisher). Title may have been "Barnwell Recorder." See <u>People's Recorder</u> [Columbia].

BLACKVILLE

BANNER AND TRI-COUNTY ADVERTISER   weekly, independent-- established 1921, ceased c. 1922. Cited once by Ayer (1922): Ed. N. Clarke (editor and publisher). *NFK*

BARNWELL COUNTY ADVERTISER   weekly, Democrat--established 1889, ceased c. 1891. Published in Bamberg as <u>Advertiser</u> (1889-1890). Cited in Blackville by Ayer 1891: D. H. Witherspoon (editor and publisher). *NFK*

BARNWELL COUNTY TIMES   weekly, Republican, black publication-- established 1871, ceased c. 1875. Cited by Rowell 1874 and 1875: Mrs. F. A. Whipper (editor and publisher). Mrs. F. A. Whipper probably relative of black politician W. J. Whipper. *NFK*

BARNWELL JOURNAL   see <u>Barnwell Journal</u> [Barnwell].

BEAUFORT TIMES   weekly, Republican, black publication--according to Woody, W. J. Whipper published this weekly in Blackville c. 1873 while treasurer of Barnwell County...Woody presumably means <u>Beaufort County Times</u>. See <u>Beaufort County Times</u> [Beaufort].

BLACKVILLE NEWS   weekly, Democrat--established 1875, ceased c. 1876. Cited once by Rowell (1876): J. H. Hammet (editor and publisher). *NFK*

BLACKVILLE SUN   weekly, Republican--established 1875, ceased c. 1876. Cited by Rowell (1876) as "Blackwell Sun." <u>Free Citizen</u> of Orangeburg (Jul 31, 1875) contains an angry letter by J. Felder Meyers (co-proprietor of the <u>Blackville Sun</u>) concerning a disagreement with Charles H. Hall (publisher of both the Blackville Sun and Free Citizen). *NFK*

COURIER   weekly, Democrat--established 1908, ceased c. 1911. Listed Ayer 1910 and 1911: W. W. Tyler (editor and publisher). *NFK*

HERALD   weekly, Democrat--established 1913, ceased c. 1916. Cited once by Ayer (1916): G. B. Herndon (editor and publisher). *NFK*

NEWS   weekly, Democrat--established 1876, ceased c. 1877. Cited once by Rowell (1877): T. D. Kennedy (editor), John D. Kennedy & Company (publisher). *NFK*

WILLISTON

WILLISTON FARMERS' ADVOCATE   weekly, Democrat--established 1890, ceased c. 1890. Cited once by Ayer (1890): E. Y. Perry (editor and publisher). *NFK*

WILLISTON WAY   weekly--established 1921. Cited by Ayer 1922 to present. Ayer 1922: J. A. Latimer (editor), Williston Publishing Company. Sep 12, 1924 = vol 4, no 16, J. A. Latimer (editor), Williston Publishing Company. Currently printed and published by Barnwell People-Sentinel. E. E. Crowson, R. S. Davies, F. L. Harper, B. P. Davies, Sr., B. P. Davies, Jr., and Robert C. Harris also associated with paper. *Files: SCL (1924-1970) 6, ((Oct 1984 +)).*

BEAUFORT COUNTY

Beaufort, one of seven judicial districts organized in 1769, assumed the name of its port city, which honors Henry Somerset (1629-1700), the first Duke of Beaufort, one of the later lords proprietors.

BEAUFORT

BEAUFORT COUNTY LEADER   weekly, Democrat--established 1916, ceased c. 1917. Cited once in Ayer (1917): C. Reid Elkins (editor), E. B. McSweeney (publisher). *NFK*

BEAUFORT COUNTY NEWS   weekly, Republican, black publication--established 1904, ceased c. 1912. Cited Ayer 1906 thru 1912: Macon B. Allen (editor and publisher). *NFK*

BEAUFORT COUNTY NEWS   weekly--established 1939, merged with Jasper County Citizen Oct 5, 1939 to form Beaufort-Jasper News, which was published briefly in Beaufort and Ridgeland. Sep 14, 1939 = vol 1, no 2, Gilbert Parks (editor and publisher). *Files: SCL orig & mfm Sep 14-28, 1939.*

BEAUFORT COUNTY REPUBLICAN   weekly--established 1869 as Beaufort Republican and Sea Island Chronicle, became Beaufort County Republican Oct 12, 1871, and then Beaufort Republican Nov 30, 1871. Oct 12, 1871 = vol 2, no 3, George W. Johnson (mgr.), Port Royal Printing Company. *Files: Beaufort CL mfm Oct 12-Nov 23, 1871.*

BEAUFORT COUNTY TIMES   weekly Republican, black publication--established 1871, ceased c. 1874. Cited Rowell 1872 and 1873. Aug 26, 1871 = vol 1, no 19, D. Thomas (editor), Beaufort County Press Company (proprietor). Dec 21, 1872 = vol 2, no 26, W. J. Whipper (proprietor), Mrs. F. A. Whipper ("editress"). According to Woody, paper printed in Charleston to May 1872, then moved to Blackville where issued at least to Mar 1874. W. J. Whipper then Barnwell County treasurer. See Beaufort Times [Blackville]. *Files: American Antiquarian Society Aug 26, 1871; New York Historical Society Dec 21, 1872. Apparently no copies in SC.*

BEAUFORT GAZETTE   weekly--established 1828, ceased c. 1830. Jan 28, 1830 = vol 2, no 79. *Files: Library of Congress Jan 28, 1830. Apparently no copies in SC.*

BEAUFORT GAZETTE   weekly, daily--began as weekly in 1897, as of Apr 30, 1973 became Mon-Fri daily. Cited Ayer 1899 to present. Ayer 1899: William Elliott, Jr. (editor), W. O. Prentiss (publisher). Jul 16, 1903 = vol 7, no 23, Neils Christensen, Jr. (editor and publisher). Also associated with paper: William P. Waterhouse, H. T. Young, S. F. Sherman, W. S. Britton, R. C. Horner, Jr., W. J. Cormack, E. O. Wilson, B. F. Davies, Jr., Howard P. Cooper, T. Miles Burbage, W. K. Pillow, John

Heath, Ken Fortenberry, and James A. Cato. *Files: Beaufort CL, Beaufort Gazette, and SCL mfm ((1903-1907)) 115, 1908-Oct 1918, 1920-1943, 1945 + ; Clemson mfm ((1903-1907)) 115, 1908-Oct 1918, 1920-1943, 1945-1973.*

BEAUFORT-JASPER NEWS   weekly--formed Oct 1939 by merger of Beaufort County News and Jasper County Citizen, ceased c. Dec 1939. Published in Beaufort and Ridgeland. Oct 26, 1939 = vol 1, no 21, Albert Rouslin (editor). *Files: SCL orig & mfm Oct 5, 26, Nov 2, 9, 1939.*

BEAUFORT REPUBLICAN   weekly--continues the Beaufort County Republican on Nov 30, 1871. In 1873 merged with Port Royal Commercial to create Port Royal Commercial and Beaufort County Republican. Beaufort Republican cited in Rowell 1871 thru 1873. Rowell 1871: George W. Johnson (editor), Port Royal Printing Company (publisher). Rowell 1872 and 1873: J. G. Thompson (editor and publisher). Thompson claimed Beaufort Republican was only paper in county. *Files: Beaufort CL mfm (Nov 30, 1871-Oct 16, 1873) 81.*

BEAUFORT REPUBLICAN AND SEA ISLAND CHRONICLE   weekly-- established 1869, became Beaufort County Republican Nov 1871. Mar 21, 1870 = vol 1, no 34, Alfred Williams and David Thomas (editors). *Files: SCL orig & mfm Mar 21, 1870.*

BEAUFORT TIMES   see Beaufort County Times c. 1871.

BEAUFORT TIMES   weekly, Democrat--established 1944, ceased c. 1946. Jun 21, 1944 = vol 1, no 1, I. S. Caldwell (editor), Caldwell-Maner Publishing Company. Caldwell, father of author Erskine Caldwell, died Aug 17, 1944, age 72. At that time he was editor of the Beaufort Times, Allendale County Citizen, Hampton County Guardian, and Jasper County Record. Erskine Caldwell succeeded his father as editor of the Beaufort Times. *Files: Beaufort CL mfm Jun 21, 1944-Dec 20, 1945.*

BEAUFORT TRIBUNE   weekly, Republican--established Nov 1874, merged with Port Royal Standard and Commercial in 1876 to create Beaufort Tribune and Port Royal Commercial. Cited Rowell 1875 and 1876: Winchell Mansfield French (editor and publisher). Jun 14, 1876 = vol 2, no 30, W. M. French (editor, proprietor, and publisher). According to the Beaufort Gazette (May 28, 1985), may be considered a black publication since William J. Whipper reportedly was part owner. *Files: Library of Congress Nov 25, 1874-Dec 20, 1876. Apparently no copies in SC.*

BEAUFORT TRIBUNE AND PORT ROYAL COMMERCIAL   weekly--established 1876 by merger of Beaufort Tribune and Port Royal Standard and Commercial, succeeded by Crescent c. 1879. Jan 4, 1877 = vol 5, no 5, W. M. French (editor), W. M. French and John N. Wallace (proprietors). *Files: SCL orig & mfm Jan-Dec 1877.*

CAMP KETTLE weekly, irregular--established 1861, ceased ? Jan 7, 1862 = vol 1, no 9, published by staff of Roundhead Regiment, 100th Pennsylvania Volunteers. *Files: SCL Jan 7, May 1, 1862.*

COUNTY DEMOCRAT weekly--established 1910, ceased c. 1912. Cited once in Ayer (1912): E. G. Sandifer (editor), Beaufort County Democrat Company (publisher). Jul 20, 1910 = vol 1, no 1, Charles J. Tindall (editor), Democrat Publishing Company. Charles Bellinger also associated with paper. *Files: Beaufort CL mfm Jul 20, 1910-Dec 1, 1911.*

CRESCENT weekly--created 1879 as successor to Beaufort Tribune and Port Royal Commercial, continues number sequence, ceased c. 1881. Cited Ayer 1880 and 1881. Sep 11, 1879 = vol 7, no 30, S. H. Rodgers (editor). Rodgers says "only paper in county." *Files: SCL orig & mfm Sep 11, 1879.*

FREE SOUTH weekly--established Jan 10, 1863, ceased c. Nov 1864. Jan 17, 1863 = vol 1, no 2, James M. Latta & Company (proprietor). J. G. Thompson also associated with paper. *Files: Beaufort CL mfm (1863-1864) 28; CLS Jan 17, 31, Feb 7, 17, 1863; SCL orig & mfm (1863-1864) 28.*

NEW SOUTH weekly--established 1862 in Port Royal, moved to Beaufort c. 1865, ceased Mar 1867 when office burned. Jun 16, 1866 = vol 4, no 33, whole no 189, L. Thompson (editor and proprietor). *Files: Beaufort CL mfm (Jun-Sep 1866) 5; SCL orig & mfm (Jun-Sep 1866) 5.*

NEW SOUTH weekly, Republican, black publication--continues Sea Island News c. 1889, ceased c. 1898. Cited Ayer 1890 thru 1898. Mar 7, 1895 = vol 16, no 35, S. J. Bampfield (editor), S. W. Anderson (business manager). See Penn, Afro-American Press and Its Editors, pp. 205-210. *Files: SCL orig & mfm Mar 7, 1895.*

PALMETTO POST weekly--established in Port Royal in 1882, moved to Beaufort c. 1906, ceased c. 1907. Cited by Ayer in Beaufort 1906 and 1907: S. H. Rodgers (editor and publisher). See also Palmetto Post [Port Royal]. *Files: Beaufort CL mfm 1906.*

PORT ROYAL STANDARD AND COMMERCIAL weekly, Republican-- created in 1874 by merger of Southern Standard and Port Royal Commercial and Beaufort County Republican, merged with Beaufort Tribune in 1877 to form Beaufort Tribune and Port Royal Commercial. Cited Rowell 1875 thru 1877: A. G. Thomas (editor and publisher). Dec 9, 1875 = vol 4, no 1. J. G. Thompson also associated with paper. *Files: SCL (1874-1876) 60, mfm Aug 20, 1874, Sep 28, 1876.*

REPUBLICAN ADVOCATE weekly, Republican, black publication--established 1895, ceased c. 1898. Cited Ayer 1896 thru 1898: James Wigg (editor and publisher). According to Beaufort Gazette (May 28, 1985), W. J. Whipper, Sammy Green, and J. I. Walsh also associated with paper. *NFK*

SEA ISLAND JOURNAL   weekly, black publication, c. 1892. Beaufort Gazette (May 28, 1985) says N. F. Campbell (editor and publisher). Not cited by Ayer. *NFK*

SEA ISLAND NEWS   weekly, Independent Republican, black publication-- established 1879, succeeded c. 1889 by New South. Cited Ayer 1880 thru 1889. According to Ayer listing and ads, P. B. Morris & Company was proprietor in 1883. Tindall says direct successor of Beaufort Tribune. Nov 15, 1884 = vol 6, no 27, new series (no personnel cited). *Files: SCL mfm Nov 15, 1884, Jun 13, Oct 17, 1885.*

SEA ISLAND NEWS   weekly, Republican, black publication--established 1910, ceased c. 1913. Cited Ayer 1911 thru 1913: R. W. Mance (editor), Alexander Meyers (publisher). *NFK*

SEA ISLANDER   semi-weekly Aug 16, 1971. Sep 13, 1968 = vol 1, no 1, St. John Enterprises of Burton, S. C. (publisher). Jan 10, 1969, Penny Carpenter (editor and publisher), St. John Enterprises (also cited as publisher). Ceased c. 1975. *Files: Beaufort CL and SCL mfm 1968-1974.*

SOUTH CAROLINA CHURCHMAN   weekly, independent, black publication-- established 1904, ceased c. 1909. Cited Ayer 1906 thru 1909: L. Ruffin Nichols (editor and publisher). *NFK*

SOUTHERN STANDARD   weekly, Republican, black publication--established 1872 by Grant wing of Republican party, by May 1874 had merged with Port Royal Commercial and Beaufort County Republican, continued by the Port Royal Standard and Commercial. Apr 11, 1873 = vol 1, no 18. Cited by Rowell 1873 and 1874: G. W. Johnson (editor and publisher). According to Woody, paper founded Dec 6, 1872 and owned all or in part by Robert Smalls. *Files: New York Historical Society Apr 11, 1873. Apparently no copies in SC.*

BLUFFTON

BLUFFTON ECCENTRIC   weekly--established 1987. Sep 17, 1987 = vol 1, no 13, Graham Bullock (editor), Village Publishing Inc. *Files: Bluffton Eccentric 1987 + .*

GRAHAMVILLE

BEAUFORT ENTERPRISE   weekly--established 1860, ceased c. 1860. Sep 26, 1860 = vol 1, no 2, A. M. Speights (proprietor). *Files: SCL orig & mfm Sep 26, Oct 10, 1860.*

HILTON HEAD ISLAND

HILTON HEAD NEWS   weekly--established 1973 by Savannah Morning News. Jul 11, 1985 = vol 12, no 40, Charles W. Martin, Jr. (editor), William Morris (publisher). Issued as supplement to Savannah Morning News, but also sold independently on Hilton

Head Island and in Beaufort. Savannah Morning News also publishes a "Carolina" section on Sat. *Files: Hilton Head News 1981 + ; also available in Savannah Morning News mfm 1973 + .*

HOSPITAL SENTINEL   according to Woody, a single sheet printed at US Army Hospital by John Wingate on Apr 22, 1865 telling how news of Lincoln's death was received. Woody says bound with copies of the New South, but fails to say where. *NFK*

HOSPITAL TRANSCRIPT   weekly--established 1865, ceased c. 1865. Jul 8, 1865 = vol 1, no 9, M. J. McKenna (editor and publisher). *Files: SCL Jul 8, 1865.*

ISLAND PACKET   weekly, semi-weekly, tri-weekly, daily--established in 1970 as independent weekly, became semi-weekly Oct 16, 1973, tri-weekly Oct 3, 1983, and daily Sep 30, 1985. Jul 9, 1970 = vol 1, no 1, Ralph Hilton (editor), Island Packet Company (publisher). Also associated with paper: John Heath, Emily Bull, Thom Fesperman, Terry Plumb, and Ben T. Banks. *Files: Hilton Head Island Branch Library and SCL mfm 1970 + .*

PARRIS ISLAND

PARRIS ISLAND NEWS   weekly--established 1926, ceased ? Aug 21, 1926 = vol 1, no 22, E. A. Duff (editor), published under the direction of US Marine Corps. Primarily for servicemen and their families. *Files: SCL Aug 21, Sep 4, 18, 1926.*

PORT ROYAL

ADVERTISER   weekly--established 1877, ceased c. 1878. Cited in Rowell 1877 and 1878: Benjamin L. Brisbane (editor and publisher). *NFK*

ADVOCATE   weekly, Democrat--established 1878, ceased c. 1879. Cited once in Rowell (1879): S. H. Rodgers (editor and publisher). May have been successor to Advertiser. In 1882 Rodgers founded the Palmetto Post. *NFK*

NEW SOUTH   weekly--established 1862, moved to Beaufort c. 1865, ceased Mar 1867 when office burned. Mar 15, 1862 = vol 1, no 1, Adam Badeau (editor), Joseph H. Sears (publisher). H. J. Winser also associated with paper. *Files: Beaufort CL mfm (1862-1865) 54; CLS Aug 23, 1862, Dec 17, 1864; SCL orig & mfm (1862-1865) 54.*

PALMETTO HERALD   weekly--established Mar 1864, ceased Dec 1864 when owner went to Savannah to found Savannah News. Mar 17, 1864 = vol 1, no 3, S. W. Mason & Company (publisher). *Files: Beaufort CL mfm (1864) 20; SCL orig & mfm (1864) 20.*

PALMETTO POST   weekly, Democrat--established 1882, moved to Beaufort c. 1906. Cited by Ayer in Port Royal 1882 thru 1905. Aug 31, 1882 = vol 1, no 34, S. H. Rodgers (editor and proprietor). Ad for paper in Ayer 1886: "Worms Can't Affect It!"

See also <u>Palmetto Post</u> [Beaufort]. *Files: Beaufort CL mfm 1882-1906; Beaufort County Museum 1882-1889; <u>Beaufort Gazette</u> mfm 1895-1898; SCL (1882-1895) 8, mfm 1895-1898.*

PORT ROYAL COMMERCIAL   weekly, Republican--established 1870, merged with <u>Beaufort Republican</u> in 1873 to form <u>Port Royal Commercial and Beaufort County Republican</u>. Cited Ayer 1874: J. G. Thompson (editor and publisher). *NFK*

PORT ROYAL COMMERCIAL AND BEAUFORT COUNTY REPUBLI-CAN   weekly--created 1873 by merger of <u>Port Royal Commercial</u> and <u>Beaufort Republican</u>, merged with <u>Southern Standard</u> in 1874 to form <u>Port Royal Standard and Commercial</u> [Beaufort]. Not listed in Rowell. Oct 23, 1873 = vol 4, no 3, E. W. Everson (role not identified). By Feb 1874, J. G. Thompson (editor). *Files: Beaufort CL mfm Oct 23, 1873-Apr 30, 1874.*

BERKELEY COUNTY

Originally created in the late 17th Century and named for two of the lords proprietors, John and William Berkeley, this region became part of Charleston District in 1768. On January 31, 1882, Berkeley County re-appeared with virtually the same boundaries it had two centuries earlier.

GOOSE CREEK

GOOSE GREEK GAZETTE   weekly, independent--established 1979. Aug 29, 1979 = vol 1, no 1, Joyce Odom (editor), Goose Creek Gazette, Inc. *Files: Goose Creek Branch Library and Goose Creek Gazette 1979 + .*

MONCK'S CORNER

BERKELEY DEMOCRAT   weekly--established 1917. Ayer 1919: P. B. Lockwood (editor), Berkeley Publishing Company. Cited by Ayer since that time. Oct 6, 1938 = vol 20, no 15, Herbert Hucks (editor and publisher). Others associated with paper include Marion F. Winter (or Winters), G. E. McCormick, G. E. McCormick, Jr., Henry Hucks, Susan H. Nowell, Fred Sheheen, Christoper Hale, Paul W. Lohnes, J. Ernie Locklair, Jeanne Blain, H. Allen Morris, Kent Brown, and Jim Bretzius. *Files: Berkeley CL 1975 + ; Berkeley Democrat 1971 + ; Charleston CL 1985 + ; SCL (1928-1951) 50.*

BERKELEY ECHO   weekly, Democrat--established 1896, merged with Berkeley Free Press c. 1899, continued by Echo and Press. Ayer 1898 and 1899: R. H. Sweeney (editor and publisher). *NFK*

BERKELEY FREE PRESS   weekly, Democrat--established 1898, merged with Berkeley Echo c. 1899, continued by Echo and Press. Ayer 1899: S. P. Driggers (editor and publisher). *NFK*

BERKELEY GAZETTE   weekly, Democrat--established 1916, ceased c. 1918. Ayer 1917 and 1918: Clifford Thompson (editor and publisher). *NFK*

BERKELEY NEWS   weekly, Democrat--established 1896, ceased c. 1897. Cited once by Ayer (1897): H. Rudloff (editor and publisher). *NFK*

ECHO AND PRESS   weekly, Democrat--created c. 1899 by merger of Berkeley Echo and Berkeley Free Press, ceased c. 1917. Ayer 1900: S. P. Driggers (editor), R. H. Sweeney (publisher). In 1902 Driggers became editor and publisher and two years later moved paper to St. Stephen, where it remained until c. 1906. Ayer 1906: Driggers (editor), W. N. Faulling (publisher). In 1906-1907 paper returned to Monck's Corner. Faulling continued as publisher until 1915, when Driggers became editor-publisher once more. Echo and Press cited by Ayer 1900 thru 1917. *NFK*

MOUNT PLEASANT

BERKELEY COUNTY GAZETTE   weekly, Democrat--established Jun 1882, issued as the Berkeley Gazette after Jan 1883. Paper, which ceased c. 1895, cited by Ayer 1883 thru 1896. Aug 31, 1882 = vol 1, no 11, H. D. Bicaise (editor), John L. Kiley (publisher). Yates Snowden, Louis A. Beaty, William M. Wilson, E. F. Tighe, and H. K. Jenkins also associated with paper. Note: From 1882 to 1895, Mount Pleasant was the county seat of newly-created Berkeley County. In 1895 that community re-joined Charleston County. *Files: SCL (1882-1885) 5.*

BERKELEY GAZETTE   see Berkeley County Gazette.

ST. STEPHEN

ECHO AND PRESS   see Echo and Press [Monck's Corner].

CALHOUN COUNTY

This county, which honors statesman John C. Calhoun, was carved from Lexington and Orangeburg counties in 1908 after a twenty-seven-year struggle to achieve independent status.

ST. MATTHEWS

CALHOUN ADVANCE weekly--created by name change Feb 15, 1908 (vol 3, no 2), continues Commercial Advance, continued by the Carolinian c. 1920. Feb 15, 1908 issue bears title "commercial CALHOUN ADVANCE"...commercial, in small letters, was dropped in succeeding weeks. At that time, J. B. Prickett (editor and proprietor), Guy B. Shockley (publisher). Cited by Ayer 1909 thru 1921. J. C. Hiott and M. L. Prickett also associated with paper. *Files: Calhoun County Museum (1909-1918) 10; SCL 1908-1919.*

CALHOUN GAZETTE weekly, Democrat--continues St. Matthews Herald c. 1897, ceased c. 1899. Cited by Ayer 1898 and 1899: J. B. McLaughlin (editor and publisher). *NFK*

CALHOUN TIMES weekly--established 1922 by name change, formerly Carolinian. Jun 15, 1922 = vol 15, no 43, T. H. Dreher (editor), D. S. Murph (business manager). Not known when title changed, but this issue states it is "successor to The Carolinian." D. E. Cohn, J. B. Morris, and Edwin C. Morris also associated with paper. *Files: Calhoun CL 1969 + ; Calhoun County Museum (1936-1942) 15, 1943-1956; Calhoun Times 1922 + ; SCL ((1922-1930)) 167, 1931-1945.*

CAROLINIAN weekly, Democrat--created by name change c. 1920, formerly Calhoun Advance, continued by Calhoun Times 1922. First cited Ayer 1922: Cliff Langford (editor and publisher). *Files: Calhoun County Museum Jan 12, May 11, 1921.*

COMMERCIAL ADVANCE weekly, Democrat--established 1903 as St. Matthews Recorder, issued as Commercial Advance 1906-1908, became Calhoun Advance Feb 15, 1908. Feb 10, 1906 = vol 1, no 1, John B. Prickett and Frank H. Cain (editors and publishers). *Files: SCL Feb 1906-Feb 1908.*

GOSPEL BANNER semi-monthly, black publication, Methodist--established 1890 by L. A. McCasland. Cited Ayer 1890 and 1891: L. A. McCasland (editor and publisher). Paper moved to Orangeburg c. 1892. *NFK*

RECORD weekly, Democrat--cited Ayer 1914-1915, published by Sims Publishing Company [Orangeburg]. No date of establishment given, ceased c. 1915. Ayer 1914: James L. Sims (editor); Ayer 1915: A. T. Wannamaker (editor). *NFK*

ST. MATTHEWS HERALD   weekly, Democrat--established 1890, became Calhoun Gazette c. 1897. Cited Ayer 1890 thru 1897. Ayer 1890: George Just Brown (editor and publisher). Oct 2, 1895 = vol 3, no 2, this number sequence reflects change of ownership in 1893. In addition to Brown, J. W. Zimmerman, M. H. Daniel, and J. B. McLaughlin associated with paper. *Files: Calhoun County Museum (1890-1894) 7; SCL Jun 27, 1894, Sep 25, Oct 2, Dec 18, 1895.*

ST. MATTHEWS RECORDER   weekly, Democrat--established 1903, became Commercial Advance in 1906. Sep 1, 1904 = vol 2, no 23, F. W. Symmes (editor), A. P. Maddox (publisher). C. A. Calvo, Jr., and Dunwody and Ponder also associated with paper. *Files: Calhoun County Museum Feb 17, Sep 1, 1904, Jun 7, Oct 20, 1905; SCL Sep 1, 1904.*

SPECTATOR   weekly--established in Branchville in 1887, ceased c. 1891. Mar 17, 1887 = vol 1, no 1, H. S. Cunningham (editor and publisher). Cited Ayer 1888 as published in St. Matthews by Cunningham. By Mar 1889 paper in Orangeburg. Issue of Mar 12, 1889 (vol 3, no 1) indicates move from St. Matthews occurred only a few weeks earlier. Ayer 1891 reports paper in Harlin City. See Spectator [Branchville and Orangeburg].

CHARLESTON COUNTY

One of seven judicial districts established in 1769, Charleston County is named for its seaport city, which honors King Charles II of England. In the early 1660s, back from exile, Charles rewarded eight of his most loyal supporters with enormous land grants that led to the first permanent settlements in South Carolina.

CHARLESTON

AFRO-AMERICAN   weekly, non-partisan, black publication--established 1954, ceased c. 1955. Cited once by Ayer (1955): John H. McCray (editor), Afro-American Publishing Company. *NFK*

AFRO-AMERICAN CITIZEN   weekly, black publication--established 1899, ceased c. 1902. Jan 17, 1900 = vol 1, no 38, L. G. Gregory (editor), Citizen Publishing Company, 71 Hasell Street. "Devoted to the Interest of the Republic and Dedicated Most Especially to the Struggling but Rising Afro-Americans." *Files: SCL mfm Jan 17, 1900.*

ASHORE AND AFLOAT   weekly c. 1918-1919--paper began as daily column for navy personnel in the News and Courier, edited by G. K. Rutledge. First weekly paper issued on Jul 31, 1918. Oct 16, 1918 = vol 1, no 21, G. K. Rutledge (editor). Paper affiliated with YMCA's Trench and Camp issued for military personnel. Not cited by Ayer. *Files: SCL Oct 16, Dec 11, 1918, Jan 1, 14, 1919.*

BIBLICAL RECORDER AND SOUTHERN WATCHMAN   weekly, religious--continues the Biblical Recorder [Raleigh, N. C.] and the Southern Watchman, and General Intelligencer [Charleston] on Mar 3, 1838 = vol 4, no 8, T. Meredith (editor). Paper has dual dateline to Jan 1839 when only Raleigh cited. Subsequently became the Biblical Recorder: Journal of the Baptist Convention of North Carolina. *Files: SCL Jul 21, 1838, mfm Mar 1838-Dec 1840.*

BLACK TIMES   weekly, black publication--issued since c. 1977 by JuJu Publishing Company [Columbia] with seven different mastheads for various communities throughout the state. Black Times is the Charleston edition. See Black News [Columbia].

BRAZEN FACE   weekly c. 1810--according to Isaiah Thomas, History of Printing (1874), J. H. Sargent was publishing this paper early in 1810. However, "Brazen Face" may have been merely the title of the editorial page of Strength of the People. See Strength of the People.

BUSY BEE   semi-monthly, literary--established 1856, ceased c. 1857. Jan 15, 1857 = vol 1, no 18, Warren Curtis (editor), published by a literary association "for the promotion of Literature, Fine Arts, and Industrial and Mechanical Pursuits." *Files: CLS Jan 15, 1857.*

CAROLINA GAZETTE   weekly--established Jan 1, 1798 by Peter Freneau and Seth Paine, ceased Sep 1840. Jan 25, 1798 = vol 1, no 4, Freneau and Paine (publishers of the City Gazette). According to Brigham, this paper, issued by the daily City Gazette to Oct 1833, contained much new material and was not merely a weekly edition. John McIver, David R. Williams, Samuel J. Elliott, Samuel Richards, Ebenezer Thomas, Samuel Skinner, Joseph Whilden, and William Gilmore Simms also associated with paper. The Charleston Courier purchased the Carolina Gazette in Oct 1833 and issued it with a new number sequence as a weekly publication until Sep 1840. *Files: CLS 1801-1802, 1810-1824, Jan 1827-Dec 1828, Oct 1838-Sep 1840; SCL (1799-1836) 94, mfm (1798-1800) 94.*

CAROLINA LABOR JOURNAL   weekly, labor--established 1914, ceased c. 1917. Cited by Ayer 1916: Clifford Thompson (editor and publisher); Ayer 1917: C. L. Wilson (editor). Not cited in 1918. *NFK*

CAROLINA LIGHTHOUSE   see Charleston Lighthouse.

CAROLINA PATRIOT   weekly--established 1813, ceased c. 1813. Sep 4, 1813 = vol 1, no 19. No other data available. *Files: SCL Sep 4, 1813.*

CAROLINA WEEKLY MESSENGER   weekly--established Nov 1, 1806 by the Charleston Courier and issued from its offices, ceased Oct 1810. Paper experienced the same editor-publisher changes as the Courier during those years. Jul 18, 1807 = vol 1, no 38. The Charleston Courier (Oct 3, 1810) announced that the Messenger would be replaced by a tri-weekly edition "for the country." *Files: CLS Feb 7, 1809; SCL Nov 3-Dec 1, 1807, Jan 19, 1808-Oct 24, 1809; SC Historical Society and SCL mfm Jul 18, Nov 3-Dec 1, 1807, Jan 19, 1808-Oct 24, 1809.*

CATALYST   bi-weekly--established 1982, published by Community Press, Inc., for the Medical University of South Carolina. Sep 2, 1982 = vol 1, no 1. *Files: Catalyst 1982 + .*

CATHOLIC ADVOCATE   weekly, religious--established Apr 1871, but soon ceased. Not cited by Rowell. *NFK*

CATHOLIC BANNER   weekly, religious--established Mar 1969, although issued prior to that date with title of "Catholic Banner," the South Carolina edition of Our Sunday Visitor of Huntington, Indiana. Mar 6, 1969 = vol 1, no 1, Calhoun Ancrum (editor). *Files: CLS Dec 4, 1960, Jul 22, 1962; SCL ((1960-1966)) 100, 1967 + .*

CHARLESTON ADVERTISER   weekly, Democrat--established Dec 22, 1877, ceased c. 1878. Cited once by Rowell (1878): V. Little & Company (editor and publisher). *Files: Duke Dec 29, 1877-May 1878. Apparently no SC files.*

CHARLESTON ADVOCATE   weekly, Methodist, Republican, black publication--established 1867, ceased 1868. Feb 23, 1867 = vol 1, no 2, A[lonzo] Webster (editor), Lewis and Webster (publishers). Paper may have been revived in 1872 as the South-Eastern Advocate (see). *Files: SCL Feb 23, Apr 27, 1867, Aug 15, 1868, mfm (1867-1868) 24.*

CHARLESTON AMERICAN   daily, Progressive Democrat--established 1916, ceased Sep 29, 1923. Aug 25, 1916 = vol 1, no 27, no editor or publisher identified; however, John P. Grace, Albert Sottile, and John H. Perry associated with paper. A Hearst-like publication, the Charleston American was politician Grace's answer to the News and Courier. *Files: CLS Jul 30, 1916-Jun 30, 1917, Jan-Mar 1918, Apr-Jun 1922, Jan-Jun 1923; SCL mfm Aug 25-Sep 1917, Nov 1917-Jun 1919, Jan 1920-Jun 1922, Jan-Sep 1923.*

CHARLESTON CATHOLIC MISCELLANY   weekly, religious--continues the United States Catholic Miscellany in Jan 1861, ceased Dec 1861. Jan 5, 1861 = vol 39, no 36, total no 1956, Harper and Calvo (printers). *Files: CLS Jan-Dec 1861; SCL mfm Jan-Dec 1861.*

CHARLESTON CHECKERBOARD   weekly, black publication--established 1964, ceased Jan 1966. Paper issued by J. John French, a navy publicist, who terminated publication when he went to Vietnam. French later founded the Charleston Chronicle. *Files: Charleston Chronicle (1964-1966).*

CHARLESTON CHRONICLE   see Daily Morning Chronicle (1873).

CHARLESTON CHRONICLE   weekly, black publication--established 1971. Aug 19, 1971 = vol 1, no 1, J. John French (editor and publisher). Cited by Ayer 1977 +. See Gladys Echols Zarif, "The Development of a Contemporary Black Newspaper: The Charleston Chronicle Newspaper of Charleston, South Carolina," MA thesis, USC 1986. Since masthead features word Chronicle, paper often is referred to by that name. *Files: Charleston Chronicle and Charleston CL 1971 + ; SCL Mar 1972-Aug 1980, 1987 + .*

CHARLESTON COMMERCIAL ADVERTISER   semi-monthly "advertising sheet"--established 1873, ceased c. 1875. Cited by Rowell 1873 thru 1875: Philip Wineman & Company (editor and publisher). Nov 1, 1873 = vol 1, no 20, printed at the offices of Edward Perry. *Files: SCL Nov 1, 1873, Jan 15, 1875.*

CHARLESTON COURIER   daily--established Jan 10, 1803 by Aaron S. Willington for Loring Andrews. Stephen C. Carpenter, Frederick Dalcho, Peter R. Marchant, and Edmund Morford also associated with paper during early years. A semi-weekly edition announced in Apr 1804 did not materialize, but a weekly edition appeared in Nov 1806 (see the Carolina Weekly Messenger). According to the Charleston Courier (Oct 10, 1810), the weekly edition would be replaced in Nov 1810 by a tri-weekly "Courier for the Country" containing "all the matter that appears on the inside pages of our daily paper."

See the Charleston Courier (tri-weekly). In 1833 Willington sold a part interest in the Charleston Courier to Richard Yeadon, Jr., and William S. King. Beginning Jul 1, 1852 paper issued as the Charleston Daily Courier. Willington died in 1862, and for a few months in 1865 the paper appeared under federal auspices as the Daily Courier and the Charleston Courier. Willington's associates resumed control on Nov 20, 1865. On Apr 3, 1873 the paper was sold at auction to the owners of the Charleston Daily News and continued by the News and Courier. See Sass, Outspoken: 150 Years of "The News and Courier." *Files: CLS Jan 1803-1858, (1859-1865) 20; Darlington County Historical Commission Jul-Sep 1861; SCL ((1803-1873)) 3000; Baptist College, Charleston CL, CLS, Citadel, Clemson, College of Charleston, Dorchester CL, Francis Marion, Furman, Greenville CL, News and Courier, SCL, USC-Coastal, Winthrop, and Wofford mfm 1803-1873; Converse mfm 1852-1873; Lander mfm 1857-1866.*

CHARLESTON COURIER   title of Charleston Daily Courier Feb-Jun 1865. See Charleston Courier.

CHARLESTON COURIER   tri-weekly--established in Nov 1810, this tri-weekly edition continued until 1873, except for a break of unknown duration in 1865. Designated simply as the "Courier" from 1810 to c. 1850, it had no masthead and consisted of inside pages from daily editions. In the early 1850s, however, this paper developed a standard masthead: Charleston Courier, with a sub-head "Tri-Weekly." By 1859 this had evolved into a full-fledged title: Charleston Tri-Weekly Courier. *Files: SCL ((1832-1871)) 300, mfm Oct 24, 1855; Sumter County Museum-Archives Jan 15, 26, 1863.*

CHARLESTON CRITIC   see Critic.

CHARLESTON DAILY COURIER   see Charleston Courier.

CHARLESTON DAILY EXPRESS   daily, Republican, c. Sep-Oct 1875. Oct 4, 1875 = vol 1, no 25, published by the Express Publishing Company..."the only Conservative Journal in Charleston." Successor to the Daily Morning Chronicle, this paper apparently was started by those critical of the editorial policy of the News and Courier, but it soon ceased. Not cited by Rowell. *Files: CLS Oct 4, 1875.*

CHARLESTON DAILY NEWS   daily--established in Aug 1865 by G. R. Cathcart, James W. McMillan, and Mandred Morton. Sep 8, 1865 = vol 1, no 23, Cathcart, McMillan, and Morton (proprietors). Paper was sold to B. R. Riordan, Francis W. Dawson, and Henry Evanson on Oct 26, 1867. These men launched a tri-weekly edition in Jan 1868 and a weekly in Jan 1870. In Apr 1873 they purchased the Charleston Daily Courier and merged the two papers as the News and Courier, also continuing tri-weekly and weekly editions. See the Charleston Tri-Weekly News, Weekly News, and News and Courier. *Files: CLS Jul 1866-Apr 1873; Clemson Apr 17, Nov 1, 1869; SCL (1865-1866) 60, 1867-1873; Sumter County Museum-Archives Jun 18, 1866. Note: Mfm reel # 1 of the News and Courier contains the Charleston Daily News Jan-Apr 5, 1873.*

CHARLESTON DAILY REPUBLICAN   daily c. 1872. Mar 2, 1872 = vol 1, no 12 (no personnel listed). According to Duke checklist, this paper was a revival in Feb 1872 of the Daily Republican. It soon ceased publication. Not cited by Rowell. The Duke checklist indicates that E. C. Seabrook, J. Felder Myers, J. Evans Britton, and E. W. Mackay were associated with this paper. *Files: CLS Mar 2, 1872.*

CHARLESTON DAILY STANDARD   daily--continues Southern Standard in Sep 1853, continued by the Charleston Standard c. 1856. Feb 21, 1854 = vol 3, no 195, L. W. Spratt and E. H. Britton (editors), Spratt, Britton & Company (publishers). This paper also issued tri-weekly and weekly editions. See the Charleston Tri-Weekly Standard and the Charleston Weekly Standard. Paper's motto: "Perseverance Keeps Honor Bright." *Files: CLS Oct 1853-Dec 1855; SCL Feb 21, 1854, Apr 5, 1855.*

CHARLESTON DISPATCH   weekly--continues Sunday Dispatch c. 1886, ceased c. 1888. Cited by Ayer 1886 thru 1888. Oct 19, 1886 = vol 17, no 29, S. D. Hutson (editor and proprietor). *Files: SCL (1886-1888) 22.*

CHARLESTON ENQUIRER   weekly, prohibition, Republican, black publication-- established 1892, ceased c. 1901. Cited by Ayer 1893/4 thru 1901: George C. Rowe (editor and publisher). According to the Charleston city directory (1896), paper was published at 245 King Street. *NFK*

CHARLESTON EVENING GAZETTE   daily, tri-weekly--established as daily on Jul 11, 1785 by Joseph V. Burd and Robert Haswell. The paper became tri-weekly on Aug 7, 1786. Last known issue, according to Brigham, is Oct 18, 1786. Greenberry Hughes also associated with paper. *Files: CLS Jul 11, 1785-Oct 18, 1786.*

CHARLESTON EVENING NEWS   daily--established Oct 1845, ceased 1861. Mar 2, 1849 = vol 8, no 1049, R. Garden Pringle (editor), W. Y. Paxton & Company (publisher). This paper also issued tri-weekly and weekly editions. See the Charleston News (tri-weekly), and the Weekly News. John Cunningham, J. N. Cardozo, and Paul Hamilton Hayne also associated with these publications. *Files: CLS Oct 1845-Jun 1849, Jan 1850-Jun 1853, Jan 1854-Dec 1856; Clemson Jun 1, 1860; SCL (1847-1861) 15, mfm (Jul-Dec 1849) 135.*

CHARLESTON EVENING POST   see the Evening Post (established 1894).

CHARLESTON EVENING POST; AND COMMERCIAL AND POLITICAL GAZETTE   daily--established Jan 1815, ceased Dec 1816. Dec 5, 1815 = vol 2, no 265, W. P. Young (publisher). *Files: SCL (1815-1816) 16.*

CHARLESTON EXAMINER   semi-weekly--established Jul 15, 1837, ceased c. 1837. Jul 15, 1837 = vol 1, no 1 (no personnel cited). *Files: American Antiquarian Society Jul 15, Aug 3, 1837. Apparently no SC files.*

CHARLESTON FREE PRESS   daily--established 1871, ceased c. 1871. Feb 16, 1871 = vol 1, no 14, J. W. De Lano (proprietor). An ill-fated attempt by De Lano (editor and proprietor of the Sunday Times) to launch a daily paper. Not cited by Rowell. *Files: SCL Feb 16, 1871.*

CHARLESTON GAZETTE, AND MERCANTILE ADVERTISER   daily--established Feb 15, 1814, ceased c. Jul 1814. Apr 25, 1814 = vol 1, no 58, John L. Wilson (publisher). According to Brigham, this paper succeeded the Investigator and probably was sold to Isaac Harby, who then established the Southern Patriot and Commercial Advertiser. The short-lived Charleston Gazette, and Mercantile Advertiser also issued a tri-weekly edition for the country. *Files: SCL Apr 25, 26, June 17, 1814.*

CHARLESTON HERALD   daily, Democrat--according to the Charleston city directory (1882), this paper was established Jul 4, 1880, J. C. Irwin (editor), J. W. De Lano (publisher). Not cited by Ayer. Ceased c. 1882. *NFK*

CHARLESTON HERALD   weekly (?) c. 1965. According to Charleston telephone directory (1965), this paper had an office at 2 Second Street, Isle of Palms. *NFK*

CHARLESTON INDEPENDENT   weekly, Republican--according to Woody, established Aug 28, 1875, ceased c. 1876. Cited once by Rowell (1876): M. R. Delany (editor), D. P. Reynolds (publisher). Jun 24, 1876 = vol 1, no 30, D. P. Reynolds (publisher). *Files: Duke Jun 24, 1876. Apparently no SC files.*

CHARLESTON INDEPENDENT   weekly c. 1884. According to Duke checklist, this paper was established in 1884 by the Independent State Committee and issued the following year as the Independent and Mercury. Not cited by Ayer. *Files: Duke Oct 17, 1884. Apparently no SC files.*

CHARLESTON INQUIRER   weekly, black publication--established 1963, ceased c. 1964. Apr 5, 1963 = vol 1, no 7, William Riley (editor and publisher). *Files: CLS May 31, Jun 21, 1963; SCL (Apr-Aug 1963) 7.*

CHARLESTON JOURNAL   weekly, black publication--established Sep 1866 by B. F. Randolph and E. J. Adams, ceased c. 1867. Oct 4, 1866 = vol 1, no 3, published at 212 King Street. *Files: Harvard Oct 4, 11, 1866. Apparently no SC files.*

CHARLESTON JOURNAL OF COMMERCE   daily--established 1876, ceased 1878. May 11, 1876 = vol 1, no 11, Charleston Publishing Company. Thomas W. Brown and R. Barnwell Rhett, Jr., associated with paper. Cited by Rowell 1877 and 1878. Early issues also advertise a weekly edition, but by Jul 1876 it is no longer listed; however, a tri-weekly did appear. *Files: CLS May 1876-Jun 1878; SCL ((May 1876-Jul 1878)) 350.*

CHARLESTON JOURNAL OF COMMERCE   tri-weekly--established 1876, ceased 1878. Aug 26, 1876 = vol 1, no 102, R. Barnwell Rhett, Jr. (editor), James R. Trueheart (associate editor). *Files: SCL Aug 26, 1876.*

CHARLESTON LIGHTHOUSE weekly, black publication--established 1939, merged with the People's Informer [Sumter] c. 1941 and continued by the Lighthouse and Informer [Charleston and Columbia]. May 14, 1939 = vol 1, no 11, John H. McCray (editor), Davis Lee (publisher). Paper listed in the 1940 Charleston city directory as the "Carolina Lighthouse," offices at 54 1/2 Line Street. Not cited by Ayer. *Files: SCL May 14, 1939.*

CHARLESTON MERCURY daily--established Jan 1, 1822 = vol 1, no 1, Edmund Morford (publisher). Not issued Feb 1865-Nov 19, 1866, ceased Nov 1868. On Oct 4, 1823, Henry Laurens Pinckney (the second publisher) launched a tri-weekly "country" edition. See the Charleston Mercury (tri-weekly). Paper issued as the Charleston Mercury and Morning Advertiser Jan 1, 1822-May 14, 1825. In addition to Morford and Pinckney, John Allan Stuart, John Milton Clapp, John E. Carew, John Heart, William R. Tabor, and Robert Barnwell Rhett (Jr. and Sr.) associated with paper. See John S. Coussons, "Thirty Years with Calhoun, Rhett, and the Charleston Mercury: A Chapter in South Carolina Politcs," PhD dissertation, LSU 1971; Granville T. Prior, "A History of the Charleston Mercury, 1822-1852," PhD dissertation, Harvard University 1946; and Ernest B. Segars, "A Study of the Charleston (S. C.) Mercury under Robert Barnwell Rhett, Senior's Tenure as Editorial Writer, 1861-1863," MA thesis, USC 1974. *Files: CLS Jan 1822-Feb 1865, Nov 1866-Nov 1868; Clemson Feb 28, 1833, Oct 4, 1864, Jan 18, 1865; Darlington County Historical Commission (1860-1861) 50; SCL ((1823-1868)) 1700; Charleston CL, CLS, Clemson, College of Charleston, Francis Marion, Furman, News and Courier, SCL, USC-Coastal, and Winthrop mfm 1822-1868; Dorchester CL mfm 1822-1845; Wofford mfm 1860-1868; USC-Spartanburg mfm Jul-Dec 1860.*

CHARLESTON MERCURY daily, Independent Democrat--appears in 1880 as vol 5, indicating may have been a continuation of the Charleston Journal of Commerce (1876-1878), ceased daily edition c. 1884 and continued for unknown time as weekly. (See Charleston Independent c. 1884). This obviously was an attempt to revive the well-known Charleston daily by the same name. Sep 11, 1880 = vol 5, no 300, Democrat Publishing Company. Masthead indicates this paper had incorporated the People's Watchman (weekly) and the Democrat (daily). Note: The Charleston Mercury and the Democrat both were published at 26 Chalmers Street. By 1881, the Democrat Publishing Company had become the Mercury Publishing Company, and publisher W. J. Oliver also was issuing a tri-weekly edition. Sometime during 1881 the Mercury absorbed a third paper, the Evening Herald, a daily established in 1878. The Charleston Mercury cited by Ayer 1880 thru 1884. *Files: SCL (1880-1884) 10.*

CHARLESTON MERCURY tri-weekly---established Oct 1823, ceased 1868. Inner pages of daily edition were issued without a masthead to 1857, then paper appeared as the Charleston Mercury with subhead, "Tri-Weekly." After Sep 1861 paper issued as the Tri-Weekly Mercury. *Files: SCL (1831-1868) 75, mfm (1860-1861) 25; Sumter County Museum-Archives (1861-1862) 6.*

CHARLESTON MERCURY   tri-weekly c. 1881-1884. *NFK*

CHARLESTON MERCURY   weekly c. 1885-1886. According to 1886 Charleston city directory, W. J. Oliver was publishing weekly edition of this former daily at 111 Meeting Street. Not cited by Ayer. Ceased c. 1886. *NFK*

CHARLESTON MERCURY AND MORNING ADVERTISER   title of Charleston Mercury Jan 1, 1822-May 14, 1825. See Charleston Mercury.

CHARLESTON MESSENGER   weekly, bi-monthly, religious, black publication-- established in 1894 by Francis P. Crum as an independent weekly, taken over by the Orphan Aid Society c. 1897, ceased c. 1946. Cited by Ayer 1899 thru 1946. Reverend D. J. Jenkins and Mrs. E. C. Jenkins associated with paper. Issued bi-monthly 1943- 1946. According to the 1938 Charleston city directory, paper was being published at 20 Franklin Street, site of offices for several decades. *NFK*

CHARLESTON MORNING POST, AND DAILY ADVERTISER   daily-- continues the South-Carolina Gazette, and Public Advertiser on Jan 18, 1786, continued by the City Gazette, and the Daily Advertiser on Nov 6, 1787. May 16, 1786 = vol 4, no 369, printed by Childs, Haswell & M'Iver [Nathan Childs, Robert Haswell, and John M'Iver]. *Files: CLS Jan 1786-Jul 1787, mfm Jan 1786-Oct 1787; SCL May 16, 1786, Feb 12, 1787, mfm Jan 1786-Oct 1787.*

CHARLESTON NEWS   tri-weekly edition of Charleston Evening News, with "Tri- Weekly" as sub-head. Dec 10, 1860 issue published by John Cunningham & Company at 119 East Bay Street. SCL files indicate tri-weekly edition published c. 1845-1861. *Files: SCL Dec 10, 1860; Sumter County Museum-Archives Feb 20, 1861.*

CHARLESTON OBSERVER   weekly, Presbyterian--established Jan 6, 1827, ceased Jul 26, 1845. Jan 6, 1827 = vol 1, no 1, B[enjamin] Gildersleve (editor and proprietor). In Aug 1845 paper merged with the Watchman of the South and was continued by the Watchman and Observer [Richmond, Va.]. *Files: CLS (1831-1839) 5; Clemson (1831- 1832) 31; SCL (1827-1845) 80, mfm 1827-1828, 1830-1845.*

CHARLESTON RECORD   weekly, Democrat--continues the Charleston County Record [Myers] in Mar 1932, ceased c. 1933. Mar 3, 1932 = vol 1, no 42, David H. Rembert (editor), John Van Cronkite (publisher). Cited once by Ayer (1933). Paper began with dual dateline: Charleston and Myers, but by Nov 1932 only Charleston cited. Charles Gething also associated with paper. *Files: SCL Mar 3, May 26, Nov 4, 1932.*

CHARLESTON RECORDER   weekly, black publication--established 1886, ceased c. 1887. Nov 6, 1886 = vol 2, no 30, Rev. J. E. Hayne (publisher). Cited by Ayer 1886 and 1887. *Files: Duke Nov 6, 1886, Aug 27, 1887. Apparently no SC files.*

CHARLESTON REPUBLICAN daily--established 1876, ceased c. 1877. Oct 21, 1876 = vol 1, no 11, Charleston Republican Publishing Company..."A Paper for the People." Cited once by Rowell (1877). *Files: SCL Oct 21, 24, 26, 1876.*

CHARLESTON REVIEW weekly--continues Seashore Review c. 1903, a pro-labor publication after 1912, ceased c. 1917. Oct 2, 1909 = vol 13, no 32, whole no 708, John L. Kiley (editor and proprietor). Cited by Ayer 1904 thru 1917. Bernard P. Carey and Clifford Thompson also associated with paper. According to Charleston city directory (1916), offices at 50 Queen Street. *Files: CLS Oct 9, 1915; SCL Oct 2, 1909.*

CHARLESTON SPECTATOR, AND LADIES' LITERARY PORTFOLIO weekly--established Jun 21, 1806, ceased Dec 1806. Aug 16, 1806 = vol 1, no 9, published by John Hoff for "Goggles, Spectacles, & Co." (editors). According to Brigham, although ostensibly a magazine, the Charleston Spectator contained current news and advertisements. *Files: College of Charleston and USC mfm (Aug-Dec 1806) 8.*

CHARLESTON STANDARD daily--continues the Charleston Daily Standard c. 1856, ceased c. 1858. Also issued a tri-weekly edition (see the Charleston Tri-Weekly Standard). Paper published by L. W. Spratt & Company in 1856. *Files: Duke Dec 5, 12, 26, 1856. Apparently no SC files.*

CHARLESTON SUN daily--continues Referee c. 1875. Cited once by Rowell (1875): William M. Thomas (editor), Charleston Printing Company. Paper ceased c. 1876. *NFK*

CHARLESTON TELEGRAPH daily--established 1875, ceased c. 1875. Cited by Rowell (1875): L. E. C. Moore & Company (editor and publisher). *NFK*

CHARLESTON TRI-WEEKLY COURIER see Charleston Courier (tri-weekly).

CHARLESTON TRI-WEEKLY NEWS tri-weekly edition of the Charleston Daily News--established Jan 1868, continued by the Tri-Weekly News and Courier (see) in Apr 1873. Feb 2, 1869 = vol 2, no 168, Riordan, Dawson & Company (publisher). *Files: SCL (1869-1871) 9.*

CHARLESTON TRI-WEEKLY STANDARD tri-weekly edition of the Charleston Daily Standard and the Charleston Standard 1853-1858. Jan 31, 1856 = vol 6, no 24, L. W. Spratt & Company (publisher). *Files: SCL Jan 31, Feb 9, 1856.*

CHARLESTON WEEKLY STANDARD weekly edition of the Charleston Daily Standard and the Charleston Standard 1853-1858. Jan 16, 1855 = vol 4, no 3, L. W. Spratt & Company (publisher). *Files: SCL (1855-1858) 9.*

CHARLESTON ZEITUNG   weekly, German--established c. Aug 1852, ceased c. Sep 1853. May 12, 1853 = vol 1, no 38, H. M. Hinck (editor and publisher). See Arndt, German Language Press of the Americas. *Files: American Antiquarian Society May 12, 1853. Apparently no SC files.*

CHARLESTONER ZEITUNG   see Die Charlestoner Zeitung.

CHARLESTOWN GAZETTE   weekly--established Aug 1778, ceased c. 1780. Jan 26, 1779 = vol 1, no 33, Mary Crouch & Company (publisher). Note: This paper is part of a 12-reel mfm collection organized by the Charleston Library Society and often referred to as "18th-century South Carolina Newspapers." See Brigham and reel #1 for pertinent details. *Files: CLS (1779-1780) 6; SCL Mar 23, 1779; Baptist College, Charleston CL, CLS, Citadel, Clemson, College of Charleston, Converse, Dorchester CL, Francis Marion, Furman, Greenville CL, Greenwood High School, Lander, News and Courier, Presbyterian, SC Archives, SC Historical Society, SCL, Summerville Public Library, USC-Beaufort, USC-Coastal, Winthrop, and Wofford mfm (1779-1780) 6.*

CHRONICLE   see Charleston Chronicle (established 1971).

CHRONICLE OF LIBERTY, OR THE REPUBLICAN INTELLIGENCER weekly--established Mar 1783 by James Mansfield (editor) and Joseph Davis (printer). Mar 25, 1783 (vol 1, no 1) available in Readex Microprint # 1846. Paper ceased c. 1783. *Files: CLS Apr 27, Jun 4, 1783; USC mp Mar 25, 1783.*

CITY GAZETTE   see the City Gazette, and the Daily Advertiser.

CITY GAZETTE AND THE COMMERCIAL DAILY ADVERTISER see the City Gazette, and the Daily Advertiser.

CITY GAZETTE & DAILY ADVERTISER   see the City Gazette, and the Daily Advertiser.

CITY GAZETTE, AND THE DAILY ADVERTISER   daily--continues the Charleston Morning Post, and Daily Advertiser on Nov 6, 1787, ceased in 1840 after numerous name changes. Nov 6, 1787 = vol 5, no 786, published by [Robert] Haswell and [John] M'Iver. In Dec 1787 title was altered to City Gazette, or the Daily Advertiser and in Jan 1792 changed to City Gazette & Daily Advertiser. In Jan 1804 title shortened to City Gazette, but in Jul 1806 reverted to City Gazette and Daily Advertiser, and in Jul 1810 paper became the City Gazette and the Commercial Daily Advertiser, continuing to appear under that title until publication ceased in 1840. In addition to Haswell and M'Iver, John Markland, Peter Freneau, Seth Paine, David R. Williams, Samuel J. Elliott, Samuel Richards, Ebenezer S. Thomas, Samuel H. Skinner, Joseph Whilden, James Haig, William Gilmore Simms, and John Geddes, Jr., associated with paper. From 1798 to Oct 1833 these various editors also issued the weekly Carolina Gazette (see) and the editorial columns indicate a tri-weekly appeared during some years. *Files:*

CLS Nov 1787-Apr 1796, Oct 1796-Jan 1, 1801, Jan 1802-Dec 1805, (1806) 5, Jan 1807-Dec 1810, Jan 1812-Apr 1833, mfm 1789, Jul-Dec 1806, 1821-1824; SCL ((1795-1826)) 1400, mfm Nov 6, 1787-Dec 1789, Jun 28-Oct 22, 1790, Jul 6-Oct 21, 1791, (Feb 8-Sep 27, 1792) 15, (Sep 15-Nov 6, 1794) 12, 1795-1805, Jul-Dec 1806, 1808, 1810, 1813-1818, 1820-1821, Jan-Sep 1823, Mar 1824-Dec 1828, Jul 1829-Jan 1831, 1832; Clemson and Furman mfm 1789.

CITY GAZETTE AND MERCANTILE ADVERTISER   daily--apparently a short-lived rival of the better-established City Gazette and the Commercial Daily Advertiser. Apr 25, 1814 = vol 1, no 58, John L. Wilson (publisher). Wilson, a lawyer, issued this paper at 236 East Bay Street, next door to the office of the City Gazette and the Commercial Daily Advertiser. He also may have produced a tri-weekly "country" edition for a brief time. Paper ceased c. 1814 . Files: SCL Apr 25, 26, Jun 17, 1814.

CITY GAZETTE EXTRAORDINARY   an unusual Sun edition announcing a treaty of friendship with Great Britain (Jay's Treaty)...really a broadside. Files: SCL Jul 12, 1795.

CITY GAZETTE, OR THE DAILY ADVERTISER   see the City Gazette, and the Daily Advertiser.

COASTAL TIMES   weekly, black publication--established 1983. Apr 16-22, 1986 = vol 4, no 16, James E. Clyburn (president and publisher). In 1983-1984 paper also maintained offices in Columbia and Summerville. Files: Charleston CL 1985 + ; Coastal Times 1983 + .

COLUMBIAN HERALD   semi-weekly, tri-weekly, daily, various title changes-- established Nov 23, 1784 by Thomas B. Bowen and John Markland as the semi-weekly Columbian Herald, or the Patriotic Courier of North-America. Issued tri-weekly Jun 6, 1785 to Nov 24, 1785 when became the semi-weekly Columbian Herald, or the Independent Courier of North-America. In the fall of 1790 paper became tri-weekly and early in 1792 changed title to the Columbian Herald, and the General Advertiser. In Sep 1792 that paper became the daily Columbian Herald & Daily Advertiser, but by Jul 23, 1793 was once more the tri-weekly Columbian Herald, and the General Advertiser. Four days later it became the Columbian Herald, or the Southern Star. As of Oct 7, 1795 paper was the daily Columbian Herald; or, the New Daily Advertiser. Paper ceased with issue no 1888 on Dec 17, 1796. In addition to Bowen and Markland, James Vandle, S---- Andrews, Isaac Silliman, and William P. Harrison were associated with paper, 1784-1796. Files: CLS Nov 1784-Oct 1786, Nov 1787-Sep 1788, Feb-Apr 1789, Aug-Oct 1790, Jul 1793-Dec 1796, mfm Nov 1784-Dec 1796; SCL (1786-1791) 4, mfm Jun 1787-Oct 1790, Jul 1793-Jun 1794, Jul-Dec 1796; Clemson, Francis Marion, Furman, and USC-Coastal mfm Jun 1787-Oct 1790.

COLUMBIAN HERALD & DAILY ADVERTISER   see the Columbian Herald.

COLUMBIAN HERALD, AND THE GENERAL ADVERTISER   see the Columbian Herald.

COLUMBIAN HERALD, OR THE INDEPENDENT COURIER OF NORTH-AMERICA   see the Columbian Herald.

COLUMBIAN HERALD; OR, THE NEW DAILY ADVERTISER   see the Columbian Herald.

COLUMBIAN HERALD, OR THE PATRIOTIC COURIER OF NORTH-AMERICA   see the Columbian Herald.

COLUMBIAN HERALD, OR THE SOUTHERN STAR   see the Columbian Herald.

COMMON SENSE   weekly, anti-prohibition--established 1908, ceased c. 1917. Jan 9, 1909 = vol 1, no 25, Paul Wierse (editor and publisher). Cited by Ayer 1909 thru 1917. *Files: CLS (1912-1913) 10; SCL (1909-1915) 5.*

COURIER   see the Charleston Courier (tri-weekly edition), often called the "Country Courier" or "Courier for the Country."

CRITIC   daily, Independent Democrat--continues the Daily Sun c. 1897, ceased c. 1898. Cited once by Ayer (1898): James H. Moore (editor), Sun Company (publisher). According to the 1898 Charleston city directory, this paper was issued as the "Charleston Critic" from offices at 47 Hayne Street. *NFK*

DAILY ADVERTISER   daily, Republican--a short-lived paper issued from the offices of the Daily Republican Sep 8-24, 1871. Not cited by Rowell. *NFK*

DAILY CHARLESTON BULLETIN   see the Evening Bulletin.

DAILY COURIER   title of Charleston Daily Courier Feb 13-23, 1865. See Charleston Courier.

DAILY DEMOCRAT   daily--established 1877, ceased c. 1878. Nov 19, 1877 = vol 1, no 17, J. D. Kennedy and H. D. Bicaise (publishers). Paper apparently revived in 1879 as the Democrat (see). Daily Democrat not cited by Rowell. *Files: Duke Nov 19, 23, 24, 1877. Apparently no SC files.*

DAILY EVENING GAZETTE AND CHARLESTON TEA-TABLE COMPANION   daily--established Jan 3, 1795, continued by the Telegraphe: and Charleston Daily Advertiser c. Mar 1795. Jan 10, 1795 = vol 1, no 7, James Carey (publisher). Eight issues are available in Readex Microprint # 1850. *Files: Furman and USC mp Jan 10, 12, 15, 16, Feb 14, 16-18, 1795.*

DAILY EXPRESS   see <u>Charleston Daily Express</u>.

DAILY MERIDIAN   daily--established 1844, ceased c. 1844. May 4, 1844 = vol 1, no 1, Richard E. Mooney & Company (publisher). Mooney promised that paper would appear every day at noon--"True as the Dial to the Sun." *Files: Library of Congress May 4, 1844. Apparently no SC files.*

DAILY MORNING CHRONICLE   daily, Republican--continues the <u>Daily Charleston Bulletin</u> on Jun 1, 1873, succeeded by the <u>Charleston Daily Express</u> in Sep 1875. Oct 1, 1873 = vol 2, no 302, J. W. De Lano (business manager). George W. De Lano associated with paper as editor in 1874. Paper also issued as the <u>Charleston Chronicle</u>. Cited by Rowell 1874 and 1875. *Files: SCL Oct 1, 3, 1873, Apr 22, May 4, 1874.*

DAILY REPUBLICAN   daily--succeeds weekly <u>South Carolina Republican</u>, which moved to Columbia in Sep 1869. Aug 19, 1869 = vol 1, no 1 (no editor or publisher listed). According to Rowell 1870-1872, paper edited by J. M. Morris and Myron Fox. The <u>Daily Republican</u> suspended operations on Sep 8, 1871 and was revived in Feb 1872 as the <u>Charleston Daily Republican</u>. *Files: CLS Aug 4, 1871; SCL mfm Aug 19, 1869-Sep 8, 1871.*

DAILY SOUTH CAROLINIAN   daily--continues daily edition of a paper established in Columbia in 1838 and published there until early in 1865. See <u>Daily South Carolinian</u> [Columbia]. With the assistance of William Gilmore Simms and Henry Timrod, F. G. De Fontaine (editor and proprietor) issued daily edition in Charleston from c. Nov 1865 to May 1866. Jan 6, 1866 = "26th Year" (no issue-vol data), F. G. De Fontaine (editor and proprietor). During these months De Fontaine experimented with morning and afternoon dailies and on Apr 23, 1866 announced plans to publish <u>Die Charlestoner Zeitung</u>, to be edited by John A. Wagener; however, that German weekly did not actually appear until Oct 1867. By Jun 1866 the <u>Daily South Carolinian</u> was back in Columbia once more. *Files: CLS Jan 30, 1866; SCL Jan 6, 1866, mfm (1865-1866) 77.*

DAILY SUN   daily, Independent Democrat--established 1887, continued by <u>Critic</u> c. 1897. Aug 15, 1887 = vol 1, no 1, John McElree (proprietor). Paper cited by Ayer 1888 thru 1897. Stanhope Sams, Ross A. Smith, and James H. Moore also associated with paper. *Files: CLS Aug-Dec 1887, Jul-Dec 1888, Jul 1889-Dec 1891, May 9, 1895; Greenville CL Aug 30, 1888; SCL (1889-1894) 4; Sumter County Museum-Archives Jan 8, 25, 1892.*

DEATH SHIP TIMES   underground monthly c. 1973-1974--published by the Defense Committee of North Charleston. The University of Connecticut has three issues, none of which contain standard publication data. *Files: University of Connecticut Feb, Apr, Jun 1974. Apparently no SC files.*

DEMOCRAT   daily--established 1879, merged with the Charleston Mercury c. 1880 and continued by that paper. Oct 30, 1879 = vol 1, no 28, Democrat Publishing Company. Not cited by Rowell. *Files: SCL Oct 30, Nov 18, 1879.*

DER TEUTONE   semi-weekly, Democrat, German--established in Apr 1844, continued by Die Deutsche Zeitung Oct 1853. According to Arndt, paper was edited by Johann Andreas Wagerer and published by J. B. Nixon. *NFK*

DEUTSCHE ZEITUNG   see Die Deutsche Zeitung.

DIE CHARLESTONER ZEITUNG   weekly, German--established Oct 1867, succeeded by Sudlicher Correspondent in Jun 1869. Oct 23, 1867 = vol 1, no 1, John A. Wagener (editor), C. G. Erckmann (publisher). On Apr 23, 1866, F. G. De Fontaine, editor of the Daily South Carolinian, announced plans to issue this weekly; however, it did not appear until eighteen months later. *Files: Library of Congress Oct 23, 1867-Oct 10, 1868. Apparently no SC files.*

DIE DEUTSCHE ZEITUNG   semi-weekly, weekly, German--continues Der Teutone in Oct 1853, ceased in 1917. According to King, paper not published 1861-1870. Die Deutsche Zeitung was issued semi-weekly to c. 1902, then weekly, and also published a weekly edition 1874 to c. 1902. See Die Wochentliche Deutsche Zeitung. Jan 3, 1876 = vol 23, no 1, Franz Melchers & Son (editors and publishers). Cited by Rowell and Ayer 1871 thru 1918. In Aug 1912 paper began to publish articles in English (perhaps because of a state political campaign) that soon developed into an English edition or supplement. In addition to Melchers, C. F. Vogler, G. Hoffmann, A. F. Melchers, Albert Orth, Henry Jensen, Wilhelm Woernle, Paul Wierse, and J. Ernest Schroeder associated with paper. See Arndt, German Language Press of the Americas. *Files: CLS Nov 22, 1913; SCL Sep 4, 11, 1873, Jun 13, 1903, mfm 1876-1900, 1905-1917. Note: These mfm files are essentially complete for years indicated, with missing issues listed at the beginning of each reel. English editions are included, 1912-1917.*

DIE WOCHENTLICHE DEUTSCHE ZEITUNG   weekly or "country" edition of Die Deutsche Zeitung--established 1874, ceased c. 1902. Jul 8, 1876 = vol 2, no 41. Cited by Rowell and Ayer 1875-1902. See Arndt, German Language Press of the Americas. *Files: American Antiquarian Society Jul 8, 1876. Apparently no SC files.*

ECHO DU SUD   tri-weekly, French--established Apr 1801, ceased c. Jul 1801, Jun 22, 1801 = vol 1, no 28, [Jean] Dacqueny and [Alexander] Bourgeois (publishers). Nine issues are available in Readex Microprint # 1851. The full title of this paper was L'Echo du Sud. Moniteur Francais. *Files: USC mp Jun 22-Jul 15, 1801.*

EVENING BULLETIN   daily, Republican--established Jan 27, 1873 by G. W. and J. W. De Lano. According to Duke checklist, paper continued by the Daily Charleston Bulletin on May 12, 1873 and by the Daily Morning Chronicle on Jun 1, 1873. *Files: Duke Jan 27-May 31, 1873. Apparently no SC files.*

EVENING COURIER   semi-weekly--established Jul 31, 1798, ceased c. Nov 1798. Jul 31, 1798 = vol 1, no 1, [Gabriel] Bounetheau and [John J.] Evans (publishers). This paper usually is called the "Evening Courier," although masthead title is the Evening Vesper Courier with "Vesper" set in a crescent under a star in the center. Twenty-nine issues are available in Readex Microprint # 1852. *Files: USC mp (Jul-Nov 1798) 29.*

EVENING HERALD   daily--established 1878, merged with the Charleston Mercury c. 1880-1881 and continued by that paper. Dec 12, 1878 = vol 1, no 1 ? , S. D. Hutson (publisher). Not cited by Rowell. *Files: Duke Dec 12, 1878. Apparently no SC files.*

EVENING NEWS AND ADVERTISER   daily--established 1898, ceased c. 1900. Cited by Ayer 1899 as a daily publication (no details given), but in 1900 listed as weekly "News and Advertiser." Not cited in 1901. *NFK*

EVENING POST   daily, tri-weekly c. 1832-1833. A short-lived paper printed by J. A. Stuart for William Grey early in 1832. By Nov 1832 the publishers were Norris and Gitsinger. The Library of Congress has scattered tri-weekly and daily editions. *Files: Library of Congress Nov 6, 1832 [daily], (Mar 1832-Sep 1833) 8 [tri-weekly]. Apparently no SC files.*

EVENING POST   daily--established Oct 1, 1894 = vol 1, no 1, Hartwell M. Ayer (editor). Cited by Ayer 1896 + . Issued as Post c. 1896-1900 and as the Charleston Evening Post 1908 to 1978. Jointly owned wtih the News and Courier [morning] since 1926, the two papers often have published cooperative special editions and since Apr 1974, when the Evening Post adopted a Mon-Fri schedule, have issued combined Sat-Sun editions. See Saturday and Sunday. W. W. Ball, Thomas R. Waring, F. H. McMaster, F. O. Emerson, R. M. Hitt, Jr., A. M. Wilcox, R. L. Schreadley, Peter Manigault, Barbara S. Williams, and Hall T. McGee, Jr., also associated with paper. *Files: Charleston CL mfm 1945 + ; CLS Mar 1907-Oct 1963, mfm 1894-1907, Nov 1963 + ; Clemson mfm 1894-1974; Evening Post mfm 1894 + ; SCL ((1897-1970)) 150, mfm 1894 +.*

EVENING POST AND GENERAL ADVERTISER   daily c. 1790--according to Brigham, the City Gazette of Jul 9, 1790 published a proposal for a new daily to be edited by James Carson. The City Gazette also mentioned this paper on Sep 7-8, 1790; however, no copies have been found. By 1791 Carson was publishing the South-Carolina Independent Gazette in Georgetown. *NFK*

EVENING SPY   weekly c. 1822. According to King, this paper was established in the same year as the Charleston Mercury. He indicates it soon ceased publication. *NFK*

EVENING VESPER COURIER   see Evening Courier.

FEDERAL CAROLINA GAZETTE   weekly--established Jan 2, 1800, ceased c. Dec 1800. This paper was published from the offices of the South-Carolina State-Gazette, and Timothy's Daily Advertiser by Benjamin F. Timothy and Thomas Sheppard.

Andrew M'Farlan also was associated with this weekly. According to Brigham, Harvard and the Library of Congress had copies in the 1930s. *Files: Harvard Feb 6, 20, 1800; Library of Congress Nov 13, Dec 25, 1800. Apparently no SC files.*

FOLLY BEACHCOMBER   weekly c. 1960-1961. Listed in Moore, Research Materials in South Carolina: A Guide (1967). *NFK*

FREE PRESS   weekly, Republican, black publication--established 1868, ceased 1868. Apr 5, 1868 = vol 1, no 2, C. D. Duval (editor), Timothy Hurley (publisher). According to King, this paper ceased publication by Oct 10, 1868. *Files: SCL mfm Apr 5, 11, 1868.*

FRENCH GAZETTE   weekly c. 1784. The Gazette of the State of South-Carolina (Aug 2, 1784) contains a proposal by Boinard and Gaillard to publish a "French Gazette." It is not known if any issues ever appeared. *NFK*

GAZETTE   weekly, Catholic, Republican--established Jan 1866 and at one time, according to Woody, was issued from the offices of the Daily Republican. Sep 12, 1868 = vol 3, no 20, J. D. Budds (proprietor). This issue indicates Budds recently had purchased the Gazette from M. Caulfield. Oct 23, 1869 = vol 4, no 25, L. C. Northrop and James Brennan (editors and proprietors). Subtitle to 1869 issue: "A First Class Irish-American Weekly Newspaper. The Only One Published in the South. Devoted to News, Irish Literature, and Catholic Intelligence." Cited once by Rowell (1869): J. D. Budds (editor and publisher). The Gazette, which may also have been issued as the Weekly Gazette, was continued by the Southern Celt in Dec 1869. *Files: University of North Carolina Sep 12, 1868, Oct 23, 1869. Apparently no SC files.*

GAZETTE OF THE STATE OF SOUTH-CAROLINA   weekly, semi-weekly--a revival in Apr 1777 of the South-Carolina Gazette suspended in Dec 1775. Apr 9, 1777 = no 2055, Peter Timothy (publisher). Following intermittent publication and the destruction of Timothy's printing office by fire, in Jun 1778 he entered into partnership with Nicholas Boden. This arrangement lasted until Feb 1780, when the paper was suspended upon approach of the British. Publication was resumed in Jul 1783 by Peter's widow, Ann Timothy, and E. Walsh. In Jul 1784 paper became a semi-weekly and on Mar 28, 1785 was continued by the State Gazette of South-Carolina. Note: This publication is part of a 12-reel mfm collection organized by the Charleston Library Society and often referred to as "18th-century South Carolina Newspapers." See Brigham and reel # 1 for pertinent details. *Files: CLS Apr 9-Nov 25, 1777, Jun 24, 1778-Dec 8, 1779, Feb 9, 1780, Jul 16, 1783-Mar 24, 1785; SCL Apr 14, 1779, Aug 2, 1784; Baptist College, Charleston CL, CLS, Citadel, Clemson, College of Charleston, Converse, Dorchester CL, Francis Marion, Furman, Greenville CL, Greenwood High School, Lander, News and Courier, Presbyterian, SC Archives, SC Historical Society, SCL, Summerville Public Library, USC-Beaufort, USC-Coastal, Winthrop, and Wofford mfm ((1777-1780)) 100.*

HAMITIC PALLADIUM   weekly, Republican, black publication--established 1902, ceased c. 1905. Cited by Ayer 1904 and 1905: Joseph E. Hayne (editor and publisher). *NFK*

HERALD   weekly, independent, black publication--established 1948, ceased c. 1955. Cited once by Ayer (1954): Arthur W. Aiken (publisher). *NFK*

HOME CIRCLE   weekly--established 1879, ceased c. 1879. Apr 25, 1879 = vol 1, no 6, Mrs. M. E. Britton (editor and publisher), Lucas and Richardson (printers). Not cited by Rowell and Ayer. *Files: Duke Apr 25, Sep 26, 1879. Apparently no SC files.*

INQUIRER   weekly, black publication c. 1901. According to a special woman's edition of the News and Courier entitled "Interlude" (Feb 1901), "Afro-American citizens" of Charleston at that time were reading the Inquirer. *NFK*

INTERLUDE   special 34-page edition of the News and Courier prepared by the Woman's Department of the South Carolina Inter-State and West Indian Exposition. Only one issue printed. *Files: SCL Feb 1901.*

INVESTIGATOR   daily--established Aug 22, 1812 by John Mackey & Company, ceased Feb 12, 1814. Sep 24, 1812 = vol 1, no 29. John L. Wilson, who was associated with Mackey, dissolved firm when latter retired in Feb 1814 and then established a new paper, the Charleston Gazette, and Mercantile Advertiser. The Investigator also issued a tri-weekly "country" edition. *Files: CLS orig & mfm Aug 22, 1812-Jun 29, 1813; SCL (1812-1813) 20, mfm Aug 22, 1812-Jun 29, 1813.*

IRISHMAN   see the Irishman and Southern Democrat.

IRISHMAN AND CHARLESTON WEEKLY REGISTER   see the Irishman and Southern Democrat.

IRISHMAN AND SOUTHERN DEMOCRAT   weekly--established Dec 1828, ceased c. 1832. May 29, 1830 = vol 2, no 1, William S. Blain (publisher). Also issued as the Irishman and Charleston Weekly Register May-Aug 1829 and the Irishman Aug 1829-May 1830. An ad for paper in the Charleston city directory (1831) indicates office was at 26 State Street. *Files: SCL Aug 24, 1831, a special edition consisting of a letter by Bishop John England. According to Gregory, Harvard University, Huntington Library, and New York Historical Society hold scattered issues.*

JAMES ISLAND JOURNAL   bi-weekly, weekly--established as an independent bi-weekly by the James Island Optimist Club on Feb 8, 1968 and subsequently issued weekly by James Island Publications, Inc. Charles P. Diggle, Jerry Sanders, Michael Baugh, and J. Fred Myers associated with the paper, which c. 1976 was continued by the Journal. Apr 30, 1986 = vol 10, no 16. *Files: Charleston CL Dec 17, 1968-Feb 10, 1982; Journal 1968 + .*

JAMES ISLAND NEWS   weekly--established 1961, ceased c. 1966. Paper listed in Charleston telephone directories from 1962 thru 1966, office at 669 Fort Sumter Drive. *NFK*

JOURNAL   see James Island Journal (established 1968).

LA PATRIOTE FRANCAIS   tri-weekly c. 1795. Jul 23, 1795 = vol 2, no 2, published by Claudius Beleurgey. Only one issue known to exist. See George Parker Winship, "French Newspapers in the United States from 1790 to 1800," Papers of the Bibliographical Society of America, XIV (1920), part 2, pp. 82-147. *Files: Brown University Jul 23, 1795. Apparently no SC files.*

LIGHTHOUSE AND INFORMER   weekly, independent, black publication--created c. 1941 by the merger of the Charleston Lighthouse and the People's Informer [Sumter]. Oct 19, 1941 = vol 5, no 18, John H. McCray (editor and publisher). Although published in Columbia, paper carried Charleston dateline in the early 1940s. See also Lighthouse and Informer [Columbia]. *Files: SCL Oct 19, 1941, Jan 10, 1943.*

L'ORACLE, FRANCAIS-AMERICAIN   semi-weekly, tri-weekly, French, French/English--established Jan 1, 1807 by John J. Negrin, ceased Dec 1807. Began as semi-weekly with French and English columns. On Feb 17, 1807 became tri-weekly L'Oracle published only in French, but on Jul 7, 1807 reverted to French/English material. Not issued regularly in Nov-Dec 1807. By Jan 1808 Negrin was publishing the L'Oracle and Daily Advertiser in New York City. *Files: CLS and SCL mfm ((1807)) 110.*

LOWCOUNTRY NEWS AND REVIEW   weekly c. 1978. Paper listed once in Charleston city directory (1978), Dewey Swain (editor and publisher), office at 103 Hasell Street. *NFK*

LUTHERAN VISITOR   weekly, religious--according to Rowell, paper published in Charleston by T. W. Dash c. 1875-1876. See Lutheran Visitor [Columbia].

METEOR   special Colonial Dames supplement to the News and Courier, only one issue published. *Files: CLS Apr 6, 1895.*

METHODIST MESSENGER   semi-monthly--established in Charleston in 1881, cited by Ayer in that city 1884 and 1885. By 1886 had moved to Orangeburg where became weekly. See Methodist Messenger [Orangeburg].

MISSIONARY RECORD   weekly, black publication--continues the South Carolina Leader on Apr 7, 1868, ceased c. 1879. Apr 1, 1876 = vol 6, no 18, Richard H. Cain (editor), South Carolina Annual Conference of the A. M. E. Church (publisher). Cited by Rowell 1869 thru 1879. Rowell 1874: "The first and only newspaper published by a colored man for any length of time, with the largest circulation in this State."

Apparently became a religious organ in 1876. *Files: SCL Apr 1, 1876, mfm Jul 5, 1873.*

MONITOR   weekly, religious, black publication--established in Columbia in 1883 as the Columbia Monitor, this paper moved to Bennettsville c. 1885 and was issued as the South Carolina Monitor; however, it soon suspended operations. The Monitor apparently was published briefly in Charleston in 1888 and is cited by Ayer 1888 and 1889 in Cheraw: C. W. McColl (editor and proprietor). This paper also may have been issued during these same years in Charlotte, N. C., and Bennettsville as the Baptist Monitor. May 26, 1888 = vol 1, no 9, C. W. McColl (editor and publisher). *Files: Duke May 26, 1888. Apparently no SC files.*

MOULTRIE NEWS   see Moultrie News [Mount Pleasant].

NATIONALIST   daily, Republican--a short-lived daily paper issued from the offices of the Daily Republican from Sep 24, 1871 to Feb 19, 1872. According to Woody, this publication was a successor to the Daily Advertiser. Not cited by Rowell. *NFK*

NEW CITIZEN   weekly, independent, black publication--established 1948, ceased c. 1952. Cited by Ayer 1949 thru 1952: W. Eugene Simmons (editor), Arthur W. Aiken (publisher). *NFK*

NEW ERA   weekly, black publication--established 1880, ceased c. 1884. Cited by Ayer 1881 thru 1884. Apr 3, 1880 = vol 1, no 3, William Holloway (publisher). *Files: Duke (1880-1884) 70. Apparently no SC files.*

NEW ERA   weekly, black publication--established c. 1927, ceased c. 1935. Not cited by Ayer. According to Who's Who in Colored America (1927), R. L. Wainwright was editor and publisher of the New Era, offices at 87 Mary Street. Behling says paper was still being issued 1934-1935. *NFK*

NEWS AND ADVERTISER   see Evening News and Advertiser.

NEWS AND COURIER   daily--continues Charleston Daily News and Charleston Daily Courier on Apr 7, 1873 = vol 10, no 2256, Riordan, Dawson & Company (publishers). J. C. Hemphill, Robert Lathan, William Watts Ball, Thomas P. Lesene, James E. Rockwell, T. R. Waring, A. M. Wilcox, R. L. Schreadley, Peter Manigault, and Hall T. McGee, Jr., also associated with paper, which continued weekly and tri-weekly editions after merger in 1873. See the Weekly News and the Tri-Weekly News and Courier. Paper launched a Sun edition in Nov 1879 (see the Sunday News), and in 1926 the owners of the Evening Post acquired a controlling interest in the News and Courier. See Herbert Ravenel Sass, Outspoken: 150 Years of "The News and Courier" (Columbia, 1953). *Files: Numerous SC depositories hold random and commemorative issues and the Charleston CL has extensive subject index, 1930 + . Charleston CL, CLS, Citadel, Clemson, College of Charleston, News and Courier, SCL, and Winthrop mfm 1873 + ; Converse mfm 1969-1976; Dorchester CL mfm 1873-1921; Furman* *mfm 1873-1966; Presbyterian mfm 1873-1889; USC-Coastal mfm 1893-1965; Voorhees mfm 1969-1972; Wofford mfm 1873-1896. Note: Reel # 1 of the* News and Courier *contains the* Charleston Daily News *Jan 1-Apr 5, 1873.*

OBSERVER   weekly (?) c. 1899--a black publication cited in the "Negro in Business," a report of a conference held at Atlanta University in May 1899. *NFK*

ORACLE   see L'Oracle. Francais Americain.

PALMETTO BATTERY   daily, pro-nullification c. 1834. According to King, this short-lived revival of the State Rights and Free Trade Evening Post was edited by James Wright Simmons. Simmons--poet, writer, and treasurer of the Republic of Texas--also was correspondent for various New York dailies during his extensive career. *NFK*

PALMETTO FLAG   semi-weekly, tri-weekly, pro-secession--Sep 12, 1851 = vol 1, no 1, Edward Councell (printer and publisher). "The period of decisive action has arrived. We have counted the cost and find nothing as deplorable as voluntary servitude." Paper ceased Oct 25, 1851. Councell published a full-page ad for his book and job printing business at 119 East Bay Street in the 1852 Charleston city directory. *Files: SCL mfm Sep 12-Oct 25, 1851.*

PALMETTO PRESS   weekly, black publication--established 1882, ceased c. 1885. Jul 8, 1882 = vol 1, no 2. According to Tindall, this paper was edited by R. L. Smith. The Charleston city directory (1885) indicates offices were located at 84 Queen Street. *Files: SCL Jul 8, 1882 (xerox copy).*

PALO ALTO   semi-weekly--Democrat publication for 1848 presidential campaign. Aug 5, 1848 = vol 1, no 1, issued from the offices of the Charleston Evening News-- "General Taylor is a man you cannot buy--a man you cannot sell--a man you cannot scare--and a man who never surrenders." *Files: SCL (Aug-Oct 1848) 12.*

PEOPLE'S WATCHMAN   weekly, black publication--established c. 1879, merged with the Charleston Mercury in Jan 1880 and continued by that paper. According to Penn, Afro-American Press and Its Editors, this was a prominent Afro-American journal. *NFK*

PORT FOLIO   weekly c. 1869. An unpublished CLS survey indicates that this paper was issued by F. W. Miller and LeRoy Hammond. *NFK*

POST   see the Evening Post (established 1894).

PROTECTIVE LEAGUE JOURNAL   weekly, black publication--established 1905, ceased c. 1909. Cited by Ayer 1907 thru 1909: Protective League Company (publisher). *NFK*

REFEREE   weekly, free "advertising sheet"--established Jun 14, 1869, continued by the Charleston Sun c. 1875.   Jul 9, 1870 = vol 2, no 5, F. Eugene Durbec (publisher). Cited by Rowell 1870 thru 1874: F. E. Durbec (editor and publisher). *Files: CLS Jul 9, 1870.*

ROYAL GAZETTE   semi-weekly--established Mar 3, 1781 (vol 1, no 1) by R. Wells & Son [Robert and John Wells]. Paper was suspended from Aug 7 to Sep 7, 1782 and ceased c. Oct 1782. Note: This paper is part of a 12-reel mfm collection organized by the Charleston Library Society and often referred to as "18th-century South Carolina Newspapers." See reel # 1 and Brigham for pertinent details. *Files: CLS ((Mar 1871-Sep 1782)) 160; Baptist College, Charleston CL, CLS, Citadel, Clemson, College of Charleston, Converse, Dorchester CL, Francis Marion, Furman, Greenville CL, Greenwood High School, Lander, News and Courier, Presbyterian, SC Archives, SC Historical Society, SCL, Summerville Public Library, USC-Beaufort, USC-Coastal, Winthrop, and Wofford mfm ((Mar 1781-Sep 1782)) 160.*

ROYAL SOUTH-CAROLINA GAZETTE   tri-weekly, semi-weekly--established as tri-weekly in Jun 1780 by James Robertson, Donald Macdonald, and Alexander Cameron. Jul 6, 1780 = vol 1, no 15. In 1781 paper became semi-weekly issued by Robertson and ceased publication on Sep 12, 1782. Note: This paper is part of a 12-reel mfm collection organized by the Charleston Library Society and often referred to as "18th-century South Carolina Newspapers." See reel # 1 and Brigham for pertinent details. *Files: CLS (1780-1782) 18; Baptist College, Charleston CL, CLS, Citadel, Clemson, College of Charleston, Converse, Dorchester CL, Francis Marion, Furman, Greenville CL, Greenwood High School, Lander, News and Courier, Presbyterian, SC Archives, SC Historical Society, SCL, Summerville Public Library, USC-Beaufort, USC-Coastal, Winthrop, and Wofford mfm (1780-1782) 25.*

SATURDAY   title of combined editions of the News and Courier and the Charleston Evening Post as of Apr 7, 1974.   See also Sunday. *Files: see mfm reels of daily News and Courier Apr 1974 + .*

SATURDAY BULLETIN, AN INDEPENDENT LITERARY AND DO-MESTIC JOURNAL   weekly--established 1837, ceased c. 1838. Aug 18, 1838 = vol 2, no 6, Thomas J. Eccles (publisher). Paper had an office at 44 Queen Street. *Files: Library of Congress Aug 18, 1838. Apparently no SC files.*

SATURDAY MORNING'S HERALD   weekly c. 1834--a prospectus appearing in Georgetown's Winyah Intelligencer (Aug 12, 1834) indicates that Benjamin R. Gitsinger, owner of the State Rights and Free Trade Evening Post, was planning to launch this new publication. *NFK*

SEASHORE REVIEW   weekly, Democrat--established c. 1900, continued by the Charleston Review c. 1903. Cited by Ayer 1901 thru 1903: B. P. Carey (editor), [John L.] Kiley and Carey (publishers). *NFK*

SENTINEL   weekly, labor--established 1907, ceased c. 1908. Cited once by Ayer (1908): E. F. Hammond (publisher). *NFK*

SOUTH-CAROLINA AND AMERICAN GENERAL GAZETTE   weekly, semi-weekly--continues the South-Carolina Weekly Gazette on Apr 4, 1764, apparently published by Robert Wells and David Bruce. John Wells (son of Robert Wells) and John Wells, Jr. (a nephew) both were associated with paper, which was suspended briefly in 1776 and again in 1779. Loyalist John Wells revived paper as a semi-weekly in Oct 1780. Early in 1781 it was succeeded by the Royal Gazette. Note: This paper is part of a 12-reel mfm collection organized by the Charleston Library Society and often referred to as "18th-century South Carolina Newspapers." See reel # 1 and Brigham for pertinent details. *Files: CLS Apr 18, 1764, May 1766-Apr 1772, Oct 22, 1772, Apr 1774-Feb 1781; Baptist College, Charleston CL, CLS, Citadel, Clemson, College of Charleston, Converse, Dorchester CL, Francis Marion, Furman, Greenville CL, Greenwood High School, Lander, News and Courier, Presbyterian, SC Archives, SC Historical Society, SCL, Summerville Public Library, USC-Beaufort, USC-Coastal, Winthrop, and Wofford mfm ((1764-1781)) 700.*

SOUTH-CAROLINA GAZETTE   weekly--established Jan 8, 1732 by Thomas Whitemarsh, suspended Sep 8, 1733, and re-established Feb 2, 1734 by Lewis Timothee [Timothy]. Timothy's widow, Ann, and their son, Peter, produced paper after Jan 1739. During succeeding decades there were numerous suspensions, and on Apr 9, 1777 paper was continued by the Gazette of the State of South-Carolina. Note: This paper is part of a 12-reel mfm collection organized by the Charleston Library Society and often referred to as "18th-century South Carolina Newspapers." See reel # 1 and Brigham for pertinent details. Also, see Hennig Cohen (compiler), A Name Index to the South-Carolina Gazette, 1732-1738 (Charleston, 1953). *Files: CLS Jan 1732-Aug 1757, Jun 1758-Dec 1775, photostat copies also available; SCL ((1732-1737)) 200, some of these issues photostats, Sep 26, 1775; Baptist College, Charleston CL, CLS, Citadel, Clemson, College of Charleston, Converse, Dorchester CL, Francis Marion, Furman, Greenville CL, Greenwood High School, Lander, News and Courier, Presbyterian, SC Archives, SC Historical Society, SCL, Summerville Public Library, USC-Beaufort, USC-Coastal, Winthrop, and Wofford mfm ((1732-1775)) 2200; USC mfm ((1732-1753)).*

SOUTH-CAROLINA GAZETTE; AND COUNTRY JOURNAL   weekly--established Dec 17, 1765, ceased Aug 1775. The first two issues of this paper, published by Charles Crouch throughout its ten-year history, appeared as the South-Carolina Gazetteer; and Country Journal. The mfm files, virtually complete, contain numerous supplements, extras, and special editions. Note: These files are part of a 12-reel mfm collection organized by the Charleston Library Society and often referred to as "18th-century South Carolina Newspapers." See reel # 1 and Brigham for pertinent details. *Files: CLS Dec 1765-Aug 1775; SCL Nov 29, 1768; Baptist College, Charleston CL, CLS, Citadel, Clemson, College of Charleston, Converse, Dorchester CL, Francis Marion, Furman, Greenville CL, Greenwood High School, Lander, News and Courier, Presbyterian, SC Archives, SC Historical Society, SCL, Summerville Public Library, USC-Beaufort, USC-Coastal, Winthrop, and Wofford mfm ((1765-1775)) 500.*

SOUTH-CAROLINA GAZETTE AND GENERAL ADVERTISER semi-weekly, tri-weekly, daily--established Mar 15, 1783 (vol 1, no 1), printed for John Miller. Issued semi-weekly (irregularly) to Jan 1, 1784 when became tri-weekly. Title changed on Oct 26, 1784 to the South-Carolina State Gazette, and General Advertiser and on Nov 30, 1784 that paper became a daily publication, the South Carolina State Gazette and Daily Advertiser. Paper ceased c. Aug 1785. *Files: CLS orig & mfm Mar 15, 1783-Jul 26, 1785; SCL mfm Mar 15, 1783-Jul 26, 1785.*

SOUTH-CAROLINA GAZETTE, AND PUBLIC ADVERTISER semi-weekly, tri-weekly--continues the South-Carolina Weekly Gazette on Mar 3, 1784 = vol 2, no 56, printed by Nathan Childs & Company, 85 Church Street. Paper issued semi-weekly except from Jul 12-Nov 23, 1785 when tri-weekly. Continued by the Charleston Morning Post, and Daily Advertiser on Jan 18, 1786. See Brigham for details. *Files: CLS orig & mfm Mar 3, 1784-Jan 14, 1786; SCL mfm Mar 3, 1784-Jan 14, 1786.*

SOUTH-CAROLINA GAZETTEER; AND COUNTRY JOURNAL see the South-Carolina Gazette; and Country Journal.

SOUTH CAROLINA LABOR LEDGER weekly--established 1944, ceased c. 1947. Cited by Ayer 1946 and 1947. Ayer 1946: Fred P. Kupfer (editor), Charles E. Silva (publisher). Ayer 1947: Bruce Hall (editor), Central Labor Union (publisher). *NFK*

SOUTH CAROLINA LEADER weekly, Republican, black publication--established Oct 7, 1865 by T. Hurley & Company in the interests of "Free Labor and General Reform." Nov 25, 1865 = vol 1, no 8, Allen Coffin (editor). H. Judge Moore, Richard Harvey Cain, Alonzo Ransier, and Robert B. Elliott also associated with paper. Continued by the Missionary Record on Apr 7, 1868. *Files: SCL mfm (1865-1866) 12.*

SOUTH CAROLINA METHODIST weekly, black publication--established 1903, ceased c. 1905. Cited by Ayer 1904 and 1906: L. Ruffin Nichols (editor), South Carolina Methodist Publishing Company. *NFK*

SOUTH CAROLINA REPUBLICAN weekly--established Oct 1868 by J. M. Morris and Myron Fox. Oct 10, 1868 = vol 1, no 1, Union Printing Company (publisher). Weekly edition moved to Columbia in Sep 1869 and local paper was replaced by the Daily Republican. *Files: SCL Oct 10, 1868, Jun 19, 1869.*

SOUTH-CAROLINA STATE-GAZETTE daily--continues the State Gazette of South-Carolina on Jan 1, 1794 (vol 55, no 4302), published by Benjamin F. Timothy and William Mason. Full title was the South-Carolina State-Gazette & Timothy & Mason's Daily Advertiser. During the next four years, according to Brigham, there were frequent title changes, two issues appearing in Jan 1795 as the State Gazette of South Carolina. As of Jan 1, 1798 Timothy gained full control and title became the South-Carolina State Gazette, and Timothy's Daily Advertiser. Paper ceased c. Sep 1802. *Files: CLS Jul 1794-Jun 1795, Oct 1795-Sep 1802; SCL May 30, 1794, Jul 13, 1801,* *mfm Jan-Jun 1794, Oct 1795-Apr 1796, Oct 1796-Feb 1797, Sep 1797-Jun 1799, Jan-Sep 1802.*

SOUTH CAROLINA STATE GAZETTE AND DAILY ADVERTISER
see the South-Carolina Gazette and General Advertiser.

SOUTH-CAROLINA STATE GAZETTE, AND GENERAL ADVERTISER
see the South-Carolina Gazette and General Advertiser.

SOUTH-CAROLINA STATE-GAZETTE & TIMOTHY & MASON'S DAILY ADVERTISER   see the South-Carolina State-Gazette.

SOUTH-CAROLINA STATE-GAZETTE, AND TIMOTHY'S DAILY ADVERTISER   see the South-Carolina State-Gazette.

SOUTH-CAROLINA TEMPERANCE ADVOCATE AND REGISTER OF AGRICULTURAL AND GENERAL LITERATURE   weekly--established in Columbia in 1839 as the South-Carolina Temperance Advocate. Paper was published briefly in Charleston c. 1852 and moved to Camden in 1853. Feb 12, 1852 = vol 13, no 33, Edwin Heriot (editor and publisher). See the South-Carolina Temperance Advocate [Columbia and Camden].

SOUTH-CAROLINA WEEKLY ADVERTISER   weekly--established Feb 19, 1783, ceased Apr 23, 1783. Feb 19, 1783 = vol 1, no 1, published by Elizabeth Boden. Feb 19-Apr 23, 1783 available in Readex Microprint # 1871. *Files: USC mp Feb-Apr 1783.*

SOUTH-CAROLINA WEEKLY CHRONICLE   weekly--established May 1787, ceased c. 1787. Oct 9, 1787 = no 21, published by John Markland, who on Jan 1, 1788 became one of the publishers of the City Gazette. *Files: CLS Oct 9, 1787.*

SOUTH-CAROLINA WEEKLY GAZETTE   weekly--established in 1758 by Robert Wells, who later entered into partnership with G. Bruce. David Bruce also associated with paper. Feb 7, 1759 = no 12, Robert Wells (publisher). According to Brigham, this copy is no longer available, but three issues can be found on mfm: Oct 31, 1759, Dec 10, 1760, and Mar 21, 1764. The 1759-1760 issues also are available in Readex Microprint # 1873. In Apr 1764 this paper was continued by the South-Carolina and American General Gazette. Note: This weekly is part of a 12-reel mfm collection organized by the Charleston Library Society and often referred to as "18th-century South Carolina Newspapers." See reel # 1 and Brigham for pertinent details. *Files: Baptist College, Charleston CL, CLS, Citadel, Clemson, College of Charleston, Converse, Dorchester CL, Francis Marion, Furman, Greenville CL, Greenwood High School, Lander, News and Courier, Presbyterian, SC Archives, SC Historical Society, SCL, Summerville Public Library, USC-Beaufort, USC-Coastal, Winthrop, and Wofford mfm (1759-1764) 3; USC mp (1759-1760) 2.*

SOUTH-CAROLINA WEEKLY GAZETTE weekly--established Feb 15, 1783 (vol 1, no 1) by Nathan Childs, who took Robert Bruce as partner the following month. On Mar 3, 1784 paper became semi-weekly and was continued by the South-Carolina Gazette, and Public Advertiser. *Files: CLS orig & mfm Feb 15, 1783-Feb 27, 1784; SCL mfm Feb 15, 1783-Feb 27, 1784.*

SOUTH-CAROLINA WEEKLY JOURNAL weekly c. 1732. A notice in the South-Carolina Gazette (Mar 22, 1735) indicates that Eleazer Phillips, Jr., published this weekly sometime prior to his death in Jul 1732. No copies have been found. See Brigham for details. *NFK*

SOUTH-EASTERN ADVOCATE bi-weekly, religious, black publication-- established 1872, ceased c. 1876. Cited by Rowell 1875 and 1876: A[lonzo] Webster (editor), Advocate Publishing Company. May have been a revival of the Charleston Advocate, 1867-1868. *NFK*

SOUTHERN BAPTIST weekly, religious--established 1846, ceased c. 1860. Jun 5, 1847 = vol 2, no 6, T. W. Haynes (editor). E. T. Winkler, J. P. Tustin, and W. B. Carson also associated with paper. *Files: SCL (1854-1857) 4, mfm Jun 1847-Dec 1860.*

SOUTHERN BAPTIST ADVOCATE weekly, religious--established 1843, ceased c. 1843. Apr 22, 1843 = vol 1, no 12, Thomas Curtis (editor), Burges and James (publishers). *Files: SCL Apr 22, 1843.*

SOUTHERN BAPTIST, AND GENERAL INTELLIGENCER weekly, religious--established Jan 1835, continued by the Southern Watchman, and General Intelligencer in Jan 1837. Jan 3, 1835 = vol 1, no 1, William Henry Brisbane (editor), printed by James S. Burges. *Files: SCL mfm Jan-Dec 1835, (Jan-Dec 1836) 44. Note: Mfm reel contains index to 1835 issues.*

SOUTHERN BOOM weekly, Democrat--established 1880, ceased c. 1880. Cited once by Ayer (1880). *NFK*

SOUTHERN CELT weekly, Catholic, Republican--continues the Gazette in Dec 1869. Apr 2, 1870 = vol 5, no 18, L. C. Northrop and James Brennan (editors and proprietors). According to Woody, this paper was suspended for several months in 1871 and revived in Feb 1872. Cited by Rowell 1871 thru 1873. Paper ceased c. 1873. G. D. Foxe also associated with the Southern Celt. *Files: SCL Apr 2, 1870.*

SOUTHERN CHRISTIAN ADVOCATE weekly, Methodist--established in Charleston in 1837 and published in various cities in South Carolina and Georgia, continued by the South Carolina Methodist Advocate in 1948. See the Southern Christian Advocate [Columbia].

SOUTHERN CHRISTIAN SENTINEL   weekly, Presbyterian--established Mar 1839, ceased Dec 1841. Sep 26, 1840 = vol 2, no 30 T[homas] Magruder (editor), B. B. Hussey (printer). According to E. T. Thompson, Presbyterians in the South, I, p. 403, Magruder advocated an independent southern church free of abolitionist "aggression." *Files: SCL Sep 26, 1840.*

SOUTHERN COURIER   weekly, black publication--established 1980, ceased c. 1981. Nov 12, 1980 = vol 1, no 11 (no personnel listed). According to Charleston city directory (1980-1981), this paper was published by Gladys Hazel at 218 Rutledge Avenue. Not cited in directories, 1982-1983. *Files: Lee Hendren [Holly Hill] Nov 12, 1980.*

SOUTHERN EVANGELICAL INTELLIGENCER   weekly, Presbyterian--established Mar 27, 1819 (vol 1, no 1) by B. M. Palmer and George Reid (editors), W. P. Young & Son (printers). Although periodical in format, this publication contains local news, obituaries, and Charleston prices current. Index available at SCL. Continued by the Southern Intelligencer in Jan 1822. *Files: SCL orig & mfm ((Mar 1819-Dec 1821)) 120.*

SOUTHERN EVANGELIST   weekly, Presbyterian, black publication--established in Charlotte, N. C., in 1874, cited by Rowell 1879 in Charleston: William A. Patton and D. J. Saunders (editors and publishers). According to North, paper merged with the African American Presbyterian of Washington, D. C., in 1879. *NFK*

SOUTHERN FREE PRESS   weekly--established 1830, ceased c. 1830. May 15, 1830 = vol 1, no 18, A. F. C. (editor and publisher). "My Press is free, and all parties will I publish for; the Athiest, the Materialist, the Christian, the Mahometan, the Jew, the Deist, the Politician, and the Visionary, if he is not included in some of the previously named sects." Note: According to Gregory, the Historical, Memorial, and Art Department of Iowa [Des Moines] held Mar 6-Nov 13, 1830 in the 1930s; however, those files are not cited in the United States Newspaper Program National Union List (1985), which includes Iowa depositories. *Files: Huntington Museum May 15, 1830. Apparently no SC files.*

SOUTHERN GAZETTE   weekly c. 1918-1919--according to the Charleston city directory (1918), this paper was being issued at 125 Meeting Street by Albert Orth. This was an obvious attempt by the former editor of Die Deutsche Zeitung (closed by World War I) to continue his journalistic career. Paper soon ceased. Not cited by Ayer. *NFK*

SOUTHERN HEBREW   weekly--established 1877, ceased c. 1878. Cited once by Rowell (1878): H. Jacobs (publisher). *NFK*

SOUTHERN INTELLIGENCER   weekly, religious--continues the Southern Evangelical Intelligencer in Jan 1822, William Riley (printer). Paper ceased c. 1826. More periodical than newspaper, it contained local news and Charleston prices current. *Files: SCL orig & mfm (Jan 5, 1822-Mar 29, 1823) 53.*

SOUTHERN INVENTOR   monthly--established Jan 15, 1858 (vol 1, no 1) by James Phynney (printer), Kellogg and Dodge (publishers). W. F. Dodge, who served as editor, notes that he issued an experimental issue entitled the "Bulletin" in Nov 1857. Paper ceased c. 1858. *Files: SCL Jan 15, 1858.*

SOUTHERN LIGHT JOURNAL   weekly, black publication--established 1962 ? Jun 4-10, 1980 = vol 18, no 25, no personnel cited. *Files: Lee Hendren [Holly Hill] Jun 4, 1980, Mar 30, 1983.*

SOUTHERN LUTHERAN   weekly, religious--established 1861, moved to Columbia in 1863. Sep 28, 1861 = vol 1, no 7, edited by a Committee of the Synod of South Carolina, James Phynney (printer). N. Aldrich and John Bachman also associated with paper. See also Southern Lutheran [Columbia]. *Files: SCL (1862-1863) 2, mfm (1861-1863) 14.*

SOUTHERN MEDIUM, AND IMPRESS OF THE TIMES   semi-weekly, Whig publication, c. 1839-1840. Jan 8, 1840 = vol 1, no 9. A pro-William Henry Harrison campaign organ, this paper was issued briefly by J. M. Simons and I. Bailey at 73 East Bay Street. *Files: Library of Congress Jan 8, 1840. Apparently no SC files.*

SOUTHERN PATRIOT   daily--continues the Southern Patriot and Commercial Advertiser in Oct 1825, ceased c. 1848. Jan 3, 1826 = vol 18, no 8309, J. N. Cardozo (publisher). Martin E. Munro and Albert G. Mackey also associated with paper, which issued a tri-weekly "country" edition. *Files: CLS Jul-Dec 1827, Jan-Jun 1829, Jan 1830-Jun 1838, Jan 1839-Jun 1840, Jan-Jun 1841, Jan 1845-Dec 1848; SCL Jul 1826-Jun 1827, (1830-1848) 9, mfm 1826, 1828, Jul 1829-Dec 1835, Jan 1841-Dec 1844.*

SOUTHERN PATRIOT   tri-weekly, "country" edition--see Southern Patriot for details. *Files: Library of Congress Mar 19/20, 1833. Apparently no SC files.*

SOUTHERN PATRIOT AND COMMERCIAL ADVERTISER   daily--established in Jul 1814 by Isaac Harby. Jul 28, 1814 = vol 1, no 3. On Oct 10, 1825 paper continued by the Southern Patriot. This paper also issued a tri-weekly, "country" edition. *Files: CLS 1815-1820, 1823, 1825; SCL ((1814)) 105, Jan-Jun 1824, mfm 1815-1818, 1821-1822, 1824.*

SOUTHERN PATRIOT AND COMMERCIAL ADVERTISER   tri-weekly, "country" edition--see the Southern Patriot and Commercial Advertiser for details. *Files: CLS Jan 4-Mar 16, 1815.*

SOUTHERN PRESBYTERIAN   weekly--established c. 1850 in Milledgeville, Ga., moved to Charleston in 1852, to Columbia in 1861, and to Clinton in 1893. This publication often is confused with the quarterly Southern Presbyterian Review (1847-1885), which sometimes used same number sequence. Apr 29, 1852 = vol 5, no 35, Washington Baird (editor). J. L. Kirkpatrick, W. P. Paxton, and H. B. Cunningham also associated with paper while in Charleston, 1852-1861. See also Southern Presbyterian [Columbia and Clinton]. *Files: SCL (1852-1860) 18.*

SOUTHERN REPORTER   weekly, Republican, black publication--established 1900, ceased c. 1920. Cited by Ayer 1904 thru 1920. According to the Charleston city directory (1903), this paper--established May 5, 1900--was being issued by I. E. Lowery from an office at 153 1/2 Coming Street. In 1919 the city directory noted that E. B. Burroughs was publishing the Southern Reporter at 19 Kracke Street. *NFK*

SOUTHERN STANDARD   daily--continues the Sun on Aug 30, 1851, continued by the Charleston Daily Standard in Sep 1853. Nov 17, 1852 = vol 2, no 120, B. C. Pressley (editor and publisher). This paper also issued tri-weekly (no masthead) and weekly editions. *Files: CLS Jul 1852-Sep 1853 [daily]; SCL Nov 17, 1852 [daily], Oct 6/7, 1851 [tri-weekly].*

SOUTHERN WATCHMAN, AND GENERAL INTELLIGENCER   weekly, religious--continues the Southern Baptist, and General Intelligencer in Jan 1837. Jan 13, 1837 = vol 4, no 2, B. Manly (editor), James Burges (publisher). William T. Brantley also associated with paper, which was continued by the Biblical Recorder and Southern Watchman in Mar 1838. *Files: SCL mfm Jan 1837-Feb 1838.*

STAR: AND CHARLESTON DAILY ADVERTISER   daily, tri-weekly-- established Mar 1783, ceased May 1794. Sep 7, 1793 = vol 2, no 123, James Carey (printer). According to Brigham, William P. Harrison was associated with this paper until Jul 27, 1793 when he became editor of the Columbian Herald. At that time, Carey transformed paper into a tri-weekly, the Star: and Charleston Public Advertiser. The South-Carolina Gazette & Timothy and Mason's Daily Advertiser (May 30, 1794) indicates that the Star had ceased publication. *Files: Furman mfm (Jul-Sep 1793) 8; SCL Sep 7, 1793.*

STAR: AND CHARLESTON PUBLIC ADVERTISER   see the Star: and Charleston Daily Advertiser.

STATE GAZETTE OF SOUTH-CAROLINA   semi-weekly, tri-weekly-- continues the Gazette of the State of South-Carolina on Mar 28, 1785. Sep 8, 1785 = vol 44, no 2331, printed semi-weekly for Ann Timothy. Following her death in Sep 1792, Benjamin Franklin Timothy became publisher and on Oct 30, 1793 paper was transformed into a tri-weekly. William Mason joined Timothy as partner in May 1793, and in Jan 1794 paper was continued by the South-Carolina State-Gazette & Timothy & Mason's Daily Advertiser. *Files: CLS Mar 1785-Dec 1786, ((1787-1788)), Aug-Nov 1790, 1791-1793; SCL (1785-1793) 25, mfm ((1789-1793)) 420.*

STATE RIGHTS AND FREE TRADE EVENING POST   daily, pro- nullification--established Oct 1831, ceased c. 1834. Oct 1, 1831 = vol 1, no 1, printed for J. A. Stuart by William Gray. James C. Norris and Benjamin R. Gitsinger purchased this paper in Nov 1832. According to King, it expired after 684 issues and was revived briefly as the Palmetto Battery. The Post also issued a tri-weekly "country" edition. *Files: CLS Oct 1831-May 1834; SCL mfm Oct 1, 1831-Jun 29, 1833.*

STRENGTH OF THE PEOPLE   tri-weekly, daily, semi-weekly--established as a tri-weekly on Jun 24, 1809 by John H. Sargent, became daily on Sep 19 and semi-weekly on Nov 16. Ceased c. Sep 1810. Seventy issues are available in Readex Microprint # 1881. Strength of the People published a column and an editorial page entitled "Brazen Face" that may have appeared as a separate publication. *Files: CLS Jun 24, 1809; SCL mfm (Jun 1809-Sep 1810) 70; USC mp (Jun 1809-Sep 1810) 70.*

SUBURBAN NEWS   weekly--established c. 1973, ceased c. 1976. Published by Charles P. Diggle, Community Press, Inc. *NFK*

SUBURBAN TIMES   weekly--established Jul 1986 by Charles P. Diggle, Community Press, Inc. Paper absorbed by Journal in Jan 1987. *Files: Journal Jul-Dec 1986.*

SUDLICHER CORRESPONDENT   semi-weekly, German--established Jun 1869, ceased in 1870 and was succeeded by Die Deutsche Zeitung. Jun 29, 1869 = vol 1, no 1, Ernest Beyer (editor), Erckmann, Beyer & Company (publisher). Cited by Rowell in 1870 as "the only German paper" in the Carolinas, Georgia, and Florida. See Arndt for pertinent details. *Files: Library of Congress Jun 29, 1869-Dec 29, 1870. Apparently no SC files.*

SUN   daily--established 1850, continued by the Southern Standard in Aug 1851. Nov 9, 1850 = vol 1, no 36, Edward Sill, Jr. (editor), H. L. Darr (printer). *Files: CLS Oct 5, 1850-Jan 25, 1851; SCL Nov 9, 1850.*

SUN   see Daily Sun c. 1887-1897.

SUNDAY   Sun edition of the News and Courier--continues News and Courier (Sunday) on Apr 7, 1974. At that time, the Charleston Evening Post inititated a five-day, Mon-Fri schedule and the two papers began issuing joint weekend editions entitled Saturday and Sunday. *Files: see mfm reels of daily News and Courier Apr 1974 + .*

SUNDAY BUDGET   weekly--established 1887, ceased Oct 7, 1891. Nov 20, 1887 = vol 2, no 41. Cited by Ayer 1889 thru 1891. Octavus Cohen, Yates Snowden, Louis A. Beaty, and Francis S. Rogers associated with this paper, which also published the World (daily) and the Weekly World. Note: Nov 20, 1887 clearly is the first issue of the Sunday Budget despite vol-issue numbering. Cohen previously worked on the staff of the "Sunday Budget" in Troy, N. Y., a well-established paper. That association may have inspired the title of this Charleston publication. *Files: CLS Nov 1887-Jul 1888, Sep 1888-Oct 1891; Greenville CL Feb 3, Jun 30, 1889; SCL mfm ((Jul 1888-Oct 1891)), filmed with daily World, files virtually complete for years indicated.*

SUNDAY DISPATCH   weekly, Independent Democrat--continues the Sunday Times c. 1883, continued by the Charleston Dispatch c. 1886. Sep 20, 1885 = vol 16, no 26, S. D. Hutson and J. W. Hammond (editors and proprietors). Cited by Ayer 1884 and 1885. *Files: SCL Sep 20, 1885.*

SUNDAY NEWS   Sun edition of the News and Courier--established Nov 1879, continued on Aug 22, 1926 by the News and Courier (same masthead as weekday edition). See also Sunday. *Files: Sun editions of the News and Courier are available on the mfm reels of the daily paper, Jan 1882 + . See News and Courier.*

SUNDAY TIMES   weekly--according to King, this paper was established on Mar 20, 1870 by J. W. De Lano. It was continued by the Sunday Dispatch c. 1883. Cited by Rowell 1871 thru 1876 and Ayer 1880 thru 1883. Mar 8, 1874 = vol 4, no 51, J. W. De Lano (proprietor). *Files: CLS Mar 8, May 31, 1874.*

TELEGRAPHE: AND CHARLESTON DAILY ADVERTISER   daily-- continues the Daily Evening Gazette and Charleston Tea-Table Companion c. Mar 1795, ceased c. 1795. Mar 16, 1795 = vol 1, no 58, James Carey (publisher). Mar 16-18, 20, 1795 available in Readex Microprint # 1882. *Files: USC mp Mar 16-18, 20, 1795.*

TEUTONE   see Der Teutone.

THIS IS CHARLESTON   bi-weekly, tourist--established 1986. Apr 30-May 13, 1986 = vol 1, no 4, B. J. Hale (managing editor), Charles P. Diggle (publisher), Community Press, Inc. *Files: This is Charleston 1986 + .*

TIMES   daily--established Oct 6, 1800 by Thomas C. Cox and Thomas Sheppard as the Times, and Political and Commercial Evening Gazette. On Nov 17, 1800 paper became the Times, City Gazette & Merchants' Evening Advertiser and on May 16, 1801 the Times. Tacitus G. Skrine, John C. Duke, Edwin C. Holland, and Samuel H. Skinner also associated with paper, which ceased Jul 14, 1821. The Times issued a tri-weekly "country" paper; however, the only known issue is Jun 30, 1817 at the Library of Congress, two of four pages blank. *Files: CLS Oct 1800-Sep 1809, Apr-Sep 1810, Apr 1811-Dec 1813, Jan 16, Apr 1, 1815, Jan 1816-Dec 1817, Jan-Jul 1821; SCL Oct 18, 1803, Jan-Jun 1804, Oct 1, 1804, ((1808-1815)) 30, Aug-Nov 1816; Charleston CL, CLS, Dorchester CL, Francis Marion, Furman, Greenville CL, SCL, and Winthrop mfm ((1800-1821)). Note: These mfm files are virtually complete for years indicated.*

TIMES, AND POLITICAL AND COMMERCIAL EVENING GAZETTE see the Times.

TIMES, CITY GAZETTE & MERCHANTS' EVENING ADVERTISER see the Times.

TRANSCRIPT   daily--established 1840, ceased c. 1848. Jul 1, 1841 = vol 2, no 197, J. N. Cardozo (publisher). According to King, the Transcript was an "auxiliary" of the Southern Patriot. Both papers, he writes, ceased c. 1848. *Files: Library of Congress Jul-Dec 1841. Apparently no SC files.*

TRI-WEEKLY MERCURY   see the Charleston Mercury (tri-weekly).

TRI-WEEKLY NEWS AND COURIER   tri-weekly--continues Tue-Thu-Sat editions of the Charleston Daily News and the Charleston Daily Courier in Apr 1873, ceased c. 1883. In effect, the Sun edition of the News and Courier launched in 1879 replaced this tri-weekly. It is last cited on the editorial page of the daily paper on Oct 30, 1883. *Files: SCL Apr 14, 1874.*

UNION   weekly, labor--according to Charleston city directories (1901 and 1902), this paper was being published at 121 Cannon Street "in the interests organized labor." Not cited by Ayer. Ceased c. 1902. *NFK*

UNION & STATE RIGHTS GAZETTE   irregular, anti-nullification sheet-- established 1831. Oct 18, 1831 = vol 1, no 2, printed by James S. Burges, 44 Queen Street. Motto: "The Virtue of an Enlightened People is the true Conservative Principle of a Republic." Paper ceased c. 1831. *Files: SCL Oct 18, 1831.*

UNITED STATES CATHOLIC MISCELLANY   weekly, religious--founded by Bishop John Ireland in 1822, suspended Jan-Dec 1823 and Jan-Jun 1826, title shortened to the Catholic Miscellany on Dec 29, 1860, continued by the Charleston Catholic Miscellany on Jan 5, 1861. Jun 5, 1822 = vol 1, no 1, Thomas Martin, Jr. (publisher). Richard Swinton Baker, Patrick N. Lynch, and James Andrew Corcoran also associated with paper. *Files: CLS Jun-Dec 1822, 1824-1825, Jul 1826-Dec 1860; SCL 1824, Jul 1826-1831, mfm Jun-Dec 1822, 1824-1825, Jul 1826-Dec 1860.*

VESPER; OR, THE EVENING COURIER   see the Evening Courier.

WEEKLY GAZETTE   see the Gazette 1866-1869.

WEEKLY NEWS   weekly edition of the Charleston Evening News--established 1851, ceased c. 1856. Mar 12, 1853 = vol 3, no 3, P[aul] H[amilton] Hayne (editor), W. Y. Paxton (publisher). John Cunningham also associated with this publication, "A Family Paper Devoted to Intelligence, Literature and Arts." By Mar 1853 the Weekly News has this running head on inside pages: "The Weekly News and Southern Literary Gazette," indicating it had absorbed that short-lived periodical by that date. A Hayne letter reproduced in Rayburn S. Moore's A Man of Letters in the Nineteenth-Century South reveals this merger occurred sometime before Dec 1852. *Files: CLS Jun 26, Jul 3, 1852; SCL Jun 29, 1854, mfm ((Mar 1853-Aug 1856)) 155.*

WEEKLY NEWS   weekly--established in Jan 1870 as the weekly edition of the Charleston Daily News and continued without title change as the weekly edition of the

News and Courier from Apr 1873 to Nov 1884 when paper became the Weekly News and Courier. Feb 18, 1874 = vol 5, no 195, Riordan, Dawson & Company (proprietor). *Files: CLS Sep 3, 1879; Clemson (1877-1884) 10; SCL (1874-1884) 30.*

WEEKLY NEWS AND COURIER   weekly--continues the Weekly News in Nov 1884, issued semi-weekly from 1889 to 1912, when ceased. Although often classified as a "weekly" after 1889, this paper actually was issued in two parts on Wed and Sat without any vol-issue data. It is last cited on the editorial page of the daily paper as a "semi-weekly" on Oct 29, 1912. *Files: Clemson (1885-1887) 4; SCL (1884-1890) 4, Jan 1897-May 1900, Jan 1901-Sep 1902, (Oct-Dec 1902) 15, Feb 1903-Jul 1908, Aug-Sep 1910.*

WEEKLY RECORD   weekly, religious--established Dec 16, 1865, ceased c. 1868. Jan 13, 1866 = vol 1, no 5, Urban Sinkler Bird and F. A. Mood (publishers). According to the Charleston city directory (1867-1868), this paper was being published at 163 Meeting Street. *Files: SCL Jan 13, Feb 3, 1866.*

WEEKLY WORLD   weekly edition of the World--established 1888, ceased 1891. Nov 2, 1888 = vol 1, no 6, World-Budget Company (publisher). Cited by Ayer 1890 and 1891: Octavus Cohen (managing editor). See World and Sunday Budget. *Files: CLS Nov 1888-Sep 1890; SCL Jun 23, Aug 4, Sep 1, 8, 1891 (all fragments).*

WESLEYAN JOURNAL   weekly, Methodist--established Oct 1825, merged with New York's Christian Advocate Mar 1827. Oct 1, 1825 = vol 1, no 1, published by a Committee of the South Carolina Conference. Stephen Olin and William Capers later were associated with this paper as editors. Motto: "To Stir You Up, By Putting You in Remembrance." *Files: Newberry College Oct 1, 1825-Feb 17, 1827; Wofford Oct 1, 1825-Mar 3, 1827; SCL mfm Oct 1, 1825-Mar 3, 1827.*

WEST ASHLEY ENTERPRISE   weekly c. 1980. Ben Boozer (publisher), 960 Morrison Drive, North Charlesto . Paper cited in Southern Bell media directory (1980), George Southern (editor). *NFK*

WEST ASHLEY JOURNAL   weekly, independent--established Mar 16, 1961 (vol 1, no 1), Jack Bass (editor), L. J. James, Jr., and Jack Bass (publishers). Paper sold to Warren Allen Frieberg in May 1963, ceased Mar 12, 1964. Cited by Ayer 1962 thru 1964. *Files: Charleston CL Mar 16, 1961-Mar 12, 1964.*

WEST ASHLEY NEIGHBOR   weekly--continues the North Charleston Banner in Oct 1980. Listed once in Charleston city directory (1981). Ceased c. 1981. *NFK*

WEST ASHLEY SUBURBAN NEWS   weekly c. 1980--Joseph E. Flint (executive editor), Charles P. Diggle (publisher). Paper cited in Southern Bell media directory (1980), merged with Journal c. 1980. *NFK*

WOCHENTLICHE DEUTSCHE ZEITUNG   see <u>Die Wochentliche Deutsche</u> <u>Zeitung</u>.

WORKING CHRISTIAN   weekly, Baptist--established in York in 1869, published in Charleston from May 19, 1870 to Oct 1871, when paper moved to Columbia. Continued by the <u>Baptist Courier</u> in 1877. May 19, 1870 = vol 1, no 46, Tilman R. Gaines and J. W. De Lano (publishers). Motto: "Diligent in Business, Fervent in Spirit, Serving the Lord." See <u>Working Christian</u> [Columbia] and <u>Baptist Courier</u> [Greenville].

WORLD   daily, Democrat--established 1888, ceased Oct 7, 1891. Began Feb 7, 1888 (no vol-issue data). Cited by Ayer 1888 thru 1891. Octavus Cohen, Yates Snowden, Louis A. Beaty, and Francis S. Rogers associated with paper, which also issued the <u>Weekly World</u> and <u>Sunday Budget</u>. *Files: CLS Feb-Jul, Sep 1888-Oct 1891; Greenville CL (Jul-Aug 1889) 4; Sumter County Museum-Archives (1889-1890) 6; SCL mfm ((Apr 1888-Oct 1891)), mfm files virtually complete for years indicated.*

CHARLESTON AIR FORCE BASE

AIRLIFT DISPATCH   weekly--established Nov 1960, published by the Community Press, Inc., for Charleston AFB personnel. Nov 13, 1963 = vol 4, no 1. Paper also has appeared at times as the <u>Charleston Airlift Dispatch</u>. Cited by Ayer 1974 + . *Files: <u>Airlift Dispatch</u> 1963 + ; Wisconsin Historical Society mfm May 1981 + .*

CHARLESTON NAVAL BASE

BOW HOOK   bi-weekly--established c. 1960 for Charleston Naval Base personnel. Apr 18, 1986 = vol 26, no 8, Susan Worsham (editor), Charles P. Diggle (publisher), Community Press, Inc. Cited by Ayer 1986 + . *Files: <u>Bow Hook</u> ((1985 +)).*

MORRIS ISLAND

SWAMP ANGEL   "semi-occasionally" c. 1864--wartime paper printed by Federal troops stationed on Morris Island in Charleston Harbor. May 26, 1864 = vol 1, no 2. *Files: SCL May 26, 1864.*

MOUNT PLEASANT

BERKELEY COUNTY GAZETTE   see the <u>Berkeley County Gazette</u> [Berkeley County].

EAST COOPER NEIGHBOR   weekly--continues the <u>East Cooper Pilot</u> on Oct 21, 1980 (vol 6, no 43), Ben Boozer (publisher). Paper not listed in Charleston city directory after 1981. Ceased c. 1981. *Files: Charleston CL Oct 21-Dec 3, 1980.*

EAST COOPER PILOT   weekly--established Jul 9, 1975 (vol 1, no 1), Tom Hamrick (editor), continued by the East Cooper Neighbor in Oct 1980. Charles Ravenel, David Rawle, George Swain, Ron Dunn, and Ben Boozer also associated with paper. *Files: Charleston CL Jul 9, 1975-Oct 14, 1980.*

MOULTRIE NEWS   weekly--established 1964. Jan 18, 1968 = vol 5, no 1, Carl E. Meynardie (editor), published by the Hanahan News for Mount Pleasant, Isle of Palms, Sullivan's Island, McClellanville, and Awendaw. Since 1973 published by Charles P. Diggle, East Cooper Publications, Inc. Christopher L. Hale and Michael Baugh also associated with paper. *Files: Charleston CL 1968 + .*

PEOPLE'S ADVOCATE   weekly, Republican, black publication--established 1903, ceased c. 1906. Cited by Ayer 1905 and 1906: H. W. B. Bennett (editor and publisher). *NFK*

SEASHORE NEWS   weekly (in summer)--established 1924, ceased ? Sep 22, 1928 = vol 5, no 16, Vernon Tobias (editor). Published four months of each year for residents of Mount Pleasant, Sullivan's Island, Isle of Palms, and Folly Beach. *Files: CLS Sep 22, 1928.*

STATE GAZETTE   weekly, Independent Democrat--established 1913, ceased 1914. According to McIver, History of Mount Pleasant, this paper was published from Nov 8, 1913 to Jun 27, 1914. Cited by Ayer 1914: Ethelbert L. Baier (editor), Palmetto Publishing Company; Ayer 1915: Percival H. Whaley (editor), Palmetto Publishing Company. *NFK*

MYERS

CHARLESTON COUNTY RECORD   weekly--established May 21, 1931 (vol 1, no 1), continued by the Charleston Record in Mar 1932. The Charleston Record (see) reveals that Albert Orth was founding editor. *Files: SCL May 21-Jun 4, 25, 1931.*

NORTH CHARLESTON

HANAHAN NEWS   weekly--established 1959. Apr 23, 1986 = vol 28, no 17, Carl E. Meynardie (editor and publisher). Paper serves Hanahan, Goose Creek, and Berkeley County area. *Files: Hanahan News 1959 + .*

LOW COUNTRY NEIGHBOR   weekly--continues North Area Neighbor, listed once in Charleston city directory (1981), ceased c. 1981. *NFK*

NORTH AREA NEIGHBOR   weekly--continues North Charleston Banner on Oct 23, 1980 = vol 22, no 48, continued by Low Country Neighbor in 1981. *Files: Charleston CL Oct 23-Dec 1980.*

NORTH CHARLESTON BANNER   weekly--established Feb 1960, continued by
Peninsula Neighbor, West Ashley Neighbor, and North Area Neighbor in Oct 1980. Feb
4, 1960 = vol 1, no 1, H. Richard De Witt (editor and publisher). George Spain, J. C.
Knight, Kenneth E. Knight, Harry Carter, Ben Boozer, David Rawle, and Charles
Ravenel also associated with paper. *Files: Charleston CL 1960-1980.*

NORTH CHARLESTONIAN   weekly, independent--established 1941, ceased c.
1961. Cited by Ayer 1951 thru 1961: Edgar Davies (editor and publisher). *NFK*

PENINSULA NEIGHBOR   weekly--continues North Charleston Banner in Oct 1980,
published by Ben Boozer, ceased c. 1981. Listed once in Charleston city directory
(1981). *NFK*

TWIN-CITY NEWS   weekly c. 1960-1964--published by Edgar Davies. J. C. Long
also associated with paper. Twin-City Publishing Company listed in Charleston
telephone directories, 1960-1964. *NFK*

PARKER'S FERRY

SOUTH-CAROLINA GAZETTE   weekly--established Apr 10, 1782, ceased c.
1782. May 15, 1782 = vol 1, no 6, printed by Benjamin F. Dunlap. This paper was
published by Revolutionary forces, and the Royal Gazette indicates that additional issues
appeared on Jun 19 and 26. The only copy located contains this ad: "Subscribers may be
furnished with this Paper weekly, at the Headquarters of his Excellency, the Governor,
the Headquarters of the Army, the Printing Offices at Parker's-Ferry, and such other
Places as Gentlemen may require...." *Files: SCL May 15, 1782.*

CHEROKEE COUNTY

Created in 1897 from parts of Spartanburg, Union, and York counties, Cherokee County is named for the well-known Indian nation of earlier times. The campaign to form this new county was led by the Gaffney Ledger.

BLACKSBURG

BLACKSBURG TIMES   weekly--established 1965 by Al Cogdale of Shelby, N. C. Dec 14, 1966 = vol 2, no 17. Not cited in Ayer. Paper purchased from Mullen Publications on Mar 5, 1968 by Gene McKown and continued by the Blacksburg Times & Cherokee Report. In addition to Cogdale, Shirley Skidmore also associated with paper. *Files: Blacksburg Times & Cherokee Tribune (1966-1968).*

BLACKSBURG TIMES & CHEROKEE REPORT   weekly, Mar 1968-1971, continues Blacksburg Times, continued by Blacksburg Times & Cherokee Tribune. Not cited in Ayer. *Files: Blacksburg Times & Cherokee Tribune ((1968-1971)).*

BLACKSBURG TIMES & CHEROKEE TRIBUNE   weekly--continues Blacksburg Times & Cherokee Report. Jan 25, 1984 = vol 19, no 4, Gene McKown (editor and publisher). *Files: Blacksburg Times & Cherokee Tribune 1971 + .*

CHEROKEE CRITIC   weekly--established 1902, ceased c. 1903. Cited once in Ayer (1903): R. J. Balfour (editor), Cherokee Critic Company (publisher). *NFK*

CHRONICLE   weekly, Democrat--established 1905, ceased c. 1908. Cited Ayer 1906 thru 1908: George R. Pfeiffer (editor), Parrott Brothers (publishers). *NFK*

NEWS   weekly, Democrat--established 1890, ceased c. 1893. Cited Ayer 1890 thru 1893/4. Ayer 1890-1891: Blacksburg Printing Company (editor and publisher). Ayer 1892-1893/4: C. P. Roberts (editor), Blacksburg Printing Company (publisher). *NFK*

NEWS   weekly--established 1925, ceased c. 1926. Listed once in Ayer (1926): W. L. Spinx (editor and publisher). *NFK*

GAFFNEY

CHEROKEE NEWS   weekly, semi-weekly--established 1899 as Laurens County News, moved to Gaffney Feb 1903 and continued as Cherokee News, ceased c. 1919. Jul 20, 1916 = vol 19, no 2, "Covers Cherokee like the Sunshine." Cited Ayer 1904 thru 1919. Ayer 1904: S. Frank Parrott (editor), Cherokee Publishing Company. Others associated with Cherokee News include J. B. Bell and F. L. Baker. *Files: SCL Mar 4, 1915 (fragment), Jul 20, 1916.*

CHEROKEE TIMES   semi-weekly, Democrat--established Aug 4, 1922, ceased c. 1930. Cited Ayer 1923 thru 1930. Jun 18, 1923 = vol 1, no 93, J. B. Bell (editor), Gaffney Publishing Company. George B. Lay (editor and publisher), 1929-1930. *Files: Cherokee CL mfm ((Aug 4, 1922-Dec 28, 1928)); SCL (1923-1929) 50.*

CHRONICLE   weekly, Baptist, black publication--established 1915, ceased c. 1923. Cited Ayer 1921 thru 1923: A. Norris (editor), Chronicle Publishing Company. *NFK*

COURIER   weekly, Democrat--established 1889, ceased c. 1892. Cited Ayer 1890 thru 1892: Frank P. Beard (editor and publisher). *NFK*

GAFFNEY CAROLINIAN   weekly, Democrat--established 1881, continued as Piedmont Inspector c. 1884. Aug 24, 1882 = vol 2, no 13, E. H. Britton and T. Stobo Farrow (publishers). Cited Ayer 1882 as Spartanburg County Carolinian and Ayer 1883 and 1884 as Carolinian. *Files: SCL Aug 24, 1882.*

GAFFNEY LEDGER   semi-weekly, tri-weekly--continues Ledger as of Nov 26, 1907. In Nov 1907, Edw. H. DeCamp (editor and publisher). S. C. Littlejohn, Jack Trueluck, Bill Gibbons, F. W. and Louis Sossamon also associated with paper. Became tri-weekly May 3, 1917. *Files: Cherokee CL mfm 1907 + ; SCL (1908-1952) 40, mfm 1907 + .*

IMMIGRATION MONTHLY   monthly--established c. 1875, ceased c. 1875. Tilman R. Gaines (editor and printer). Cited by Moss, Old Iron District (p. 246). Moss also mentions two more early papers, the Gaffney Register and the Gaffney City Bulletin, but provides few pertinent details. *NFK*

LEDGER   semi-weekly--continues Weekly Ledger as of Jun 1896, continued by Gaffney Ledger Nov 1907. Jun 4, 1896 = vol 3, no 17, R. O. Sams (editor), Limestone Publishing Company. *Files: Cherokee CL mfm 1896-1907; SCL (1896-1901) 5, mfm 1896-1907.*

LYCEUM   weekly--established 1888, ceased c. 1888. Not cited by Ayer. Sep 1, 1888 = vol 1, no 1, Tilman R. Gaines (editor), Lyceum Publishing Company. *Files: Dr. Bobby G. Moss [Gaffney] Sep 1, 1888.*

NEGRO JOURNAL   weekly, independent, black publication--established 1915, ceased c. 1920. Cited Ayer 1917 thru 1920: Perry Little (editor), Negro Journal Company. *NFK*

NEWS   weekly, Democrat--established 1893, ceased c. 1894. Cited once in Ayer (1893/4): T. W. Adams (editor and publisher). *NFK*

PIEDMONT INSPECTOR   weekly, Democrat--continues Gaffney Carolinian c. 1884, ceased c. 1885. Cited once in Ayer (1885) as a weekly established in 1881. No editor or publisher cited, but H. P. Griffith of the Piedmont Inspector joined the SC Press Association in 1885. *NFK*

SPARTANBURG COUNTY CAROLINIAN   see Gaffney Carolinian.

SUN   weekly, black publication--established 1905, ceased c. 1906. Cited once in Ayer (1906): Dr. H. M. Dougherty (editor), R. C. Corry and A. B. Champion (publishers). *NFK*

WEEKLY BULLETIN   weekly, Democrat--established 1884, ceased c, 1888. Cited Ayer 1885 thru 1888. Ayer 1885-1886: S. P. Britton (proprietor). Ayer 1887-1888: W. W. Galloway (editor and proprietor), Bulletin Publishing Company. Ayer cites as both Bulletin and Weekly Bulletin. *NFK*

WEEKLY LEDGER   weekly--established 1894, continued by Ledger Jun 1896. Feb 16, 1894 = vol 1, no 1, R. O. Sams (editor), Limestone Printing and Publishing Company. *Files: Cherokee CL mfm Feb 1894-May 1896; SCL Jul 27, 1894, mfm Feb 1894-May 1896.*

CHESTER COUNTY

Chester District, now Chester County, was organized in 1798 when old Camden District was split into five parts. It is named for its county seat, settled by pioneer families from Chester, Pennsylvania, which, in turn, was named for Chester, England.

CHESTER

CHESTER BULLETIN   weekly, Democrat--established as State Bulletin in 1879, continued as Chester Bulletin c. 1882, ceased c. 1899. Dec 15, 1882 = vol 4, no 42, Thomas W. Clawson, Jr., and George W. Gage (editors). F. T. Morgan also associated with paper. Cited in Ayer 1883 thru 1899. *Files: SCL orig & mfm (1882-1892) 15.*

CHESTER NEWS   semi-weekly, weekly--continuation of Semi-Weekly News established 1913, changed name to Chester News Sep 1917 (retaining number sequence of Semi-Weekly News), merged with Chester Reporter Sep 1971 to form News and Reporter. In 1917, Chester News was semi-weekly, Democrat. Oct 2, 1917 = vol 4, no 79, W. Ward Peagram and Stewart L. Cassells (owners and publishers). Circa 1942 became weekly. *Files: Chester CL mfm 1917-1923, 1925, 1927-1971; SCL (1922-1928) 4, 1930-1939, (1943-1950) 40, 1951-1962, 1970-1971, mfm 1917-1923, 1925, 1927-1971.*

CHESTER REPORTER   weekly, semi-weekly--established 1869, merged with Chester News Sep 1971 to form News and Reporter. Began weekly, became semi-weekly c. 1909. Nov 3, 1870 = vol 2, no 38, John A. Bradley, Jr. (editor and proprietor). Others associated with paper include E. C. McLure, John H. Buchanan, J. C. Hardin, W. J. Irwin, J. T. Perkins, Julian Starr, Jr., Paul League, and Don McKeown. Great Falls Reporter, a mid-week supplement, continued by News and Reporter. *Files: Chester CL mfm 1906-Nov 1930, 1931-1971; Clemson mfm May 1874-Jun 1906; Lancaster News mfm 1920-1966; News and Reporter 1960-1971; SCL ((1870-1971)) 210, mfm (1870-1872) 6, May 1874-Jun 1906, (1909-1928) 9, 1929-1971.*

CHESTER PALMETTO STANDARD   weekly--established 1849, continued by the Palmetto Standard c. 1850. Jan 16, 1850 = vol 1, no 7, C. Davis Melton and R. W. Murray (publishers). *Files: Duke Jan 16, 1850. Apparently no files in SC.*

CHESTER STANDARD   weekly, semi-weekly--continues Palmetto Standard c. 1853, ceased c. 1869 and succeeded by the Chester Reporter. Began weekly, also published semi-weekly edition c. 1869. Jan 21, 1854 = vol 5, no 2, C. Davis Melton and Samuel W. Melton (proprietors), Samuel W. Melton (editor). Also associated with paper: Charles S. Brice, J. Belton Mickle, George Pither, C. J. McDaniel, E. C. McLure, and John Bradley, Jr. McLure and Bradley reportedly founded the Chester Reporter. *Files: Chester CL mfm 1854-1857; SCL (1856-1868) 10, mfm 1854-1857, (1859-1868) 8.*

DAILY SOUTH CAROLINIAN   daily--a Columbia newspaper that published several single-sheet editions in Chester and Charlotte, N. C., Mar-Apr 1865. An ad in Apr 19 issue (vol 16, no 75) indicates F. G. De Fontaine began publication in Chester on Apr 2, 1865. See Daily South Carolinian [Columbia]. *Files: SCL Mar 7, 14, 1865 [Charlotte], Apr 19, 1865 [Chester].*

DRUGGIST   weekly--established 1886, ceased c. 1886. Aug 18, 1886 = vol 1, no 1, A. H. Davega (publisher). *Files: SCL orig & mfm Aug 18, 1886.*

ENTERPRISE   weekly, Democrat--established 1890, ceased c. 1891. Cited once in Ayer (1891): W. J. Boylin and J. T. Bigham (editors and publishers). *NFK*

LANTERN   semi-weekly, Independent Democrat--established 1897, ceased c. 1913. Oct 8, 1897 = vol 1, no 1, J. T. Bigham (editor and proprietor). Also associated with paper: W. F. Caldwell, T. Dana Jones, J. Otis Hull, C. N. Wrenshaw, J. E. Nunnery, S. L. Cassells, and W. Ward Peagram. *Files: Chester CL mfm Oct 1897-Oct 1898, 1901, 1904, 1906-1909; SCL (1897-1913) 95, mfm Oct 1897-Oct 1898, 1901, 1904, 1906-1909, (1911-1913) 82.*

NEWS AND REPORTER   semi-weekly--created Sep 1971 by merger of Chester News and Chester Reporter. Publishes Great Falls Reporter as a mid-week supplement. Sep 1, 1971 = vol 102, no 35, Don McKeown (editor), Paul League (publisher). Richard Gannaway also associated with paper. *Files: Chester CL 1982 + ; News and Reporter 1971 + ; SCL mfm 1971-1984.*

PALMETTO STANDARD   weekly--continues Chester Palmetto Standard c. 1850, continued by the Chester Standard c. 1853. Dec 3, 1851 = vol 2, no 49, whole no 101, C. Davis Melton (editor and proprietor). *Files: SCL Sep 10 (fragment), Dec 3, 1851.*

PALMETTO STANDARD   weekly, Suffragette--established 1895, ceased c. 1895. May 28, 1895 = vol 1, no 1, Mrs. J. J. Stringfellow (editor), published by Chester Presbyterian Church ladies "as supplement to Palmetto Standard." *Files: SCL mfm May 28, 1895.*

PUBLIC OPINION   semi-monthly, prohibition--established 1891, ceased c. 1891. Aug 29, 1891 = vol 1, no 12, Bob Jaggers (editor and proprietor)..."devoted to prohibition, moral, social, and political reform." *Files: SCL orig & mfm Aug 29, 1891.*

SEMI-WEEKLY NEWS   semi-weekly--established 1913, continued by Chester News Oct 1917. Successor to Lantern, but new name, new number sequence. Ayer 1915: J. E. Nunnery (editor and publisher). Nov 2, 1915 = vol 2, no 49, W. W. Peagram, Stewart L. Cassells, and J. H. Williamson (owners and publishers). *Files: Chester CL mfm Jul 1915-Sep 1917; SCL Aug 4, 25, 28, Sep 11, 1914, Apr 30, 1915, mfm Jul 1915-Sep 1917.*

SOUTH CAROLINA HERALD   weekly, black publication--established 1891, ceased c. 1894. Produced by African Methodist Episcopal Church. Cited Ayer 1893/4: W. A. Walker (editor and publisher). *NFK*

STATE BULLETIN   weekly, Democrat--established 1879, c. 1882 became <u>Chester Bulletin</u> (see). Mar 23, 1880 = vol 1, no 59, T. W. Clawson & Company (publisher). *Files: SCL orig & mfm Mar 23, Apr 20, 1880.*

TEMPERANCE WORKER   semi-monthly--established 1883 in Columbia, published in Sumter 1885-1887, ceased c. 1887. Issues for Sep-Dec 1887 bear dual dateline [Sumter and Chester] after H. F. Chreitzberg (editor) moved to Chester. See <u>Temperance Worker</u> [Columbia and Sumter].

TORCHLIGHT   weekly, Democrat--established 1906, ceased c. 1907. Cited once by Ayer (1907): Bishop James H. Carey (editor), Torchlight Publishing Company. *NFK*

GREAT FALLS

GREAT FALLS COURIER   weekly, independent--established 1949, ceased c. 1952. Cited Ayer 1951: William Mason (editor), Tri-County Publishing Company; Ayer 1952: Mrs. A. B. Ford (editor), Tri-County Publishing Company. *NFK*

GREAT FALLS REPORTER   weekly--established c. 1957. By 1969 was mid-week supplement to <u>Chester Reporter</u>. Not cited in Ayer. Sep 24, 1969 = vol 100, no 39, William C. Breedin (editor). *Files: SCL Aug 27, 1969-Apr 25, 1973. <u>Note</u>: See also files of <u>Chester Reporter</u> and <u>News and Reporter</u>.*

CHESTERFIELD COUNTY

Chesterfield District, now Chesterfield County, came into existence in 1798 when old Cheraws District was divided into three parts: Chesterfield, Darlington, and Marlborough districts. It is named for Philip Dormer Stanhope (1694-1773), the fourth Earl of Chesterfield, a noted 18th century politician, wit, and writer of letters.

CHERAW

CAROLINA CITIZEN weekly, Democrat--established 1903, ceased c. 1906. Listed in Ayer 1905 and 1906: John F. Meehan (editor and publisher). *NFK*

CAROLINA NEWS weekly, Republican, black publication--established 1909, ceased c. 1914. Cited Ayer 1911 thru 1914: John C. Hillian (editor and publisher). *NFK*

CAROLINA SUN weekly, Democrat--established 1880, merged with Marlboro Monitor of Bennettsville c. 1883 to form Sun and Monitor bearing dual place names: Cheraw and Bennettsville. Cited Ayer 1880 thru 1883. Sep 9, 1880 = vol 1, no 27, R. H. Pegues (editor). *Files: SCL Sep 9, 1880, Jun 28, 1883.*

CHERAW CHRONICLE weekly--established 1896. First cited Ayer 1897: J. N. Stricklin (editor and publisher). Others associated with paper include W. J. Stricklin, Joe Lindsay, J. N. Stricklin, Jr., P. H. Hearn, James and Christine Law, A. M. Secrest, Edward M. Sweatt, and Thomas A. MacCallum. *Files: Cheraw Chronicle ((1920-1922)), 1948 + ; SCL (1905-1976) 27, ((1984 +)).*

CHERAW DAILY daily c. 1911--according to special edition of Cheraw Chronicle (May 28, 1975), Joseph Stricklin, publisher of the weekly Cheraw Chronicle, launched this daily Jun 12, 1911. It ceased publication within a year. Not cited in Ayer. *NFK*

CHERAW GAZETTE weekly--established Nov 17, 1835, continued by Cheraw Gazette and Pee Dee Farmer Nov 21, 1838. Nov 17, 1835 = vol 1, no 1, Murdoch McLean (editor and proprietor). *Files: SCL ((1835-1837)) 104, mfm Nov 1836-Nov 1837.*

CHERAW GAZETTE weekly--continues Farmers' Gazette c. 1845. Library of Congress has Cheraw Gazette Nov 23, 1847 = N. S. vol 5, no 36, whole no 562. However, by 1851 Editor James Powell was using old style number sequence based upon original Cheraw Gazette of the 1830s. Sep 13, 1851 = vol 13, no 26, James Powell (editor). *Files: SCL Sep 23, 1851, May 13, Jun 3, 1857, Aug 24, 1859, mfm Jun 23, 1858, Aug 24, 1859.*

CHERAW GAZETTE AND PEE DEE FARMER weekly--established as Cheraw Gazette in 1835, became Cheraw Gazette and Pee Dee Farmer Nov 21, 1838 and Farmers' Gazette and Cheraw Advertiser Nov 15, 1839. Nov 21, 1838 = vol 4, no 1,

Murdoch McLean (editor and proprietor). Note: McLean states name changes were designed to appeal to agricultural interests and to please groups such as the Pee Dee Agricultural Society. *Files: SCL orig & mfm Nov 21, 1838-Nov 8, 1839.*

CHERAW INTELLIGENCER AND SOUTHERN REGISTER   weekly-- established Jun 5, 1823, ceased Mar 10, 1826, when merged with Pee Dee Gazette and Cheraw Advertiser to form Pee Dee Gazette and Cheraw Intelligencer. Jun 5, 1823 = vol 1, no 1, William Poole & Company (publisher). On Jun 4, 1824, James Conover (editor since paper began) became editor and publisher. On Mar 10, 1826, Conover sold out to Mason R. Lyon, publisher of the Pee Dee Gazette and Cheraw Advertiser. *Files: CLS Mar 5, 1824, May 27, 1825; SCL (1823-1824) 6, mfm Jun 5, 1823-Mar 10, 1826.*

CHERAW REPORTER   weekly, Democrat--established 1885, became Star c. 1896. Cited Ayer 1886 thru 1896. Ayer 1887: J. N. Stricklin (editor). Ayer 1888-1896: A. G. Kollock (editor and publisher). Mar 20, 1888 = vol 3, no 29, A. G. Kollock (publisher). Local sources indicate Stricklin founded paper (forerunner of Cheraw Chronicle) on Jul 9, 1885. *Files: SCL (1888-1895) 6.*

CHERAW REPUBLICAN   weekly, pro-nullification--prospectus in Sumter Gazette and Constitutional Advocate (Feb 6, 1830) announced that this paper would begin publication in Jan 1830. Jul 21, 1832 = vol 3, no 13, whole no 117, John G. Bowman (editor). Paper ceased c. 1833. *Files: SCL Jul 21, 1832.*

CHERAW SPECTATOR   see South-Carolina Spectator.

CHESTERFIELD COUNTY SHOPPER   weekly--established 1982. First cited in Ayer 1985. Jun 16, 1982 = vol 1, no 1, Charles H. Watson and David Linton (editors and publishers). First such publication in South Carolina to offer total market coverage. *Files: Chesterfield County Shopper 1982 + .*

CHESTERFIELD DEMOCRAT   weekly, Democrat--established 1868, ceased c. 1877. Listed Rowell 1869 thru 1877. Rowell 1869: Worley & Company (editor and publisher). Rowell 1870: W. L. T. Prince (editor and publisher). Rowell 1871-1877: Valcour Little (editor and publisher). According to local history, this was leading paper in community c. 1870. *NFK*

FARMERS' GAZETTE   weekly--established 1843, continues Farmers' Gazette and Cheraw Advertiser with new number system. Sep 24, 1844 = N. S. vol 2, no 28, whole no 398, John Stubbs (editor). Name changed to Cheraw Gazette by Nov 1847 and paper continued under that title. *Files: SCL Sep 24, 1844, Jan 28, 1845.*

FARMERS' GAZETTE AND CHERAW ADVERTISER   weekly--created Nov 15, 1839, successor to Cheraw Gazette and Cheraw Gazette and Pee Dee Farmer, continued by Farmers' Gazette in 1843. Nov 15, 1839 = vol 5, no 1, M. Maclean (editor and proprietor). *Files: SCL Nov 15, 1839-Feb 14, 1843.*

MONITOR   weekly, religious, black publication--established in Columbia in 1883 as the Columbia Monitor, published c. 1885 in Bennettsville as the South Carolina Monitor by Rev. C. W. McColl. Ceased operations c. 1885, revived as Monitor in Cheraw c. 1888 and cited by Ayer in Cheraw 1888 and 1889; however, copy at Duke indicates paper was being issued in Charleston. Later issued as the Baptist Monitor in Charlotte, N. C., and Bennettsville c. 1889-1890. Various versions ceased c. 1891. See Monitor [Charleston].

NEWS   weekly--established 1878, ceased c. 1879. Listed once in Rowell (1879): W. D. Upchurch (publisher). *NFK*

PEE DEE GAZETTE AND CHERAW ADVERTISER   weekly--established 1820, merged with Cheraw Intelligencer and Southern Register Mar 1826 to create Pee Dee Gazette and Cheraw Intelligencer. According to Brigham, a copy of Pee Dee Gazette and Cheraw Advertiser (Jun 13, 1821 = vol 1, no 30, James Lyon, publisher) was found in State Department records indicating paper was established Sep 1820. Photostat copies of that issue are at the Library of Congress and the American Antiquarian Society. Aug 10, 1824 = vol 4, no 25, whole no 180, Mason Risley Lyon (proprietor). This issue contains a prospectus for the Religious Spectator, a weekly Lyon planned to launch in Nov 1824. *Files: SCL mfm Aug 10, 1824.*

PEE DEE GAZETTE AND CHERAW ADVERTISER   weekly--established as a new publication in 1833, ceased ? Apparently did not last long since Cheraw Gazette appears in 1835. Aug 13, 1833 = vol 1, no 2, Matthew Lyon (publisher). *Files: SCL Dec 24, 31, 1833, mfm Aug 13, 1833.*

PEE DEE GAZETTE AND CHERAW INTELLIGENCER   weekly--created by merger of Pee Dee Gazette and Cheraw Advertiser and Cheraw Intelligencer and Southern Register in 1826. Lasted only a few issues under this title (Mar 21-May 16, 1826), Mason Risley Lyon (publisher). The issue of May 16, 1826 was edited by C. F. Daniels, recently arrived "from a northern port" with ideas and plans for a new publication. That publication was the South-Carolina Spectator, which continued the Pee Dee Gazette and Cheraw Intelligencer. *Files: SCL mfm (Mar 21-May 16, 1826) 9.*

PEE DEE HERALD   weekly, semi-weekly--established 1856, ceased c. 1859. Jul 1, 1856 = vol 1, no 4, W. L. T. Prince and J. Randolph Malloy (editors and proprietors). Ellen says issued both weekly and semi-weekly editions and notes that paper ceased Jun 1859. *Files: Matheson Memorial Library [Cheraw] Jun 17, 1856; SCL Jul 1, 1856, mfm Jun 17, 1856-Apr 7, 1857.*

PEE DEE NEWS   weekly--established c. 1910, purchased by J. P. Tucker c. 1911 and merged with Pageland's Scout to form News and Scout. Not cited in Ayer. *NFK*

SOUTH-CAROLINA SPECTATOR   weekly--established May 23, 1826, continues Pee Dee Gazette and Cheraw Intelligencer, ceased ? May also have appeared as the Cheraw Spectator. May 23, 1826 = vol 6, new series, no 1, whole no 274, C. F.

Daniels (editor), Mason R. Lyon (proprietor). *Files: Library of Congress May 23-Dec 29, 1826. Apparently no files in SC.*

SOUTHERN CHRISTIAN HERALD   weekly, Presbyterian--established in Columbia in 1834, moved to Cheraw Apr 3, 1836 = vol 3, no 2, M. McLean (editor and publisher), G. H. Taylor (printer), ceased c. 1838. R. S. Gladney and Samuel Weir also associated with paper. *Files: Newberry College Mar 26, 1835-Mar 24, 1837; SCL Mar 18, 1834-Mar 19, 1835, (1836-1838) 50, mfm Mar 30, 1836-Mar 24, 1837.*

SOUTHERN RADICAL   weekly--established Aug 22, 1828, ceased ? May be successor to South-Carolina Spectator.   An anti-Jackson, anti-Adams, "strict constructionist" publication edited by Harris Smith Evans and A. N. MacDonald, both of whom were candidates for the state legislature. *Files: Library of Congress Aug 22, 29, 1828. Apparently no files in SC.*

STAR   weekly, Democrat--established as Cheraw Reporter 1885, became Star c. 1896, ceased c. 1897. Cited once in Ayer (1897): Herman B. Crosland (editor and publisher). *NFK*

SUN AND MONITOR   weekly, Democrat--created c. 1883 by merger of Carolina Sun and Bennettsville's Marlboro Monitor, bearing dual date lines: Cheraw and Bennettsville. May have become Chesterfield Advertiser, which appears in Ayer 1885 citing founding date of 1880 (same as that of Carolina Sun). Nov 28, 1883 = vol 4, no 35, Thomas & Breeden (editors and publishers)..."only newspaper in Chesterfield County." *Files: Cheraw Chronicle Nov 28, 1883; SCL Nov 28, 1883.*

CHESTERFIELD

ADVERTISER-JOURNAL   weekly--created by merger of Chesterfield Advertiser and Pageland Journal Jun 1978, ceased Oct 1, 1980, when both papers resumed independent status. Denny Truesdale (editor), c. 1978-1980, Banner Publishing Company. During merger, Pageland section sometimes issued as "Pageland Panorama." *Files: Pageland Progressive-Journal Jan-Sep 1980.*

CAROLINA ARGUS   weekly, Democrat--according to Rowell 1877, established 1844 [sic], George D. Smith (editor and publisher). Only time cited, not found in Gregory. *NFK*

CHESTERFIELD ADVERTISER   weekly--established 1880, merged with Pageland Journal Jun 1978 to form Advertiser-Journal, resumed independent status Oct 1980. May be successor to Cheraw-Bennettsville Sun and Monitor. First cited Ayer 1885 as founded 1880. Ayer 1887: D. M. Barentine (editor), Barentine and Laudie (publishers). Others associated with paper include G. J. Redfearn, John H. Walsh, J. B. Swinnie, F. M. Cannon, John T. Meehan, R. D. Marsh, Paul R. Hearn, C. S. and L. B. Britton, Mrs. C. S. Britton, Clarence M. Ford, Kenneth Webb, Milton Belkin, Caroline Goforth, Jane L. Burch, Joye C. Pierce, Denny Truesdale, Tom Taylor, and Mary Jean Crawley. *Files:*

Chesterfield Advertiser Sep 8, 1902, 1928-1958, 1968-1978, 1980 + ; *Chesterfield CL* 1985 + ; *SCL (1904-1944) 25, mfm (1904-1934) 18.*

CHESTERFIELD BANNER   weekly--established 1880, ceased c. 1880. Cited once in Ayer (1880). *NFK*

CHESTERFIELD COUNTY BULLETIN   weekly, monthly, quarterly, independent--established 1928, ceased c. 1937. Began as weekly, became quarterly c. 1932 and c. 1937 changed title to Agricultural Bulletin, a monthly. Cited Ayer 1929 thru 1937. Ayer 1929: R. A. Hanna (editor), Bulletin Publishing Company. *NFK*

JEFFERSON

CAROLINA CITIZEN   weekly, Democrat--established 1903, ceased c. 1909. Cited Ayer 1907: John T. Meehan (editor and publisher). Ayer 1908 and 1909: R. D. Marsh (editor), Jefferson Printing and Publishing Company. *NFK*

JEFFERSONIAN   weekly--established 1912, ceased c. 1920. Aug 22, 1913 = vol 2, no 12. Cited Ayer 1913 thru 1920. Ayer 1912-1915: G. W. McCarthy (editor), Carolina Printing Company. Ayer 1916: E. E. Goodson (editor), The Jeffersonian (publisher). Ayer 1917: W. A. Edmonds (editor), The Jeffersonian (publisher). Ayer 1918-1920: A. R. Wallack (editor and publisher). *Files: SCL Aug 22, 1913.*

MC BEE

MC BEE COURIER   weekly--established 1912, ceased ? Not cited in Ayer. Sep 26, 1912 = vol 1, no 2, J. E. Gardner (editor and manager), McBee Publishing Company. *Files: SCL Sep 26, 1912, Sep 4, 1913.*

PAGELAND

NEWS AND SCOUT   weekly, Democrat--created c. 1910 by merger of Cheraw's Pee Dee News and Scout, became Pageland Journal Dec 12, 1911. May 2, 1911 = vol 1, no 6, J. P. Tucker (editor), J. P. and C. M. Tucker (publishers). *Files: Pageland Progressive-Journal Apr-Dec 1911.*

PAGELAND JOURNAL   weekly--created Dec 1911 when News and Scout became Pageland Journal. Merged with Chesterfield Advertiser Jun 1978 to form Advertiser-Journal, resumed independent status Oct 1980, and merged with Pageland Progressive Jun 1981 to form Pageland Progressive-Journal. First issue, Dec 12, 1911 = vol 2, no 13, C. M. Tucker (editor), C. M. and J. P. Tucker (publishers). R. S. Latimer, B. T. Sanders, G. D. Sanders, H. E. Carraway, J. W. Richards, Jon O. Fulenwider III, and Mrs. Betty Sowell also associated with paper. *Files: Pageland Progressive-Journal 1911-1978; SCL ((1923-1973)) 150.*

PAGELAND PROGRESSIVE   weekly--established 1978, merged with <u>Pageland Journal</u> Jun 1981 to form <u>Pageland Progressive-Journal</u>. Aug 8, 1978 = vol 1, no 1, Brian K. Hough (editor). *Files: <u>Pageland Progressive-Journal</u> 1978-1981.*

PAGELAND PROGRESSIVE-JOURNAL   weekly--created Jun 1981 by merger of <u>Pageland Progressive</u> and <u>Pageland Journal</u>. Jun 30, 1981 = vol 1, no 1, Brian K. Hough (editor). *Files: <u>Pageland Progressive-Journal</u> 1981 + ; SCL ((1984 +)).*

SCOUT   weekly--established 1910, merged with Cheraw's <u>Pee Dee News</u> c. Apr 1911 to form <u>News and Scout</u>. Not cited in Ayer. Oct 27, 1910 = vol 1, no 7, J. P. Tucker (editor). *Files: <u>Pageland Progressive-Journal</u> 1910-1911.*

CLARENDON COUNTY

Formed from part of Sumter District in 1855, Clarendon County is named for Edward Hyde (1609-1674), the first Earl of Clarendon, one of the original lords proprietors.

MANNING

CLARENDON BANNER   weekly--established 1858, ceased c. 1865. Founded by John Witherspoon Ervin, who in Aug 1859 quit to teach school. Sep 11, 1860 = vol 3, no 11, Machen & Son (publishers). According to Duke checklist, Robert H. Machen and W. J. N. Hammett were the publishers in 1861, and H. D. Machen was editor in 1862. *Files: SCL (1860-1865) 20, mfm Sep 11, 1860, Jul 29, 1862.*

CLARENDON BANNER--OF FREEDOM   single issue, Yankee broadside-- published by "an Association of Printers from the 25th and 107th Ohio Reg'ts" at Manning on Apr 9, 1865. An editorial notes that General Potter did not intend to burn the town, "but if we have our way, this office [the Clarendon Banner] shall no more poison the political atmosphere of the country with its foul odors. The newspapers of the South have done more towards bringing about the Rebellion than aught else, and they should not be spared." Sheet also contains an account of the Yankee occupation of Camden and an ad seeking 800 "able bodied American citizens of African descent" eager to become U. S. soldiers. The recruiting officer in Georgetown promised each man a $300 bounty and rations, clothing, and monthly pay "the same as white soldiers." *Files: CLS Apr 9, 1865.*

CLARENDON CHRONICLE   weekly, established Mar 23, 1973, ceased c. 1983. Ray Hamilton (publisher) in 1973. Aug 17, 1977 = vol 4, no 23, Mabel Hinson (editor), Clarendon Publishers, Inc. Hinson also cited as co-publisher in 1978. Not listed in Ayer. *Files: Clarendon CL ((Aug 1977-Nov 1981)).*

CLARENDON ENTERPRISE   weekly--established 1881, ceased c. 1895. Ayer cites founding date of 1881, then 1867. Ayer ad (1887) says Enterprise was "twenty years old," thus successor to Clarendon Press founded 1867. Nov 16, 1882 = vol 15, no 41, S. A. Nettles (proprietor and editor), G. J. Brown (publisher). M. J. Haynesworth, D. H. Witherspoon, J. H. Lesesne, and E. A. Lowry also associated with paper. *Files: Greenville CL May 15, 1889; SCL Nov 9, 1882-Feb 17, 1887, Feb 21, 1889.*

CLARENDON NEWS   weekly, Democrat--appears c. 1895 with founding date of 1867, thus successor to Clarendon Press and Clarendon Enterprise, ceased c. 1896. Cited Ayer 1895 and 1896: S. E. Ingram (editor), News Publishing Company. *NFK*

CLARENDON PRESS   weekly--established 1867, continued as Clarendon Enterprise c. 1881. Aug 6, 1868 = vol 2, no 16, Lucas, David, and Lucas (publishers). Mar 23, 1871 = vol 4, no 47, Melvin B. Lucas (publisher), W. T. Lesesne (editor). Rowell

1879: J. E. Scott (editor), Melvin B. Lucas (publisher). *Files: SCL Aug 6, 1868, Mar 23, Jul 13, 1871, Aug 12, 1880.*

CLARENDON RECORDER   weekly, Democrat--established Oct 6, 1865 by same individuals who produced Clarendon Banner, ceased c. 1866. Oct 13, 1865 = vol 1, no 2, H. D. Machen (editor), R. H. Machen (proprietor). *Files: SCL Oct 13-27, Dec 1, 8, 22, 1865.*

CLARENDON SENTINEL   weekly, Democrat--appears c. 1907, continuation of Farmer (established 1899), ceased c. 1907. Listed once in Ayer (1907): F. E. Bradham (editor), Manning Publishing Company. *NFK*

FARMER   weekly, Democrat--established 1899, continued by Clarendon Sentinel c. 1907. Cited Ayer 1901 thru 1906. Ayer 1902: E. J. Browne (editor), Manning Publishing Company. F. E. Bradham and A. S. Todd also associated with paper. *NFK*

HERALD   weekly, Independent Democrat--established 1913, ceased c. 1919. Jun 25, 1914 = vol 1, no 38, J. K. Breedin (editor), Herald Publishing Company. Listed in Ayer 1914 thru 1919. *Files: SCL Jun 18 (fragment), 25, 1914, mfm Jul 13, 1916.*

MANNING TIMES   weekly--established 1884. Formerly Spirit of the Times [Sumter]. Oct 7, 1885 = vol 1, no 43, B. S. Dinkins (editor and proprietor). Others associated with paper include A. Levi, S. A. Nettles, Louis Appelt, Clara H. Appelt, S. Vallye Appelt, Martha B. Appelt, Kendrick R. Johnson, G. D. Sanders, E. D. Medlock, Douglas Birkhead, Carleton Naylor, Carole Kronberg, James De Roy, and J. Alan Young. *Files: Clarendon CL ((1978 +)); Greenville CL Jul 3, 24, 31, 1889; Manning Times 1938 + ; SCL ((1885-1887)) 107, 1888-1891, 1894 + .*

RISING STAR   weekly--established 1908, ceased c. 1911. Ayer 1910 and 1911: T. J. M. Dinkins (editor and publisher). Not cited 1912. *NFK*

SUMMERTON

ADVANCE   weekly, non-political--established 1906, ceased c. 1907. Cited once in Ayer (1907): Elliott Bourquin (editor and publisher). *NFK*

COLLETON COUNTY

First created in 1682 when the Carolina province was divided into three counties, Colleton re-emerged as a separate entity in 1798. Formerly part of Charleston District, it is named for Sir John Colleton, one of the original lords proprietors.

JACKSONBORO

GAZETTE   According to the Journal of the South Carolina House of Representatives (1782) and Charleston's Royal Gazette (Mar 13, 1782), the Gazette was published at Jacksonboro Mar 1, 1782. No copy ever found...may have been a broadside. Pendleton Messenger (Aug 25, 1827) says the press used was part of the equipment of General Greene. See Brigham for details. *NFK*

WALTERBORO

COLLETON AND BEAUFORT SUN   weekly--established 1858, ceased ? Dec 25, 1860 = vol 3, no 18, whole no 122, V. Stanton (editor), Stanton and Hyrne (publishers), V. Stanton and Henry Hyrne, Jr., (proprietors). *Files: American Antiquarian Society Dec 25, 1860. Apparently no copies in SC.*

COLLETON COURIER   weekly, Democrat--established 1892, ceased c. 1896. Cited Ayer 1892 thru 1896: D. H. Behre (editor), Behre and Rich (publishers). In 1897 Behre was editor of the Low Country News. *NFK*

COLLETON DEMOCRAT   weekly--established 1877, became Colleton Press c. 1880, which in 1890 merged with the Colleton Standard to form the Press and Standard. Latter now uses 1877 as founding date. Jul 18, 1879 = vol 2, no 49, B. Stokes (editor), W. S. Teague (publisher). *Files: Colleton CL mfm (1879-1880) 13; Press and Standard orig & mfm (1879-1880) 13; SCL mfm (1879-1880) 13.*

COLLETON GAZETTE   weekly, Republican--established 1872, ceased c. 1873. Cited once in Rowell (1873): George F. McIntyre & Company (editor and publisher). *NFK*

COLLETON NEWS   semi-weekly, weekly--established 1908, ceased c. 1911. Began as semi-weekly, became weekly Mar 1909. Cited Ayer 1909 thru 1911. Jul 14, 1908 = vol 1, no 1, John W. Hammond (editor and manager). E. F. Hammond and John E. Moore also associated with paper. *Files: Colleton CL mfm Jul 1908-Jun 1910; Press and Standard orig & mfm Jul 1908-Jun 1910; SCL mfm Jul 1908-Jun 1910.*

COLLETON PRESS   weekly, Democrat, Farmers' Alliance--established 1877 as Colleton Democrat, became Colleton Press c. 1880, merged with Colleton Standard in 1890 to form Press and Standard. Oct 4, 1882 = vol 6, no 5. No editor or publisher identified until 1890 when B. G. Price, Jr. is cited as editor and publisher. By that date

Colleton Press was the official organ of the Colleton County Alliance. Cited Ayer 1881 thru 1890, which first lists Price as editor-publisher in 1887. *Files: Colleton CL mfm (1882-1890) 9; Greenville CL Jan 2, 9, Feb 13, May 29, 1889; Press and Standard orig & mfm (1882-1890) 9; SCL mfm (1882-1890) 9.*

COLLETON REPUBLICAN   weekly, Republican--established 1874, ceased 1875. Successor to Colleton Gazette. According to Woody, founded by George Francis McIntyre. Not cited in Rowell. McIntyre, a Charleston native and an army veteran, served in the Reconstruction legislature and held various Colleton County offices during the 1870s. *NFK*

COLLETON STANDARD   weekly, Democrat--established 1889, merged with Colleton Press in 1890 to form the Press and Standard. Aug 15, 1889 = vol 1, no 1, C. C. Tracy (editor). Cited only once in Ayer (1890). *Files: Colleton CL mfm (1889-1890) 22; Press and Standard orig & mfm (1889-1890) 22; SCL mfm (1889-1890) 22.*

COLLETON TIMES   weekly, independent--established 1964, ceased c. 1967. Cited Ayer 1966 and 1967: Robert F. Hartley (editor and publisher). *NFK*

LOW COUNTRY NEWS   weekly, Democrat--established 1896, ceased c. 1897. Cited once in Ayer (1897): D. R. Behre (editor), L. M. Fripp (publisher). *NFK*

PRESS AND STANDARD   weekly--created in 1890 by merger of Colleton Press and Colleton Standard. Press and Standard dates origin from 1877 when Colleton Democrat--the Colleton Press after 1880--was founded. Issued briefly (1974-1975) as semi-weekly. Jun 24, 1891 = vol 14, no 38, B. G. Price, Jr. (editor and publisher). Also associated with paper: J. L. B. Warren, James E. Peurifoy, William Wrightman Smoak, R. M. Jefferies, James F. Risher, F. L. Morrow, William W. Smoak, Jr., W. Wrightman Smoak III, and Estelle Sullivan Smoak. *Files: Colleton CL mfm (1891-1905) 16, 1906 + ; Press and Standard orig & mfm (1891-1905) 16, 1906 + ; SCL Dec 4, 1901, mfm (1891-1905) 16, 1906 + .*

SOUTHERN STAR   weekly--established 1885, ceased c. 1887. Cited once in Ayer (1887): W. B. Gruber (editor and publisher). According to the Charleston Dispatch (Jan 22, 1888), the Colleton Press bought the Southern Star and ended its career. *NFK*

WALTERBORO NEWS   weekly, Republican--established 1873, ceased c. 1877. Cited in Rowell 1874 thru 1877: A. C. Shaffer & Company (editors and publishers). Aug 2, 1873 = vol 1, no 2, A. C. Shaffer & Company (proprietors). Paper's slogan: "With Malice toward None, with Charity for All." *Files: Colleton CL mfm (1873-1875) 89; Press and Standard orig & mfm (1873-1875) 89; SCL mfm (1873-1875) 89.*

DARLINGTON COUNTY

This county was created in 1798 when old Cheraws District was split into three parts: Darlington, Chesterfield, and Marlborough. The source of the name is unclear, although it may honor a Revolutionary War colonel or perhaps be derived from Darlington in Durham County, England.

DARLINGTON

BUILDER   weekly--established 1924, ceased c. 1926. Cited Ayer 1925 and 1926: Thomas H. Coker (editor), Builder Publishing Company. Jun 12, 1924 = vol 1, no 19, Thomas H. Coker (editor), Thomas E. Stokes (manager). *Files: SCL Jun 12, 1924.*

CAROLINA PLANTER   monthly, agricultural, family newspaper--established in Florence as a semi-monthly in 1895, moved to Darlington c. 1897, and cited by Ayer once in Darlington (1897): W. D. Woods (editor), B. O. Bristow (publisher). Ceased c. 1898. *NFK*

CONFEDERATION   weekly, anti-secession c. 1860. According to Ervin and Rudisill's <u>Darlingtoniana</u>, this paper was established in 1860 by James H. Norwood and ceased in 1861 when it was sold to the <u>Darlington Southerner</u>. <u>Horry Dispatch</u> (Apr 11, 1861) contains a prospectus for weekly "Southern Confederation" to be published in Darlington by James H. Norwood, William C. Zimmerman, and Jessee E. Norwood. *NFK*

COUNTY MESSENGER   weekly--established in Hartsville as <u>Hartsville Messenger</u> Mar 8, 1893, moved to Darlington Mar 17, 1898, and became <u>County Messenger</u>. In 1903 moved back to Hartsville and in 1909 became the <u>Hartsville Messenger</u>. May 5, 1898 = vol 6, no 8, T. J. Drew (editor and publisher). Note: This issue contains precise data on establishment and move to Darlington. *Files: Darlington County Historical Commission (1900-1907) 10; SCL May 5, 1898 (fragment), Jan 18, 1900.*

DAILY INDEX   daily--established Jun 1896, ceased c. 1896. Not cited in Ayer. Jun 29, 1896 = vol 1, no 1, C. F. Sansbury (editor). *Files: Darlington County Historical Commission Jun 29, 1896.*

DAILY OBSERVER   daily--established Jul 1912, ceased c. 1912. Not cited in Ayer. Jul 26, 1912 = vol 1, no 3, Stokes Printing Company. *Files: Darlington County Historical Commission (Jul-Sep 1912) 25.*

DAILY RECORD   daily--established Sep 1896 by owners of semi-weekly <u>Darlingtonian</u>, soon ceased. Not cited in Ayer. Sep 9, 1896 = vol 1, no 3. *Files: Darlington County Historical Commission Sep 9, 1896.*

DARLINGTON DEMOCRAT   weekly--established 1868 by E. P. Lucas (editor and publisher), ceased 1871. Clarendon Press (Aug 6, 1868) contains proposal by Lucas to start Darlington Democrat about Aug 19. Nov 18, 1868 = vol 1, no 8, E. P. Lucas (publisher). Cited in Rowell 1869 and 1870. According to Camden Weekly Journal (fragment), Darlington Democrat was sold early in 1871 and succeeded by the Darlington Index. *Files: Darlington County Historical Commission (Oct 1869-Jul 1870) 10; SCL Nov 18, 1868, Jan 26, 1870.*

DARLINGTON FLAG   weekly--established 1851, ceased 1861. Mar 5, 1851 = vol 1, no 1, J. H. Norwood (editor), John F. DeLorme (publisher). By Oct 1851 Norwood and DeLorme (publishers). For a brief time in 1850s issued as Family Friend (see). According to Ervin and Rudisill's Darlingtoniana, T. C. Evans, F. F. Warley, and A. J. Rugg also associated with paper. Rugg, who purchased the Darlington Flag in 1858, ceased operations in 1861. He planned to move his press to Marion after the war, but died in battle. *Files: Darlington County Historical Commission (1851-1860) 30; Florence CL mfm Mar 5, 1851-Apr 15, 1852; News and Press Apr 11, 1861; SCL (1851-1860) 9, mfm Mar 5, 1851-Apr 15, 1852.*

DARLINGTON HERALD   weekly--established Jul 16, 1890, destroyed by fire Dec 15, 1890, re-established Feb 11, 1891, ceased c. 1895. Cited by Ayer 1890 thru 1895. Ayer 1890: A. S. McIver (editor and publisher). Sep 30, 1891 = vol 2, no 4, W. D. Woods and T. J. Drew (editors and proprietors). *Files: Darlington County Historical Commission ((1892-1894)); SCL Sep 30, 1891, Apr 6, 13, 1894.*

DARLINGTON INDEX   weekly--established May 1871, ceased c. 1871. Not cited by Rowell. Jul 13, 1871 = vol 1, no 10, Ira E. Hill (editor), John R. Liles and Thomas W. Westbury (proprietors). *Files: SCL Jul 13, 20, Aug 10, Sep 14, Oct 5, Nov 2, 1871.*

DARLINGTON NEWS   weekly--established 1875 by J. W. Hammond, merged with Darlington Press Apr 20, 1909 to form News and Press. Nov 28, 1878 = vol 4, no 44, J. W. Hammond (publisher and proprietor). Cited in Rowell and Ayer 1877 thru 1909. W. and Henry T. Thompson, George W. Brown, D. D. Evans, and Alex G. Kollock also associated with paper. *Files: Darlington County Historical Commission ((1878-1909)); Florence CL ((1886-1895)), mfm Jun 1890-Dec 1895; Francis Marion mfm Nov 28, Dec 26, 1878; SCL (1879-1907) 9, mfm Nov 28, Dec 26, 1878, (1886) 48, 1888-1895; Sumter County Museum-Archives Apr 1, 1897.*

DARLINGTON PRESS   weekly--established 1903 as New Era, changed name to Darlington Press Jul 4, 1906 = vol 3, no 32, A. J. Bethea (editor), merged with Darlington News in 1909 to create News and Press. In addition to Bethea, Thomas H. Coker, Jr., S. C. King, T. E. Stokes, and J. Monroe Spears also associated with paper. *Files: Darlington County Historical Commission (1906-1908) 10; SCL mfm Jul 1, 1906-Dec 16, 1907.*

DARLINGTON SOUTHERNER   weekly--established 1859 by J. M. Brown, ceased c. 1883. Cited by Rowell and Ayer 1869 thru 1883. Apr 6, 1863 = vol 4, no 1, J. M.

Brown (publisher)..."Dedicated to the South, Literature, etc." F. F. Warley, Charles A. Brown, S. A. Brown, and D. P. Reynolds also associated with paper. Rowell and Ayer indicate may have been issued as Southerner in 1870s and 1880s. *Files: Darlington County Historical Commission (1860-1880) 25; Florence CL Oct 19, 1866; SCL (1862-1876) 7, mfm Apr 6, 1863, Mar 25, 1864, Oct 19, 1866.*

DARLINGTON VINDICATOR   weekly, Democrat--established 1884, ceased c. 1886. Cited by Ayer 1884 thru 1886. Jul 9, 1884 = vol 1, no 6, Charles A. Brown (publisher and proprietor), Brown and Early (proprietors). *Files: Darlington County Historical Commission Jul 9, 1884.*

DARLINGTONIAN   weekly, semi-weekly--established 1895, ceased c. 1902. Cited by Ayer 1896 thru 1899 and in 1902. Ayer 1896: Charles A. Brown (editor and publisher). May 28, 1897 = vol 2, no 44, C. A. Brown (editor and publisher). By 1899 was semi-weekly. May have suspended operations c. 1900, but was cited again by Ayer 1902 as weekly. *Files: Darlington County Historical Commission (1895) 10; SCL Dec 25, 1895, May 28, 1897, Dec 1, 1898.*

FAMILY FRIEND   title of weekly Darlington Flag c. 1857. May 27, 1857 = vol 1, no 5, Law and Calvo (publishers). By Dec 30, 1857, F. F. Warley (editor), C. B. Brooks (proprietor). Scattered files indicate Family Friend continued the Darlington Flag in Apr 1857 and was continued by that paper c. 1858. *Files: News and Press May 27, 1857; SCL Dec 30, 1857.*

FARMERS COURIER   weekly, Republican, black publication--established 1905, ceased c. 1916. Cited in Ayer 1906 thru 1916: A. Jonathan Jefferson (editor and publisher). *NFK*

GOSSIP   weekly (?) According to Ervin and Rudisill's Darlingtoniana, published briefly c. 1887 by a local merchant, S. A. Woods. Not cited in Ayer. *NFK*

NEW ERA   weekly, Republican--established 1865, ceased c. 1866. Aug 1, 1865 = vol 1, no 3, B. F. Whittemore (editor), John W. Tarbox (publisher)..."Devoted to the Restoration, Reconstruction, and Union of the States." According to Ervin and Rudisill's Darlingtoniana, James H. Norwood took over the paper in 1866 and changed its political views. *Files: Darlington County Historical Commission Jul 18, 25, Sep 26, Dec 5, 1865 (photostats); Florence CL and SCL mfm Aug 1-22, Oct 3-17, 1865.*

NEW ERA   weekly--established 1903, became Darlington Press Jul 4, 1906. Mar 2, 1905 = vol 2, no 24, A. J. Bethea (editor and proprietor). Cited by Ayer 1904 thru 1906. Ayer 1904: A. M. Brown (publisher), E. C. Dennis and T. J. Drew (editors). *Files: Darlington County Historical Commission (1904-1906) 4; SCL mfm Mar 2, 1905-Jun 28, 1906.*

NEWS AND PRESS   weekly--created by merger of Darlington News and Darlington Press in 1909. Cited Ayer 1910 to present. At first had number sequence based upon

Darlington Press. Dec 21, 1911 = vol 4, no 3, but Feb 11, 1985 = vol 117, no 25. J. Monroe Spears (editor) at time of merger in 1909, Darlington Press Company (publisher). Others associated with paper include Earl R. Baxter, J. E. Norment, Guy Coffee, Mrs. Sara G. Coffee, Fred L. Willis, Morrell L. Thomas, Jr., and Dwight Dana. *Files: Clemson mfm ((1911-1919)) 219, 1920-1939; Darlington County Historical Commission ((1910-1914)); Darlington CL 1914 + ; Francis Marion mfm ((1911-1919)) 219, 1920-1939; News and Press 1928 + ; SCL (1911-1952) 75, 1953 + , mfm ((1911-1919)) 219, 1920-1939.*

PEE DEE WATCHMAN   weekly--established 1877, ceased c. 1879. Cited Rowell 1877 and 1878: A. A. and F. A. Gilbert (editors and publishers). Sep 13, 1877 = vol 1, no 22, A. A. and F. A. Gilbert (editors), A. A. Gilbert (proprietor). *Files: SCL Sep 13, Oct 4, 25, Nov 2, 1877, Sep 19, 1878.*

REFORM SENTINEL   weekly, Farmers' Alliance--established 1893, ceased c. 1895. Cited Ayer 1893/4 and 1895: George Just Brown (editor and publisher). Jan 18, 1894 = vol 1, no 47. *Files: Darlington County Historical Commission Jan 18, 1894.*

SOUTHERNER   see Darlington Southerner.

UNION   weekly, black publication, Baptist--according to Behling, published c. 1950. Not cited in Ayer. *NFK*

HARTSVILLE

DARCO NEWS & BUYERS GUIDE   weekly--established 1982. Sep 4, 1985 = vol 4, no 36, E. Donald McElveen (publisher). *Files: Darco News & Buyers Guide 1982 + .*

DARLINGTON COUNTY TRIBUNE   semi-weekly, weekly, independent-- established Aug 21, 1972, ceased c. 1979. Aug 21, 1972 = vol 1, no 1, E. Donald McElveen (publisher). Issued semi-weekly 1972-1973, then weekly. Winston H. McElveen also associated with paper. *Files: Darlington County Historical Commission ((1972-1978)); SCL Sep 21, 1972.*

HARTSVILLE HERALD   weekly, Democrat--established 1899, ceased c. 1900. Cited Ayer 1900: W. Eugene Cook (editor and publisher). *NFK*

HARTSVILLE MESSENGER   weekly, semi-weekly--established Mar 8, 1893, moved to Darlington Mar 17, 1898, and continued by County Messenger. In 1903 moved back to Hartsville and in 1909 resumed original name, Hartsville Messenger. Oct 18, 1894 = vol 2, no 33, T. J. Drew (editor and publisher). In 1974 became semi-weekly. Also associated with paper: Frank A. Miller, D. R. Coker, Thomas H. Coker, Jr., Myron Green, C. E. Prescott, A. L. M. Wiggins, and Joseph L. Wiggins. *Files: Darlington County Historical Commission (1895-1897, 1909) 30, 1910-1975; Hartsville*

Library mfm (1894-1907) 10, 1908 + ; Hartsville Messenger 1961 + ; SCL (1895-1952) 50, mfm (1894-1907) 10, 1908 + .

HARTSVILLE NEWS   semi-weekly--established 1938, ceased c. 1938. Not cited in Ayer. Apr 2, 1938 = vol 1, no 1, Thomas H. Coker (editor). *Files: SCL Apr 2-26, 1938.*

LAMAR

LAMAR BULLETIN   weekly--established 1891. According to Rudisill, First One Hundred Years: Lamar, South Carolina, 1872-1972, created by local businessmen, ceased c. 1892. Jan 28, 1892 = vol 1, no 16. *Files: Darlington County Historical Commission Jan 28, 1892.*

LAMAR LEADER   weekly c. 1898. According to Rudisill, First One Hundred Years: Lamar, South Carolina, 1872-1972, established 1898, but soon ceased. *NFK*

LAMAR SENTINEL   weekly--established 1922, ceased c. 1926. Cited Ayer 1923 thru 1926: Jack Wells (editor and publisher). *NFK*

PRESENT TRUTH   weekly, Seventh Day Adventist--established c. 1900, ceased c. 1904. Cited Ayer 1901 thru 1904: A. B. Cargile (editor and publisher). Printed at office of Lamar Leader. *NFK*

X RAYS   weekly--established 1897, ceased c. 1898. Cited once in Ayer (1898): Walter L. Wilson (editor and publisher). *NFK*

SOCIETY HILL

SOCIETY HILL NEWS   weekly, black publication, Republican--established 1910, ceased c. 1911. Sep 23, 1910 = vol 1, no 23, S. B. Thompson (editor and publisher). Cited once in Ayer (1911): S. B. Thompson (editor and publisher). *Files: Darlington County Historical Commission Sep 23, 1910.*

DILLON COUNTY

This county, carved out of Marion County in 1910, is named for James W. Dillon (1826-1913), an Irish merchant who led the movement to build the Wilson Short Cut Railroad.

DILLON

DILLON CENTURY DAWN   weekly, black publication--established 1902, ceased c. 1906. Listed in Ayer 1904 and 1905: A. W. Bethea, Jr. (editor and publisher). *NFK*

DILLON COUNTY ADVERTISER   weekly--established 1906, ceased c. 1907. Cited once in Ayer (1907): Elihu Muldrow (editor), Dillon Advertiser Company (publisher). *NFK*

DILLON HERALD   weekly, semi-weekly--established 1895. First cited Ayer 1896: S. S. Rozier (editor), Southern Publishing Company. Since 1955 issued semi-weekly. Those associated with paper during past century also include R. S. Churchill, A. B. Jordan, Jr., A. B. Jordan, Sr., J. D. Blizzard, R. J. Weirich, B. S. Tillinghast, Robert Robinson, Jr., and Paul Jones. Earliest issue at SCL (Jan 7, 1904 = vol 8, no 52) says founded 1895...current issues cite 1894 founding date. *Files: Dillon CL 1935 + ; Dillon Herald 1919 + ; Dunbar Library [Dillon] 1969 + ; SCL 1940-1945, (1946) 46, 1947 + , mfm ((1904-1939)), complete files for some years.*

PEE DEE TOBACCO JOURNAL   weekly--established 1899, ceased c. 1901. Cited once in Ayer (1901): Hamilton and Gasque (editors and publishers). *NFK*

LATTA

DEWEY EAGLE   weekly, independent--established 1898 in Lake City and cited by Ayer 1900 in that community: W. H. Kirton (editor), W. H. Kirton and W. H. Edwards (publishers). Ayer 1901 lists Dewey Eagle in Latta: W. H. Kirton (editor and publisher). Soon ceased, not listed in 1902. *NFK*

LATTA NEWS   weekly, non-political--established 1910, ceased c. 1910. Cited once in Ayer (1910): Smith and Bethea (editors and publishers). *NFK*

LATTA OBSERVER   weekly, monthly--established 1910, ceased c. 1983. Apr 3, 1910 = vol 3, no 10, B. H. Atkinson (publisher). First cited in Ayer 1911: B. H. Atkinson (editor and publisher). Others associated with paper include J. C. Shepard, J. W. McSweeney, H. D. Watson, and Linda Page Watson Sawyer. Latta Observer issued monthly c. 1982-1983. *Files: Dillon CL (1979-1983) 40; SCL Apr 3, 1912.*

LATTA SUN   weekly--established 1892, ceased c. 1894. Listed in Ayer 1892 thru 1893/4: James H. Evans (editor and publisher). *NFK*

DORCHESTER COUNTY

In 1697, Joseph Lord led a group of settlers from Massachusetts and Connecticut who established a frontier town named for Dorchester, Massachusetts, site of their "mother" church. That community, in turn, had been named for a town in Dorset County, England. Two centuries later, in 1897, Dorchester County was created from parts of Berkeley and Colleton counties.

ST. GEORGE

CAROLINA FREEMAN   weekly, black publication--established 1901, ceased c. 1903. Cited Ayer 1902 and 1903: T. H. Pinckney (editor), W. E. Summers (publisher). *NFK*

COLLETON CITIZEN   weekly, Democrat--established 1895, but soon changed name to Dorchester Democrat. Cited once in Ayer (1897) as Colleton Citizen, John J. Howell (editor and publisher). *NFK*

COLLETON REPUBLICAN   weekly--established 1896, ceased c. 1897. Cited once in Ayer (1897): John Z. Crook (editor and publisher). *NFK*

COUNTY RECORD   weekly--established 1922, ceased c. 1924. Listed Ayer 1923 and 1924: County Record Company (publisher). *NFK*

DORCHESTER COUNTY PROGRESS   weekly--established 1945, ceased c. 1946. Not cited in Ayer. Aug 15, 1945 = vol 1, no 1, Harland Edwards (editor), B. P. Davies, Jr., (publisher). *Files: Dorchester Eagle-Record Aug 15, Oct 24, 1945.*

DORCHESTER COUNTY RECORD   weekly, Independent Democrat--established 1927, merged with Dorchester Eagle in 1934 to form Dorchester Eagle-Record. Cited Ayer 1928 thru 1935. Oct 20, 1927 = vol 1, no 7, George R. Koester (editor), Record Publishing Company. Edward C. Powers, E. R. Berry, W. H. Twyford, and H. B. Magill also associated with paper. *Files: Dorchester Eagle-Record Sep 1927-Oct 1928, Jun 12, 1930, Jun 1932-Dec 1933; SCL ((1927-1934)) 105.*

DORCHESTER DEMOCRAT   weekly--established 1895 as Colleton Citizen, soon became Dorchester Democrat, ceased c. 1905. Listed in Ayer 1898 thru 1905: John J. Howell (editor and publisher). *NFK*

DORCHESTER EAGLE   weekly--established 1899, merged with Dorchester County Record in 1934 to form Dorchester Eagle-Record. Cited Ayer 1901 thru 1935. Ayer 1901: Marvin P. Felder (editor and proprietor). Oct 20, 1911 = vol 13, no 42, Felder (editor and proprietor). W. B. Tarkington and Emily Howell Klauber also associated with paper. *Files: Dorchester Eagle-Record Apr 1928-Aug 1930; SCL ((1911-1932)) 103.*

DORCHESTER EAGLE-RECORD   weekly--created 1934 by merger of Dorchester Eagle and Dorchester County Record. First joint issue: Dec 13, 1934 = vol 34, no 41, H. Boyd Magill (editor), Burgess and Magill (publishers). In 1967, William M. and Doris M. Owens became publishers and c. 1968 assumed editorial duties as well. *Files: Dorchester Eagle-Record 1934-1936, 1938, 1940 + ; SCL (1934-1942) 11, 1984 + .*

EXPOSITOR   weekly--established 1903, ceased c. 1905. Cited once in Ayer (1905): R. L. Weeks (editor and publisher). *NFK*

ST. GEORGE'S NEWS   weekly, Democrat--established 1885, ceased c. 1895. Cited in Ayer 1886 thru 1895. Ayer 1885-1887: J. Otey Reed (editor), J. C. McDaniel (publisher). Ayer 1888-1895: J. C. McDaniel (editor and publisher). *NFK*

SUMMERVILLE

AMERICAN NATIONALIST PARTY NEWS   irregular--an underground paper published by Charles White (national party leader) in 1970s. *Files: University of Connecticut issue # 67 (1977). Apparently no copies in SC.*

COASTAL TIMES   weekly, black publication--established 1983, produced by PIC Publications. Sep 7, 1983 = vol 1, no 10, James E. Clyburn (president and publisher), Gladys M. Hazel (editor and publisher). In 1983 listed Summerville and Columbia offices. Moved Summerville office to 701 East Bay Street, Charleston, c. 1984. See Coastal Times [Charleston].

SUMMERVILLE ADVERTISER   weekly, Democrat--established 1909, ceased c. 1924. Cited Ayer 1911 thru 1924. Ayer 1911-1922: S. P. Driggers (editor and publisher). Ayer 1923-1924: Grover R. Driggers (editor and publisher). Jun 11, 1909 = vol 1, no 1, S. P. Driggers (editor). *Files: SCL May 13, 1921, mfm (1909-1921) 40.*

SUMMERVILLE FORESTER   weekly--established 1927, ceased c. 1928. Cited once in Ayer (1928): Katherine Drayton Simons (editor), Eagle Publishing Company, St. George. Oct 12, 1927 = vol 1, no 2, Simons (editor), Eagle Publishing Company. *Files: SCL orig & mfm Oct 12, 1927, May 16, 1928.*

SUMMERVILLE HERALD   weekly, Independent Democrat--established 1884, ceased c. 1886. Cited Ayer 1884 thru 1887: George Tupper (editor), Herald Publishing Company. Nov 5, 1884 = vol 1, no 32, George Tupper (editor). *Files: SCL orig & mfm Nov 5, 1884, Aug 15, 1885.*

SUMMERVILLE JOURNAL   weekly, independent--established 1924, ceased c. 1926. Cited Ayer 1926 and 1927. Files indicate John Samsey (editor and publisher) c.

1924-1925, George R. Grist (editor and publisher) c. 1925-1926. *Files: Dorchester Eagle-Record Jul 1924-Jun 1925.*

SUMMERVILLE JOURNAL   weekly--established 1972, merged with Summerville Scene Apr 1977 to form Summerville Journal-Scene. Sep 27, 1972 = vol 1, no 1, William C. Collins (editor and publisher). Not cited in Ayer. *Files: SCL and Summerville Public Library mfm 1972-1977; Summerville Journal-Scene orig & mfm 1972-1977.*

SUMMERVILLE JOURNAL-SCENE   semi-weekly, created 1977 by merger of Summerville Journal and Summerville Scene. First joint issue Apr 20, 1977 = vol 5, no 30, William C. Collins (editor and publisher). *Files: SCL and Summerville Public Library mfm 1977 + ; Summerville Journal-Scene orig & mfm 1977 + .*

SUMMERVILLE NEWS   weekly--established 1888, ceased c. 1909. Cited Ayer 1888 thru 1909. Ayer 1888-1900: R. H. Sweeney (editor and publisher). Ayer 1901: George Tupper (editor), S. P. Driggers (publisher). Ayer 1902-1908: W. R. Dehon (editor), Summerville Publishing Company. Ayer 1909: E. Julian Carroll (editor), Summerville Publishing Company. Sep 20, 1901 = vol 14, no 27, Dehon (editor). *Files: SCL Sep 20, 27, Nov 1, 1901, mfm (1901-1908) 10.*

SUMMERVILLE SCENE   weekly, independent--established 1946, merged with Summerville Journal Apr 1977 to form Summerville Journal-Scene. Tom Hamrick (editor and publisher) 1946-Mar 1949; Jack Button (editor and publisher) Mar 1949-Oct 1972; Philip Mace (editor), Banner Publishing Company, Oct 1972-Apr 1977. Apr 20, 1950 = vol 4, no 40, Button (editor and publisher). *Files: SCL ((1950-1952)) 106, 1953-1972.*

TRIDENT PRESS   weekly--established Oct 1984. Jul 24, 1985 = vol 1, no 24, Deborah Bagley (editor), Dennis Ashley (publisher), Trident Press, Inc. Publishes Ladson and Goose Creek editions. *Files: Trident Press 1984 + .*

EDGEFIELD COUNTY

Organized in 1798 when old Ninety Six District was split into five parts, Edgefield District, now Edgefield County, may have been so named because its county seat arose on the borders of "Cedar Fields," the plantation home of Colonel Arthur Simkins. Simkins, one of that town's founding fathers, sold house lots carved out of his lands.

EDGEFIELD

ANTI-MONARCHIST, AND SOUTH-CAROLINA ADVERTISER weekly--established May 28, 1811, ceased ? Sep 9, 1811 = vol 1, no 16, Thomas M. Davenport (publisher). Only four issues located: Sep 9, 21, 28, Nov 2, 1811. Founded as a pro-War of 1812 publication. According to South Carolina Law Reports, Davenport continued to publish this paper in Cambridge [Ninety Six] in 1812, also producing a pamphlet that same year. In Apr 1819 he inserted a proposal in a Mobile newspaper to establish a paper in Tuscaloosa. Charleston Daily Courier (Jul 14, 1857) says he moved his press back to Edgefield c. 1820 and sold it to Benjamin McNary, who established the South-Carolina Republican. Four issues available in Readex Microprint # 1891. See Harry L. Watson, "Early Newspapers of Abbeville District, 1812-1834," Proceedings, SC Historical Association (1940), pp. 18-35. *Files: SCL Sep 9, 28, Nov 2, 1811; USC mp Sep 9, 21, 28, Nov 2, 1811.*

CAROLINIAN weekly--established 1829, formerly Edgefield Hive [Pottersville], became Edgefield Advertiser in Feb 1836. Jun 6, 1829 = vol 1, no 13, [F. H.] Wardlaw and [S. Warren] Mays (publishers). According to the Charleston Daily Courier (Jul 14, 1857), Mays soon died and paper passed to Wardlaw and Bacon. Circa 1831, Arthur Wingfall became editor and proprietor, followed by John Wimbish and then J. P. Carroll. Early in 1836, James Jones and Maximilian LaBorde acquired the Carolinian and changed its name to Edgefield Advertiser. *Files: Clemson Nov 27, 1830, Oct 29, Nov 26, 1831, Apr 14, 1832, Aug 22, 1833; SCL (1829-1835) 35.*

EDGEFIELD ADVERTISER weekly--established Feb 11, 1836, continues Carolinian. Feb 11, 1836 = vol 1, no 1, [Maximilian] LaBorde and [James] Jones (editors), G. Whitfield Goodrich (printer). Jones, according to the first issue, had marched off to Florida at the head of the "True Blues," a volunteer company of his regiment. Others associated with paper include Pierre Fabian LaBorde, William Francis Durisoe, Joseph Abney, William Caine Moragne, Arthur Simkins, John Edmund Bacon, Elijah Keese, Daniel Roper Durisoe, Thomas John Adams, Julian Landrum Mims, and William Walton Mims. See Eleanor Elizabeth Mims, "The Editors of the Edgefield Advertiser, Oldest Newspaper in South Carolina, 1836-1930," MA thesis, USC, 1930. *Files: Edgefield Advertiser 1928 + ; Edgefield Archives 1838-1870, 1915 + , mfm ((1836-1902)): Clemson Jun 9, 1836, mfm 1856-1868; Furman mfm ((1836-1902)); Greenville CL Jun 27, Jul 25, Sep 5, 26, 1889, mfm ((1836-1902)); Greenwood CL mfm 1856-1868; Lander mfm ((1836-1902)); SCL ((1837-1959)) 2600, 1960 + , mfm*

((1836-1902)); Winthrop mfm ((1836-1902)); Wofford mfm ((1836-1902)). *Note: SCL orig files complete for 1917, 1919-1922, 1925-1930, 1932-1933, 1936-1939, 1947-1948, 1952, 1960 + . SCL has no orig files 1840-1879. All mfm files cited are from same source and are similar in coverage: 1836-1868, (1869-1879) 32, ((1892-1902)) 228.*

EDGEFIELD CHRONICLE   weekly--established 1881, ceased 1925. Aug 3, 1881 = vol 1, no 1, Durisoe and Daley (proprietors), J. S. Daley (editor). Others associated with paper include James T. Bacon and Louis W. Cheatham. *Files: Edgefield Archives 1890-1917, mfm ((1881-1892)) 488; Furman mfm ((1881-1892)) 488; SCL ((1882-1894)) 614, 1895-1898, (1899) 49, 1900-1904, (1905) 42, 1906-Apr 1925, mfm ((1881-1892)) 488; Winthrop mfm ((1881-1892)) 488.*

EDGEFIELD COUNTY NEWS   weekly--established 1972 by Amelia Reece, merged with Edgefield County Press and Ridge Citizen in 1982 to form Citizen News [Johnston]. Jan 4, 1979 = vol 7, no 33, Amelia Reece (editor and publisher). *Files: Edgefield CL 1979-1981.*

EDGEFIELD COUNTY PRESS   weekly, independent--established 1977, ceased 1982 when merged with Edgefield County News and Ridge Citizen to form Citizen News [Johnston]. Cited by Ayer 1981 thru 1984: Emily Bull (editor and publisher). *NFK*

EDGEFIELD FARMER   weekly, Farmers' Alliance--established 1892, ceased c. 1894. Cited Ayer 1892 thru 1894: James T. Parks (editor), Parks and Durisoe (publishers). Oct 12, 1892 = vol 1, no 27, James T. Parks (editor). *Files: SCL Oct 12, 1892, mfm Aug 2, 1893.*

EDGEFIELD INFORMER   weekly--established 1856, ceased 1856. Apr 3, 1856 = vol 1, no 9, C. W. Styles & Company (publisher). According to Ellen, founded by Styles on Feb 1, 1856, ceased Oct 1856. *Files: SCL Apr 3, 1856.*

EDGEFIELD NEWS   weekly, Democrat--established 1907, ceased c. 1909. Cited Ayer 1908 and 1909: W. P. Calhoun (editor), W. P. Calhoun and W. R. Covar (publishers). *NFK*

SOUTH-CAROLINA REPUBLICAN   weekly--established c. 1820, moved to Pottersville c. 1824. According to Charleston Daily Courier (Jul 14, 1857), Benjamin McNary bought Anti-Monarchist, and South Carolina Advertiser from Thomas M. Davenport c. 1820 and changed name of paper to South-Carolina Republican. Apparently no copies exist of the South-Carolina Republican issued in Edgefield (1820-1824)...if any were printed. See South-Carolina Republican [Pottersville]. *NFK*

JOHNSTON

CITIZEN NEWS   weekly--created 1982 by merger of Ridge Citizen, Edgefield County News, and Edgefield County Press. May 20, 1982 = vol 1, no 3, J. L. Aull (managing editor), Edgefield Communications, Inc. Peggy H. Aull, Bettis C. Rainsford, Joanne F. Rainsford, and Pauline D. Patrick also associated with paper. *Files: Citizen News and Edgefield CL 1982 + ; SCL ((1984 +)).*

EDGEFIELD WEEKLY MONITOR   weekly, Democrat--established 1877, became Weekly Monitor c. 1900, and merged with Johnston News c. 1906 to form Johnston News-Monitor. Rowell 1879: E. W. McLenna and P. B. Waters (editors and publishers). Mar 10, 1881 = vol 4, no 18, E. W. McLenna (editor and publisher). J. S. Daley, W. Alvin McLenna, and Charles J. Terrell also associated with paper. *Files: SCL mfm ((1881-1899)) 130.*

JOHNSTON HERALD   weekly, Democrat--established Sep 1923, ceased Apr 1947. Cited Ayer 1924 thru 1947. Ayer 1924: O. F. Armfield (editor), Armfield Brothers (publishers). S. N. Loft, George G. Waters, and W. W. Mims also associated with paper. *Files: Citizen News 1939; SCL (1932-1939) 5, mfm (1935-1942) 8.*

JOHNSTON NEWS   weekly, independent--established 1903, merged with Weekly Monitor c. 1906 to form Johnston News-Monitor. May 27, 1903 = vol 1, no 23, W. Toney (editor). Cited Ayer 1904 thru 1906. Ayer 1904 and 1905: A. F. Perkins (editor and publisher). Ayer 1906: H. C. Bailey (editor and publisher). *Files: SCL (1903-1905) 40.*

JOHNSTON NEWS-MONITOR   weekly, Democrat--created c. 1906 by merger of Johnston News and Weekly Monitor, ceased c. 1915. Lexington News (Jun 2, 1915) states that the News-Monitor suspended operations "some time ago." Cited Ayer 1907 thru 1916. Ayer 1907: Ira C. Carson (editor), Monitor Publishing Company. Issues for 1908 cite H. C. Bailey as editor, but give no vol number. W. S. Stokes also associated with paper. *Files: SCL Jun 17, Sep 2, 1908, May 31, 1911, Aug 27, 1913.*

JOHNSTON TIMES   weekly, Independent Democrat--established 1915, ceased c. 1918. Cited Ayer 1916 thru 1918. Ayer 1916 and 1917: J. Rutledge McGhee (editor and publisher). Ayer 1918: J. Rutledge McGhee (editor), Western Carolina Publishing Company. *NFK*

RIDGE CITIZEN   weekly--established 1947, merged with Edgefield County News and Edgefield County Press in 1982 to form Citizen News. Cited Ayer 1948 thru 1982. Mar 20, 1947 = vol 1, no 6, J. L. Aull (editor and publisher). Mar 25, 1948 issue has memorial to George G. Waters (1879-1947), indicating ties to Johnston Herald. *Files: Citizen News 1947-1982; Edgefield CL 1979-1982; SCL Mar 20, 1947, Mar 25, 1948.*

WEEKLY MONITOR   weekly, Democrat--created c. 1900 by name change, formerly Edgefield Weekly Monitor. Merged with Johnston News c. 1906 to form the Johnston News-Monitor. Mar 7, 1901 = vol 24, no 15, Charles E. Terrell (editor and proprietor). According to records of the Saluda Sentinel, in Feb 1902 Terrell purchased that paper, but following a fire a short time later he returned to the Weekly Monitor. *Files: SCL Mar 7, 1901 (fragment), Oct 8, 1903, mfm Jul 14, 1904, May 25, 1905.*

POTTERSVILLE

EDGEFIELD HIVE   weekly--created Mar 1827 by name change, formerly the South-Carolina Republican continued as Carolinian [Edgefield] c. Mar 1829. South-Carolina Republican (Feb 17, 1827) announced that Abner Landrum and William Brazier, Sr., would take over that paper on Mar 1, 1827. According to the Charleston Daily Courier (Jul 14, 1857), they changed the name of the paper to the Edgefield Hive and in 1829 sold out to F. H. Ward and Warren Mays, who moved the paper to Edgefield and changed name to Carolinian. Gregory says that the American Antiquarian Society has Apr 7, 1827; however, that issue is not reported in the US Newspaper Program National Union List (1985). *NFK*

EDGEFIELD HIVE   weekly--established Dec 1829 by Abner Landrum, co-publisher of a weekly by the same name (1827-1829), ceased c. Dec 1830. Jan 12, 1830 = vol 1, no 3, Abner Landrum (publisher). This publication, more periodical than newspaper, published ads on separate sheets, an innovation the Camden Journal said was "quite a novelty, and we more than half like it." In Feb 1831, Landrum was publishing the Columbia Free Press and Hive [Columbia], so the Edgefield Hive presumably ceased in Dec 1830. *Files: SCL Jul 23, Sep 3, 1830, mfm Jan 12-Dec 24, 1830.*

POTTERSVILLE HIVE   monthly--established Apr 1981, ceased c. Dec 1981. Apr 1981 = vol 1, no 1, Carlee T. McClendon (editor and publisher). Paper has Edgefield mailing address, despite title and Pottersville address on masthead. *Files: Edgefield Archives Apr-Oct 1981; SCL Apr-Dec 1981.*

SOUTH-CAROLINA REPUBLICAN   weekly--established 1824, became Edgefield Hive c. Mar 1827. Jul 2, 1825 = vol 2, no 70, published by Abner Landrum and John Lofton. According to the Charleston Daily Courier (Jul 14, 1857), this successor to the Anti-Monarchist, and South Carolina Advertiser was published by Benjamin McNary as the South-Carolina Republican in Edgefield, 1820-1824. If so, no copies exist from those years. In 1824 the paper was purchased by Abner Landrum and John Lofton and moved to Pottersville. On Mar 1, 1827, Landrum and William Brazier, Sr. assumed control of the paper and changed its name to Edgefield Hive. *Files: SCL Jul 2, Oct 22, 1825, Feb 17, 1827.*

FAIRFIELD COUNTY

Created in 1798 when old Camden District was split into five governmental units, Fairfield District (now Fairfield County) reportedly was named by a judge who recalled an exclamation uttered by General Cornwallis when his army camped in this region during the Revolutionary War: "What fair fields!"

RIDGEWAY

ADVERTISER   weekly--established 1890, ceased c. 1892. Cited Ayer 1891 and 1892: W. J. Johnson (editor and publisher). *NFK*

ENTERPRISE   weekly, Republican--established 1898, ceased c. 1899. Cited once in Ayer (1899): John C. P. Williams (editor and publisher). *NFK*

FAIRFIELD NEWS   weekly, Democrat--established 1909, ceased c. 1915. Cited Ayer 1910 thru 1915. Sep 1, 1909 = vol 1, no 1, H. D. Rantin (president), Fairfield Publishing Company. Subsequent issues list no publisher but these staff members: W. B. Rook, H. E. Coleman, G. P. Edmonds, and W. C. Edmonds. Ayer 1912-1915: William M. Oxner (editor and publisher). *Files: SCL (1909-1914) 10.*

WINNSBORO

ADVOCATE   weekly, Democrat--established 1891, ceased c. 1894. Cited Ayer 1892 thru 1893/4. Ayer 1892: P. B. Lockwood (editor), Crosby & McMeekin (publishers); Ayer 1893/4: P. B. Lockwood and J. R. Turner (editors), Advocate Publishing Company. Not listed in Ayer 1895. *Files: SCL Sep 9, 1891.*

DAILY NEWS   daily--established Feb 1865, soon suspended, perhaps after one week. Became Tri-Weekly News Mar 1865. Feb 13, 1865 = vol 1, no 1, J. E. Britton (editor and publisher). Britton states in first issue that he is starting the News because the Herald and Register are no longer being published. *Files: SCL Feb 13-18, 1865.*

DAILY REGISTER   daily--established 1850 by E. H. Britton, became Register (tri-weekly) after 1854. Jan 18, 1851 = vol 1, no 85, E. H. Britton (publisher). By 1854, F. Gaillard and D. W. Aiken publishing paper. *Files: SCL Jan 18, 1851, Mar 2, 1854.*

FAIRFIELD COURIER   weekly--established Mar 1865, only one or two issues published. Interim publication between Daily News and Tri-Weekly News. Mar 23, 1865 = vol 1, no 1, J. E. Britton (publisher). *Files: SCL Mar 23, 1865.*

FAIRFIELD HERALD   weekly, Democrat--established 1849 by E. H. Britton. Jul 21, 1849 = vol 1, no 22, E. H. Britton (editor and proprietor). In 1858 A. Desportes was publisher and proprietor. Paper suspended operations during the Civil War and resumed publication Jun 20, 1866 = vol 1, no 1, H. A. Gaillard (editor), Gaillard,

Desportes & Company (publisher). Rowell 1869: Benjamin R. Stewart (editor), Desportes, Williams & Company (publisher). Desportes and Williams (editors and publisher) 1870-1874, succeeded by Williams and Davis in 1875. During these years, 1866-1876, Fairfield Herald (weekly) and News: Tri-Weekly published in same office by same staff. At the end of 1876 the two papers merged to form the News and Herald. *Files: Clemson Jul 21, 1849; Fairfield CL mfm 1866-1876; SCL Feb 7, Dec 30, 1858, Mar 14, May 2, 1861, mfm 1866-1876.*

FAIRFIELD INDEPENDENT   weekly--established Apr 12, 1979 (vol 1, no 1), printed for Fairfield Publishers, Inc., by Bruner Printers, Lexington. Staff included Emmy S. Fellers, Faye J. Johnson, and Thomas E. Robertson. Merged with News and Herald Feb 1982 to create the Herald-Independent. *Files: Fairfield CL and SCL mfm 1979-1982.*

FAIRFIELD NEWS AND HERALD   see News and Herald.

FARMERS' INTEREST   weekly, Democrat--established 1890, ceased c. 1890. Cited only once in Ayer (1890): G. W. Buchanan and J. H. Tillman (editors), Fairfield Publishing Company. *NFK*

HERALD-INDEPENDENT   weekly--established Mar 1982 by merger of News and Herald and Fairfield Independent. Mar 4, 1982 = vol 1, no 1, Michael Avery (editor), Faye J. Johnson (publisher). *Files: Fairfield CL mfm 1982 + ; SCL mfm 1982-1984.*

NEWS. FAIRFIELD AND CHESTER ADVERTISER   weekly--established 1844, ceased c. 1844. Sep 11, 1844 = vol 1, no 13, George W. Hopkins (editor and proprietor). Ad seeks partner with $500, less if "a regular bred printer." *Files: SCL Sep 11, 1844.*

NEWS: TRI-WEEKLY   tri-weekly--created Jun 19, 1866 by name change, formerly Tri-Weekly News. Jun 19, 1866 = vol 3, no 60, Gaillard, Desportes & Company (publisher). Rowell 1869 says established 1863. Merged with Fairfield Herald in 1876 to create the News and Herald. Both papers produced in the same office by the same staff, 1866-1876. *Files: SCL Jun-Dec 1866, (1869-1872) 4.*

NEWS AND HERALD   tri-weekly, semi-weekly, weekly--also known at times as the Fairfield News and Herald. Created by merger of News: Tri-Weekly and Fairfield Herald in 1876, in turn merged with Fairfield Independent in 1982 to form the Herald-Independent. Continued to publish both tri-weekly and weekly editions from 1876 to c. 1900, then became semi-weekly and c. 1918 weekly. Oct 12, 1876 = vol 1, no 1, John S. Reynolds (editor). Others associated with paper include E. B. Ragsdale, R. M. Davis, W. E. McDonald, F. M. Bruce, W. D. Douglas, J. Q. Davis, J. Frank Fooshe, J. M. McNaull, W. S. Stokes, J. E. Stokes, O. E. Crowson, Thomas M. Seawell, P. M. Dees, G. M. Ketchin, M. G. Brown, Faye J. Johnson, Fred R. Sheheen, and Michael Avery. *Files: James W. Green III [Route 4, Winnsboro] 1943–1981; Greenville CL Jul 9, 1879; Fairfield CL and SCL mfm 1876-1906, (1907-1919) 24, 1920-1982.*

REGISTER   tri-weekly--established 1850 by E. H. Britton as daily, became tri-weekly c. 1855, and ceased sometime during the Civil War, probably before 1863. Dec 11, 1856 = vol 6, no 337, Frank Gaillard (publisher). A. Desportes, H. A. Gaillard, W. Clarke, and D. M. Clarke also associated with paper. *Files: SCL (1856–1861) 8.*

SATURDAY POST   weekly c. 1833--prospectus published in Columbia Telescope (Oct 29, 1833) states that Francis S. Bronson will publish the Saturday Post as soon as he gets enough subscribers. *NFK*

TRI-WEEKLY NEWS   tri-weekly--created Apr 1865, formerly Daily News, continued by News: Tri-Weekly Jun 19, 1866. Apr 4, 1865 = vol 1, no 8, J. E. Britton (publisher). Gaillard, Desportes & Company also associated with paper. *Files: SCL ((Apr 4, 1865-Jun 16, 1866)) 120.*

FLORENCE COUNTY

In 1854, W. W. Harllee, the first president of the Wilmington & Manchester Railroad, bestowed the name of his six-year-old daughter upon a new rail depot. Florence, who grew up to become that community's first librarian, in turn, had been named for a fictional character in Dombey and Son by Charles Dickens. In 1888, Florence County, created from parts of Marion, Darlington, Williamsburg, and Clarendon counties, adopted the name of that depot, now a growing little city of considerable regional importance.

FLORENCE

ADVOCATE   see Reform Advocate.

BANNER MESSENGER   weekly--created 1896 by merger of County Banner and Florence Messenger. Feb 6, 1896 = vol 1, no 1, H. L. Darr (manager), H. L. Brunson (editor). This issue states that the County Banner was established Sep 27, 1894, the Florence Messenger, Oct 4, 1889. Circa 1896 the Banner Messenger merged with the Florence Times and was issued by the Florence Daily Times as the weekly Times-Messenger. *Files: Darlington County Historical Commission Feb 6, 1896 (xerox copy).*

BAPTIST CHRONICLE   semi-monthly, monthly, black publication--established c. 1896, ceased c. 1920. Cited Ayer 1897 and 1898: E. R. Roberts (editor and publisher), semi-monthly. Not listed in Ayer 1899-1905, but reappears in 1906 as Chronicle, E. R. Roberts (editor and publisher), monthly. Ayer 1911 says established 1902, again becomes Baptist Chronicle c. 1916. Not cited in Ayer 1921. *NFK*

BAPTIST-HERALD   semi-monthly, black publication--established 1889, ceased c. 1895. Cited Ayer 1890 thru 1895. Ayer 1890-1894: C. H. Prince (publisher). Ayer 1895: H. M. Ayer (publisher). *NFK*

BLACK SUN   weekly, black publication--published in Columbia for the Florence region by Redfern II, JuJu Publications. See Black News [Columbia].

CAROLINA PLANTER   semi-monthly, monthly, agricultural, family newspaper--established 1895, ceased c. 1898. Cited Ayer 1896: W. D. Woods (editor), R. C. Starr (publisher), semi-monthly. Moved to Darlington c. 1897 and cited there in Ayer 1897 as a monthly: W. D. Woods (editor), B. O. Bristow (publisher). *NFK*

CHRONICLE   see Baptist Chronicle.

COMMONWEALTH   weekly--established 1913, ceased c. 1919. Ayer 1914-1916: L. D. Bass (editor and publisher). Ayer 1917-1919: Hartwell M. Ayer (editor and publisher). *NFK*

COUNTY BANNER   weekly--established Sep 27, 1894 in Bishopville by H. L. Darr, moved to Florence c. 1895 and merged with Florence Messenger to create Banner Messenger. Cited by Ayer in both Bishopville and Florence in 1896, only in Florence in 1897: H. L. Darr (editor and publisher). *NFK*

DAILY TIMES   see Florence Daily Times.

EVENING HERALD   daily except Sun--established 1903, soon merged with Florence Daily Times. Evening Herald Mar 2, 1904 = vol 1, no 69, J. W. Ragsdale (editor and publisher). Florence Daily Times (May 11, 1904) has sub-head "and Evening Herald." By Sep 1904 this sub-head has disappeared. *Files: Darlington County Historical Commission Mar 2, 8, 11, 1904; SCL Mar 19, 1904, mfm Mar 2, 8, 11, 1904.*

EXAMINER   weekly, semi-weekly--established Feb 1977, ceased c. 1978. Feb 16, 1977 = vol 1, no 1, William B. Williams (editor and publisher). Began as Wed weekly, issued semi-weekly (Jun-Jul 1978), then became a Fri weekly. Also published Lake City and Timmonsville editions. Not cited by Ayer. *Files: Florence CL and SCL Feb 16, 1977-Oct 27, 1978.*

FARMERS' FRIEND   weekly--established in Timmonsville in 1887. Cited in Florence by Ayer 1889: J. W. Hammond (editor and publisher). Became Florence Messenger c. 1889. See Farmers' Friend [Timmonsville].

FLORENCE ADVERTISER   weekly--established 1932, ceased c. 1932. Not cited by Ayer. Aug 6, 1932 = vol 1, no 2, W. B. King (editor), J. I. Barr (publisher). *Files: SCL mfm Aug 6, 1932.*

FLORENCE COUNTY NEWS & SHOPPER   see News & Shopper.

FLORENCE DAILY TIMES   daily except Sun--established 1894, absorbed Evening Herald in 1904, merged with Morning News Review Mar 27, 1925. Also issued as Daily Times. Aug 27, 1894 = vol 1, no 20, John P. Coffin (editor). Hartwell M. Ayer, James D. Evans, and Mason C. Brunson also associated with paper. *Files: Darlington County Historical Commission ((1898)), 1911; Florence CL mfm ((1895-1899)) 870; SCL (1904-1924) 60, mfm ((1894-1923)) 1000.*

FLORENCE EVENING STAR   daily except Sun--established 1939, continued by the Florence Star Mar 1941. Aug 4, 1939 = vol 1, no 1, John Zeigler (editor), Melvin Purvis (publisher). Cited in Ayer 1940 and Ayer 1941. *Files: Darlington County Historical Commission ((Oct 1939-Mar 1941)); Florence CL ((Aug 1939-Mar 1941)).*

FLORENCE GAZETTE   weekly c. 1869. Cited once in Rowell (1869), but no data provided by the Gazette. Ceased c. 1869. *NFK*

FLORENCE JOURNAL weekly--established c. 1978, ceased c. 1983. Not cited in Ayer. Frank Martin (publisher). According to J. B. Harris (publisher of News & Shopper), Florence Journal lasted for about fifteen months. *NFK*

FLORENCE MESSENGER weekly--established in Timmonsville in 1887 as Farmers' Friend, moved to Florence c. 1888, became Florence Messenger Oct 4, 1889. Merged with County Banner in 1896 to create Banner Messenger and then with Florence Times to create Times-Messenger. Cited Ayer 1890 thru 1897. Oct 16, 1891 = vol 5, no 16, J. W. Hammond (editor and publisher). *Files: Darlington County Historical Commission (1891-1894) 4; Florence CL (1894-1896) 6; SCL mfm Oct 16, 1891, May 25, 1894, Dec 6, 1895.*

FLORENCE MONITOR weekly--established 1883, ceased c. 1885. Cited once in Ayer (1885), no personnel listed. *NFK*

FLORENCE MORNING NEWS daily except Mon, daily--created 1929 by name change, formerly Morning News Review. On Feb 3, 1929 (vol 34, no 571) became Morning ("Florence" on a globe) News, J. B. Parnell (president), J. M. McDowd (secretary and treasurer), Mason C. Brunson (editor), Florence Printing Company. On Dec 2, 1945 (vol 22, no 592) became Florence Morning News. Issued daily except Mon until Aug 8, 1949, when became daily. James A. Rogers, Joe W. Rickenbaker, Richard G. Moisio, Thom Anderson, and Tenney S. Griffin also associated with paper. Note: Volume 34 (1929) is based upon founding date of the Florence Daily Times (1894), which merged with the Morning News Review in 1925. Florence Morning News now cites founding date of 1922. *Files: Darlington County Historical Commission 1929-1981; Clemson, Florence CL, Florence Morning News, and SCL mfm 1929 + .*

FLORENCE OBSERVER daily, evenings except Sun--established 1931, ceased c. 1935. Cited by Ayer 1933 and 1934: W. J. Stricklin (editor), Pee Dee Printing Company. *NFK*

FLORENCE PIONEER weekly--established 1872, ceased c. 1876. Cited Rowell 1873 thru 1876. Jul 18, 1873 = vol 1, no 31, Jerome P. Chase (editor), W. W. McDiarmid (proprietor). Pioneer offered for sale in this issue. According to Rowell 1874-1876, William Little (editor and publisher). *Files: Florence CL Jul 18, 1873; SCL mfm Jul 18, 1873.*

FLORENCE REFLECTOR weekly, Democrat--established 1892, ceased c. 1894. Published in Conway as Horry Monitor and in Kingstree as Alliance Ladder. Cited once in Ayer (1893/4): T. C. Willoughby (editor and publisher). *NFK*

FLORENCE STAR daily, evening--established as Florence Evening Star Aug 1939, became Florence Star Mar 1941, ceased c. 1941. First issue Mar 21, 1941 = vol 3, no 69, Star Publishing Company. *Files: Darlington County Historical Commission ((Mar-Oct 1941)); Florence CL ((Mar-Oct 1941)).*

FLORENCE TIMES   weekly--according to Rowell 1877 thru 1879, this paper was established in 1876. Paper later would claim founding date of 1865. Cited Rowell and Ayer 1877 thru 1897. Rowell 1877: Chase, Brunson, and Hart (editors and publishers). Merged with Florence Messenger in 1896 to create Times-Messenger, weekly edition of the Florence Daily Times. Jan 7, 1884 = vol 27, no 14, C. H. Prince (editor and proprietor). Hartwell M. Ayer and John P. Coffin also associated with paper. *Files: Florence CL (1893-1895) 15, mfm (1884, 1894-1895) 31; SCL Sep 15, 1887, mfm (1884, 1894-1895), 31.*

FLORENCE TIMES   weekly--established 1965, ceased c. 1970. Sep 30, 1965 = vol 1, no 1, Mark W. Buyck, Jr., (president), Morrell L. Thomas (editor), Panorama Publishing Company. Cited Ayer 1966 thru 1978. Ayer 1966-1969: Morrell Thomas (editor), Panorama Publishing Company; Ayer 1970-1978: Jimmy Howle (editor), Panorama Publishing Company. Chester A. Martin also associated with paper. *Files: Darlington County Historical Commission ((1967-1969)); Florence CL ((1965-1970)).*

FLORENTINE   weekly c. 1958. Lem Winesett (editor and publisher). Cited by State Chamber of Commerce publications, 1958. *NFK*

JOINT ENTERPRISE   semi-monthly, black publication--established 1910, ceased c. 1910. Cited once in Ayer (1911): Joint Enterprise Publishing Company. *NFK*

KEY   weekly, black publication c. 1979-1980. Printed in Florence largely for markets outside of the community. *NFK*

MORNING NEWS   see Florence Morning News.

MORNING NEWS REVIEW   daily except Mon--established Mar 1922 as Weekly News Review, c. Mar 1923 became Morning News Review. Jun 9, 1923 = vol 1, no 49, J. A. Zeigler (editor), J. B. Parnell (manager). Note: All existing Jun 1923 issues are "no 49." Merged with Florence Daily Times Mar 27, 1925, but retained name of Morning News Review until Feb 3, 1929, when paper became the Morning [Florence] News. Continued by the Florence Morning News on Dec 2, 1945. J. A. Zeigler (editor, 1923-1928). Mason C. Brunson also associated with paper. *Files: Darlington County Historical Commission 1924-1929; SCL (1923) 18; Clemson, Florence CL, Florence Morning News, and SCL mfm 1924-1929.*

NEWS & SHOPPER   weekly--established Nov 10, 1982, J. B. Harris (editor and publisher). *Files: News & Shopper 1982 + .*

NEWS & SHOPPER   weekly--regional edition of News & Shopper published in Myrtle Beach for Williamsburg County and lower Florence County c. 1977-1986. Continued by Williamsburg-Florence Journal Nov 1986. See News & Shopper [Myrtle Beach] and the Myrtle Beach Journal.

REFORM ADVOCATE   weekly--established as a Farmers' Alliance publication in 1893, ceased c. 1914. Cited Ayer 1893/4 thru 1914. Ayer 1893/4: W. F. Clayton (editor), Miller and Sansbury (publishers). Apr 4, 1895 (no vol no), W. F. Clayton (editor), Reform Publishing Company. G. R. Pettigrew, George Galletly, J. W. Ragsdale, J. S. Abercrombie, and Hartwell M. Ayer also associated with paper. Cited by Ayer 1905-1914 as the Advocate. *Files: SCL Apr 4, 1895.*

SUNDAY NEWS REVIEW   title of Sun edition of Morning News Review c. 1925-1929--see Morning News Review.

TIMES-MESSENGER   weekly--created 1896 by merger of Florence Times and Banner Messenger, ceased c. 1919. Issued as weekly edition of the Florence Daily Times. Cited by Ayer 1896 thru 1919. Oct 8, 1896 = vol 1, no 26, H. L. Darr (manager), H. A. Brunson (editor). Hartwell M. Ayer also associated with paper. *Files: Florence CL mfm (1896-1899) 40; SCL mfm (1896-1919) 48.*

WEEKLY NEWS REVIEW   weekly--established Mar 18, 1922, by Mar 1923 had become Morning News Review, daily except Mon. Jun 15, 1922 = vol 1, no 7, J. A. Zeigler (editor), Florence Printing Company. *Files: Darlington County Historical Commission Dec 14, 1922; SCL Jun 15, 22, 1922.*

WILLIAMSBURG-FLORENCE JOURNAL   weekly--established Jun 1986, continues News & Shopper. See News & Shopper [Myrtle Beach] and the Myrtle Beach Journal. *Files: Myrtle Beach Journal 1986 + .*

LAKE CITY

COUNTY NEWS   see Rutledge County News.

DEWEY EAGLE   weekly, independent--established 1898, moved to Latta c. 1900. Cited in Lake City by Ayer 1900: W. H. Kirton (editor), W. H. Kirton and W. H. Edwards (publishers). *NFK*

LAKE CITY NEWS   weekly, independent--established 1895, ceased c. 1896. Listed in Ayer (1896): Southern Publishing Company. No personnel cited. *NFK*

LAKE CITY NEWS   weekly, semi-weekly, tri-weekly--established 1910, merged with the Lake City Post in May 1972 to create the Lake City News and Post. Sep 1, 1910 = vol 1, no 20. Cited Ayer 1912 thru 1977. Ayer 1912: W. S. Stokes (editor and publisher). J. S. Stokes, George S. Coadery, W. F. Tolley, L. H. Cromer, Jr., A. W. Wimberly, Mrs. A. M. Parker, Morrell L. Thomas, Jr., and Gordon B. Gardener also associated with paper. Issued weekly except 1920 (semi-weekly) and 1971-1972 (tri-weekly). During the 1930s paper cited a founding date of 1900, by 1950, 1888. *Files: Darlington County Historical Commission Feb 19, 1931; Lake City News and Post 1970-1972; SCL (1917-1954) 75, mfm Sep 1, 1910 (fragment), Feb 19, 1931.*

LAKE CITY NEWS AND POST   tri-weekly, weekly--established May 1972 by merger of Lake City News and Lake City Post. First joint issue May 1, 1972 = vol 67, no 131, Greg Smith (general manager), Banner Publishing Company. Barry Myers also associated with paper, which issues the Penny Pincher (weekly shopper). *Files: Lake City News and Post ((1972-1978)), 1979 + .*

LAKE CITY POST   weekly, semi-weekly--established Jul 1968, merged with Lake City News May 1972 to form Lake City News and Post. Jul 1, 1968 = vol 1, no 1, Jimmie Howle (editor), Chester A. Martin (publisher). *Files: Lake City News and Post 1968-1972.*

LAKE CITY TIMES   weekly--established 1895, ceased c. 1899. Cited Ayer 1896 thru 1899. Ayer 1896: Frank Carter (editor), Times Publishing Company. Carl W. Hill and W. H. Kirton also associated with paper. *NFK*

LAKE CITY WEEKLY   weekly--established 1889, ceased c. 1889. Cited once in Ayer (1889): W. L. Bass (editor and publisher). *NFK*

PENNY PINCHER   see Lake City News and Post.

RURAL EXPONENT   weekly--established 1890, ceased c. 1891. Cited Ayer 1890 and 1891: M. L. Rodgers (editor and publisher). *NFK*

RUTLEDGE COUNTY NEWS   weekly--established 1908, ceased c. 1910. Cited Ayer 1909 and 1910: Stewart Starr (editor and publisher). Mar 6, 1908 = vol 1, no 6, no personnel listed. Hartwell M. Ayer also associated with this unsuccessful effort to create "Rutledge County." May also have been issued as County News. *Files: SCL mfm Mar 6, 1908, Aug 6, 1909.*

SOUTH CAROLINA BAPTIST   weekly--printed in several South Carolina communities. According to Ayer, established in Lake City by A. McA. Pittman in 1898. Had moved to Greenwood by 1899. See South Carolina Baptist [Greenwood].

TIMES-HERALD   weekly, semi-weekly--established 1949, ceased c. 1967. Began weekly, issued semi-weekly Apr 1950-Jan 1951, then weekly again. Cited Ayer 1951 thru 1967. Jan 6, 1950 = vol 1, no 24, Anderson-Fowler Printers. Ayer 1951: C. L. Anderson (editor), D. Howard Anderson (publisher). Julia S. Parker and Arthur M. Parker also associated with paper. *Files: SCL ((1950-1959)) 350, 1960-1966.*

OLANTA

OLANTA OBSERVER   weekly--established 1915, ceased c. 1920. Cited Ayer 1916 thru 1920. Ayer 1916: M. D. Myers (editor and publisher). Feb 22, 1917 = vol 2, no 30, no personnel listed. W. M. Wall, S. J. Tomlinson, and Frank McCormick also associated with paper. *Files: SCL Feb 22, 1917.*

SCRANTON

NEWS   weekly--established 1900, ceased c. 1902. Cited Ayer 1901 and 1902: W. Eugene Cooke (editor), W. Hampton Edwards (publisher). *NFK*

TIMMONSVILLE

ADVERTISER   weekly--established 1934, ceased c. 1934. Oct 10, 1934 = vol 1, no 1, no personnel listed. Not cited in Ayer. *Files: SCL Oct 10, 1934.*

BATTLE AX   weekly--established 1901, ceased c. 1902. Cited Ayer 1902: Apple and Berger (editors and publishers). *NFK*

CAROLINA PLANTER   weekly, monthly--established 1902, ceased c. 1909. Cited by Ayer 1904 thru 1909: Charles F. Sansbury (editor and publisher). Listed as weekly (1904), monthly (1905-1909). May be revival of earlier publication by same name. See Carolina Planter [Florence and Darlington]. *NFK*

FARMERS' FRIEND   weekly--established 1887, moved to Florence c. 1888 and became Florence Messenger. Dec 15, 1887 = vol 1, no 23, Farmers' Friend Company. Cited Ayer 1888 in Timmonsville: J. W. Hammond (editor and publisher). *Files: Darlington County Historical Commission Dec 15, 1887.*

FLORENCE COUNTY JOURNAL   weekly--established 1925, ceased c. 1929. Cited Ayer 1925 thru 1929. Ayer 1925: D. E. Stokes (editor and publisher). Mar 10, 1927 = vol 3, no 10, J. P. Ward (editor). *Files: Darlington County Historical Commission Jan 6, Mar 10, 1927.*

GOSPEL BUGLE   weekly, evangelical--established 1892, ceased c. 1893. Cited once in Ayer (1892): W. B. Duncan (editor and publisher). *NFK*

JOINT STOCK NEWS   semi-monthly, black publication--established 1914, ceased c. 1915. Cited once in Ayer (1915): N. G. Sparks (editor), Joint Stock News Company (publisher). *NFK*

PEE DEE WATCHMAN   weekly, black publication--established 1909, merged with [Sumter] Defender in 1913 to form the Pee Dee Watchman and Defender. Cited in Ayer 1911 thru 1914: H. C. Asbury (editor), Watchman Publishing Company (publisher). According to the Watchman and Defender, the Pee Dee Watchman was established Dec 16, 1909. *NFK*

PEE DEE WATCHMAN AND DEFENDER   weekly, black publication--created Feb 23, 1913 by merger of Pee Dee Watchman and [Sumter] Defender. Cited Ayer 1915 thru 1919: H. C. Asbury (editor), Watchman Publishing Company. Continued c. 1920 as Watchman and Defender. *NFK*

TIMMONSVILLE ENTERPRISE   weekly--established 1895, ceased c. 1925. Oct 11, 1895 = vol 1, no 19, J. W. Ragsdale (editor and proprietor). Cited Ayer 1897 thru 1925. Ayer 1897: J. W. Ragsdale (editor and proprietor). W. E. Lea, J. E. Boskin, Charles F. Sansbury, J. W. McLendon, T. E. Stokes, Louis W. Sansbury, Roy Swindelle, Jack Wells, and J. A. Zeigler also associated with paper. *Files: Darlington County Historical Commission (1904-1920) 30; Florence CL Oct 11, 1895, Sep 17, 1896; SCL Oct 28, 1897 (vol 3, no 22), a souvenir edition, not a real issue.*

TIMMONSVILLE NEWS   weekly--established 1873, ceased c. 1876. Cited Rowell 1874 thru 1876. Rowell 1874: L. B. McQueen (editor and publisher)..."only pure democratic [sic] paper in Darlington County." Rowell 1875 and 1876: J. W. Hammond (editor and publisher). *NFK*

TIMMONSVILLE NEWS   weekly--established 1891, ceased c. 1893. Cited once in Ayer (1892): Henry J. Gasque (editor and publisher). *NFK*

TIMMONSVILLE NEWS   weekly--established 1925, ceased c. 1933. Erratic citations in Ayer. Cited 1927 as established 1925, no personnel listed. Not cited 1928. Cited 1929 and 1930 as established 1925: L. H. Cromer, Jr. (publisher). Not listed 1930 and 1931. Cited 1933 as established 1928: Lewis H. Wallace (editor), L. H. Cromer, Jr. (publisher). Jun 7, 1928 = vol 1, no 33, L. H. Cromer, Jr. (publisher). *Files: Darlington County Historical Commission Jun 7, 1928, Jan 2, 1930.*

TIMMONSVILLE NEWS   weekly--established 1964, ceased c. 1972. Apr 29, 1964 = vol 1, no 6, Rutledge Printing Company. Cited in Southern Bell media handbook 1967 thru 1971. T. V. Rutledge, Charles A. Martin, and Phyllis A. Valentin associated with paper. Not cited in Ayer. *Files: Darlington County Historical Commission Apr 29, Oct 28, 1964.*

TIMMONSVILLE NEWS-ARGUS   weekly--established 1937, ceased c. 1937. Not cited in Ayer. Feb 19, 1937 = vol 1, no 6, Charles F. Sansbury (editor). *Files: Darlington County Historical Commission Feb 19, Apr 30, 1937.*

TIMMONSVILLE TIMES   weekly--established Jun 7, 1946, ceased c. 1958. Cited Ayer 1948 thru 1958. Ayer 1948: Mason C. Brunson, Jr., (editor), Timmonsville Times, Inc. A. M. Parker, H. E. Carraway, A. A. Hennon, and James O. Howle also associated with paper. Jun 7, 1946 = vol 1, no 1, F. F. Williams (publisher). *Files: Darlington County Historical Commission ((1946-1957)); SCL Jul 14, 1955.*

WATCHMAN AND DEFENDER   weekly, black publication--created by name change c. 1920, continues Pee Dee Watchman and Defender, ceased c. 1931. Cited Ayer 1920 thru 1931: H. C. Asbury (editor and publisher). Jul 23, 1920 = vol 7, no 12, H. C. Asbury (editor). *Files: Darlington County Historical Commission Jul 23, 1920.*

GEORGETOWN COUNTY

Georgetown District, now Georgetown County, was one of seven judicial districts created in 1769. Like most of these new governmental units, Georgetown District assumed the name of its most important community, the port city that honors the memory of England's King George II.

ANDREWS

ANDREWS HERALD   weekly c. 1958. Martin Meadows (editor and publisher). Cited in State Chamber of Commerce literature. *NFK*

ANDREWS NEWS   weekly, independent--established 1918, ceased c. 1924. Jan 3, 1918 = vol 1, no 1, E. N. Beard (editor), Beard Publishing Company. Cited in Ayer 1919 thru 1924. Ayer 1919-1920: E. N. Beard (editor and publisher). Ayer 1921-1924: H. Douglas Oswald (editor), Eastern Carolina Publishing Company. *Files: Georgetown CL and SCL mfm Jan 31, 1918-Sep 2, 1921.*

ANDREWS NEWS   weekly--established 1949, ceased c. 1950. Not cited by Ayer. Mar 30, 1949 = vol 1, no 1. J. J. Hinds identified as publisher in next issue. *Files: Georgetown CL and SCL mfm Mar 30, 1949-Mar 30, 1950.*

ANDREWS STAR   weekly, independent--established 1954, ceased c. 1958. Cited Ayer 1955 thru 1958. Sep 2, 1954 = vol 1, no 1, Mrs. J. D. Howle (editor), A. A. Hennon (publisher). James O. Howle and Mrs. C. C. Blake also associated with paper. *Files: SCL Sep 2, 1954-Aug 25, 1955.*

COASTAL CHRONICLE   weekly, Democrat--established 1922, ceased c. 1927. Cited Ayer 1924 thru 1927. Issued with Andrews and Georgetown datelines c. 1926-1927. Nov 23, 1922 = vol 1, no 1, Archie Lewis (manager and publisher), Palmetto Printing Company. Louis J. McConnell also associated with paper. *Files: Georgetown CL and SCL mfm Nov 23, 1922-Dec 25, 1924, Apr 8, 1926-Jun 24, 1927.*

GEORGETOWN

CAROLINA AMERICAN, AND GEORGETOWN GAZETTE   semi-weekly c. 1813. Apr 10, 1813 = vol 16, no 1434, Thomas Tolman (publisher). Continues Georgetown Gazette, and Commercial Advertiser, continued by Georgetown Gazette. *Files: SCL mfm Apr 10, 17, 1813.*

CAROLINA FIELD   weekly--established 1905, ceased c. 1905. Not cited by Ayer. May 3, 1905 = vol 1, no 1, James Henry Rice, Jr. (editor), Field Publishing Company. *Files: Georgetown CL and SCL mfm May 3-Dec 27, 1905.*

COASTAL CHRONICLE see Coastal Chronicle [Andrews].

COMET AND NEWS weekly, semi-weekly--created 1877 by merger of Georgetown Comet and Horry News [Conway], by Sep 1878 had merged with Georgetown Times, continued by Times and Comet. Oct 3, 1877 = vol 4, no 2, Moses L. Dorrill (proprietor). Not cited in Rowell. *Files: Clemson, Francis Marion, and Georgetown CL mfm Oct 3, 1877; SCL Jan 25, 1878, mfm Oct 3, 1877.*

DAILY AMERICAN daily except Sun--established 1973, merged with Grand Strand Journal Jun 1973, continued by Grand Strand Journal American with offices in Georgetown and Myrtle Beach. Mar 7, 1973 = vol 1, no 1, Lucien Agniel (editor), United Communications Company. *Files: SCL (Mar 7-Jun 23, 1973) 80.*

GEORGETOWN ADVOCATE weekly, black publication--established 1902, ceased c. 1905. Jun 7, 1902 = vol 1, no 1, R. B. Salters, G. E. Herriot, W. P. Carolina (editors), Georgetown Advocate Company. Motto: "God bless all our people, both white and black." Cited by Ayer 1904 and 1905. *Files: Georgetown CL and SCL mfm (Jun 7, 1902-Jun 6, 1903) 39.*

GEORGETOWN AMERICAN weekly, semi-weekly--established 1839, ceased Mar 3, 1841. Nov 9, 1839 = vol 1, no 1, William Chapman (editor and publisher). Dec 1840 Chapman sold paper to Eleazer Waterman, who announced plans to publish the Winyah Observer. During its brief career, the Georgetown American vacillated between weekly and semi-weekly status. *Files: Georgetown CL and SCL mfm (Nov 9, 1839-Mar 3, 1841) 72.*

GEORGETOWN CHRONICLE, AND SOUTH-CAROLINA ADVERTISER semi-weekly c. 1797--continues Georgetown Chronicle, and South-Carolina Weekly Advertiser, ceased c. 1798. Changed title sometime in the summer of 1797. Sep 23, 1797 = vol 7, no 345, James Smylie (printer). *Files: SCL mfm Sep 23, Nov 1, 1797.*

GEORGETOWN CHRONICLE, AND SOUTH-CAROLINA WEEKLY AD-VERTISER weekly--continues South-Carolina Independent Gazette, and Georgetown Chronicle, no change in number sequence. According to Brigham, title changed between 1792 and 1796. In summer of 1797 continued by Georgetown Chronicle, and South-Carolina Advertiser. Mar 22, 1796 = vol 6, no 262, James Smylie (printer). *Files: SCL mfm Mar 22, 1796, Jan 19, 1797.*

GEORGETOWN COMET weekly--established 1874, merged with Horry News [Conway] in 1877, continued by Comet and News. Cited by Rowell 1875 thru 1877. Rowell 1875: M. L. Dorrill and E. H. Williams (editors and publishers). Dec 20, 1876 = vol 3, no 13, Moses L. Dorrill (editor and proprietor), C. W. Rouse (publisher). *Files: Clemson, Francis Marion, Georgetown CL, and SCL mfm Dec 20, 1876.*

GEORGETOWN DAILY ITEM daily--established 1907, ceased c. 1913. May 1, 1907 = vol 1, no 1, C. W. Rouse (manager), Georgetown Daily Item Company. Circa

1910 absorbed Sunday Outlook, which became Sun edition of paper. *Files: Georgetown CL and SCL mfm May 1, 1907-Sep 30, 1912.*

GEORGETOWN ENQUIRER weekly, Democrat--established 1880, ceased 1889. Oct 13, 1880 = vol 1, no 1, Walter Hazard (editor and proprietor). On Oct 30, 1889, Hazard sold paper to Josiah Doar, editor and publisher of the Georgetown Times. *Files: Francis Marion, Georgetown CL, and SCL mfm Oct 13, 1880-Oct 30, 1889.*

GEORGETOWN EVENING CHRONICLE weekly, black publication-- established 1903, ceased c. 1906. Cited by Ayer 1905 and 1906: R. B. Salters (editor), Chronicle Company. *NFK*

GEORGETOWN GAZETTE weekly, semi-weekly--established May 8, 1798 by ----- Elliott and John Burd. Continued in 1806 by the Georgetown Gazette, and Commercial Advertiser. Andrew M'Farlan and Joseph Hamilton also associated with paper. Issued semi-weekly from Sep 1798-Jan 1799, 1800-1806. *Files: CLS May 15, 1798-Dec 27, 1800; Francis Marion and Georgetown CL mfm ((1799-1806)) 108; SCL Nov 6, 1799, Jul 30, 1806, mfm ((1798-1806)) 110. Note: Semi-weekly edition for 1801 complete on mfm reels.*

GEORGETOWN GAZETTE semi-weekly c. 1814-1815--continues Carolina American, and Georgetown Gazette, continued by Georgetown Gazette, and Mercantile Advertiser. Apr 27, 1814 = vol 17, no 1536, Edward B. Cooke (publisher). *Files: SCL mfm Apr 27, 1814.*

GEORGETOWN GAZETTE semi-weekly--established 1823, ceased c. 1826. Feb 23, 1824 = vol 1, no 36, H. C. Flagg and Benjamin Green (editors), G. W. Addison & Company (publisher). Oct 19, 1824 (vol 2, no 1) notes that two inner pages of semi-weekly editions were issued each Fri as the "Country Paper" at $3 per annum. *Files: CLS Oct 18, 1825-Oct 13, 1826; SCL mfm (1824-1825) 10.*

GEORGETOWN GAZETTE [For the Country] weekly c. 1824-1826. Inner pages of semi-weekly edition. *Files: Library of Congress (Feb-Apr 1824) 3. Apparently no files in SC.*

GEORGETOWN GAZETTE, AND COMMERCIAL ADVERTISER semi-weekly c. 1806-1810--continues Georgetown Gazette, continued by Carolina American, and Georgetown Gazette. Jun 20, 1807 = vol 10, no 858, Francis M. Baxter (publisher). *Files: Francis Marion and Georgetown CL mfm Jun 20, 27, Jul 1, 1807, Feb 17, 1810; SCL Jun 20, 27, Jul 1, 1807, Feb 17, 1810, mfm (1806-1810) 18.*

GEORGETOWN GAZETTE, AND MERCANTILE ADVERTISER semi-weekly c. 1815-1817--continues Georgetown Gazette, continued by the Winyah Intelligencer. Jul 5, 1815 = vol 18, no 1511, ----- Baxter and Eleazer Waterman (publishers). *Files: Francis Marion and Georgetown CL mfm Jun 5, 1816; SCL mfm ((Jul 5, 1815-Feb 8, 1817)) 116.*

GEORGETOWN HERALD   semi-weekly--established 1918, ceased 1918. Mar 22, 1918 = vol 1, no 1, L. B. Steele (editor), Georgetown Herald, Inc. When Steele quit on Sep 10, 1918, operations ceased. Cited once by Ayer (1919). *Files: Georgetown CL and SCL mfm (Mar 22-Sep 10, 1918) 40.*

GEORGETOWN INDEX   weekly--established Mar 12, 1920, E. N. Beard (editor). Merged with Georgetown Times Apr 2, 1920, continued by Georgetown Times-Index. *Files: Georgetown CL and SCL mfm Mar 12-26, 1920.*

GEORGETOWN JOURNAL   weekly--established Jun 1986, continues News & Shopper [Myrtle Beach]. See Myrtle Beach Journal. *Files: Myrtle Beach Journal 1986 + .*

GEORGETOWN PLANET   weekly, Republican, black publication--established 1873, ceased c. 1875. May 31, 1873 = vol 1, no 10, James A. Bowley (editor), R. O. Bush (associate editor), Planet Publishing Company. Cited by Rowell 1873 thru 1875. *Files: Georgetown CL mfm Oct 17, 1874; SCL mfm May 31, 1873, Oct 17, 1874.*

GEORGETOWN SEMI-WEEKLY TIMES   semi-weekly--Jan-Aug1893, continues Georgetown Times, continued by Georgetown Times: Semi-Weekly Edition. Jan 4, 1893 = vol 27, no 44, Josiah Doar (editor). Motto: "Chained to no party's arbitrary sway, we'll cleave to truth where'er she leads the way." *Files: Clemson, Georgetown CL, and SCL mfm Jan-Aug 1893.*

GEORGETOWN SEMI-WEEKLY TIMES   semi-weekly--Mar 1894-Dec 1904, continues Georgetown Times, continued by Georgetown Times. Mar 10, 1894 = vol 28, no 103, Josiah Doar (editor). *Files: Clemson, Georgetown CL, and SCL mfm Mar 1894-Dec 1904.*

GEORGETOWN TIMES   weekly--established 1866, merged with Comet and News c. 1878, continued by Times and Comet. Jun 17, 1869 = vol 4, no 14, John W. Tarbox (publisher). Jan 22, 1874 = vol 8, no 47, new series, established 1817, "the only paper that circulates among white men of Georgetown County." Paper currently cites founding date of 1797. *Files: Clemson, Francis Marion, Georgetown CL mfm Jun 17, 1869, Feb 8, 1877; SCL (1869-1875) 5, mfm Jun 17, 1869, Feb 8, 1877.*

GEORGETOWN TIMES   weekly--1880-1892, continues Times and Comet, continued by Georgetown Semi-Weekly Times. Sep 2, 1880 = vol 15, no 26, Joseph Sessions (proprietor). Josiah Doar also associated with paper. *Files: Clemson, Francis Marion, Georgetown CL, and SCL mfm Sep 2, 1880, Jan 11, Nov 7, 1885, Oct 1889-Dec 1892.*

GEORGETOWN TIMES   semi-weekly--Aug 1893-Mar 1894, continues Georgetown Times: Semi-Weekly Edition, continued by Georgetown Semi-Weekly Times. Aug 19,

1893 = vol 28, no 48, Josiah Doar (editor). *Files: Clemson, Georgetown CL, and SCL mfm Aug 1893-Mar 1894.*

GEORGETOWN TIMES   semi-weekly, weekly--Jan 1905-Mar 1920, continues Georgetown Semi-Weekly Times, continued by Georgetown Times-Index. Jan 4, 1905 = vol 39, no 86, Josiah Doar (editor), published and printed by J. Benjamin Doar and Russell Doar. Paper issued semi-weekly to Jan 1920, then weekly. *Files: Georgetown CL and SCL mfm Jan 1905-Mar 1920*

GEORGETOWN TIMES   weekly, semi-weekly, tri-weekly--1921 to present, continues Georgetown Times-Index. Sep 9, 1921 = vol 126, no 39, A. T. Wendt (publisher). J. P. LaBruce, L. H. Wallace, J. J. Hinds, L. C. Davis, Thomas Petigru Davis, Lawrence L. McConnell, Robert D. Gorman, and Samuel R. Marshall also associated with paper. Issued weekly to Mar 27, 1973, semi-weekly to Nov 4, 1983, then tri-weekly. In 1985 masthead title (but not inside running heads) shortened to Times. *Files: Georgetown Times 1956 + ; Georgetown CL and SCL mfm 1921 + .*

GEORGETOWN TIMES: SEMI-WEEKLY EDITION   semi-weekly--Aug 5-16, 1893, continues Georgetown Semi-Weekly Times, continued by Georgetown Times. Aug 5, 1893 = vol 27, no 43, Josiah Doar (editor). *Files: Clemson, Georgetown CL, and SCL mfm Aug 5-16, 1893.*

GEORGETOWN TIMES-INDEX   weekly--created by merger of Georgetown Times and Georgetown Index Apr 1920, continued by Georgetown Times Sep 9, 1921. First three issues contain no vol-issue data. Apr 23, 1920 = vol 124, no 4, E. N. Beard (editor). This sequence is based upon the Georgetown Gazette of the 1790s. *Files: Georgetown CL mfm 1920-1921; SCL (1920-1921) 40, mfm 1920-1921.*

GEORGETOWN UNION   weekly--established 1830, ceased c. 1839. Jul 12, 1831 (fragment) = vol 1, no 73. John Matthews & Company cited as publisher in 1835. *Files: Georgetown CL mfm (Sep 1837-Aug 1839) 88; SCL Jul 12, 1831, May 23, 1835, mfm (Sep 1837-Aug 1839) 88.*

GRAND STRAND JOURNAL AMERICAN   see Grand Strand Journal American [Myrtle Beach].

HARVEST   weekly, semi-weekly c. 1827-1828. Oct 17, 1828 = vol 1, no 9, A. B. Shackelford (publisher). *Files: American Antiquarian Society Oct 17, Dec 12, 19, 1828. Apparently no files in SC.*

JOURNAL AMERICAN   see Journal American [Myrtle Beach].

NEWS & SHOPPER   see News & Shopper [Myrtle Beach].

OUTLOOK weekly, Democrat--established Jan 1901, continued by Sunday Outlook Dec 1901. Jan 25, 1901 = vol 1, no 1, C. W. Wolfe (editor), C. W. Wolfe Publishing Company. *Files: Georgetown CL and SCL mfm 1901.*

PEE DEE TIMES weekly--established 1853, ceased c. 1861. Mar 9, 1853 = vol 1, no 9, R. Dozier, E. Waterman, Jr., and J. W. Tarbox (publishers and proprietors). *Files: Georgetown CL mfm Mar 1853-Jul 1858, (1859-1861) 5; SCL Dec 26, 1860, mfm Mar 1853-Jul 1858, (1859-1861) 5.*

PROGRESSIVE DEMOCRAT weekly, Democrat--established 1913, ceased c. 1916. Nov 13, 1913 = vol 1, no 1, Arthur L. King (editor), Thomas W. Barfield (owner and publisher). C. W. Rouse also associated with paper. *Files: Georgetown CL mfm Nov 1913-Feb 1916; SCL (1914-1915) 9, mfm Nov 1913-Feb 1916.*

SOUTH-CAROLINA INDEPENDENT GAZETTE, AND GEORGETOWN CHRONICLE weekly--established 1791, continued by Georgetown Chronicle, and South-Carolina Weekly Advertiser sometime between 1792 and 1796. May 21, 1791 = vol 1, no 8, James Carson (printer). Eight issues available in Readex Microprint # 1894. *Files: SCL mfm (1791-1792) 8; USC mp (1791-1792) 8.*

SUNDAY OUTLOOK Sun weekly, Democrat--continues Outlook. Dec 1, 1901 = vol 2, no 20, J. Walter Doar (editor), Outlook Printing Company. Circa 1910 became Sun edition of the Georgetown Daily Item. Cited by Ayer 1903 thru 1913. Ceased c. 1913. C. W. Rouse also associated with paper. *Files: Georgetown CL mfm Dec 1901-Jun 1911; SCL (1901-1907) 8, mfm Dec 1901-Jun 1911.*

TIMES see Georgetown Times c. 1985.

TIMES AND COMET weekly, Democrat--created by merger of Georgetown Times and Comet and News c. 1878, continued by Georgetown Times c. 1880. Sep 19, 1878 = vol 13, no 29, Josiah Doar (proprietor), Moses L. Dorrill and Joseph Sessions also associated with paper. *Files: Clemson, Francis Marion, and Georgetown CL mfm (1878-1880) 8; SCL Sep 11, 25, 1879, Jul 1, 8, 1880, mfm (1878-1880) 8.*

TRUE REPUBLICAN weekly--established 1849, ceased Dec 1852 when purchased by owners of the Winyah Observer. Feb 13, 1850 = vol 1, no 13, Leonard Dozier (editor). *Files: SCL mfm Feb 13, 1850.*

WINYAH INTELLIGENCER semi-weekly, weekly--established 1817, ceased c. 1835. Nov 15, 1817 = vol 1, no 11, Eleazer Waterman (publisher). James Smith, John A. Keith, W. A. Norris, and William B. Toler also associated with paper. Issued semi-weekly to Aug 1833, then weekly. Eighty-nine issues available in Readex Microprint # 1895. *Files: CLS orig & mfm 1825, 1827, Jan 1832-Jun 1833; Clemson Oct 20, Nov 10, 1832, Feb 23, 1833; Georgetown CL mfm (Sep-Dec 1819) 12, (1834-1835) 27; SCL Mar 11, Aug 12, 1834, mfm ((1817-1835)) 264; USC mp (1817-1820) 89.*

WINYAH OBSERVER   weekly, semi-weekly--established 1841, ceased 1852. Issued weekly during summer months.   Mar 10, 1841 = vol 1, no 1, Eleazer Waterman (publisher).   Eleazer Waterman, Jr., J. W. Tarbox, and Richard Dozier also associated with paper.   On Dec 29, 1852 owners announced purchase of the True Republican and plans to launch the Pee Dee Times. *Files: Georgetown CL mfm ((1841-1844)) 220, 1845-1852; SCL Nov 8, 1845, mfm ((1841-1844)) 220, 1845-1852.*

MURRELL'S INLET

MURRELL'S INLET-GARDEN CITY NEWS   weekly c. 1983. Only 4 issues printed. *NFK*

PAWLEY'S ISLAND

COASTAL OBSERVER   weekly--established 1982.   Jul 1, 1982 = vol 1, no 1, Charles R. Swenson (editor), Bruce C. Hunter (publisher). Zane Wilson also associated with paper. *Files: Coastal Observer 1982 + .*

PAWLEY'S ISLAND PERSPECTIVE   monthly, irregular--established 1980, ceased c. 1980.   Jun 1980 = vol 1, no 4, Heidi Hall (editor), Jean H. Thompson (publisher). *Files: SCL Jun, Aug-Sep, 1980.*

GREENVILLE COUNTY

Created in 1798 when old Washington District was split into two parts, Pendleton and Greenville districts, the latter assumed the name of its most important trading center. Yet the origin of the name "Greenville" remains obscure. For many years it was attributed to either Revolutionary War hero Nathaniel Greene or to Isaac Green, an early settler who owned a mill on Reedy River. However, Greene was not popular with Up Country veterans of the late 18th century and Green the miller had lived in the region only a few months before the name appeared. Thus the most acceptable theory is that the luxuriant, verdant growth of the area created the name "Greenville."

BEREA

BEREA REGALIA   weekly--established 1979, ceased c. 1980. Not cited by Ayer. Dec 14, 1979 = vol 1, no 6, no personnel listed. *Files: Greenville CL Nov 9, 1979-May 3, 1980.*

CAMP SEVIER

TRENCH AND CAMP   weekly, YMCA-sponsored paper for WWI army personnel--established Oct 8, 1917, ceased c. 1919. Printed and distributed by daily newspapers located near major camps. Several issues available in mfm reels of Greenville Daily News (Sun editions). *Files: Greenville Daily News (Feb-May 1918) 10.*

FOUNTAIN INN

FOUNTAIN INN NEWS   weekly--established 1921, ceased c. 1923. Cited by Ayer 1922 and 1923: P. W. Smith (editor and publisher). *NFK*

FOUNTAIN INN TRIBUNE   weekly--continues News and Notions Feb 19, 1911, merged with Simpsonville Times Dec 1957, continued by Tribune-Times c. 1964. Cited Ayer 1912 thru 1964. Feb 9, 1911 = vol 3, no 29, Ford Todd Cox and Robert Quillen (editors and publishers). Marvin S. Sipe, W. W. Kellett, Marcelle Quillen, and Mark Nelson also associated with paper. Under the editorial direction of Robert Quillen this was one of the nation's best-known weeklies during the 1920s and 1930s. *Files: Lander mfm Feb-Dec 1911, 1928, 1930-1948; SCL (1925-1949) 53, mfm Feb-Dec 1911, 1928, 1930-1948; Tribune-Times Feb-Dec 1911, 1928, 1930-1951, mfm Feb-Dec 1911, 1928, 1930-1948.*

JOURNAL   weekly--established 1906, ceased c. 1907. Cited Ayer 1907: Fountain Inn Printing Company. According to Robert Quillen, this paper was launched by the publisher of the Belton Times, George E. Clarke. *NFK*

NEWS AND NOTIONS   weekly, Democrat--established 1908, continued by Fountain Inn Tribune 1911. Cited Ayer 1909 thru 1911. Ayer 1909: G. H. Waddell (editor and publisher). Ayer 1910: H. M. Burgard and R. W. Davis (editors and publishers). Ayer 1911: F. T. Cox and James M. Richardson (editors and publishers). Jun 23, 1910 = vol 2, no 49, F. T. Cox and J. M. Richardson (editors and publishers). *Files: Lander mfm Jan 5-Feb 2, 1911; SCL Jun 23, Aug 10, 1910, mfm Jan 5-Feb 2, 1911; Tribune-Times orig & mfm Jan 5-Feb 2, 1911.*

TRIBUNE-TIMES   weekly--continues Fountain Inn Tribune and Simpsonville Times c. 1964. Jan 6, 1965 = vol 53, no 54, G. Bradley Jones (general manager). F. Louis Grant, Jack Trim, Dave R. Everett, Allen Riddle, Teri Hammond, and Ben Davis also associated with paper. Published in Mauldin c. 1972-1980. *Files: Greenville CL ((1973 +)); SCL mfm 1965, 1967, 1969; Tribune-Times 1968-1974, 1978, 1981 + .*

GREENVILLE

ADVERTISER   semi-monthly, Farmers' Alliance--established 1891, ceased c. 1891. Not cited by Ayer. Jun 1, 1891 = vol 1, no 5, James H. Berry (publisher). *Files: SCL Jun 1, 1891.*

BAPTIST COURIER   weekly, religious--established in York in 1869 as Working Christian, published in Charleston 1870-1871 and in Columbia under that title until Sep 20, 1877 when continued by Baptist Courier. Sep 20, 1877 = vol 9, no 37, vol 1, no 1 (new series), C. M. McJunkin (editor and proprietor). Published in Greenville since 1879. Note: SCL classifies as a periodical after 1897. *Files: Baptist Courier 1910 + ; Erskine mfm 1965 + ; Furman Sep 26, 1878-Apr 17, 1898, Oct 13, 1898-Sep 28, 1899, 1900 + , mfm 1877 + ; Greenville CL (1893-1907) 25; SCL ((1882-1947)), mfm 1877-1967.*

BLACK STAR   weekly, irregular, black publication--established c. 1976. May 30, 1980 = vol 3, no 71, Redfern II (president), JuJu Publishing Company. Issued by Columbia publisher with different titles for different cities. See Black Times [Columbia]. *Files: SCL Mar 24, May 10, 30, 1980.*

CAROLINA NEWS AND GUIDE   weekly, black publication--established 1963, ceased c. 1964. Not cited by Ayer. May 1, 1963 = vol 1, no 1, David Carter (editor and publisher). *Files: Greenville CL mfm (Mar-Aug 1963) 15; SCL orig & mfm (Mar-Aug 1963) 15.*

CAROLINA TEXTILE JOURNAL   weekly--established 1923, ceased c. 1925. Cited Ayer 1924 and 1925: Claude A. Graves and D. W. Hiott, Jr. (editors and publishers). *NFK*

CAROLINIAN   weekly, Democrat--established 1887, ceased c. 1888. Cited Ayer 1888: Carolinian Publishing Company. *NFK*

COHEN'S WEEKLY   weekly, official organ of Cohen's Chain Stores--established 1926, ceased c. 1926. Apr 22, 1926 = vol 1, no 1. *Files: Greenville CL orig & mfm Apr-Jul 1926; SCL mfm Apr-Jul 1926.*

COTTON PLANT   monthly, semi-monthly, agricultural, Grange, Farmers' Alliance--established in Marion in 1883.   Published in Greenville 1887-1890, Orangeburg 1891, Columbia 1892-1896, Spartanburg 1897, Laurens 1898, Greenville 1899-1904. Merged with Progressive Farmer in 1904, continued by Progressive Farmer and Southern Cotton Plant, later Progressive Farmer and Southern Ruralist [Raleigh and Birmingham].   Apr 15, 1888 = vol 5, no 13, James A. Hoyt and W. W. Keys (proprietors). J. W. Bowden, J. W. Stokes, and A. M. Howell also associated with paper. See also Cotton Plant [Marion]. *Files: Greenville CL (1892-1903) 9, mfm (1887-1902) 8; SCL (1887-1902) 50, mfm (1887-1902) 8.*

COUNTY FARE   weekly--established 1984. Apr 4, 1984 = vol 1, no 8, Rupen G. Avakian (editor), Greenville News-Piedmont (publisher). Continued by the County Fare and the Poinsett Register in 1986. *Files: Greenville CL Apr 4, 1984; Greenville News-Piedmont 1984-1986.*

COUNTY FARE AND THE POINSETT REGISTER   weekly--continues County Fare in 1986. Jul 29, 1987 = vol 4, no 20, Clifford L. Gray (editor), Greenville News-Piedmont (publisher). *Files: Greenville News-Piedmont 1986 + .*

DAILY ENTERPRISE   daily edition of the Enterprise and Mountaineer--established 1876, ceased c. 1876. Not cited by Rowell. *Files: CLS Aug 6-Dec 14, 1876; Greenville CL Aug 6, Nov 30, 1876.*

DAILY HERALD   daily, afternoons Mon-Fri and Sun morning--continues Greenville Daily Herald c. 1906, continued by Evening Piedmont c. 1907. Sep 12, 1906 = vol 7, no 231. Also issued weekly edition in 1906. *Files: Greenville CL mfm Sep 12, 1906; SCL orig & mfm Sep 12, 1906.*

DAILY PIEDMONT   daily--continues Evening Piedmont c. 1908, continued by Piedmont and Mountaineer c. 1911. Sep 28, 1908 = vol 12, no 88. Ayer 1908 and 1909: Marshall Moore (editor), Piedmont Company (publisher). Ayer 1910: J. Rutledge McGehee (editor and publisher). *Files SCL orig & mfm Sep 28, 1908 (fragment).*

ENTERPRISE   weekly, Republican, black publication--established 1906, ceased c. 1908. Cited Ayer 1908: S. N. Cassell (editor), Enterprise Publishing Company. *NFK*

ENTERPRISE AND MOUNTAINEER   weekly--created Jun 18, 1873 by merger of Greenville Enterprise and Greenville Mountaineer, continued by Greenville Mountaineer c. Jan 1893. Jun 18, 1873 = vol 20, no 7, John C. Bailey (editor and proprietor).. Edward Bailey and James A. Hoyt also associated with paper. Issued daily edition briefly in 1876. See Daily Enterprise. *Files: CLS ((1875-1889, 1891)), files* *are essentially complete for years indicated; Furman mfm (1873-1880) 70; Greenville CL (1873-1885) 9, mfm (1873-1889) 74; SCL ((1873-1892)) 100, mfm (1873-1889) 79; Wofford mfm (1873-1880) 70.*

EVENING OBSERVER   daily--established 1900, ceased c. 1900. Not cited by Ayer. Mar 16, 1900 = vol 1, no 10, ------ Williams and J. F. Richardson (publishers). Mill village newspaper. *Files: Greenville CL mfm Mar 16, 20, 1900; SCL orig & mfm Mar 16, 20, 1900.*

EVENING PIEDMONT   daily--continues Daily Herald c. 1907, continued by Daily Piedmont c. 1908. Jul 18, 1907 = vol 10, no 43. According to Ayer 1907, issued evenings Mon-Fri and Sun morning. *Files: Greenville CL mfm Jul 18, 1907; SCL orig & mfm Jul 18, 1907.*

EVENING STAR   evenings except Sun, Democrat--established 1880, ceased c. 1881. Cited in Ayer 1881. *NFK*

FOCUS   weekly, black publication--established Sep 5, 1973, continued by Focus News Jun 16, 1976. Sep 5, 1973 = vol 1, no 1, John E. Bishop (president), B & S Properties (publisher), "Black Perspective in the Piedmont." Jeanne Mansell, Damali Bashira, and Jimmie Sanders also associated with paper. Focus taken over in Jul 1975 by Jill Media Group and new number sequence instituted. Aug 12, 1975 = vol 1, no 3, David A. Crossman (editor). Not cited by Ayer. *Files: Greenville CL (1973-1976); SCL (Jan 1975-Jun 1976) 50.*

FOCUS NEWS   weekly, black publication--continues Focus on Jun 16, 1976 = vol 2, no 24, Patricia Byrd (managing editor), Jill Media Group. After Jan 1980 published by the Genesis Media Group of Duncan, S. C. Ceased c. 1981. Not cited by Ayer. *Files: Greenville CL (1976-1980); SCL (Jun 1976-Apr 1977) 35.*

GREENVILLE ADVERTISER   weekly, Democrat--established 1879, ceased c. 1881. Cited by Ayer 1880 and 1881, but no details given. *NFK*

GREENVILLE AMERICAN   weekly, black publication c. 1952. Cited by Behling, no details given. Not cited by Ayer. *NFK*

GREENVILLE CHRONICLE   weekly, Democrat--established 1880, ceased c. 1880. Listed in Ayer 1880, but no details given. According to North, ceased May 1880. *NFK*

GREENVILLE COUNTY OBSERVER   weekly--established 1928, continued by Greenville Observer c. 1932. Aug 14, 1930 = vol 2, no 51, D. W. Hiott (president), J. B. Southern (editor), Greenville County Observer Company. Although formerly the Parker Progress, began new number system in 1928, but by Nov 1930 had adopted sequence based upon earlier paper--Nov 6, 1930 = vol 5, no 11. *Files: SCL (1930-1931) 5.*

GREENVILLE DAILY HERALD   daily, evenings except Sun--established 1902, continued by Daily Herald c. 1906. Apr 12, 1903 = vol 1, no 95. According to the Greenville News (Jun 26, 1962), founded by A. D. Brewer. Cited Ayer 1903 thru 1906: Herald Company (publisher). *Files: Greenville CL mfm Apr 12, 1903; SCL orig & mfm Apr 12, 1903.*

GREENVILLE DAILY NEWS   daily, weekly, semi-weekly--established 1874 by A. M. Speights. Published both daily and weekly editions until c. 1890 when weekly became semi-weekly. Also published weekly again Jan 1914-Mar 1915. Semi-weekly ceased c. 1919. See Greenville Semi-Weekly News and Greenville Weekly News. Greenville Daily News continued by Greenville News Oct 26, 1920. Sep 2, 1874 (no vol number), A. M. Speights (publisher). A. M. Howell, A. C. Garlington, G. W. Bruner, Jr., J. Rion McKissick, W. W. Wallace, J. K. Blackman, R. W. Simpson, Jr., and B. H. Peace also associated with paper. *Files: Clemson mfm 1900-1920; Furman mfm 1881, 1900-1920; Greenville CL (1879-1918) 5, mfm (1874-1900) 30, 1881, 1900-1920; Greenville News-Piedmont mfm 1881, 1900-1920; SCL (1874-1918) 70, mfm (1874-1900) 30, 1881, 1900-1920.*

GREENVILLE DAILY PIEDMONT   daily, evenings except Sun--continues Piedmont and Mountaineer c. 1912, continued by Piedmont in 1916. Jun 1, 1912 = vol 82, no 154, Harold C. Booker (editor). *Files: SCL (1912-1915) 22.*

GREENVILLE DEMOCRAT   daily--established 1891, ceased c. 1895. Ayer 1892: evenings except Sun, with Tue weekly edition, J. L. Gantt (editor), B. F. Perry & Son (publishers). Ayer 1893/4 and 1895 indicate weekly only. Feb 14, 1894 = vol 3, no 1 (new series), John C. Bailey (editor), Greenville Democrat Stock Company. Not listed in Ayer 1896. See also Weekly Democrat. *Files: CLS Feb 15, 1893-May 2, 1894; Greenville CL Sep 27, 1893, mfm Feb 14, 1894; SCL orig & mfm Feb 14, 1894.*

GREENVILLE ENTERPRISE   weekly 1866--continues Southern Enterprise, continued by Southern Enterprise. Feb 8, 1866 = vol 12, no 36, John C. Bailey & Company (editor and proprietor). Publishers of Southern Enterprise apparently experimented briefly with name change. *Files: SCL Feb 8, 1866.*

GREENVILLE ENTERPRISE   weekly--continues Southern Enterprise c. 1870, merged with Greenville Mountaineer Jun 1873, continued by Enterprise and Mountaineer. Mar 9, 1870 = vol 16, no 42, John C. and Edward Bailey (proprietors). *Files: CLS Feb 7-Dec 21, 1870, Jan 4, 1871-Dec 25, 1872; Furman mfm (1871-1873) 67; Greenville CL (1870-1871) 13, mfm (1871-1873) 67; SCL (1870-1873) 11, mfm (1871-1873) 67.*

GREENVILLE GAZETTE   weekly c. 1825. Prospectus dated Jan 1, 1825, John G. Hewitt (proprietor), published in the Columbia Telescope (Mar 4, 1825). *NFK*

GREENVILLE MOUNTAINEER   weekly--continues Mountaineer Jan 1830, merged with Southern Patriot Dec 1855, continued by Patriot and Mountaineer. Jan 16, 1830 = vol 2, no 1, B. F. Perry (editor), O. H. Wells (publisher). William H. Thomas,

C. F. Townes, H. Nelson Wheaton, and J. R. Gossett also associated with paper. See J. L. West, "Early Backwoods Humor in the Greenville Mountaineer, 1826-1840," *Mississippi Quarterly* (Winter, 1971), pp. 69-82. *Files: Bob Jones Jan 16, 1830-Jan 11, 1850; CLS (1832-1845) 20, Oct 23, 1846-Dec 14, 1849; Greenville CL Oct 19, 1838; SCL (1830-1855) 55; Clemson mfm ((1830-1850)) 480; Furman, Greenville CL, Greenville News-Piedmont, SCL, and Wofford mfm 1830-1850.*

GREENVILLE MOUNTAINEER   weekly--continues Patriot and Mountaineer 1866, continued by Mountaineer Dec 1866. Aug 2, 1866 = vol 15, no 19, G. E. Elford (editor and proprietor). Also issued semi-weekly edition, see Semi-Weekly Mountaineer. *Files: SCL Aug 2, Nov 22, 29, 1866.*

GREENVILLE MOUNTAINEER   weekly--continues Mountaineer 1872, merged with Greenville Enterprise 1873, continued by Enterprise and Mountaineer. Jun 3, 1873 = vol 21, no 36, whole no 1086, G. E. Elford (editor and proprietor), G. G. Wells (associate editor). *Files: SCL Jun 3, 1873.*

GREENVILLE MOUNTAINEER   weekly, semi-weekly--continues Enterprise and Mountaineer c. Jan 1893, continued by Mountaineer Dec 31, 1902. Jan 4, 1893 = vol 68, no 32, James A. Hoyt (editor and publisher). Became semi-weekly in Jan 1895. "A Democratic Newspaper--'Unawed by Power and Unbribed by gain.'" *Files: CLS 1893-1894; Greenville CL ((1893-1902)); SCL (1893-1902) 20; Greenville CL and SCL mfm 1893-1898, 1900, (1901) 2, 1902.*

GREENVILLE NEWS   daily--continues Greenville Daily News Oct 26, 1920 = vol 46, no 297, B. H. Peace (editor), Greenville News Company. Roger C. Peace, Wayne W. Freeman, James H. McKinney, Jr., J. Kelly Sisk, John S. Pittman, Rhea T. Askew, and W. de B. Mebane also associated with paper. "Palmetto Edition" (state) issued as News in 1987. *Files: Clemson, Greenville CL, Greenville News-Piedmont, and SCL mfm 1920 + ; Furman mfm 1920-1931, 1942 + ; North Greenville College mfm 1970-1984 ; Winthrop mfm 1972 + .*

GREENVILLE NEWS: SEMI-WEEKLY EDITION   see Greenville Semi-Weekly News.

GREENVILLE NEWS-PIEDMONT   title of combined Sat-Sun editions of Greenville News and Greenville Piedmont 1973 + . Also issued as Greenville News / Greenville Piedmont. See Greenville News.

GREENVILLE OBSERVER   weekly--continues Greenville County Observer c. 1932, continued by Observer Mar 8, 1935. Jan 29, 1932 = vol 6, no 22, George R. Koester (editor), D. W. Hiott (publisher). *Files: SCL ((1932-1935)) 137.*

GREENVILLE PIEDMONT   daily--continues Piedmont Mar 12, 1927. According to the Greenville News (Jun 26, 1962), Ralph B. Chandler bought the Piedmont in 1926 and the following year sold it to B. H. Peace, publisher of the Greenville News. Others associated with the paper include R. C. Peace, Wayne Freeman, William R. Gaines, F. C. McConnell, J. Kelly Sisk, J. S. Pittman, and R. T. Askew. *Files: Clemson mfm 1927-1945; Furman mfm 1927-1932, 1941 + ; Greenville CL, Greenville News-Piedmont, and SCL mfm 1927 + .*

GREENVILLE REPUBLICAN   weekly--established 1826, ceased 1828. Jul 12, 1826 = vol 1, no 1, W. C. Young and ------ Timme (publishers). Charles W. D'Oyley and O. H. Wells also associated with paper. *Files: Bob Jones Jul 12, 1826-Aug 30, 1828; Furman, Greenville CL, Greenville News-Piedmont, and Wofford mfm Jul 12, 1826-Aug 30, 1828; SCL (1826-1827) 60, mfm Jul 12, 1826-Aug 30, 1828.*

GREENVILLE REPUBLICAN   weekly--established 1873, sold to Greenville Daily News c. 1874. May 6, 1873 = vol 1, no 12, A. Blythe (editor). Cited by Rowell 1873 thru 1875. R. McKay and James M. Runion also associated with paper. *Files: SCL May 6, 1873.*

GREENVILLE SEMI-WEEKLY NEWS   semi-weekly--established c. 1890 as Tue-Fri edition of Greenville Daily News, continued by Greenville Weekly News Jan 1914. Published in 1890s as Greenville News: Semi-Weekly Edition. Apr 14, 1891 = new series, no 6, J. F. Richardson (manager). No vol data given. *Files: SCL (1891-1912) 21, mfm 1907-1913.*

GREENVILLE SEMI-WEEKLY NEWS   semi-weekly--continues Greenville Weekly News on Mar 2, 1915 (vol 1, no 1), George W. Brunson, Jr. (editor), ceased c. 1919. Note: Some 1915 issues mistakenly dated "1914." *Files: SCL mfm Mar 1915-Dec 1918.*

GREENVILLE WEEKLY NEWS   weekly--established 1874 as weekly edition of Greenville Daily News, continued by Greenville Semi-Weekly News c. 1890. Paper edited by A. C. Garlington and A. M. Howell c. 1878-1879, no vol-issue data provided. *Files: Greenville CL mfm (1878-1879) 7; SCL (1878-1888) 70, mfm (1878-1879) 7.*

GREENVILLE WEEKLY NEWS   weekly--continues Greenville Semi-Weekly News Jan 1914, continued by Greenville Semi-Weekly News Mar 1915. Jan 7, 1915 = vol 2, no 1, George W. Brunson, Jr. (editor). Note: Some 1915 issues mistakenly dated "1914." *Files: Greenville CL and SCL mfm Jan-Feb 1915.*

GREENVILLE WORLD   weekly, black publication--established 1932, ceased c. 1941. Cited Ayer 1936 thru 1940: E. B. Holloway (editor), Eugene Smith (publisher). *NFK*

INDUSTRIAL NEWS AND SOUTHERN FARMER   weekly--established 1906, ceased c. 1908. Cited Ayer 1908: Union Printing and Publishing Company. *NFK*

LABOR PRESS   weekly--established 1914, ceased c. 1918. Cited Ayer 1918: Labor Press Company. *NFK*

LANCET   weekly, black publication--established 1890, ceased c. 1891. Cited Ayer 1890 and 1891: E. B. Holloway and A. Robertson (editors and publishers). *NFK*

LONG FELT WANT   weekly--established 1919, ceased c. 1920. Cited Ayer 1920: S. E. Bomar (editor), Southeastern Publishing Company. *NFK*

MIDDLE EARTH FREE PRESS   semi-monthly--established 1965, ceased ? Sep 9-23, 1969 = vol 5, no 1. *Files: USC mfm Sep 9-23, 1969. See Underground Newspaper Collection, reel 38.*

MILL LIFE   weekly--established 1915, ceased c. 1916. Cited Ayer 1916: Peter Hollis and Associates (editors), Mill Life Company. *NFK*

MILL WORKERS' WORLD   weekly--established 1907, ceased c. 1910. Cited Ayer 1909 and 1910: World Publishing Company. *NFK*

MOUNTAIN CITY ECHO   weekly c. 1891. Nov 14, 1891 = vol 1, no 2, no personnel listed. Not cited by Ayer. *Files: SCL Nov 14, 1891.*

MOUNTAINEER   weekly--established Jan 1829, continued by <u>Greenville Mountaineer</u> Jan 1830. Jan 17, 1829 = vol 1, no 2, O. H. Wells (publisher). *Files: Bob Jones Jan 17, 1829-Jan 9, 1830; Clemson mfm (1829-1830) 33; Furman, Greenville CL, <u>Greenville News-Piedmont</u>, SCL, and Wofford mfm Jan 17, 1829-Jan 9, 1830.*

MOUNTAINEER   weekly--continues <u>Greenville Mountaineer</u> Dec 1866, continued by <u>Greenville Mountaineer</u> 1872. Feb 14, 1867 = vol 15, no 47, G. E. Elford (editor and proprietor). *Files: SCL (1867-1871) 44, mfm (1870-1871) 21.*

MOUNTAINEER   semi-weekly, weekly--continues <u>Greenville Mountaineer</u> Dec 1902, issued as independent semi-weekly to 1907, then as weekly and semi-weekly editions of <u>Evening Piedmont</u> and <u>Daily Piedmont</u> from 1907 to 1911, continued by <u>Piedmont and Mountaineer</u> c. 1911. Dec 31, 1902 = vol 78, no 73, James A. Hoyt (editor and proprietor). Note: Number system erratic. James E. Sanders also associated with paper. *Files: CLS Dec 17, 1904-Jan 11, 1905; Greenville CL orig & mfm (1902-1906) 87; SCL (1903-1904) 5, mfm (1902-1906) 87.*

NEW SOUTH WEEKLY   weekly, independent--established 1881, ceased c. 1882. Cited by Ayer 1881 and 1882. *NFK*

NEWS   see <u>Greenville News</u>.

OBSERVER   weekly, bi-weekly--continues <u>Greenville Observer</u> Mar 1935, ceased c. 1967. Jan 3, 1936 = vol 13, no 18, George R. Koester (editor). D. W. Hiott, J. D.

Daniels, and James A. Klosky also associated with paper. Issued bi-weekly 1966-1967. *Files: Greenville CL Aug 17, 1945; SCL (1936, 1944, 1965) 35.*

PALMETTO LEADER   weekly, black publication--established 1945 ? Paper said to be a "revival" of an earlier publication, perhaps the Palmetto Leader published in Columbia c. 1927-1961. Jan 4, 1985 = vol 40, no 1, Norman Pearson (editor and publisher). *Files: Palmetto Leader 1985 + .*

PALMETTO TIMES   weekly, Democrat--established 1953, ceased c. 1964. Cited Ayer 1956 thru 1964. Ayer 1956: T. Max Lawson (editor and publisher). H. K. Ripley also associated with paper. May have been published in Travelers Rest. *NFK*

PARKER PROGRESS   weekly--established 1925, continued by Greenville County Observer 1928. Mar 6, 1925 = vol 1, no 1, Judson W. Chapman (editor), D. W. Hiott, Jr. (publisher). Cited by Ayer 1926 thru 1928. *Files: Greenville CL orig & mfm Mar 1925-Sep 1927; SCL mfm Mar 1925-Sep 1927.*

PATRIOT AND MOUNTAINEER   weekly--created Dec 13, 1855 by merger of Southern Patriot and Greenville Mountaineer, continued by Greenville Mountaineer 1866. Continues numerical sequence of Southern Patriot. Feb 7, 1856 = vol 5, no 51, whole no 259, B. F. Perry (editor), G. E. Elford (proprietor). C. F. Elford also associated with paper. *Files: SCL (Jan 1856-Oct 1861) 82.*

PEOPLE'S RECORD   weekly, black publication--established 1901, ceased c. 1909. Cited by Ayer 1906 thru 1909: L. B. Langford and W. R. Saxon (editors and publishers). *NFK*

PIEDMONT   daily, afternoons except Sun--continues Greenville Daily Piedmont 1916, continued by Greenville Piedmont Mar 1927. Oct 7, 1916 = vol 86, no 263. George R. Koester, J. Rion McKissick, and R. B. Chandler associated with paper. *Files: Greenville CL (1918-1919) 5; SCL ((1916-1925)) 350; Furman, Greenville CL, Greenville News-Piedmont, and SCL mfm 1926-1927.*

PIEDMONT AND MOUNTAINEER   daily, weekly--continues Daily Piedmont and Mountaineer c. 1911, continued by Greenville Daily Piedmont c. 1912. Ayer 1911: Piedmont and Mountaineer evenings except Sun and Fri (weekly), J. Rutledge McGehee (editor) Daily Piedmont Company (publisher). *NFK*

SEMI-WEEKLY MOUNTAINEER   semi-weekly edition of Greenville Mountaineer c. 1866. Mar 6, 1866 = vol 14, no 48, G. E. Elford (editor and proprietor). *Files: Greenville CL mfm Mar 6, 1866; SCL orig & mfm Mar 6, 1866.*

SEMI-WEEKLY TIMES   semi-weekly--established 1899, ceased c. 1900. Dec 26, 1899 = vol 1, no 41, D. Barnett Foster (editor), Foster Brothers (publishers). See Sunday Times. *Files: Greenville CL mfm Dec 26, 1899; SCL orig & mfm Dec 26, 1899.*

SOUTHERN CHRISTIAN ADVOCATE   weekly, Methodist--established in Charleston 1837, published in various places, including Greenville 1895-1898, 1912-1914. Jan 3, 1895 = vol 58, no 29, John O. Willson (editor), James A. Hoyt (printer for the Methodist Episcopal Church, South). Moved to Columbia Jan 1899. Sep 12, 1912 = vol 76, no 13, S. A. Nettles (editor), Southern Christian Advocate (publisher). Moved to Anderson Jan 1915. Note: Now classified as a periodical at SCL. See Southern Christian Advocate [Columbia].

SOUTHERN CRUSADER   weekly, black publication--established 1942 by J. H. Smith (owner and president), ceased ? Not cited by Ayer. Feb 7, 1943 = vol 2, no 12, E. B. Holloway (chairman of the board and chief reporter). *Files: Greenville CL mfm Feb 7, Mar 7, 1943; SCL orig & mfm Feb 7, Mar 7, 1943.*

SOUTHERN ENTERPRISE   weekly--established 1854, continued by Greenville Enterprise 1866. Jun 2, 1854 = vol 1, no 3, W. P. Price (editor and proprietor), W. P. and T. J. Price (publishers). J. C. Bailey, C. F. Townes, and C. M. McJunkin also associated with paper. *Files: CLS May 19, 1854-May 6, 1858, May 12-Jul 21, 1859, Dec 1, 1859-Dec 20, 1860, Oct 10-31, 1861, 1863; Greenville CL Jan 22, Jul 23, 1863; SCL (1854-1864) 18, mfm Jun 30, 1859.*

SOUTHERN ENTERPRISE   weekly--continues Greenville Enterprise 1866, continued by Greenville Enterprise c. 1870. Sep 22, 1869 = vol 16, no 18, John C. Bailey (proprietor), C. F. Townes (editor). *Files: CLS 1867-1868, Jan 13-Dec 1869; SCL (1866-1870) 7.*

SOUTHERN ENTERPRISE   weekly, black publication--established 1914, ceased ? Not cited by Ayer. Mar 6, 1926 = vol 13, no 23, C. C. Clarkson (editor), E. B. Holloway, Henry M. L. James, I. E. Lowery, and S. M. Brown also associated with paper. *Files: SCL Mar 6, 1926 (xerox fragment).*

SOUTHERN HERALD AND WORKING MAN   semi-monthly, immigration--established 1874, ceased ? Not cited by Rowell. Produced in New York City and Greenville to promote immigration. Jan 1, 1876 = vol 3, no 2, Tilman R. Gaines (editor). *Files: Greenville CL and SCL mfm Jan 1, 1876, Oct 18, 1877.*

SOUTHERN PATRIOT   weekly--established 1851, merged with Greenville Mountaineer Dec 1855 to create Patriot and Mountaineer. Feb 28, 1851 = vol 1, no 1, B. F. Perry and C. J. Elford (editors and publishers). See also Tri-Weekly Southern Patriot. *Files: Bob Jones and CLS Feb 28, 1851-Feb 17, 1853; Furman, Greenville CL, Greenville News-Piedmont, and SCL mfm Feb 28, 1851-Feb 17, 1853; Greenville CL mfm Mar 10, 1853, Mar 29, May 19, 1855; SCL Oct 18, 25, Nov 8, 1855, mfm Mar 10, 1853, Mar 29, May 19, 1855.*

SOUTHERN SENTINEL   weekly c. 1832, pro-nullification. Aug 4, 1832 = vol 1, no 7, Turner Bynum (editor), B. Bynum and G. E. W. Nelson (printers). Motto:

"Quick to Discern, and Ready to Defend." True to his word, Editor Bynum attacked the Greenville Mountaineer's stand on the tariff, which led to his death in a duel with B. F. Perry on Aug 17, 1832. *Files: Clemson Aug 18, 1832, mfm Aug 4, 1832. Note: Copy filmed with the Greenville Mountaineer.*

SUNDAY TIMES   daily, semi-weekly--established 1899, ceased c. 1900. Cited in Ayer 1900: Times Publishing Company. May 28, 1899 = vol 1, no 4, D. Barnett Foster (editor and publisher). At that time issuing evening, Tue-Fri, and Sun editions. See Semi-Weekly Times. *Files: Greenville CL mfm May 28, 1899; SCL orig & mfm May 28, 1899.*

TRI-WEEKLY SOUTHERN PATRIOT   tri-weekly--established Apr 22, 1851, ceased Feb 16, 1852. May 10, 1851 = vol 1, no 9, B. F. Perry and C. J. Elford (publishers). Weekly edition of Southern Patriot merged with the Greenville Mountaineer in 1855 to create the Patriot and Mountaineer. *Files: Greenville CL mfm May 10, Jul 28, Aug 18, 1851; Greenville News-Piedmont mfm Apr 22, 1851-Feb 16, 1852; SCL (1851) 7, mfm (1851) 5.*

WEEKLY DEMOCRAT   weekly edition of Greenville Democrat--established 1892, ceased c. 1895. May 10, 1892 = vol 1, no 13, B. F. Perry & Company (publisher). See also the Greenville Democrat. *Files: Greenville CL mfm Apr 26, May 10, 1892; SCL orig & mfm Apr 26, May 10, 1892.*

WEEKLY FLAG   weekly c. 1879. Not cited by Rowell. *Files: SCL Jan 10, 1879.*

GREER

GREER CITIZEN   weekly, semi-weekly--established May 10, 1917, presumably by P. W. Smith. Cited by Ayer 1919 + . Apr 7, 1922 = vol 4, no 45, P. W. Smith (publisher). W. G. Hazel, James N. Benton, J. J. Fair, C. A. Herlong, R. F. Read, M. G. Lewis, C. P. Smith, Mrs. P. W. Smith, Tup Lucas, H. B. Ver Standig, E. A. Burch, Leland E. Burch, and Walter M. Burch also associated with paper. According to Ayer, issued semi-weekly 1925-1927. *Files: Greenville CL ((1973 +)); Greer Branch Library 1983 + ; Greer Citizen 1980 + ; SCL ((1922-1976)) 100, 1985 + .*

GREER NEWS-LEADER   semi-weekly, weekly, Democrat--established 1910 as semi-weekly, issued weekly after 1912, ceased c. 1915. Cited by Ayer 1911 thru 1915. Ayer 1911: J. Stuart Price (editor and publisher). *NFK*

GREER OBSERVER   weekly--established 1905, suspended c. 1913-1915, ceased c. 1918. Cited Ayer 1907-1912, 1916-1918. Dec 9, 1909 = vol 5, no 24, N. C. Remsen (editor). *Files: SCL Dec 9, 1909.*

GREER TRIBUNE AND THE INDUSTRIAL NEWS   weekly, Independent Democrat--established 1924, ceased c. 1935. Cited Ayer 1930 thru 1935. May 23, 1929

= vol 5, no 15, C. B. Vaughn (editor). C. A. Herlong also associated with paper. *Files: SCL (1929-1933) 8.*

MARIETTA

COMMUNITY NEWS   weekly--established 1970, continued by Greenville County Monitor in 1973. Larry Atkins (editor and publisher) put out a single issue of the "Community News" to honor the local basketball team when it won state honors. He had no intention of establishing a weekly paper, but ads flowed in and he did. *Files: Travelers Rest Monitor ((1970-1972)).*

GREENVILLE COUNTY MONITOR   weekly--continues Community News in 1973, continued by the Mountain Monitor in 1979. Larry Atkins (editor and publisher). *Files: SCL Feb 3-17, 1977; Travelers Rest Monitor ((1973-1978)).*

MOUNTAIN MONITOR   weekly--continues Greenville County Monitor in 1979, continued by the Travelers Rest Monitor in 1985. Larry Atkins (editor and publisher) substituted Travelers Rest in title to avoid confusion with Marietta, Ga. *Files: Travelers Rest Monitor (1979-1984)).*

TRAVELERS REST MONITOR   weekly--continues Mountain Monitor in 1985. Larry Atkins (editor and publisher). *Files: Travelers Rest Monitor 1985 + .*

MAULDIN

TRIBUNE-TIMES   see Tribune-Times [Fountain Inn].

PIEDMONT

BRIDGE   monthly--established 1918, ceased c. 1925. Not cited by Ayer. Oct 1918 = vol 1, no 1, A. S. Rowell (publisher). *Files: SCL ((Oct 1918-Oct 1925) 60, xerox copies only.*

SALUDA VALLEY RECORD   weekly--established 1962, ceased c. 1965. Not cited by Ayer. Jul 12, 1962 = vol 1, no 1, Larry Ayers (editor), Saluda Valley Publishing Company. *Files: SCL mfm ((Jul 1962-Feb 1965)) 130.*

SUN   weekly, independent--established 1896, merged with Herald [Pelzer] c. 1900, continued by Sun-Herald. Cited by Ayer 1897 thru 1899. Ayer 1897-1898: John R. Dortch (editor and publisher). Ayer 1899: A. S. Rowell (editor and publisher). *NFK*

SUN-HERALD   weekly--created c. 1900 by merger of Sun [Piedmont] and Herald [Pelzer], ceased c. 1900. Cited by Ayer 1900: A. S. Rowell (editor and publisher). *NFK*

SIMPSONVILLE

GOLDEN STRIP JOURNAL   weekly c. 1959.   Cited by State Chamber of Commerce literature. *NFK*

SIMPSONVILLE TIMES   weekly--established 1955, merged with Fountain Inn Tribune Dec 19, 1957, continued by Fountain Inn Tribune, which c. 1964 became the Tribune-Times "serving the Golden Strip of South Carolina"...Fountain Inn, Simpsonville, and Mauldin. *NFK*

TAYLORS

PEOPLE'S PAPER   weekly, independent--established 1967, ceased c. 1971.   Cited by Ayer 1970 and 1971:   Harry McVeety (publisher). *NFK*

TRAVELERS REST

HOMETOWN MUSIC NEWS   monthly, gospel music--established 1980, continued by Southland Gospel News Feb 1985.   Allen Riddle (editor and publisher). *Files: Southland Gospel News 1980-1985.*

NORTHWEST SENTINEL   weekly--established by the Pickens Sentinel in 1980. Apr 30, 1980 = vol 1, no 1, Bill Williams (editor), Ben Bagwell and Jerry Alexander (publishers).   Published in Travelers Rest since 1983 by Jean Owens and Pat and Leslie Rowell. *Files: Northwest Sentinel 1984 + ; Pickens Sentinel Apr 30, 1980.*

PALMETTO TIMES   see Palmetto Times [Greenville].

SOUTHLAND GOSPEL NEWS   monthly, gospel music--continues Hometown Music News Feb 1985.   Oct 1985 = vol 6, no 8, Allen Riddle (editor), Hometown Music News Inc. *Files: Southland Gospel News 1985 + .*

TRAVELERS REST TIMES   weekly c. 1963.   Cited in Southern Bell media directory, Mrs. J. F. Daugherty (editor and publisher). *NFK*

GREENWOOD COUNTY

Formed from parts of Abbeville and Edgefield counties in 1897, Greenwood County takes its name from its major trading center. That city, in turn, was named for "Green Wood," the summer home built in 1823 by John C. McGehee, a Cambridge lawyer. The site of this two-room cabin reportedly was 509 East Cambridge Avenue in Greenwood. About 1830, the McGehee family moved to Florida where Mr. McGehee became a circuit judge.

GREENWOOD

BAPTIST PRESS   weekly--continues South Carolina Baptist on Aug 2, 1905 = vol 8, no 47, Victor L. Master and Louis J. Bristow (editors and proprietors). Paper moved to Union on Nov 7, 1906. *Files: SCL Aug 1905-Oct 1906.*

CHRISTIAN APPEAL   weekly, Methodist--established 1903, ceased c. 1914. Cited by Ayer 1903 thru 1914. Ayer 1903: C. W. Creighton (editor and publisher). *NFK*

DAILY INDEX   daily except Mon--established Jul 22, 1902, continues Greenwood Index, ceased Dec 1902. Jul 22, 1902 = vol 1, no 1, H. L. Watson (editor and publisher). An ill-fated attempt by the Greenwood Index to become a daily. Reverted to weekly status Dec 1902. *Files: Erskine, Greenwood CL, Index-Journal, and SCL mfm Jul 22-Nov 19, 1902.*

EVENING INDEX   daily except Sun--continues Greenwood Index, became daily Jan 14, 1918, and changed name to Evening Index Jan 31, 1918 = vol 21, no 73, H. L. Watson (president), Index Publishing Company. Continued tri-weekly subscriptions, although (according to Ayer) reader simply got Mon-Wed-Fri issues each week, not a true tri-weekly edition. Merged with Greenwood Daily Journal Feb 6, 1919 to form the Index-Journal. *Files: Greenwood CL, Index-Journal, and SCL mfm Jan-Dec 1918.*

GREENWOOD ADVOCATE   weekly c. 1894. According to the Abbeville Press and Banner (Apr 25, 1894), this pro-Tillman paper was established in Greenwood by W. W. Thompson & Son to oppose the Greenwood Leader. On May 3, 1894, Thompson (who had been associate editor of the Greenwood Leader) shot that paper's editor, P. E. Rowell, during a disagreement over a railroad pass. Rowell, who subsequently died from his wounds, claimed the pass had been issued to the Greenwood Leader, not to Thompson. A few weeks later, R. B. Wilson purchased the Greenwood Advocate, which he renamed the Greenwood Journal. *NFK*

GREENWOOD ATLAS   weekly c. 1891-1892. According to a history of area journalism published in the Index-Journal (Jun 27, 1937), S. P. Britton printed this short-lived newspaper. Not cited by Ayer. *NFK*

GREENWOOD DAILY JOURNAL   evenings except Sun--continues Greenwood Journal, which on Apr 13, 1911 became daily. Apr 13, 1911 = vol 1, no 1, G. W. Gardner and G. W. Gardner, Jr. (editors), G. W. Gardner (proprietor). Merged with Evening Index Feb 6, 1919 to create the Index-Journal. *Files: SCL Jun 1, 1912, Jul 10, 1917, Jan 8-12, 1919; Greenwood CL, Index-Journal, and SCL mfm Apr 1911-Apr 1912, Apr 1914-Apr 1917.*

GREENWOOD INDEX   weekly, tri-weekly--established Nov 11, 1897, in 1902 issued briefly as Daily Index (see), then reverted to weekly status until Feb 27, 1917, when became tri-weekly. In Jan 1918 became Evening Index. Nov 11, 1897 = vol 1, no 1, W. G. Chaffee (editor and proprietor). In Aug 1898 Chaffee went off to war and was succeeded by S. H. McGhee. H. L. Watson, J. Rutledge McGhee, and Joel S. Bailey also associated with paper. *Files: Erskine mfm 1897-1905, 1907-1915; Greenwood CL, Index-Journal, and SCL mfm 1897-1905, 1907-1918.*

GREENWOOD JOURNAL   weekly, semi-weekly--established Aug 1, 1894 as weekly, issued semi-weekly c. 1898-1902, then weekly. On Apr 13, 1911 became Greenville Daily Journal. Sep 12, 1895 = vol 2, no 7, R. B. Wilson (editor), Greenwood Publishing Company. F. M. Allen, J. L. Carr, and George W. Gardner also associated with paper. *Files: Greenwood CL and Index-Journal mfm (1895-1897) 85, 1901, 1903-1905, 1907-1911; SCL Sep 24, 1896, Aug 28, 1908, mfm (1895-1897) 85, 1901, 1903-1905, 1907-1911.*

GREENWOOD LEADER   weekly c. 1894. According to the Abbeville Medium (Feb 22, 1894), the first issue of the Greenwood Leader had appeared--P. E. Rowell (editor), W. W. Thompson (associate editor). A few months later, Thompson shot and killed Rowell. See the Greenwood Advocate. *NFK*

GREENWOOD LIGHT   weekly--established 1885, ceased c. 1886. Not cited by Ayer. Nov 20, 1885 = vol 1, no 7, E. S. F. Giles (editor). H. S. Cunningham also associated with paper. *Files: Erskine, Greenwood CL, and SC Historical Society mfm Nov 20, Dec 11, 1885, Jan 1, 29, 1886.*

GREENWOOD PLAIN DEALER   weekly, independent--established 1939, ceased c. 1949. May 12, 1939 = vol 1, no 2. This issue indicates paper founded on May 5, 1939 by John Allyn Cheshire. Cited by Ayer 1940 thru 1949: J. A. Cheshire (editor), Plain Dealer Publishing Company. *Files: SCL (1939-1941) 9.*

GREENWOOD TIMES   weekly--established 1889, ceased c. 1890. Aug 23, 1889 = vol 1, no 14, Fitz Hugh McMaster (editor), Greenwood Printing House. Cited once in Ayer (1889). *Files: Erskine, Greenwood CL, and SC Historical Society mfm Aug 23, 1889; SCL Dec 11, 1889.*

GREENWOOD TRIBUNE   weekly, independent--established 1885, ceased c. 1890. Sep 23, 1886 = vol 1, no 51, J. S. Daley and R. G. McLees (editors and publishers). W. K. Blake, William F. Carter, E. C. McCants, and W. P. Barratt also associated with paper. Cited by Ayer 1886 thru 1890. *Files: Erskine, Greenwood CL, and SC Historical Society mfm (1886-1888) 20; SCL Jul 6, 1888.*

INDEX-JOURNAL   daily--created by merger of <u>Evening Index</u> and <u>Greenwood Daily Journal</u> Feb 6, 1919 = vol 1, no 1, H. L. Watson (editor), Index-Journal Company (publisher). According to Ayer, until 1944 <u>Index-Journal</u> used Mon-Wed-Fri issues as tri-weekly. In addition to Watson, J. E. Chafin, James A. Cato, William C. Collins, R. Frank Mundy, and Mrs. Eleanor Mundy associated with paper. *Files: Clemson mfm 1924-1945; Lander mfm 1921-1922, 1950 + ; Greenwood CL, <u>Index-Journal</u>, and SCL mfm 1919 + .*

MILL VISITOR   weekly--established 1916, ceased ? Not cited by Ayer. Apr 7, 1916 = vol 1, no 5 (no personnel listed). *Files: SCL Apr 7, 1916.*

NEW ERA   weekly--established 1875, moved to Ninety Six in 1876 and became the <u>Ninety Six Herald</u>. Rowell (1875): W. K. Blake (editor), New Era Publishing Company. *NFK*

NEWS AND VIEWS   weekly, semi-weekly--established 1903, ceased c. 1906. Cited by Ayer 1904 thru 1906. Jun 1, 1905 = vol 3, no 22, J. R. Pittman (editor), News and Views Company. "A Journal of the DEEDS and INDEX to the NEEDS of all our PEOPLE." *Files: Erskine, Greenwood CL, and SC Historical Society mfm Jun 1, Jul 6, Aug 11, 1905.*

NEWS SCIMITER   weekly--established 1911, ceased c. 1913. May 20, 1912 = vol 1, no 38 (also has Laurens dateline), W. T. Crews and W. P. Beard (editors), News Scimiter Publishing Company. Not cited by Ayer. In Jul 1914 Beard founded the <u>Scimitar</u> in Abbeville. *Files: SCL May 20, Jul 4, 1912.*

PIEDMONT VOICE   weekly, black publication--established 1910, ceased c. 1913. Cited by Ayer 1911 thru 1913, no personnel listed. *NFK*

SALUDA ARGUS   weekly--established 1881, ceased c. 1884. Cited by Ayer 1882 thru 1884. Apr 17, 1884 = vol 3, no 48, whole no 152, John H. Hogan (editor), Hogan and Tolbert (proprietors). W. P. Calhoun represented this paper at the SC State Press Association meeting in 1884. Reportedly became the <u>Abbeville Messenger</u> in 1884 (see). *Files: Erskine, Greenwood CL, and SC Historical Society mfm Apr 17, May 1, Aug 7, 1884.*

SENTINEL   weekly, black publication--established 1903, ceased c. 1904. Cited by Ayer 1902 thru 1904: D. Timothy McDaniel (editor), James C. White (publisher). *NFK*

SOUTH CAROLINA BAPTIST   weekly--established in Lake City in 1897 by A. McA. Pittman, soon moved to Greenwood, became <u>Baptist Press</u> Aug 2, 1905. Cited by Ayer 1899 thru 1905. May 28, 1898 = vol 1, no 38, R. W. Sanders and J. W. Perry (editors), Pittman, Gardner & Company (proprietor). *Files: SCL (1905) 7, mfm (1898-1902) 29.*

NINETY SIX

ANTI-MONARCHIST, AND SOUTH-CAROLINA ADVERTISER weekly--established in Edgefield in 1811, but according to McCord and Nott's law reports was published in Cambridge [Ninety Six] in 1812. Not known when ceased. See Anti-Monarchist, and South-Carolina Advertiser [Edgefield] and Harry L. Watson, "Early Newspapers of Abbeville District, 1812-1834," Proceedings, SC Historical Association (1940), pp. 18-35. *Files: none known for 1812, four issues exist for Edgefield (1811).*

NINETY SIX GUARDIAN weekly--established 1877, ceased c. 1879 when moved to Hampton and continued as the Hampton County Guardian. May 30, 1878 = vol 2, no 1, M. B. McSweeney (proprietor). Note: McSweeney served as governor, 1899-1903. *Files: Erskine, Greenwood CL, and SC Historical Society mfm (1878-1879) 50.*

NINETY SIX HERALD weekly--established 1876, ceased c. 1877. Cited by Rowell 1876 and 1877: W. K. Blake (editor and publisher). Formerly the New Era [Greenwood]. *NFK*

NINETY SIX NEWS weekly, independent--established 1957, ceased c. 1960. Cited by Ayer 1958 thru 1960. Ayer 1958: Jack Brewster (publisher). Ayer 1959 and 1960: Charles Byars (publisher). For a brief time in 1960, the Ninety Six News was published as a supplement to Greenwood's Index-Journal. *NFK*

STAR weekly, Democrat--established 1906, ceased c. 1909. Cited by Ayer 1907 thru 1909: E. A. McDowell (editor and publisher). Aug 16, 1906 (vol 1, no 1) listed on contents of mfm reel held by Erskine, Greenwood CL, and SC Historical Society, but not reproduced. *NFK*

STAR-COUNTY REVIEW weekly--established Sep 1981 by Don Goforth (editor), Don Goforth and James Graves (publishers). Feb 27, 1985 = vol 4, no 23, James Graves (editor and publisher). *Files: Star-County Review 1981 + .*

WARE SHOALS

OBSERVER weekly--established 1981. Apr 15, 1981 = vol 1, no 1, Dan Branyon (editor and publisher). *Files: Observer and Ware Shoals Library 1981 + .*

WARE SHOALS LIFE weekly, bi-monthly--established 1922, ceased 1984. Mar 26, 1926 = vol 4, no 13, M. B. Camack (editor), published by the "Ware Shoals School and Community." Produced as a semi-house organ of Riegel Corporation for many years. Became bi-monthly in 1984, ceased in Nov 1984. Hugh L. Phillips and Mrs. Judy Abrams also associated with paper. *Files: SCL (1926-1934, 1944-1948) 55; Ware Shoals Library 1947-1984. Note: SCL classifies Ware Shoals Life as a periodical.*

WARE SHOALS NEWS   weekly (?) -- title listed in history of area journalism published in the <u>Index-Journal</u> (Jun 27, 1937). No details given. Not cited by Ayer. *NFK*

HAMPTON COUNTY

Formed in 1878 from part of Beaufort County, Hampton County is named for Wade Hampton, Confederate general and governor of South Carolina, 1876-1879.

BRUNSON

HAMPTON COUNTY ELEVATOR semi-monthly, Republican, black publication--established 1891, ceased c. 1893. Cited once in Ayer (1892): R. E. Primus (editor), Colored Publishing Company of Hampton County. *NFK*

HAMPTON COUNTY NEWS HERALD weekly, independent--established 1887, ceased c. 1890. Cited by Ayer 1888 thru 1890. Ayer 1888 and 1889: Ben S. Williams (editor and publisher). Ayer 1890: Julius P. Youmans (editor and publisher). *Files: Greenville CL Aug 22, 1888, Apr 10, 1889.*

NEW LIGHT semi-monthly, black publication--established 1896, ceased c. 1897. Cited once in Ayer (1897): J. C. Eubanks and M. P. Harvey (editors and publishers). *NFK*

TRUE SOUTH weekly--established 1875, ceased c. 1875. Cited once in Rowell (1875): Benjamin L. Brisbane (editor and publisher). Apr 8, 1875 = vol 1, no 9, Benjamin L. Brisbane (editor, publisher, and proprietor). *Files: SCL Apr 8, 1875.*

ESTILL

ESTILL HERALD weekly, Democrat--established 1914, ceased c. 1915. Cited once in Ayer (1915): F. Earle Bradham (editor and publisher). *NFK*

ESTILL PROGRESS weekly c. 1909. According to Both Sides of the Swamp (Hampton County Tricentennial Commission, 1970), this paper was established by Henry Lee Solomons in 1909. Not cited by Ayer. *NFK*

HAMPTON

FARMER'S REVIEW weekly, Democrat--established 1911, ceased c. 1913. Cited once in Ayer (1912): E. F. Hammond (editor), W. T. Johns (publisher). Jan 4, 1912 = vol 1, no 16. *Files: SCL Jan 4, 1912.*

HAMPTON COUNTY DEMOCRAT weekly--established 1937 in Yemassee as a monthly, but soon became a weekly. According to Ayer, issued in Hampton c. 1948 to Oct 3, 1951, when absorbed by the Hampton County Guardian. Subsequently revived and once more cited in Ayer 1969 to 1978, when apparently ceased. Jul 22, 1949 = vol 12, no 23, W. O. Miller (editor and publisher). In addition to Miller, B. P. Davies, Jr., Jack Mette, and John W. Mette also associated with paper. *Files: Hampton CL (1949-1951) 60.*

HAMPTON COUNTY GUARDIAN   weekly--established in 1879 by Miles B. McSweeney, editor and publisher and later governor (1899-1903). McSweeney previously published the Ninety Six Guardian (1877-1879). In 1919, his son, Eugene B. McSweeney, moved operations to Allendale, where he also published the Allendale County Citizen. Others associated with the paper include Florence Humphries McSweeney, Erskine Caldwell, Mr. and Mrs. W. L. Maner, Tom O'Connor, Martha Young O'Connor, Pat Tyler, Wayne Zurenda, Martha Bee Anderson, and Linda Mixon. *Files: Allendale CL mfm 1950-1960, 1962-1980; Greenville CL (1888-1889) 8; Hampton County Guardian 1975 + ; Hampton CL 1912-1913, 1950, 1956, 1982 + , mfm 1914-1960, 1962-1981; SCL ((1882-1979)) 260, mfm 1914-1960, 1962-1981.*

HAMPTON COUNTY HERALD   weekly--established 1916, ceased c. 1919. Cited by Ayer 1917 thru 1919. Mar 3, 1916 = vol 1, no 1, Thomas M. Seawell (manager), Randolph Murdaugh (president), Hampton County Herald Publishing Company. *Files: Hampton CL (1916-1917) 30; SCL mfm Nov 23, 1916.*

HAMPTON COUNTY NEWS   weekly, Democrat--established 1910, ceased c. 1913. Jul 21, 1911 = vol 1, no 26, J. W. Manuel (associate editor). Ayer lists under Brunson, but Jul issue has Hampton dateline. Cited by Ayer 1911 thru 1912. *Files: SCL mfm Jul 21, 1911.*

VARNVILLE

HAMPTON DEMOCRAT   weekly--established 1878, ceased c. 1879. Listed once in Rowell (1879): T. H. Marshall (editor and publisher). *NFK*

VARNVILLE ENTERPRISE   weekly, Democrat--established 1892, ceased c. 1899. Cited by Ayer 1894 thru 1898. Oct 23, 1895 = vol 3, no 27, T. P. Miller (editor and publisher). Mrs. Virginia D. Young also associated with paper. *Files: SCL Oct 9, 23, 30, 1895.*

VARNVILLE MESSENGER   weekly--established 1880, ceased c. 1881. Cited by Ayer 1880 and 1881. No editor or publisher listed. *NFK*

YEMASSEE

HAMPTON COUNTY DEMOCRAT   monthly, weekly--established 1937 as monthly, but soon issued weekly. Apr 1938 = vol 1, no 8, Jack Mette (editor and publisher). According to Ayer, issued in Hampton after 1948. *Files: SCL (1938-1940) 40.*

HORRY COUNTY

Formerly Kingston County within Georgetown District, in 1801 Horry District (now Horry County) achieved separate status. Named for a Revolutionary War officer, Peter Horry (1743-1815), what is now the state's largest county long was a region of subsistence farming known as "The Independent Republic." As this nickname indicates, until quite recently Horry County led a quiet, isolated existence, cut off from the rest of South Carolina by swamps, rivers, and poor roads.

CONWAY

FIELD   weekly, semi-weekly--established 1903, merged with Horry Herald in 1964, continued by Field and Herald. Cited by Ayer 1906 thru 1964. Issued semi-weekly c. 1954-1957. Ayer 1906: Edwin J. Sherwood (editor), Horry Publishing Company. Apr 17, 1913 = vol 10, no 17, Power W. Bethea (editor), Horry Publishing Company. J. O. Norton, E. S. C. Baker, B. St. L. Sommerlyn, Eldridge Thompson, John Sikes, Larry Boulier, and Mark C. Garner also associated with paper. *Files: SCL (1913-1924) 13; Horry CL and SCL mfm ((1924-1952)) 228, 1954-1964.*

FIELD AND HERALD   weekly--created by merger of Field and Horry Herald on Jul 29, 1964 = vol 105, no 11, Eldridge Thompson (editor), Mark C. Garner (owner and publisher). Larry Boulier, James A. Cato, Steve Robertson, Coyte White, Ben Morris, and Robert L. Reeves also associated with paper. *Files: SCL Jun 16, 1967; Horry CL, SCL, and Sun-News mfm 1964 + .*

HORRY DISPATCH   weekly--established 1861, ceased c. 1863. Apr 11, 1861 = vol 1, no 6, A. A. Gilbert and H. L. Darr (publishers). N. G. Osteen also associated with paper. Horry Dispatch, owned by the Sumter Watchman, had been the Sumter Dispatch (1860-1861). *Files: SCL (1861-1862) 15; Horry CL, SCL, and USC-Coastal mfm (1861-1862) 25.*

HORRY HERALD   weekly, Democrat--established 1886, continued by Independent Republic c. 1897. Jan 20, 1887 = vol 1, no 26 (no personnel cited). Listed in Ayer 1887 thru 1897. Ayer 1887: E. R. Beatty (publisher). Evans Norton, E. W. Nolley, and John W. Hammond also associated with paper. *Files: SCL May 12, 19, 1887; Francis Marion, Horry CL, SCL, and USC-Coastal mfm ((Jan 1887-Nov 1894)) 176, Jan-May 1897.*

HORRY HERALD   weekly--continues Independent Republic c. 1899, merged with Field in 1964, continued by Field and Herald. Jan 5, 1899 = vol 2, no 32, E. W. Nolley (editor and manager), Conway Publishing Company. Aug 17, 1899 = vol 14, no 5, based upon founding date of 1886. H. H. Woodward, Clarence W. Atkinson, Lem Winesett, Martin Meadows, Eldridge Thompson, Larry Boulier, and Mark C. Garner also associated with paper. *Files: Francis Marion mfm Jan 5, 1899, Jun 1899-Jul 1906;*

Horry CL mfm Jan 5, 1899, Jun 1899-1964; USC-Coastal mfm Jan 5, 1899, Jun 1899-1954; SCL ((1930-1934)) 130, mfm Jan 5, 1899, Jun 1899-1964.

HORRY INDEPENDENT   weekly--established 1980. Jul 7, 1981 = vol 2, no 15, Steve Robertson (editor and publisher). *Files: Horry Independent 1980 + .*

HORRY MONITOR   weekly, Democrat--established 1892, ceased c. 1894. Part of each edition of the Florence Reflector was published as the Horry Monitor [Conway] and the Alliance Ladder [Kingstree]. Cited once in Ayer (1893/4): T. C. Willoughby (editor and publisher). *NFK*

HORRY NEWS   weekly, independent--established 1869, merged with the Georgetown Comet 1877, continued by the Comet and News. Cited in Rowell 1870: T. W. Beatty (editor), S. R. Rhodes (publisher). Jul 14, 1871 = vol 3, no 28, T. W. Beatty (editor). *Files: Francis Marion, Horry CL, and USC-Coastal mfm ((1871, 1874-1877)) 120; SCL orig & mfm ((1871, 1874-1877)) 120.*

HORRY PROGRESS   weekly, Democrat--continues the Telephone c. 1883, ceased c. 1888. Mar 5, 1886 = vol 10, no 10, Henry Hardee (editor), James W. Ogilvie (publisher). According to Ogilvie's reminiscences (Horry Herald, Oct 25, 1909), the Horry Progress ceased c. 1886; however, Ayer indicates it was published in Loris c. 1887-1888 by Ogilvie. *Files: SCL Mar 5, 1886 (fragment).*

HORRY SENTINEL   weekly, Democrat--established 1868, ceased c. 1869. Printed by Marion Crescent. Cited by Rowell 1869: Sidney E. McMillan (editor and publisher). *NFK*

INDEPENDENT REPUBLIC   weekly, Democrat--continues Horry Herald c. 1897, continued by Horry Herald c. 1899. Mar 17, 1898 = vol 1, no 42, S. Frank Parrott (editor), Conway Publishing Company. Cited Ayer 1898: J. O. Norton (editor), D. A. Spivey (publisher). E. W. Nolley represented paper at 1898 session of the SC Press Association. Apparently a temporary name change of the Horry Herald. *Files: Clemson Mar 17, 1898.*

NEWS & SHOPPER   see News & Shopper [Myrtle Beach].

TELEPHONE   weekly, Democrat--established 1878, continued by Horry Progress c. 1883. Cited by Rowell 1879 and Ayer 1880 thru 1882. Dec 6, 1879 = vol 2, no 39, whole no 91, Landy Wood (editor and proprietor). *Files: Horry CL mfm Dec 6, 1879, Apr 3, 1880; SCL orig & mfm Dec 6, 1879, Apr 3, 1880.*

TIMES   see Times [Myrtle Beach].

WEST HORRY JOURNAL   weekly--established 1986. Published by the Myrtle Beach Journal for western Horry County. Continues regional edition of News & Shopper. *Files: Myrtle Beach Journal 1986 + .*

GARDEN CITY

WILD FLOWER   weekly, irregular--established 1977, ceased c. 1980. Dec 14, 1977 = vol 1, no ? , ------- Garrett (editor), Winesett Publishing Company [Marion]. Weekly paper for Garden City, Surfside Beach, Murrell's Inlet, Litchfield Beach, and Pawley's Island. *Files: SCL Dec 14, 1977, Aug 29, 1979.*

LORIS

HORRY COUNTY NEWS   weekly, Democrat--established Feb 20, 1936, continued by Horry County News and Loris Sentinel in Jun 1952. Nov 4, 1949 = vol 14, no 49 (no personnel listed). Ayer 1939: F. S. Radspinner (editor), Field Publishers and Printers [Conway]. Phil Wright, J. L. King, Edwin Tichenor, and Rod Sparrow also associated with paper. *Files: Horry CL and SCL mfm ((Nov 1949-May 1952)) 112.*

HORRY COUNTY NEWS AND LORIS SENTINEL   weekly--continues Horry County News Jun 1952, continued by Loris Sentinel Jan 1955. No merger involved. On Jun 5, 1952 (vol 16, no 25) paper announced title change, Fenton Miller (editor), Atlantic Publishing Company. Edwin B. Tichenor, W. Horace Carter, and Mark C. Garner also associated with paper. *Files: Horry CL mfm Jun 1952-Jul 1954; Loris Sentinel 1952-1954; SCL mfm Jun 1952-Jul 1954.*

HORRY PROGRESS   weekly, Democrat--continues Telephone c. 1883, ceased c. 1888. Published in Conway 1883-1886. According to Ayer 1887-1888, published in Loris by James W. Ogilvie. See Horry Progress [Conway].

LORIS NEWS   weekly c. 1910. According to Horry Herald (Apr 3, 1910), the Loris News had suspended operations because of financial difficulties. *NFK*

LORIS NEWS   weekly, Democrat--established 1912, ceased c. 1915. Cited by Ayer 1913 thru 1915: Sam T. Creech (editor), Loris Publishing Company. *NFK*

LORIS OBSERVER   weekly--established 1928, ceased c. 1929. Cited once in Ayer (1929): B. H. Prince (editor), Loris Observer (publisher). Organ of those agitating for a new county with Loris as the county seat. See the Independent Republic Quarterly (Jul 1976). *NFK*

LORIS SENTINEL   weekly--continues Horry County News and Loris Sentinel on Jan 5, 1955 = vol 19, no 21, Rod Sparrow (editor). "Horry County News" dropped from masthead, but continued for a time on editorial page. Rupert Blocker, V. Laverne Ward, W. Horace Carter, Bob Bloodworth, Edward Boyd, Laura Phelps, Anne Trainer, and

Davis O. Heniford also associated with paper. *Files: Horry CL mfm 1955 + ; Loris Sentinel 1955 + ; SCL mfm 1955 + .*

MYRTLE BEACH

GRAND STRAND JOURNAL   weekly--published Aug 1972-Jun 1973, continues Myrtle Beach Journal. On Jun 21, 1973 merged with Daily American [Georgetown], continued by Grand Strand Journal American. Aug 31, 1972 = vol 1, no 38, Henry O. Counts (editor), United Communications Company. *Files: Horry CL mfm Aug 1972-Jun 1973; SCL orig & mfm Aug 1972-Jun 1973.*

GRAND STRAND JOURNAL AMERICAN   daily--created Jun 1973 by merger of Grand Strand Journal and Daily American [Georgetown], continued by Journal American Aug 1973. Jun 28, 1973 = vol 1, no 97, Bruce Humphrey (editor), United Communications Company. Offices in Myrtle Beach and Georgetown. *Files: Horry CL mfm (Jun-Aug 1973) 40; SCL orig & mfm (Jun-Aug 1973) 40.*

JOURNAL AMERICAN   daily--continues Grand Strand Journal American in Aug 1973, ceased c. 1975. Aug 13, 1973 = vol 1, no 136, John H. Sumner (editor), United Communications Company. John Carriker and R. H. Cunningham also associated with paper. Offices in Myrtle Beach and Georgetown. *Files: Horry CL mfm Aug 1973-Dec 1974; SCL orig & mfm Aug 1973-Dec 1974.*

MYRTLE BEACH DAILY NEWS   daily c. 1956--continues Myrtle Beach News, continued by Myrtle Beach News. Jan 3, 1956 = vol 21, no 88, W. LeRoy Harrelson (editor and publisher). Ill-fated attempt by weekly to become a daily publication. *Files: Horry CL, SCL and Sun-News mfm Jan-Jun 1956.*

MYRTLE BEACH JOURNAL   weekly--established 1971, continued by Grand Strand Journal Aug 1972. Dec 30, 1971 = vol 1, no 3, William E. Black (editor and publisher), Journal Publishing Company. *Files: SCL (Dec 1971-Jul 1972) 20.*

MYRTLE BEACH JOURNAL   weekly--established 1982. Mar 17, 1982 = vol 1, no 1, Chad Buffkin (editor), Atlantic Publications. Cindy Buffkin also associated with paper. Also publishes the West Horry Journal, Williamsburg-Florence Journal, Georgetown Journal, and North Myrtle Beach Journal--all established in 1986. *Files: Chapin Memorial Library 1982 + ; Horry CL mfm 1982 + ; Myrtle Beach Journal 1982 + .*

MYRTLE BEACH NEWS   weekly--established 1935, continued by Myrtle Beach Daily News c. 1956. Jan 30, 1936 = vol 1, no 36, J. C. Macklen (owner and publisher). W. G. Hazel, C. L. Phillips, James L. Platt, and W. LeRoy Harrelson also associated with paper. "Coastal Carolinian" in small type incorporated in masthead c. 1948-1949, but not true title change. Published at that time by the Coastal Carolinian Press. *Files:*

Horry CL and Sun-News mfm Jan 1938-Jun 1939, Jul 1949-Dec 1955; SCL ((1936-1941)) 123, mfm Jan 1938-Jun 1939, Jul 1949-Dec 1955.

MYRTLE BEACH NEWS   weekly, semi-weekly--continues Myrtle Beach Daily News c. 1956, merged with Myrtle Beach Sun and Ocean Beach News Aug 1961, continued by Sun-News. Sep 29, 1960 = vol 29, no 17, John E. Jones (editor), Grand Strand Publishing Company. *Files: Horry CL and Sun-News mfm Sep 1960-Jul 1961; SCL Apr 6, 1961, mfm Sep 1960-Jul 1961.*

MYRTLE BEACH SUN   weekly, Independent Democrat--established 1950. Jun 16, 1950 = vol 1, no 1, Mark C. Garner (editor), Atlantic Publishing Company. Merged with Ocean Beach News Jan 1956 to create the Myrtle Beach Sun and Ocean Beach News. *Files: Horry CL and SCL mfm 1950-1955.*

MYRTLE BEACH SUN AND OCEAN BEACH NEWS   weekly--created Jan 1956 by merger of Myrtle Beach Sun and Ocean Beach News. Both papers apparently founded by Mark C. Garner in 1950. Merger not announced in first joint issue, Jan 4, 1956 = vol 6, no 28. Paper merged with Myrtle Beach News Aug 1961, continued by Sun-News. Larry Boulier also associated with paper. *Files: Horry CL and SCL mfm 1956-1961.*

NEWS & SHOPPER   weekly--established 1977, Terri Harris and Wayne Weible (publishers). Until 1986 published four regional editions: Grand Strand, West Horry, Georgetown, and Williamsburg-Lake City. These shoppers were acquired by the Myrtle Beach Journal (Atlantic Publications) in 1986 and converted into these weekly newspapers: West Horry Journal, Georgetown Journal, and Williamsburg-Florence Journal. *Files: Myrtle Beach Journal 1977-1986.*

SOUTH CAROLINA BEACHCOMBER   weekly, seasonal, Easter to Labor Day--established 1985, Chad Buffkin (editor), Atlantic Publications. *Files: Chapin Memorial Library and Myrtle Beach Journal 1985 + .*

SUN-NEWS   weekly, semi-weekly, tri-weekly, daily--created by merger of Myrtle Beach Sun and Ocean Beach News and Myrtle Beach News on Aug 16, 1961 = vol 12, no 9, Eldridge Thompson (editor), Mark C. Garner (publisher). Thom Billington, Ken Hare, Ben Morris, Jim D'Avignon, and Jerry Ausband also associated with paper. Sun-News issued weekly to Feb 2, 1969, semi-weekly to Nov 7, 1972, tri-weekly to Nov 19, 1973, and daily since that date. *Files: Chapin Memorial Library 1970 + ; Horry CL, SCL, and Sun-News mfm 1961 + .*

TIMES   weekly--established 1986. May 28-Jun 3, 1987 = vol 1, no 33, Catherine Perkins Black (editor), Barbara Easterling (advertising manager). Paper publishes three editions with same title serving Myrtle Beach, Conway, and the Surfside Beach-Garden City-Socastee area. *Files: Times 1986 + .*

WEEKLY JOURNAL   weekly, black publication--established 1975, ceased c. 1976. Oct 16, 1975 = vol 1, no 2, Carnell C. Midgette (editor and publisher). *Files: Horry CL and SCL mfm Oct 16, 1975.*

WEEKLY OBSERVER   weekly, black publication--established 1974, ceased c. 1977. Dec 4, 1975 = vol 2, no 9, Thom H. Billington (editor), Minority Associates, Inc. *Files: Horry CL and SCL mfm Dec 1975-Nov 1976.*

MYRTLE BEACH AIR FORCE BASE

STRAND SENTRY   weekly--established 1968, published by the Sun-News for U. S. Air Force personnel. *Files: Strand Sentry 1985 + , microfiche 1958-1984; Wisconsin Historical Society mfm May 1981 + .*

NORTH MYRTLE BEACH

COASTAL COURIER   weekly--established 1987 and issued by owners of the Loris Sentinel. Mar 26, 1987 = vol 1, no 1, Anne Trainer (managing editor), Ricky Hardee (publisher). *Files: Coastal Courier 1987 + .*

NORTH MYRTLE BEACH JOURNAL   weekly--established Nov 1986 by Atlantic Publications (publisher of Myrtle Beach Journal). *Files: Myrtle Beach Journal 1986 + .*

NORTH MYRTLE BEACH TIMES   weekly, semi-weekly--established Feb 24, 1971 = vol 1, no 1, Pauline Lowman (managing editor). Tommy Grant and Elbert Marshall also associated with paper. *Files: Horry CL mfm 1971 + ; North Myrtle Beach Times 1971 + ; SCL mfm 1971 + .*

OCEAN BEACH

OCEAN BEACH NEWS   weekly, Independent Democrat--established 1950. Cited by Ayer 1954 thru 1956: Mark C. Garner (editor), Atlantic Publishing Company. Merged with Myrtle Beach Sun Jan 1956, continued by the Myrtle Beach Sun and Ocean Beach News. *NFK*

SURFSIDE BEACH

SOUTH STRAND DAILY NEWS   daily c. 1980. Only one issue published, presumably by Bob Cunningham, Pawley's Island. *NFK*

SOUTH STRAND HERALD   weekly--established Jun 1984, continued Jun 1985 by Coastal Observer [Pawley's Island]. Apr 30, 1985 = vol 1, no 46, Charles R. Swenson (editor and publisher). Regional edition of Coastal Observer. *Files: Coastal Observer 1984-1985.*

TIMES   see Times [Myrtle Beach].

JASPER COUNTY

Formed in 1912 from parts of Beaufort and Hampton counties, Jasper County is named for Sergeant William Jasper, who was mortally wounded during the seige of Savannah in October 1779.

HARDEEVILLE

LOW COUNTRY WEEKLY weekly--established 1980. Oct 16, 1980 = vol 1, no 1, Debra Butler and Donna Floyd (editors and publishers). William Hornung and Julie and Dewey Kundson also associated with paper. Not cited by Ayer. *Files: Debra Butler 1980-1983; Hardeeville Community Library 1980 + ; Low Country Weekly 1984 + .*

TRI-CITY MIRROR weekly--established 1972, ceased Aug 1980. Jan 10, 1980 = vol 7, no 39, Paul Hayes (editor and publisher). Hayes also founded paper. Not cited by Ayer. *Files: Hardeeville Community Library (1980) 28.*

RIDGELAND

BEAUFORT-JASPER NEWS weekly--formed Oct 1939 by merger of the Beaufort County News and the Jasper County Citizen, ceased c. Dec 1939. Published in Beaufort and Ridgeland. Oct 26, 1939 = vol 1, no 21, Albert Rouslin (editor). *Files: SCL orig & mfm Oct 5, 26, Nov 2, 9, 1939.*

JASPER COUNTY CITIZEN weekly--established 1939, merged with Beaufort County News Oct 1939 to form Beaufort-Jasper News. Ayer 1940: Jack Mette (editor and publisher). *NFK*

JASPER COUNTY NEWS weekly--established 1956. Ayer 1956: G. Wesley Frame (editor and publisher). May 14, 1963 = vol 7, no 38, G. Wesley Frame (publisher), D. N. Rivers (editor). Mrs. D. N. Rivers, Sr., Cynthia Smith, and St. Julien G. Rivers also associated with paper. *Files: Jasper County News ((1963 +)); SCL ((1984 +)).*

JASPER COUNTY RECORD weekly--established 1924, absorbed by Hampton County Guardian Aug 1, 1951. Cited by Ayer 1926 thru 1952. Ayer 1926: Eugene B. McSweeney (editor and publisher). Jun 20, 1930 = vol 6, no 39, Eugene B. McSweeney (editor and publisher). Tom O'Connor also associated with paper. *Files: SCL (1928-1944) 50.*

JASPER HERALD weekly--established 1911, ceased 1919. Cited by Ayer 1912 thru 1919. Ayer 1912: R. N. Jefferies (editor), Ridgeland Printing Company. Dec 8, 1915 = vol 5, no 50, James D. Archer (editor), C. E. Perry (proprietor), Ridgeland Printing Company. E. L. Perry also associated with paper. Ceased when office burned on May 20, 1919. *Files: SCL Dec 8, 1915.*

LOW COUNTRY SENTINEL   weekly, independent--established 1971, ceased c. 1972. Not listed in Ayer. Eugene Able (editor and publisher) reportedly had files in late 1970s. *NFK*

TRUE LIGHT   semi-monthly, black publication--established 1899, ceased c. 1900. Cited once in Ayer (1899). No editor or publisher listed. *NFK*

KERSHAW COUNTY

Created in 1798 when old Camden District was divided into five parts, Kershaw District (now Kershaw County) is named for Colonel Joseph Kershaw, Revolutionary War leader and founder of Camden. Kershaw, born in England about 1728, was a prominent back-country merchant and perhaps owner of this state's first flour mill. He died in 1791.

BETHUNE

BETHUNE ENTERPRISE weekly, Democrat--established 1900, ceased c. 1902. Cited by Ayer 1901 and 1902: J. E. Gardner (editor and publisher). Not cited in 1903. Jul 4, 1901 = vol 1, no 41, J. E. Gardner (editor and proprietor). *Files: Camden Archives Jul 4, 1901.*

BETHUNE OBSERVER weekly, Democrat--established 1913, 1916, and 1922 with a new number sequence for each series. Cited by Ayer 1914 and 1915, 1917 thru 1921, 1923. Ayer 1914: L. A. McDowell (editor), Bethune Publishing Company. Jul 9, 1914 = vol 2, no 11, J. E. Gardner (editor). Gardner listed by Ayer as editor and publisher 1917-1921, 1923. Paper ceased c. 1923. *Files: SCL (1914-1923) 13.*

CAMDEN

CAMDEN AND LANCASTER BEACON weekly, pro-nullification--established in Lancaster as Lancaster Beacon in 1830, moved to Camden in 1831 and continued as the Camden and Lancaster Beacon, ceased c. 1832. First Camden issue Mar 15, 1831 = vol 1, no 21, James D. Cocke (editor), George P. Cocke (printer). See also the Camden Republican, and Lancaster Beacon. *Files: Camden Archives Nov 15, 1831; Clemson Apr 3, 1832 (fragment); SCL Mar 1831-Oct 1832.*

CAMDEN BEE weekly, Republican, black publication--established 1907, moved to Columbia c. 1911. Cited by Ayer in Camden 1909 thru 1911: C. C. Clarkson (editor), Camden Bee Publishing Company. *NFK*

CAMDEN CHRONICLE weekly, semi-weekly, tri-weekly, daily--established 1888, merged with Camden Independent May 1981 to create the Chronicle-Independent. Cited by Ayer 1889 thru 1981. Ayer 1889: W. L. McDowell (publisher), B. B. Clarke (editor). Nov 6, 1891 = vol 3, no 27, W. L. McDowell and B. B. Clarke (editors and proprietors). This issue states that T. J. Kirkland and W. L. Villepigue have purchased the paper. According to Ayer, issued weekly to 1952, semi-weekly 1952-1956, tri-weekly 1956-1979, daily 1980-1981. Others associated with paper include H. D. Niles, E. N. McDowell, Da Costa Brown, Harold C. Booker, C. William Calk, C. M. Ford, Fred D. Sheheen, Ted Smiley, J. B. Harris, Bill Bryant, J. S. DeRoy, and Robert F. Coppage. *Files: Camden Archives 1912, 1914, 1916-1946, 1948-Jun 1978, mfm Nov 1891-Nov 1893, 1895-Mar 1959, 1979-1981; Clemson mfm Nov 1891-Nov 1893,*

1895-Mar 1950; SCL (1913-1921) 13, 1926-1930, 1934-1935, (1938) 18, 1939-1940, (1941-1946) 25, mfm Nov 1891-Nov 1893, 1895-Mar 1950.

CAMDEN CITIZEN   weekly, Democrat--established 1953, ceased c. 1955. Cited once by Ayer (1955). Apr 9, 1953 = vol 1, no 10, George E. Stuart, Jr. (editor), Fred C. Mergner, Jr. (publisher). Pete Chaney also associated with paper. *Files: Camden Archives Apr 9, 1953; SCL Nov 25, 1953, Jan 7, 21, 1954.*

CAMDEN COMMERCIAL COURIER   weekly--established 1837, ceased c. 1838. May 6, 1837 = vol 1, no 1, Mordecai M. Levy (editor), L. M. Jones & Company (publisher). *Files: Camden Archives May 6, 1837; SCL mfm May 6, 1837-Jun 16, 1838.*

CAMDEN CONFEDERATE   weekly--established 1861. Nov 1, 1861 = vol 1, no 1, J. T. Hershman (publisher). Hershman noted that the Camden Weekly Journal had suspended operations as of Nov 1861. Paper issued Apr-Sep 1864 as the Camden Weekly Confederate (see). Merged with the Camden Journal Mar 1865, continued by the Journal and Confederate. *Files: Camden Archives (1862-1865) 15; SCL mfm Nov 1, 1861-Dec 11, 1863.*

CAMDEN DAILY JOURNAL   daily except Sun--established Jul 1864, ceased Dec 1864. Jul 6, 1864 = vol 1, no 4, D. D. Hocott (publisher). Beginning Jan 1865 issued weekly and tri-weekly editions. In Mar 1865 merged with Camden Confederate, continued by Journal and Confederate. See also the Camden Journal and the Tri-Weekly Journal. *Files: Camden Archives Dec 10, 13, 1864; SCL (1864) 70.*

CAMDEN GAZETTE   weekly--established Apr 4, 1816, printed by P. W. Johnston for proprietors. On Nov 21, 1818 continued by Camden Gazette and Mercantile Advertiser. William Langley and George W. B. Harby also associated with paper. *Files: Camden Archives, SCL, and York CL mfm Apr 11, 1816-Nov 14, 1818.*

CAMDEN GAZETTE AND MERCANTILE ADVERTISER   weekly-- continues Camden Gazette Nov 1818, ceased Feb 1822. Nov 21, 1818 = vol 3, no 136, Fisher Moses (publisher). Wilie Vaughan and John Cambridge also associated with paper. Motto: "The public will our guide--the public good our end." Succeeded by the Southern Chronicle and Camden Gazette. *Files: Camden Archives, SCL, and York CL mfm Nov 21, 1818-Apr 8, 1819, Jun 3, 1819-Feb 7, 1822.*

CAMDEN INDEPENDENT   weekly--established 1978, merged with Camden Chronicle May 1981, continued by Chronicle-Independent. May 1, 1978 = vol 1, no 1, Glenn Tucker and Michael Mischner (publishers). *Files: Camden Archives and Chronicle-Independent mfm 1978-1981.*

CAMDEN INTELLIGENCER   weekly c. 1803. According to the centennial issue of the Charleston News and Courier (1903), the Camden Intelligencer appeared Jun 5, 1803, John B. Hood (editor). *NFK*

CAMDEN JOURNAL   weekly, semi-weekly, tri-weekly, daily except Sun-- established 1826, ceased 1891. Frequent mergers, suspensions, and name changes. Jan 21, 1826 = vol 1, no 1, Charles A. Bullard (publisher). Bullard had purchased the Southern Chronicle. In 1834 paper merged with the Southern Whig [Sumter] to create the Camden Journal and Southern Whig, which was issued from May 1834 to Dec 1835. In Jan 1836 the Camden Journal was revived and then suspended from Mar 1837 to Dec 1839. On Jan 9, 1850 paper expanded to a semi-weekly and announced plans to become tri-weekly. From 1853 to 1861 issued as the Camden Weekly Journal, then operations suspended once more. Revived in Jan 1864 as the Camden Journal (weekly). Issued as a single sheet Camden Daily Journal Jul-Dec 1864, while continuing to publish a weekly edition as well. Beginning in Jan 1865 issued as Weekly Journal and Tri-Weekly Journal until merged briefly with the Camden Confederate to create the Journal and Confederate Mar-May 1865. With military occupation publishers once more issued the Weekly Journal and Tri-Weekly Journal, which subsequently became the Camden Weekly Journal and the Camden Journal. Paper merged with the Kershaw Gazette in Jul 1877 to create the Journal and Gazette, a union that lasted only a month. Issued as Camden Journal 1877-1891. In addition to Bullard, these individuals were associated with paper: W. J. Grant, C. F. Daniels, J. C. West, Robert T. M'Knight, Thomas J. Warren, G. W. Addison, Thomas W. Pegues, C. A. Price, Daniel D. Hocott, J. T. Hershman, W. D. Trantham, J. T. Hay, D. C. Kirkley, William B. Johnston, Thurlow Caston, and John Kershaw. Cited by Rowell and Ayer 1869 thru 1890. *Files: Camden Archives (1829-1879) 80, mfm 1842-1847; SCL ((1826-1891)) 1300, mfm 1842-1847; York CL mfm 1842-1847.*

CAMDEN JOURNAL AND SOUTHERN WHIG   weekly, anti-nullification-- created by merger of Camden Journal and Southern Whig [Sumter] in May 1834. Continues number sequence of Camden Journal. May 3, 1834 = vol 9, no 18, Thomas W. Pegues (publisher). Ceased Dec 1835 and Camden Journal revived in Jan 1836. *Files: Camden Archives Jun 28, 1834; SCL May 1834-Dec 1835.*

CAMDEN MORNING CALL   daily except Mon--established 1887, ceased c. 1887. Aug 9, 1887 = vol 1, no 73, N. T. Adams (editor, publisher, and proprietor). Not cited by Ayer. *Files: SCL Aug 9, 12, 1887.*

CAMDEN NEWS   weekly, Democrat--established 1909, ceased Jan 1913 when sold to the Camden Chronicle. Aug 4, 1909 = vol 1, no 1, J. W. Hamel (editor). Cited by Ayer 1911 thru 1913. *Files: Camden Archives (1909-1913) 6; SCL (1909-1912) 50.*

CAMDEN NEWS   weekly, independent--established 1956, ceased c. 1962. Cited by Ayer 1957 thru 1962. Mar 20, 1956 = vol 1, no 1, Harold C. Booker (editor and publisher). Priscilla Buckley and Mrs. William F. Buckley also associated with paper. *Files: Camden Archives Mar 20, 1956-Dec 31, 1958.*

CAMDEN REPUBLICAN, AND LANCASTER BEACON   weekly c. 1832- 1833. Mar 5, 1833 = vol 1, no 1 (new series), Samuel Weir (publisher). Revival of

Camden and Lancaster Beacon under slightly different title. *Files: Clemson Mar 5, 16, Jun 25, 1833; SCL Jun 25, 1833 (fragment).*

CAMDEN WEEKLY CONFEDERATE   weekly--established 1861 as the Camden Confederate by J. T. Hershman. After brief suspension early in 1864, issued as the Camden Weekly Confederate Apr-Sep 1864. Then resumed original title and in Mar 1865 merged with the Camden Journal to create the Journal and Confederate. Apr 6, 1864 = vol 3, no 1, J. T. Hershman (publisher). See Camden Confederate. *Files: Camden Archives (Apr-Jun 1864) 10; SCL (Apr-Sep 1864) 20.*

CAMDEN WEEKLY JOURNAL   title of Camden Journal at various times from 1853 to 1871. Jan 4, 1853 = vol 14, no 1, Thomas J. Warren (publisher). See also the Camden Journal. *Files: SCL ((1853-1871)) 250.*

CAROLINA JOURNAL   weekly c. 1802. According to Brigham, an issue of Oct 19, 1802 was found many years ago but has since disappeared. The editor was John Martin Slump. *NFK*

CHRONICLE-INDEPENDENT   daily, tri-weekly--created May 1981 by merger of the Camden Chronicle and the Camden Independent. May 11, 1981 = vol 1, no 1, Glenn Tucker and Michael Mischner (publishers). Issued daily May 1981-Oct 1982, then became tri-weekly. *Files: Camden Archives mfm May 1981 + ; Chronicle-Independent May 1981 + ; SCL ((1986 +)).*

DAILY BULLETIN   daily except Sun--established May 1864, ceased c. Aug 1864. May 9, 1864 = vol 1, no 1, W. K. Rodgers (publisher). Single sheet publication. *Files: SCL May 9, 16, Jun 8, Jul 1, 1864.*

JOURNAL   weekly, independent--established 1894, ceased c. 1895. Attempt to revive old Camden Journal. Cited once by Ayer (1895): G. G. Alexander (editor and publisher). *NFK*

JOURNAL AND CONFEDERATE   weekly, tri-weekly--created Mar 1865 by merger of Camden Journal and Camden Confederate. Circa Jun 1865 the Camden Journal resumed publication of weekly and tri-weekly editions under its own name. Journal and Confederate began as a weekly, but by Apr 1865 was tri-weekly. Mar 10, 1865 = vol 23, no 39 (new series, vol 2, no 19), J. T. Hershman and D. D. Hocott (editors). Apr 3, 1865 = vol 1, no 22, a single-sheet tri-weekly. *Files: SCL (Mar-May 1865) 19.*

JOURNAL AND GAZETTE   weekly--established Jul 5, 1877 by merger of Camden Journal and Kershaw Gazette. Within a month both papers resumed independent status. Jul 5, 1877 = vol 1, no 1, (new series), vol 35, no 51 (old series), William D. Trantham and Frank P. Beard (editors and proprietors). *Files: Camden Archives Jul 26, 1877; SCL Jul 5-26, 1877.*

KERSHAW GAZETTE   weekly, semi-weekly, daily except Sun--established as a weekly in 1873, merged briefly with the Camden Journal in 1877, became daily except Sun c. 1886-1887, issued semi-weekly and weekly editions in 1888, ceased c. 1888. Feb 3, 1874 = vol 1, no 18, Frank P. Beard (editor and proprietor). L. W. R. Blair and G. G. Alexander also associated with paper. *Files: Camden Archives (1874, 1876, 1883) 19; SCL ((1873-1887)) 200.*

PEOPLE   weekly, Democrat--established 1904, ceased c. 1911. Oct 12, 1905 = vol 2, no 37, W. A. Shrock (editor and publisher). Cited by Ayer 1905 thru 1911. *Files: Camden Archives Aug 6, 13, 20, 1908; SCL (1905-1909) 25.*

SOUTH-CAROLINA TEMPERANCE ADVOCATE   weekly--established in Columbia in 1839, published in Charleston in 1852 and in Camden 1853-1854, ceased c. 1854. Aug 4, 1853 = vol 15, no 1, Thomas J. Warren (publisher). See also South-Carolina Temperance Advocate [Columbia and Charleston]. *Files: Camden Archives (1853) 4; SCL orig & mfm 1853-1854.*

SOUTHERN CHRONICLE   see Southern Chronicle and Camden Gazette.

SOUTHERN CHRONICLE AND CAMDEN AEGIS   see Southern Chronicle and Camden Gazette.

SOUTHERN CHRONICLE AND CAMDEN GAZETTE   weekly--established 1822. Mar 14, 1822 = vol 1, no 5, George W. Tarbox (publisher). Also issued as the Southern Chronicle Sep 18, 1822-Mar 24, 1824, Southern Chronicle and Camden Aegis Mar 31, 1824-Jan 29, 1825, and the Southern Chronicle and Camden Literary and Political Register Feb 5-c. Dec 1825. Succeeded by the Camden Journal Jan 1826. In addition to Tarbox, G. W. Addison and Charles A. Bullard associated with these papers. *Files: Camden Archives Jan 7, 1824; SCL Mar 1822-Aug 1825.*

SOUTHERN CHRONICLE AND CAMDEN LITERARY AND POLITICAL REGISTER   see Southern Chronicle and Camden Gazette.

SOUTHERN REPUBLIC   weekly--established Jun 1851, ceased Oct 1851. According to Ellen, founded by C. A. Price on Jun 14, 1851. Jun 21, 1851 = vol 1, no 2, C. A. Price (publisher). *Files: Duke (1851) 16. Apparently no files in SC.*

SUN   weekly, Republican--established 1896, ceased c. 1897. Cited once by Ayer (1897): Sun Publishing Company. *NFK*

TEMPERANCE ADVOCATE   weekly--established in Columbia in 1870, published briefly in Orangeburg c. 1872, moved to Camden in 1873, to Columbia c. Oct 1873, ceased c. 1876. Cited by Rowell in Camden in 1873. May 20, 1873 = vol 3, no 27, Frank P. Beard (editor and proprietor). See Temperance Advocate [Columbia].

TRI-WEEKLY JOURNAL   tri-weekly--continues <u>Camden Daily Journal</u> Jan 1865, also publishing <u>Weekly Journal</u>. Merged with <u>Camden Confederate</u> Mar 1865 and issued as <u>Journal and Confederate</u> Mar-May 1865, then resumed former title. Jan 2, 1865 = vol 1, no 1, D. D. Hocott (publisher). J. T. Hershman (editor of the <u>Camden Confederate</u>) associated with paper after Mar 1865. See <u>Camden Journal</u> and <u>Journal and Confederate</u>. *Files: Camden Archives Jan 1, Jun 23, 1865; SCL (1865) 25.*

WATEREE MESSENGER   weekly, Democrat--established 1884, ceased c. 1942. Cited by Ayer 1885 thru 1942. Nov 27, 1888 = vol 4, no 9, C. W. Birchmore (proprietor). *Files: Camden Archives (1902-1934) 14; SCL ((1888-1935)) 275.*

WEEKLY JOURNAL   title of weekly edition of <u>Camden Journal</u> c. 1865-1866. See <u>Camden Journal</u>.

LANCASTER COUNTY

Lancaster District, now Lancaster County, was formed in 1798 when old Camden District was split into five parts. It assumed the name of its most prominent settlement, a town created by pioneer families who had moved south from Lancaster, Pennsylvania.

HEATH SPRINGS

AGE-HERALD   weekly, Democrat--established 1932, ceased c. 1935. Cited by Ayer 1934 and 1935: Louis Ellsworth Jaeckel (editor and publisher). *NFK*

KERSHAW

COMET   weekly, Democrat--established 1888, ceased c. 1889. Cited once in Ayer (1889): R. F. Willeford (editor), Comet Publishing Company. *NFK*

KERSHAW ERA   weekly--established 1889, ceased c. 1938. Cited by Ayer 1889 thru 1942. Ayer 1890: L. F. Stratton (editor), Era Publishing Company. Jan 20, 1903 = vol 14, no 21, J. W. Hamel (editor and proprietor). James H. Hamel also associated with paper. *Files: Camden Archives (1932-1933) 4; SCL ((1902-1935)) 145, mfm (1913-1936) 17.*

KERSHAW NEWS-ERA   weekly--established 1946. Oct 11, 1946 = vol 1, no 1, H. E. Carraway and J. W. Richards (publishers). Cited by Ayer 1950 + . Melverda O. Gaskin, Pam McKeown, and Jim McKeown, Jr., also associated with paper. *Files: Camden Archives 1983 + ; Kershaw News-Era 1946 + ; Kershaw Memorial Library, Lancaster CL, and SCL mfm 1946 + .*

KERSHAW TIMES   weekly--established 1938, ceased c. 1939. Nov 16, 1938 = vol 1, no 45, J. W. and J. M. Barton (publishers). Not cited by Ayer. *Files: Kershaw Memorial Library, Lancaster CL, and SCL mfm Nov 16, 1938.*

LANCASTER

CAROLINA REVIEW   weekly, Democrat--established 1878, became Lancaster Review c. 1880. Nov 6, 1878 = vol 1, no 2, Benjamin F. Welsh and J. J. Hall (editors and publishers). *Files: SCL mfm (Nov 1878-Feb 1879) 9.*

LANCASTER BEACON   weekly, pro-nullification--established 1830, moved to Camden Feb 1831 and became the Camden and Lancaster Beacon. Twenty issues published in Lancaster (1830-1831), James D. Cocke (editor), George P. Cocke (printer). *NFK*

LANCASTER CITIZEN   semi-weekly--continues Lancaster County Citizen c. 1923. Jun 21, 1923 = vol 8, no 49, Gilmore Lynn Nisbet (editor and publisher). Cited by Ayer 1924 and 1925. Ceased c. 1925. *Files: SCL Jun 21, 1923.*

LANCASTER COUNTY CITIZEN   weekly--established 1916, continued by Lancaster Citizen. Feb 1, 1917 = vol 1, no 34, W. C. Corcoran (editor), Corcoran and Davis (publishers). Cited by Ayer 1917 thru 1923. Circa 1923 Gilmore Lynn Nisbet became editor-publisher and changed title to Lancaster Citizen (semi-weekly). *Files: SCL Feb 1, 1917.*

LANCASTER ENTERPRISE   weekly, semi-weekly--established 1891 as a Farmers' Alliance publication, later Democrat. Merged with Lancaster Ledger and Lancaster Review in 1905 to form the Lancaster News. Began as a weekly, issued semi-weekly 1898-1902. Cited by Ayer 1891 thru 1905. Feb 10, 1892 = vol 1, no 48, A. J. Clark and T. Y. Williams (editors), Enterprise Publishing Company. *Files: Lancaster CL mfm (1892, 1897) 7; SCL mfm ((1892, 1897-1904)) 450; USC-Lancaster mfm ((Apr 1897-Sep 1903)) 425.*

LANCASTER JOURNAL   weekly--established 1906, ceased c. 1907. Cited once by Ayer (1907): F. W. Mindrop (editor), Journal Publishing Company. *NFK*

LANCASTER LEDGER   weekly, semi-weekly--established 1852, merged with Lancaster Enterprise and Lancaster Review in 1905 to form the Lancaster News. Began weekly, by 1900 was semi-weekly. Feb 12, 1852 = vol 1, no 1, R. W. Bailey (editor and proprietor). David J. Carter and Thurlow Carter also associated with paper. *Files: Lancaster CL mfm ((1852-1905)) 1300; SCL (1862-1896) 21, mfm ((1852-1905)) 1300.*

LANCASTER NEWS   semi-weekly, tri-weekly--established 1905 by merger of the Lancaster Enterprise, Lancaster Ledger, and Lancaster Review. Began as semi-weekly, became tri-weekly in 1972. Oct 4, 1905 = vol 1, no 1, Charles T. Connors (editor), Lancaster Publishing Company. This issue contains brief histories of the Enterprise and Ledger. Also see the Lancaster News (Oct 31, 1952). In addition to Connors, these individuals have been associated with this paper: R. W. Wylie, W. C. Cauthen, J. M. Riddle, Jr., A. J. Clark, Juanita Wylie, Luther Ellison, George Bulla Craven, Ira B. Jones, Sr., Ira B. Jones, Jr., R. D. Hudson, Robert Kelsey, J. A. Gallimore, Harold Booker, Morrell Thomas, Warren Koon, Julian Starr, Z. Bright Tucker, Paul League, Richard M. Gannaway, and Scott C. Kearns. *Files: Lancaster CL mfm ((1905-1919)) 1025, 1920 + ; Lancaster News 1920 + , mfm ((1905-1919)) 1025, 1920 + ; SCL (1912-1965) 60, Jun 1985 + , mfm ((1905-1919)) 1025, 1963-1970, 1973-1981; USC-Lancaster mfm ((1905-1919)) 1025.*

LANCASTER REVIEW   weekly--established in 1878 as the Carolina Review, became the Lancaster Review c. 1880, merged with the Lancaster Enterprise and the Lancaster Ledger in 1905 to form the Lancaster News. Jun 17, 1885 = vol 7, no 17, Charles T. Connors (editor), Riddle and Connors (proprietors). *Files: Lancaster CL mfm (1885-1899) 10; SCL (1882-1905) 20.*

LAURENS COUNTY

Created on 1798 when old Ninety Six District was split into five parts, Laurens District (now Laurens County) is named for Henry Laurens (1724-1792), a famous statesman of the Revolutionary War era.

CLINTON

CLINTON CHRONICLE weekly--established 1901. Cited by Ayer 1902 to present. Ayer 1902: C. C. Little (editor), Chronicle Publishing Company. Jan 2, 1919 = vol 19, no 1, Wilson W. Harris (editor), Chronicle Publishing Company. J. R. Jacobs, H. D. Rantin, Clair Hayes, A. O'Daniel, V. L. Loehr, Mrs. W. W. Harris, Cordelia Harris, Mrs. George Senn, and Donnie Wilder also associated with paper. *Files: Clinton Chronicle mfm 1919, 1924-1927, 1929 + ; Laurens CL mfm 1966-1969; Presbyterian mfm 1919, 1924-1927, 1929 + ; SCL (1924-1970) 19, mfm 1919, 1924-1927, 1929 + .*

CLINTON ENTERPRISE weekly--established 1887, ceased c. 1888. Cited by Ayer 1887 and 1888. May 3, 1887 = vol 1, no 4, J. B. Parrott and W. B. Crews (editors), T. B. Crews & Company (proprietor). *Files: SCL orig & mfm May 1887-Mar 1888.*

CLINTON WEEKLY GAZETTE weekly--established 1888, ceased c. 1918. Cited by Ayer 1888 thru 1918. Ayer 1888: W. J. Denby (editor and publisher). Sep 26, 1889 = vol 1, no 47, W. J. Denby (publisher). J. F. Cromer, T. M. Workman, and G. M. Rumple also associated with paper. *Files: Duke Sep 26, 1889. Apparently no files in SC.*

NEWS weekly, Democrat--established 1899, ceased c. 1900. Cited once in Ayer (1900): S. Frank Parrott (editor), Clinton Publishing Company. *NFK*

SOUTHERN PRESBYTERIAN weekly--established c. 1850 in Milledgeville, Ga., subsequently published in Charleston and Columbia and also in Clinton 1893-1908. Clinton editors include W. S. Bean, J. F. and W. S. Jacobs. Cited by Ayer in Clinton 1893/4 thru 1905. Apr 6, 1893 = vol 27, no 14 (new series), whole no 1418, William S. Bean (editor), Presbyterian Publishing Company. Often confused with Southern Presbyterian Review (1847-1885). Some depositories classify as periodical. Ceased c. 1908 when absorbed by the Presbyterian of the South. See Southern Presbyterian [Charleston and Columbia].

THORNWELL MESSENGER weekly--established 1910, ceased c. 1917. Cited by Ayer 1911 thru 1917: J. B. Branch (editor and publisher). *Files: Thornwell Home for Children 1910-1917.*

TRUE WITNESS   weekly--established 1866, ceased c. 1867. Founded by W. P. Jacobs. Later developed into an agricultural magazine, Farm and Garden, which in 1872 became Our Monthly. *NFK*

CROSS HILL

GAZETTE   weekly, Democrat--established 1917, ceased c. 1918. Cited once by Ayer (1918): J. F. Croomer [sic] (editor and publisher). This is probably the same J. F. Cromer who was publishing the Gazette in Whitmire and the Clinton Weekly Gazette...or perhaps these papers had moved to Cross Hill. *NFK*

GRAY COURT

GRAY COURT-OWINGS HERALD   weekly--established 1909, ceased c. 1910. Cited once by Ayer (1910): J. Archie Willis (editor and publisher). *NFK*

LAURENS

CITY GOSSIP   evenings except Thu and Sun--established 1890, ceased c. 1891. Cited once by Ayer (1891): J. B. Lockwood and W. T. Crews (editors and publishers). Ill-fated attempt by Crews (publisher of the Laurensville Herald) to move toward a daily schedule. *NFK*

COTTON PLANT   monthly, semi-monthly, agricultural--established 1883, published in various places, including Laurens c. 1897-1898. Cited in Laurens by Ayer (1898): W. T. Crews (editor and publisher). Mrs. Susan B. Pluss of Laurens represented this paper at the SC Press Association meeting in 1897. See Cotton Plant [Marion and Greenville].

LAURENS ADVERTISER   weekly, semi-weekly--established 1885, became semi-weekly Nov 15, 1971, changed name to Laurens County Advertiser Apr 18, 1973. Aug 26, 1885 = vol 1, no 4, J. C. Garlington (publisher). W. W. Ball, Samuel E. Boney, Arthur and Alison Lee, D. A. Harman, Ken Garfield, Jim Klutz, Grant Vosburgh, and W. J. Brown also associated with paper. *Files: Laurens County Advertiser mfm & orig ((1885-1902)) 570, 1903-Aug 1906, Aug 1907 + ; Laurens CL mfm ((1885-1902)) 570, 1903-Aug 1906, Aug 1907 + ; Presbyterian 1977 + ; SCL ((1885-1974)) 200, mfm ((1885-1902)) 570, 1903-Aug 1906, Aug 1907 + .*

LAURENS COUNTY ADVERTISER   see Laurens Advertiser.

LAURENS COUNTY NEWS   weekly, Democrat--established 1899, moved to Gaffney Feb 1903 and continued as the Cherokee News. Cited Ayer 1901 thru 1904. May 24, 1900 = vol 1, no 47, S. Frank Parrott (editor), Parrott Brothers (publishers). This issue says that a daily edition is planned during the "county campaign." *Files: Laurens CL May 24, 1900.*

LAURENS HERALD   see Laurensville Herald.

LAURENSVILLE HERALD   weekly--continues Laurensville Weekly Herald c. Apr 1848, issued briefly as the Laurens Herald c. 1932, ceased c. 1933. Jun 16, 1848 = vol 3, no 30, S. A. Godman (editor and proprietor). Motto: "Devoted to the Rights of the South, Morals, News, Agriculture, Literature and Science." John D. Wright, Robert M. Stokes, W. L. Hudgens, Homer L. McGowan, James Hollingsworth, J. Perkins Hoyt, T. B. Crews, John Wells Simpson, Jr., B. W. Ball, R. C. Watts, W. T. Crews, J. Archie Willis, W. L. Taylor, B. Y. Culbertson, and Thomas C. McCants also associated with paper. *Files: Clemson Feb 15, 1856; Greenville CL Jan 28, 1859; Laurens CL (1854) 40, mfm ((1848-1929)) 3000; SCL (1861, 1898, 1900, 1909, 1932) 7, mfm ((1848-1929)) 3000. Note: No files 1862-1865.*

LAURENSVILLE WEEKLY HERALD   weekly--established 1845, continued by Laurensville Herald c. 1848. Nov 26, 1845 = vol 1, no 1, N. V. Bailey (editor), R. S. Bailey, Jr. (publisher). *Files: Laurens CL mfm (1845-1846) 56; SCL mfm (1846) 50.*

MERCHANT AND FARMER   weekly, Democrat--established in Marion in 1875, moved to Laurens c. 1883, cited by Ayer in Laurens 1884 and 1885, ceased c. 1885. J. D. McLucas (editor and publisher) in Marion. May have been succeeded by the Laurens Advertiser. See Merchant and Farmer [Marion].

MR. SUN   weekly--established 1982, published by the Laurens County Advertiser. Distributed free throughout the county. Aug 13, 1985 = vol 4, no 7. *Files: Laurens County Advertiser 1982 + .*

NEWS SCIMITER   see News Scimiter [Greenwood].

PEOPLE'S RECORD   weekly, non-political, black publication--established 1901, ceased c. 1905. Cited by Ayer 1902 thru 1905: L. B. Langford and W. R. Saxon (publishers). *NFK*

VIDETTE   weekly--established 1905, ceased c. 1907. Cited once by Ayer (1907): W. T. Crews and W. C. Irby, Jr. (editors and publishers). *NFK*

LEE COUNTY

Lee County, named for General Robert E. Lee of Virginia, was formed in 1902 from parts of Darlington, Kershaw, and Sumter counties.

BISHOPVILLE

AFRO-AMERICAN RECORDER   weekly, black publication--established 1907, ceased c. 1909. Cited once by Ayer (1909): J. Miles Carson (editor), Afro-American Publishing Company. *NFK*

BISHOPVILLE EAGLE   weekly--established 1888, ceased c. 1893. Cited by Ayer 1890 thru 1892: J. D. Shaw (editor). In 1890 produced by the Bishopville Publishing Company, but then taken over by the People's Publishing Company, obviously an Alliance/Populist organ after that time. Masthead: "Here shall the Press the People's Rights maintain, unawed by influence and unbribed by gain." Aug 27, 1891 = vol 3, no 12, S. J. McMichael (editor and business manager). *Files: Greenville CL Aug 29, 1889; SCL orig & mfm Aug 27, 1891.*

BISHOPVILLE ENTERPRISE   weekly, Democrat--established 1886, ceased c. 1888. Cited by Ayer 1887 and 1888: P. G. Bowman, Jr. (editor and publisher). Aug 15, 1888 = vol 2, no 31, Shephard Nash (editor). An ad indicates that Nash was preparing to reopen Bishopville High School. *Files: SCL Aug 15, 1888.*

BISHOPVILLE GRAPHIC   weekly, independent--established 1959, ceased 1959. Oct 21, 1959 = vol 1, no 1, William L. King (editor and publisher). Only five issues printed. *Files: William L. King Oct-Nov 1959; Lee County Historical Society Oct 21, 1959.*

BISHOPVILLE LEADER   weekly--established Apr 1902 by A. B. Cargill, but soon bought out by the Lee County Vindicator and continued as the Leader and Vindicator. Leader and Vindicator (Jul 8, 1903) indicates that the papers merged in the fall of 1902. *NFK*

COUNTY BANNER   weekly--established Sep 27, 1894 by H. L. Darr (editor and publisher), but soon moved to Florence. Cited in both communities by Ayer in 1896...as a Thu weekly in Bishopville (established 1893) and as a Wed weekly in Florence (established 1895). Not listed in Bishopville in 1897. Merged with Florence Messenger Feb 1896 to create the Banner Messenger. First issue of the Banner Messenger says that the County Banner was established Sep 27, 1894. *NFK*

LEADER AND VINDICATOR   weekly, Democrat--created 1902 by merger of the Bishopville Leader and the Lee County Vindicator, became the Lee County Messenger Feb 15, 1923. May 20, 1903 = vol 2, no 8, H. S. Cunningham (editor). *Files: Coker* *mfm Sep 1902-1920, (1921-1923) 40; Lee County Observer 1920-1923; SCL (1903-1922) 50, mfm Sep 1902-1920, (1921-1923) 40.*

LEE COUNTY LEDGER   weekly--established 1898, ceased c. 1899. Cited once by Ayer (1899): W. L. Wilson (editor and publisher). *NFK*

LEE COUNTY MESSENGER   weekly--created by name change in 1923, continues number system of Leader and Vindicator, absorbed by Lee County Observer Mar 24, 1982, continued as Lee County Observer. Jan 1, 1925 = vol 22, no 1, W. J. Stricklin (editor and manager). Stricklin and Charles J. Cappleman took over the Leader and Vindicator in 1920 as co-publishers. When Stricklin gained complete control, he changed the title to the Lee County Messenger. *Files: Lee CL 1937, 1939, 1942, 1946-1971, mfm 1923-1982; Lee County Observer 1923-1982; SCL mfm 1923-1982.*

LEE COUNTY OBSERVER   weekly--established Apr 1977, after nine issues suspended until Nov 23, 1977. Apr 28, 1977 = vol 1, no 1, Robert Berryhill (editor), Lee County Observer, Inc. Acquired Lee County Messenger Mar 1982, continued as Lee County Observer. Roger McKenzie also associated with paper. *Files: Lee County Historical Society and Lee County Observer 1977 + ; Lee CL and SCL mfm Mar-Sep 1982.*

LEE COUNTY RECORDER   weekly--established 1898, ceased c. 1900. Cited by Ayer 1899 and 1900: Recorder Publishing Company. No personnel listed. *NFK*

LEE COUNTY VINDICATOR   weekly, Democrat--established 1902, merged with Bishopville Leader Sep 1902 to form the Leader and Vindicator. Mar 14, 1902 = vol 1, no 1, H. S. Cunningham (editor). *Files: Coker mfm Mar 14-Aug 20, 1902, Sep 16, 23, 1903; SCL orig & mfm Mar 14-Aug 20, 1902, Sep 16, 23, 1903. Note: The 1903 issues were published after the Leader and Vindicator was formed. Lee County Vindicator appears on the masthead; Leader and Vindicator, on inside pages.*

MIRROR   weekly, non-partisan--established 1896, ceased c. 1897. Cited once by Ayer (1897): Mirror Publishing Company. No personnel listed. Probably successor to the Bishopville Eagle since it bears virtually the same motto. Jun 2, 1896 = vol 1, no 11, editor not identified. *Files: SCL orig & mfm Jun, Aug 25-Sep 8, Nov 17, 1896.*

NEW ERA   weekly c. 1904. *Files: Sumter County Museum-Archives Jul 8, 1904.*

NEWS   weekly--established c. 1892. Cited once in Ayer (1893/4): W. L. McDowell (editor), News Publishing Company. According to Ayer (1895), McDowell was editor of the Camden Chronicle. *NFK*

LYNCHBURG

MESSENGER   weekly, non-partisan--established 1910, ceased c. 1911. Cited once in Ayer (1911): Joseph J. Baker (editor and publisher). *NFK*

LEXINGTON COUNTY

Carved out of Orangeburgh District in 1804, Lexington District (now Lexington County) honors the first battle of the Revolutionary War in Lexington, Massachusetts.

BATESBURG

BATESBURG ADVOCATE   weekly, Democrat--established Jan 1901, formerly Saluda Advocate, ceased Oct 27, 1911 when acquired by Leesville News and continued by the News-Advocate [Leesville]. Jan 23, 1901 = vol 1, no 2, John Bell Towill (editor), Advocate Publishing Company. N. Rogers Bayly and J. O. Eargle also associated with paper. *Files: SCL orig & mfm ((1901-1911)) 250.*

BATESBURG HERALD   weekly--established 1912, merged with News-Advocate [Leesville] Jan 1913, continued by the Batesburg Herald and Leesville News-Advocate. *NFK*

BATESBURG HERALD AND LEESVILLE NEWS-ADVOCATE   weekly-- created by merger of the Batesburg Herald and the News-Advocate [Leesville] Jan 1913, ceased c. 1918. Feb 19, 1914 = vol 20, no 14, Herald Publishing Company. Cited by Ayer 1914 thru 1918. Ayer 1914: Thomas M. Seawell (editor); Ayer 1915-1918: J. Rutledge McGhee (editor and publisher). *Files: SCL (1914-1917) 13, mfm (1916-1917) 10.*

BATESBURG-LEESVILLE NEWS   weekly--established 1913 as the Leesville Twin-County News, became the Batesburg-Leesville News (with dual dateline) on Oct 19, 1921, William N. Oxner (editor and publisher). Oct 19, 1921 = vol 9, no 1. Cited by Ayer 1922 thru 1924. Ceased c. 1924. *Files: SCL Oct 1921-Oct 1923.*

BATESBURG NEWS   weekly, Democrat--founded in 1882 as the Monthly/Weekly News [Gilbert Hollow and Lewiedale], became the Batesburg News c. 1888 and the Batesburg Sentinel c. 1889. Batesburg News cited once by Ayer (1889): Wade Leaphart (editor and publisher). *NFK*

BATESBURG SENTINEL   weekly--continues Batesburg News, created Mar 1889 by name change, ceased c. 1889. Not cited by Ayer. Mar 14, 1889 = vol 7, no 9, M. S. Hallman (editor and business manager), Sentinel Publishing Company. *Files: SCL orig & mfm Mar 14, 21, Apr 4, 1889.*

BATESBURGH MONITOR   weekly--established 1877, ceased c. 1878. Cited once in Rowell (1878): E. M. McLenna (editor and publisher). *NFK*

ENTERPRISE   weekly--established 1910, moved to Lexington c. 1913. Cited once in Ayer (1912). Dec 1, 1910 = vol 1, no 1, John Bell Towill (editor), Enterprise Publishing Company. *Files: SCL orig & mfm (1910-1912) 25.*

PEOPLE'S ADVOCATE   weekly--established Oct 1895, became Weekly Advocate Dec 10, 1895, ceased c. 1896. Not cited by Ayer. Oct 22, 1895 = vol 1, no 1, Josiah B. Game and J. J. Andrews (editors). *Files: SCL orig & mfm Oct 22-Dec 3, 1895.*

SOUTHERN HEADLIGHT   weekly--established Mar 1924, became Summerland Headlight Apr 21, 1924. Mar 24, 1924 = vol 1, no 3, W. L. Spinks (president and general manager), Ira C. Carson (editor). *Files: SCL orig & mfm Mar 24, 31, 1924.*

SUMMERLAND HEADLIGHT   weekly--continues Southern Headlight Apr 1924, continued by Twin-City News May 21, 1925. Apr 21, 1924 = vol 1, no 7, W. L. Spinks (president and general manager), Ira C. Carson (editor). *Files: SCL orig & mfm Apr 21, 1924-May 14, 1925.*

THIS WAY   weekly, monthly, YMCA--established in 1894 as a weekly, became monthly in 1896, ceased c. 1897. Not cited by Ayer. Oct 1, 1894 = vol 1, no 1, John Lake (editor). Dec 19, 1894 also is vol 1, no 1. Although YMCA organ, contains local news as well. *Files: SCL (1894-1897) 50, mfm (1894-1895) 25.*

TWIN-CITY NEWS   weekly--continues Summerland Headlight May 1925. May 21, 1925 = vol 2, no 11, Will W. Bruner (editor), Bruner Press. Also associated with paper: Mr. and Mrs. Douglas N. Bruner, Douglas N. Bruner, Jr., Mrs. Sara Bruner, and Virginia Sprinkle. *Files: Lexington CL ((1927-1939)), 1940 + ; SCL ((1925-1935)) 400, ((1984 +)), mfm May 21-Dec 18, 1925; Twin-City News 1931, 1934, 1939, 1955 + .*

WEEKLY ADVOCATE   weekly--established Oct 1895 as People's Advocate, became Weekly Advocate Dec 10, 1895, ceased c. 1896. Not cited by Ayer. Changed name to avoid confusion with the People's Advocate [Anderson]. Dec 10, 1895 = vol 1, no 8, Josiah B. Game and J. J. Andrews (editors). *Files: SCL orig & mfm Dec 10, 17, 1895.*

BROOKLAND

BROOKLAND-CAYCE NEWS   weekly Nov-Dec 1931. According to Earl Fulmer, "History of Journalism in Lexington County," State (Jul 21, 1935), this paper was established on Nov 13, 1931 with Charles L. Watkins as managing editor. Only four issues were printed. *NFK*

SOUTHLAN   monthly, non-political--established Apr 1895, ceased c. 1896. Cited once by Ayer (1896): C. M. Dempsey (editor and publisher). Apr 1895 = vol 1, no 1, C. M. Dempsey (editor and proprietor). "Published monthly at Brookland, a suburban [sic] of Columbia." *Files: SCL (1895-1896) 4.*

CAYCE

BROOKLAND-CAYCE NEWS   see Brookland-Cayce News [Brookland].

WEST COLUMBIA-CAYCE JOURNAL   see Journal [West Columbia].

CHAPIN

CAROLINA NEWS   weekly--established 1896, ceased c. 1904. Cited by Ayer 1897 thru 1904. Mar 24, 1897 = vol 1, no 33, Clarence L. Beard (editor), Chapin Publishing Company (proprietor). H. A. Gasque and H. C. Bailey also associated with paper. *Files: SCL orig & mfm (1897-1899, 1903) 25.*

CHAPIN TIMES   weekly--established 1976. Feb 25, 1976 = vol 1, no 1, Thad Bruner (editor and publisher). Jul 1976 issue cites Bruner Publishing Company as publisher. Not cited by Ayer. Bud Timmons also associated with paper. *Files: Chapin Times 1976 + ; Lexington CL [Chapin] 1978 + ; SCL ((1976-1979)) 160.*

GILBERT HOLLOW

WEEKLY NEWS   weekly--established as Monthly News in 1882 by Wade Leaphart, soon became Weekly News, and c. 1888 continued by Batesburg News. Cited by Ayer 1882 as Monthly. Ayer 1883-1885: Weekly News. Moved to Lewiedale c. 1886. Ayer ad (1883) says published by "Wade Leaphart & Bro." See Weekly News [Lewiedale].

IRMO

CHRISTIAN CITIZEN   weekly, temperance--established in 1900 by J. S. Abercrombie (editor and publisher). Cited once in Ayer (1902). Ceased c. 1902. *NFK*

INDEPENDENT NEWS OF IRMO   weekly--established 1978 as the Irmese Independent, continued by the Independent News of Irmo in Aug 1980. Aug 14, 1980 = vol 3, no 1, Luanne Hicks (editor), Percival Publishing Company, Inc. Fred Sheheen and Nancy McEwan also associated with paper. *Files: Independent News of Irmo ((1980 +)).*

IRMESE INDEPENDENT   weekly--established Sep 27, 1978 (vol 1, no 1) by Ronald G. Dunn, continued by the Independent News of Irmo in Aug 1980. Connie Leslie and Scott Sargent also associated with paper. *Files: Independent News of Irmo (1979-1980) 20; SCL (1978-1980) 20.*

LEESVILLE

BATESBURG-LEESVILLE NEWS   see Batesburg-Leesville News [Batesburg].

LEESVILLE LANCET   semi-monthly, Silver Democrat--established 1897, ceased c. 1898. Feb 27, 1897 = vol 1, no 3, S. R. Bridges (editor). W. P. Coker also associated with paper. *Files: SCL Feb 27, Mar 15, 1897 (fragments).*

LEESVILLE NEWS   weekly--created Apr 1906 by merger of Our News Letter [Summit] and Leesville Sun, merged with the Batesburg Advocate Nov 1911, continued by the News-Advocate. Apr 4, 1906 = vol 12, no 26, Hare and [J. O.] Eargle (publishers and proprietors). *Files: SCL Apr 1906-Sep 1909, (1909-1911) 35, some photostat copies.*

LEESVILLE SEMI-MONTHLY TRIBUNE   semi-monthly, weekly--established 1889, ceased c. 1890. Cited by Ayer 1889 and 1890. Mar 15, 1889 = vol 1, no 10, D. B. Busby and L. E. Busby (editors and proprietors). *Files: SCL Mar 15, 1889.*

LEESVILLE SUN   weekly, Democrat--established 1905, merged with Our News Letter [Summit] in Apr 1906 to form the Leesville News. Sep 14, 1905 = vol 1, no 6, W. Aug. Shealy (editor), J. W. Cooner, Jr. (publisher). *Files: SCL Sep 14, 1905-Mar 29, 1906.*

LEESVILLE TWIN-COUNTY NEWS   weekly, Democrat--established 1913, continued by the Batesburg-Leesville News Oct 19, 1921. Cited by Ayer 1914 thru 1921. Aug 27, 1913 = vol 1, no 1, William M. Oxner (editor and publisher). *Files: SCL Aug 27, 1913-Oct 12, 1921.*

NEWS-ADVOCATE   weekly--created Nov 1911 by merger of the Leesville News and Batesburg Advocate, Jan 1913 merged with the Batesburg Herald, continued by the Batesburg Herald and Leesville News-Advocate. Nov 16, 1911 = vol 18, no 6, J. O. Eargle (editor and publisher). *Files: SCL (1911-1913) 9.*

LEWIEDALE

WEEKLY NEWS   weekly, Democrat--established as Monthly or Weekly News [Gilbert Hollow] in 1882, moved to Lewiedale c. 1885, continued by the Batesburg News c. 1888. Oct 26, 1887 = vol 5, no 47, Wade Leaphart (publisher). W. M. Jones also associated with paper. *Files: SCL orig & mfm (1887-1888) 16.*

LEXINGTON

DISPATCH-NEWS   weekly--continues Lexington Dispatch-News on Nov 12, 1919 = vol 50, no 3, Sligh and Walker (publishers), G. M. Harman (associate editor). Despite change, "Lexington Dispatch-News" remains as running head on inside pages. Ira Sligh and Thornleigh Walker took over paper on Aug 6, 1919 from Harman, who--according to issue of Aug 30, 1919--founded the Lexington Dispatch on Sep 17, 1870. That issue also notes that the Lexington Dispatch was ravaged by fire on Apr 23, 1894 and Mar 27, 1916. Dispatch-News cited by Ayer 1920 +. W. W. Bruner, W. T. Bruner, Don Bruner, Mark Ethridge, Jerry Bellune, and Macleod Bellune also associated with paper. *Files: Dispatch-News 1925-1928, 1969 + ; Lexington CL 1950 + ; SCL ((1919-1961)) 1000, 1962 + .*

ENTERPRISE weekly, Democrat--established in Batesburg in 1910, moved to Lexington c. 1913, ceased c. 1915. Cited by Ayer 1914 and 1915: John Bell Towill (editor), Enterprise Publishing Company. Jul 16, 1914 = vol 4, no 27. *Files: SCL Jul 16, 1914.*

LEXINGTON DISPATCH weekly--established Sep 17, 1870, merged with Lexington News on Mar 7, 1917 to create the Lexington Dispatch-News. Jan 31, 1872 = vol 2, no 17, Godfrey M. Harman (publisher), W. D. M. Harman and H. W. Rice (editors). C. D. and D. R. Haltiwanger also associated with paper. *Files: Dispatch-News 1894-1913; SCL ((1873-1917)) 215, mfm ((1872-1916)) 310.*

LEXINGTON DISPATCH-NEWS weekly--created by merger of Lexington Dispatch and Lexington News on Mar 7, 1917. Issued as Dispatch-News after Nov 12, 1919. Jun 13, 1917 = vol 47, no 33, G. M. Harman (editor), Lexington Dispatch-News Publishing Company. Cited by Ayer 1918 and 1919. Ira M. Sligh and Thornleigh Walker also associated with paper. *Files: SCL (1917-1919) 60, mfm (1917-1919) 10.*

LEXINGTON FLAG weekly--established 1857, ceased c. 1860. Mar 12, 1857 = vol 1, no 5, E. J. H. Dreher (senior editor), Dreher and [J. H. G.] Leppard (proprietors). George Adolphus Fink also associated with paper. *Files: SCL mfm (1857-1860) 20.*

LEXINGTON NEWS weekly, Democrat--established 1915, merged with the Lexington Dispatch on Mar 7, 1917, continued by Lexington Dispatch-News. May 19, 1915 = vol 1, no 1, S. J. Leaphart and M. G. Sarratt (publishers). *Files: SCL (1915-1917) 50.*

LEXINGTON TELEGRAPH weekly, Democrat--established 1853, ceased c. 1856. Nov 3, 1853 = vol 1, no ? (unclear), Henry A. Meetze (editor), W. J. Randolph (proprietor). J. C. DeGraffarelli also associated with paper. *Files: SCL Mar 11, 1856, mfm Nov 3, 1853, May 31, 1855, Apr 8, 1856.*

SOUTH CAROLINA TEMPERANCE STANDARD semi-monthly--established 1854, ceased c. 1855. Jul 1, 1854 = vol 1, no 1, W. J. Randolph (publisher), S. E. Caughman, J. R. Breare, and Simeon Corley (editors and proprietors). *Files: SCL orig & mfm (1854-1855) 11.*

SOUTH CAROLINA TEMPERANCE STANDARD weekly--established 1877, ceased c. 1877. Not cited by Rowell. Official organ of the Sons of Temperance and Good Templars of South Carolina. Also contains local news. Apr 12, 1877 = vol 1, no 6, C. B. Brady and D. H. Witherspoon (proprietors). *Files: SCL orig & mfm Apr 12, Jun 14, 1877.*

SUMMIT

OUR NEWS LETTER weekly--established 1894, merged with the Leesville Sun in 1906 to form the Leesville News. Oct 1, 1894 = vol 1, no 1, E. C. Shealy and C. I.

Morgan (editors). Cited by Ayer 1896 thru 1906: News Letter Company (publisher). *Files: SCL Oct 1, 1894-Mar 28, 1906.*

SUMMIT COURIER   weekly, Democrat--established 1875, ceased c. 1880. Oct 17, 1877 = vol 2, no 42, D. I. Hendrix (editor), D. I. Hendrix & Company (proprietor and publisher). Cited by Rowell and Ayer 1876 thru 1880. A. L. Crouse also associated with paper. *Files: SCL Oct 17, 1877, Jul 23, 1879, Sep 15, 1880.*

WEST COLUMBIA

CONGAREE CHRONICLE   weekly--established 1941, ceased c. 1942. Not cited by Ayer. Jan 30, 1942 = vol 1, no 27 ? (copy torn), J. P. Gramling (publisher). *Files: SCL Jan 30, 1942.*

JOURNAL   weekly, semi-weekly--continues Coumbia Suburban News [Five Points] c. 1955 as West Columbia-Cayce Journal, but title soon shortened to Journal. Issued weekly except c. 1973-1977 when semi-weekly. Cited by Ayer 1956 thru 1983. Apr 12, 1962 = vol 11 (no issue number), N. Felicia Sisk (editor), West Columbia Publishing Company. Glenn Tucker, Tom Barnes, Louise Hermanson, Sandra Boozer, and Jerry Bellune also associated with paper. *Files: Journal 1955 + ; Lexington CL 1958 + ; SCL Apr 12, 1962, Oct 28, 1981, ((1984 +)).*

TRIANGLE   weekly c. 1948-1949. Cited in Columbia city directory (1949), M. Eliza Lucas (editor), offices at 134 State Street, West Columbia. *NFK*

WEST COLUMBIA-CAYCE JOURNAL   see Journal.

MC CORMICK COUNTY

Created in 1916 from parts of Abbeville and Greenwood counties, McCormick County is named for inventor Cyrus W. McCormick, who once owned thousands of acres of land in this region.

MC CORMICK

ADVANCE   weekly, Democrat--established 1885, ceased c. 1887. Cited by Ayer 1886 and 1887. Mar 19, 1885 = vol 1, no 1, T. M. Scott (editor and publisher). *Files: Erskine, Greenwood CL, and SC Historical Society mfm (1886-1887) 8; SCL mfm Mar 19, 1885-Apr 21, 1887.*

HERALD   weekly--established 1898, ceased c. 1902. Cited by Ayer 1898 thru 1902: R. G. McGowan (editor and publisher). *NFK*

INDUSTRIAL ENTERPRISE   semi-monthly, black publication--established 1908, ceased c. 1912. Cited by Ayer 1910 thru 1912: Brannum & Berry (editors and publishers). *NFK*

MC CORMICK MESSENGER   weekly--established May 1902. Sep 29, 1904 = vol 3, no 18, Jouett P. Smith (editor). Motto: "True to Ourselves, Our Neighbors, Our Country and Our God." In addition to Smith, J. M., Edmond, and John McCracken, Ken Fortenberry, and Stephen Jackson associated with paper. *Files: McCormick Messenger 1974 + ; SCL (1904-1949) 50. Note: In 1985, John McCracken (former owner and subsequently county assessor) held some pre-1974 files.*

MC CORMICK NEWS   weekly, Democrat--established 1887, ceased c. 1894. Cited by Ayer 1888 thru 1893/4. Mar 29, 1888 = vol 1, no 25, J. A. Harmon (editor and proprietor). Jun 21, 1888 = vol 1, no 37, Harmon and Calhoun (editors and proprietors). *Files: SCL Mar 29, Jun 21, 1888.*

MC CORMICK TIMES   weekly, Independent Democrat--established 1894, ceased c. 1897. Cited by Ayer 1896 and 1897: A. M. Carpenter (editor and publisher). *NFK*

MC CORMICK TIMES   weekly--established 1973, merged with McCormick Messenger in 1974, continued as McCormick Messenger. Apr 25, 1974 = vol 1, no 43, Homer Drinkard (editor and publisher). *Files: McCormick Messenger (1973-1974) 75.*

MARION COUNTY

Marion District, now Marion County, came into existence in 1798 when it split off from Georgetown District, created in 1769. At first called "Liberty District," in 1800 its name was changed to honor General Francis Marion (1732-1795), the legendary "Swamp Fox" of the American Revolution.

MARION

COTTON PLANT   monthly, agricultural--established in 1883 by W. J. McKerrall & Son. Mar 1885 = vol 2, no 9. Cited by Ayer 1884-1886 in Marion, moved to Greenville c. 1887. See Cotton Plant [Greenville]. *Files: Clemson Mar 1885; Greenville CL Nov 1884.*

CRESCENT   weekly, Democrat--established 1865, ceased c. 1872. Nov 14, 1866 = vol 2, no 1, Sidney E. McMillan (editor and publisher). In Aug 1869 the Crescent claimed a founding date of 1848, "being the purchaser and successor of the Old District Paper" and thus "the OLDEST JOURNAL in the Eastern part of the State." Apparently this boast was inspired by rivalry with the Marion Star. The meaning of the words "Old District Paper" is unclear. *Files: Marion CL mfm Nov 1866-Feb 1870; SCL orig & mfm Nov 1866-Feb 1870.*

FARMER   weekly, Democrat--established 1894, ceased c. 1896. Cited by Ayer 1895 and 1896: James T. Parks (editor and publisher). *NFK*

HERALD   weekly, Democrat--established 1917, ceased c. 1919. Cited by Ayer 1918 and 1919: Joseph H. Angel (editor and publisher). *NFK*

MARION OBSERVER   weekly--established c. 1874, ceased c. 1875. Fred. D. Bryant (publisher). Information based upon photostat fragment, vol 1, May ? 1874. Not cited by Rowell. *Files: SCL May ? 1874 (fragment).*

MARION OBSERVER   weekly, semi-weekly, Democrat--established 1904, ceased c. 1909. Mar 17, 1904 = vol 1, no 1, O. E. Crowson and J. V. Rowell (publishers). M. Stackhouse, E. Y. Hughes, and J. C. Mace also associated with paper. Cited by Ayer 1905 thru 1909. *Files: Marion CL mfm Mar 1904-Dec 1907; SCL May 2, 30, 1905, mfm Mar 1904-Dec 1907.*

MARION STAR   weekly--established 1846. Files begin May 4, 1852 (vol 1, no 1), when paper was reorganized with C. W. Miller (editor), V. Little (publisher). Predecessor (also the Marion Star) was published c. 1850-1852 by Joseph R. N. Tennet and J. B. LaBorde. Tennet notes in issue of May 4, 1852 that he had lived in Marion for three years. Tennet is listed in Marion's 1850 census as a 28-year-old Charleston native; LaBorde is not cited. They imply that their paper got into trouble because it was "too political." The Marion Star now claims a founding date of 1846. The original editor and publisher are not known, although a USC Journalism School survey (without giving source) states that A. J. Requier, a Charleston lawyer, may have started the paper in 1846. The Marion Star was issued as the Star and Southern Real Estate Advertiser Jul 7, 1869-May 25, 1870. Other individuals associated with this paper include A. Q. McDuffie, C. D. Evans, J. T. Bethea, W. J. McKerall, S. G. Owens, W. W. Nesmith, T. M. Harllee, Junius H. Evans, Charles E. Smith, M. Stackhouse, J. D. Montgomery, M. L. Clark, E. C. Coker, Palmer W. Johnson, John C. Mace, Lem Winesett, W. G. Perkins, Robert J. Weirich, Martha Beaver, Tom Miller, G. Frank Smith, Joan Jordan, Claire Connors Wharton, and Phil R. Byrd. *Files: Clemson Jul 31, 1872, Dec 10, 1941; Florence CL mfm ((1852-1864)) 275, 1866-1974; Francis Marion mfm ((1852-1864)) 275, 1866-1947, 1981 + ; Marion CL mfm ((1852-1864)) 275, 1866 + ; Marion Star 1897-1899, ((1921-1927)), 1947 + ; SCL (1862-1937) 25, mfm ((1852-1864)) 275, 1866 + . Note: Only three Civil War issues are available at SCL--Aug 6, 1862, Aug 31, Nov 16, 1864.*

MERCHANT AND FARMER   weekly--established 1875, moved to Laurens c. 1883. Oct 13, 1875 = vol 1, no 36, C. H. Prince (publisher), J. D. McLucas & Company (proprietor). *Files: SCL Oct 13, 1875, Aug 24, 1882.*

MONITOR   weekly--established Sep 1978, ceased c. 1981. Oct 3, 1978 = vol 1, no 2, John O. Lewis (editor and publisher). Not cited by Ayer. *Files: Marion CL and SCL mfm (Oct 3, 1978-Mar 17, 1981) 65.*

PEE DEE INDEX   weekly--established 1882, ceased c. 1894. Aug 22, 1882 = vol 1, no 1, W. J. Montgomery (editor), J. N. Stricklin (publisher). P. B. Hamer and W. T. Crews also associated with paper. Cited by Ayer 1883 thru 1894. *Files: SCL Oct 27, 1886, Nov 23, 1887; Marion CL and SCL mfm Aug 1882-Aug 1884, Aug 1885-Aug 1890, Dec 3, 1890.*

PEE DEE OBSERVER   weekly, black publication--established in Marion in 1981 by Oliver Lewis to serve communities of Marion, Bennettsville, Dillon, Florence, and Darlington. Aug 25-31, 1985 = vol 5, no 34, Oliver Lewis (publisher). *Files: Marion CL 1984 + ; Pee Dee Observer 1981 + .*

PLANE   weekly, black publication, independent--established in 1905, ceased c. 1907. Cited once by Ayer (1906): E. W. Stratton (editor), R. B. Phillips (publisher). *NFK*

STAR AND SOUTHERN REAL ESTATE ADVERTISER   weekly--title of Marion Star Jul 7, 1869-May 25, 1870. See Marion Star.

MULLINS

ENTERPRISE   weekly, semi-weekly--established 1898. Cited by Ayer 1901 + . Ayer 1901: J. Lee Pratt (editor and publisher). Dec 7, 1904 = vol 7, no 32. Mrs. L. B. McCormick, Maywood Rogers, J. Keith McMillan, Greg Smith, Edward M. Sweatt, Joe Chaleux, Margaret W. Anderson, and Leslie Stroud also associated with paper. The Enterprise, weekly throughout most of its career, was issued semi-weekly c. 1936 and again c. 1948-1949. *Files: Enterprise Dec 7, 1904, Jan 9, 1908, 1953 + ; Mullins Public Library mfm 1963 + ; SCL Sep 24, 1970, mfm ((1914-1956)) 215, 1963 + .*

MESSENGER weekly--established 1896, ceased c. 1898. Ayer 1897: Byrd and Reaves (editors and publishers). Ayer 1898: W. F. Norton (editor and publisher). *NFK*

MESSENGER weekly, Democrat--established 1910, ceased c. 1916. Cited by Ayer 1911 thru 1916. Jan 19, 1911 = vol 1, no 34. No personnel identified by Ayer or in 1911 issue. *Files: SCL Jan 19, 1911.*

MARLBORO COUNTY

Marlborough District (now Marlboro County) was created in 1798 when old Cheraws District was split into three parts: Marlborough, Chesterfield, and Darlington districts. It is named for John Churchill (1650-1722), first Duke of Marlborough, commander of allied forces fighting the French during the War of Spanish Succession and hero of the Battle of Blenheim.

BENNETTSVILLE

BAPTIST MONITOR   weekly, religious, black publication--revival of South Carolina Monitor, published briefly in Bennettsville c. 1885. Paper also issued by Rev. C. W. McColl as the Monitor. Cited by Ayer 1889 in Charlotte, N. C., and Cheraw, McColl editing various editions for Charlotte, Fayetteville, Cheraw, and Bennettsville. Listed by Ayer 1891 in Bennettsville: Rev. C. W. McColl (editor) Marlboro Baptist Publishing Company. Ceased c. 1892. See Monitor [Charleston].

BENNETTSVILLE BANNER   weekly, Farmers' Alliance--continues the Pee Dee Argus in Oct 1891, continued by the Pee Dee Advocate in 1895, apparently by means of a merger with the Bennettsville Review. Cited by Ayer as the Bennettsville Banner 1892 thru 1896. Oct 29, 1891 = vol 1, no 3, T. I. Rogers (editor), Simeon Gibson (proprietor). Bennettsville Banner (Oct 29, 1891) quotes a comment from the Marlboro Democrat to the effect that J. P. Gibson has sold the Pee Dee Argus to his brother, Simeon, who has revived the paper under a new name (Bennettsville Banner). Late in 1892, W. E. and R. B. Anderson acquired the Bennettsville Banner and started a new number system--Feb 2, 1893 = vol 1, no 5, W. E. Anderson (editor), R. B. Anderson (publisher). *Files: SCL (1891-1893) 6, mfm Oct 29, 1891.*

BENNETTSVILLE JOURNAL   weekly, Democrat--established 1866, ceased c. 1870. Oct 25, 1867 = vol 2, no 39, William Little (editor), Albert A. Stubbs (publisher), Stubbs & Little (proprietors). Cited by Rowell in 1869 and 1870. Rowell 1869: Stubbs and Little (editors and publishers). Rowell 1870: William Little (editor), Robert J. Cannon (publisher). *Files: Marlboro Herald-Advocate Oct 4, 1867; SCL orig & mfm Oct 25, 1867.*

BENNETTSVILLE REVIEW   weekly, Democrat--established 1894, became Pee Dee Advocate in 1895, apparently as result of merger with Bennettsville Banner. Apr 19, 1894 = vol 1, no 12, J. W. Graham (editor and publisher). H. H. Covington also listed as editor and proprietor. Bennettsville Review cited by Ayer 1895 and 1896. Early in 1895 J. P. Gibson became editor and publisher and altered number sequence to reflect his ownership of the Pee Dee Alliance--Mar 14, 1895 = vol 7, no 6, J. P. Gibson (editor). Ayer indicates that during 1895 Gibson acquired the Bennettsville Banner (successor to his Pee Dee Alliance) and combined the two papers to form the Pee Dee Advocate. *Files: SCL (1894-1895) 6, mfm Apr 19, Jul 12, 1894.*

CAROLINA MESSENGER   weekly, black publication--established c. 1974, became the Community Observer c. 1978. Number system erratic. Aug 29, 1974 = vol 1, no 9, Richard Lee (publisher). Jul 23, 1977 = vol 2, no 157, Julian B. Wright (editor), Grover McQueen (publisher). Not cited by Ayer. *Files: SCL (1974-1978) 8; Winthrop Jun 19, 1976.*

CHRONICLE   weekly, Democrat--established 1885, became Marlboro Chronicle c. 1886. Cited by Ayer 1886. Jul 31, 1885 = vol 1, no 23, W. L. Thomas (editor). *Files: SCL Jul 31, 1885, Aug 21, 1886.*

COMMUNITY OBSERVER   weekly, black publication--established c. 1974 as the Carolina Messenger, continued by the Community Observer c. 1978, ceased c. 1981. Jun 10, 1978 = vol 6, no issue number, G[rover] McQueen (president). Subsequent issues list Community Observer, Inc. (publisher). *Files: SCL (1978-1980) 9.*

CYCLONE MACK'S RECUSANT   monthly, revivalist organ--established 1929, ceased c. 1931. Also issued as the Recusant. Aug 27, 1929 = vol 1, no 5, Baxter F. McLendon (editor). Not cited by Ayer. *Files: SCL (1929-1931) 4, mfm Aug 1931.*

EASTERN CAROLINA NEWS   semi-weekly--established 1910 as the Bennettsville edition of Marlboro Times, became the Eastern Carolina News c. 1913, ceased c. 1914. Cited once by Ayer (1914): O. E. Crowson (editor and publisher). Dec 23, 1913 = vol 5, no 52, O. E. Crowson (president), Marlboro Times Company. Page 1 of Feb 24, 1914 issue reproduced in the Marlboro Herald-Advocate (Oct 7, 1974). *Files: Marlboro Herald-Advocate Feb 24, 1914; SCL Oct 3, Dec 23, 1913, mfm Dec 23, 1913.*

FARMERS' FRIEND   weekly, Democrat--established 1876 as the Marlborough Planter, became the Farmers' Friend c. 1880 and the Marlboro Democrat c. 1882. Cited by Ayer 1881 and 1882. Mar 22, 1882 = vol 7, no 11. *Files: Marlboro Herald-Advocate Mar 22, 1882.*

FINE PRINT NEWS   weekly, black publication--established 1982. Aug 15, 1985 = vol 3, no 39, N. T. Robinson III (editor). *Files: Fine Print News ((1982 +)).*

MARLBORO CHRONICLE   weekly--established 1885 as Chronicle, became Marlboro Chronicle c. 1886, ceased c. 1888. Cited by Ayer 1887 and 1888. Aug 8, 1888 = vol 4, no 21, J. DuPre Alsbrook (editor). Page 1 of Nov 30, 1887 issue (vol 3, no 37) reproduced in the Marlboro Herald-Advocate (Oct 7, 1974). *Files: Marlboro Herald-Advocate Nov 30, 1887; SCL Aug 8, 1888.*

MARLBORO COUNTY HERALD   weekly, semi-weekly--established Sep 3, 1931, became semi-weekly in 1948, merged with the Pee Dee Advocate in 1951, continued by the Marlboro Herald-Advocate. Aug 25, 1932 = vol 1, no 52, W. L. Kinney (editor and manager). Cited by Ayer 1936 thru 1952: W. L. Kinney (editor),

Marlboro Publishing Company. *Files: Marlboro CL ((1936-1950)); Marlboro Herald-Advocate 1931-1951; SCL Aug 25, 1932, Apr 7, 1950, mfm Aug 25, 1932.*

MARLBORO DEMOCRAT   weekly--established in 1876 as the Marlborough Planter, issued as the Farmers' Friend 1880-1882, became the Marlboro Democrat c. 1882, and was purchased by the Pee Dee Advocate in 1908. However, several issues exist from 1911, indicating that the paper continued for a time after 1908. Ceased c. 1911 ? Cited by Ayer 1882 thru 1908. Feb 25, 1885 = vol 10, no 11, S. A. Brown & Company (publisher). Percy M. Dees and R. L. Freeman also associated with paper. *Files: SCL orig & mfm ((1885-1911)) 250.*

MARLBORO HERALD-ADVOCATE   semi-weekly--created Sep 1951 by the merger of the Marlboro County Herald and the Pee Dee Advocate. Sep 4, 1951 (first issue) = vol 66, no 21, W. L. Kinney (editor and manager), Marlboro Publishing Company. W. L. Kinney, Jr., also associated with paper. *Files: Marlboro CL ((1951 +)); Marlboro Herald-Advocate and SCL 1951 + .*

MARLBORO MONITOR   weekly--established 1882, merged with the Carolina Sun [Cheraw] c. 1884 to form the Sun and Monitor, bearing dual date lines: Cheraw and Bennettsville. Jan 24, 1883 = vol 1, no 13, W. L. Thomas (proprietor), C. B. Brady (publisher). *Files: SCL orig & mfm Jan 24, 1883.*

MARBORO SHOPPER   weekly--established in 1984 by the Marlboro Herald-Advocate. Aug 28, 1985 = vol 1, no 44. *Files: Marlboro Herald-Advocate 1984 + .*

MARLBORO TIMES   weekly--established 1871, ceased c. 1876. Cited by Rowell 1871 thru 1876. Rowell 1871: J. Wesley Smith (editor and publisher). Marlboro Herald-Advocate (Oct 7, 1974) reproduced page 1 of Apr 14, 1876 (vol 6, no 10), J. Wesley Smith (publisher). *Files: Marlboro Herald-Advocate Apr 14, 1876.*

MARLBORO TIMES   weekly, Democrat--established in McColl in 1908, expanded to Bennettsville in 1910. Mar 18, 1910 = vol 1, no 5, Buford Jackson (editor), O. E. Crowson (publisher). At this time paper was publishing a Tue edition for McColl and a Fri edition for Bennettsville. Circa 1913 the Bennettsville edition became the Eastern Carolina News. *Files: SCL (1910) 5, mfm (1910) 4.*

MARLBOROUGH PLANTER   weekly, Democrat--established in 1876, c. 1880 became the Farmers' Friend. Page 1 of May 2, 1879 (vol 4, no 19) reproduced in the Marlboro Herald-Advocate (Oct 7, 1974). Cited by Rowell and Ayer 1877 thru 1880. Rowell 1877: C. W. Dudley (editor and publisher). *Files: Marlboro Herald-Advocate May 2, 1879.*

NEWS AND SHOPPER   weekly--established in 1983. Aug 28, 1985 = vol 2, no 35, Marion G. Brown (editor and publisher). *Files: News and Shopper 1983 + .*

PEE DEE ADVOCATE weekly--created c. 1895 by merger of the Bennettsville Review and the Bennettsville Banner. Early in 1895 J. P. Gibson acquired the Bennettsville Review and altered number sequence to reflect that of the Pee Dee Alliance, which he had founded in 1888. Ayer indicates that during that same year (1895) he acquired the Bennettsville Banner, successor to his Pee Dee Alliance, and combined the two papers under a new name. Dec 5, 1895 = vol 8, no 12, J. P. Gibson (editor and proprietor). Pee Dee Advocate merged with the Marlboro County Herald in Sep 1951 to form the Marlboro Herald-Advocate. Issued daily edition 1913-1914. See Pee Dee Daily. *Files: Marlboro CL ((1926-1951)); SCL ((1895-1951)) 2000, mfm ((1895-1939)) 570. Note: SCL orig files virtually complete 1902-1915, 1920-1923, 1934, 1937-1951, mfm files virtually complete for same years to 1939.*

PEE DEE ALLIANCE weekly, Farmers' Alliance--established 1888, continued by Pee Dee Argus c. 1890. Jul 11, 1889 = vol 1, no 31, J. Preston Gibson (editor). *Files: Marlboro Herald-Advocate Apr 10, 1890; SCL Jul 11, 1889, Apr 17, 1890.*

PEE DEE ARGUS weekly, Farmers' Alliance--continues Pee Dee Alliance c. 1890, continued by the Bennettsville Banner in Oct 1891. Mar 26, 1891 = vol 3, no 18, J. P. Gibson (proprietor). Cited by Ayer 1891: J. P. Gibson (editor and publisher). The Bennettsville Banner (Oct 29, 1891) notes a comment in the Marlboro Democrat to the effect that J. P. Gibson has sold the Argus to his brother, Simeon, who has revived paper under a new name: Bennettsville Banner. *Files: Duke Mar 28, 1891. Apparently no files in SC.*

PEE DEE DAILY daily except Thu and Sun, Democrat--established May 1913, ceased Sep 1914. May 19, 1913 = vol 1, no 1, R. L. Freeman (editor), Pee Dee Advocate (publisher). *Files: SCL orig & mfm May 1913-Sep 1914.*

PEE DEE EDUCATOR semi-monthly, black publication--established 1890, ceased c. 1900. Cited by Ayer 1890 thru 1900. Jul 4, 1890 = vol 1, no 13, E. J. Sawyer (editor), Pee Dee Publishing Company. *Files: SCL Jul 4, 1890.*

RECUSANT see Cyclone Mack's Recusant.

SONS OF TEMPERANCE weekly c. 1858-1859. Front page of Sep 8, 1859 (vol 1, no 47) reproduced in the Marlboro Herald-Advocate (Oct 7, 1974). *Files: Marlboro Herald-Advocate Sep 8, 1859.*

SOUTH CAROLINA MONITOR weekly, religious, black publication--established in Columbia in 1883 by Rev. C. W. McColl as the Columbia Monitor, moved to Bennettsville c. 1885. Paper suspended c. 1885, but later revived by McColl as the Monitor [Cheraw and Charleston c. 1888] and the Baptist Monitor in Charlotte and Bennettsville. See Monitor [Charleston] and Baptist Monitor [Bennettsville]. Various versions ceased c. 1892.

SUN AND MONITOR   weekly--created c. 1883 by merger of the Carolina Sun [Cheraw] and the Marlboro Monitor, continued by the Sun and Monitor bearing dual date line. Ceased c. 1884. Nov 23, 1883 = vol 4, no 25, Thomas and Breeden (editors and publishers). Cited once by Ayer (1884) in Cheraw. *Files: Cheraw Chronicle and SCL Nov 28, 1883.*

CLIO

CHRONICLE   weekly, Democrat--established 1910, ceased c. 1911. Cited once by Ayer (1911): P. A. George (editor and publisher). *NFK*

NEWS   weekly, non-partisan--established 1896, ceased c. 1897. Cited once by Ayer (1897): D. T. Hargrove (editor), B. F. Roper (publisher). *NFK*

MC COLL

MC COLL DISPATCH   weekly--established 1924, ceased c. 1925. Cited once by Ayer (1925): Dispatch Publishing Company. Apr 30, 1924 = vol 1, no 1, George W. Mitchell (president), Dispatch Publishing Company. *Files: SCL (1924-1925) 30.*

MC COLL MESSENGER   weekly, Democrat--established 1899, ceased c. 1900. Cited once by Ayer (1900): J. D. Craighead (editor and publisher). *NFK*

MC COLL MESSENGER   weekly, independent--established 1948. Cited by Ayer 1949 + . Ayer (1949): W. S. Minor (editor), C. A. Martin (publisher). Published by the Marlboro Herald-Advocate [Bennettsville] since 1953. Jan 12, 1984 = vol 37, no 2. L. M. Wright, Laverne Prosser, W. L. Kinney, Dorothy Snyder, Mrs. H. W. Brown, and W. L. Kinney, Jr., also associated with paper. *Files: Marlboro Herald-Advocate 1978 + .*

MC COLL TIMES   weekly, Democrat--established 1901, ceased c. 1902. Cited once by Ayer (1902): Charles F. Sansbury (editor and publisher). *NFK*

MARLBORO NEWS   weekly--established 1926, ceased c. 1926. Not cited by Ayer. Jul 9, 1926 = vol 1, no 5, Fred Abernethy (editor), Paul P. Creech (publisher). *Files: SCL Jul 9, 1926 (fragment).*

MARLBORO TIMES   weekly--established 1908, by 1911 was publishing a Tue edition for McColl and a Fri edition for Bennettsville. Sep 9, 1909 = vol 1, no 45, O. E. Crowson (editor), Times Publishing Company. Circa 1913 became the semi-weekly Eastern Carolina News [Bennettsville]. *Files: SCL (1909-1910) 10.*

SUN   weekly--established 1902, ceased c. 1903. Cited once by Ayer (1903): Sun Publishing Company. *NFK*

NEWBERRY COUNTY

Newberry District, now Newberry County, was created in 1798 when old Ninety Six District was divided into five parts. The source of its name is unclear. It may honor Captain John Newberry of Revolutionary War fame or perhaps trace its origins to Newbury, England. A third theory is that the name comes from muscadine grapes and berries that grow profusely in that region.

NEWBERRY

CONSERVATIST   weekly--established 1858, ceased c. 1861. Feb 2, 1858 = vol 1, no 1, William F. Nance (editor), Johns and Blats (publishers). Successor to the <u>News Mirror</u>. James Drayton Nance (editor c. 1861) was killed in Virginia in 1864 (Newberry <u>Rising Sun</u>, May 11, 1864). *Files: SCL ((Feb 1858-Jan 1861)) 100.*

EVENING TELEGRAM   daily--established 1904, ceased 1904. Ayer 1905: John K. Aull (editor), E. H. Aull (publisher). May 11, 1904 = vol 1, no 1 (no personnel listed). Produced by the Newberry <u>Herald and News</u>. An ill-fated effort to create a daily edition. *Files: SCL May 11-Dec 12, 1904.*

HERALD AND NEWS   semi-weekly, weekly--title of <u>Newberry Herald and News</u> as of Oct 20, 1903, E. H. Aull (editor), no volume-issue data cited. Paper issued weekly c. 1932-1937. Became <u>Newberry Daily Herald</u> Feb-Oct 1937, then sold to the <u>Newberry Observer</u> and continued by the <u>Newberry Observer and Herald & News</u>. O. F. and Ira B. Armfield also associated with paper. *Files: <u>Citizen News</u> [Johnston] 1903-1925; SCL 1903-1910, Jan-Apr 1911, 1912, 1917-1922, (1924) 1, 1925-May 1930, ((Jun 1930-May 1935)) 100, mfm 1903-1922, (1924) 1, 1925-1929, ((1930-1933)) 100.*

LUTHERAN VISITOR   weekly, religious--established in Columbia in 1868 and continued by the <u>Lutheran Church Visitor</u> in that city on Sep 15, 1904. Developed from the <u>Southern Lutheran</u> (established c. 1861) and the <u>Lutheran and Visitor</u> (established 1868), both published in Columbia. Latter soon became the <u>Lutheran Visitor</u> (Sep 22, 1869 = vol 2, no 6, new series, vol 4, no 58, old series) and moved to Prosperity c. 1879. Ayer cites as published in Newberry 1882-1904; however, files bear Prosperity dateline as late as 1887. Apparently J. Hawkins (editor c. 1879-1895) lived in Prosperity; William P. Houseal (publisher), in Newberry. Jan 20, 1887 = vol 20, no 20, whole no 943. A. J. Rude, W. J. Duffie, E. H. Aull, and S. T. Hallman also associated with paper. *Files: Newberry College 1868-1904, mfm 1868-1874; SCL (1887-1899) 75.*

NEWBERRIAN   tri-weekly--according to Ellen, founded in Dec 1853 by J. S. Reid and W. C. Wilson. On Feb 9, 1855 name changed to <u>News Mirror</u>, which ceased c. 1858 and was succeeded by the <u>Conservatist</u>. *NFK*

NEWBERRY DAILY HERALD   daily--established Feb 1937 when S. L. Goodman and Kerr L. Thompson bought the News and Herald from Otto F. Armfield and converted the paper into a daily. Paper sold to the Newberry Observer in Oct 1937, continued by the Newberry Observer and Herald & News. Newberry Daily Herald not cited by Ayer. Information concerning paper comes from first issue of the Newberry Observer and Herald & News (Oct 12, 1937). *NFK*

NEWBERRY HERALD   weekly, Democrat--continues Newberry Weekly Herald on Aug 30, 1865, merged with the Newberry News Aug 28, 1884, continued by the Newberry Herald and News. Aug 30, 1865 = vol 1, no 36, Thomas F. and R. H. Greneker (editors and proprietors). *Files: Newberry College mfm 1878-1879, Mar-Dec 1883; Newberry CL mfm 1865-1883; Newberry Observer and Herald & News mfm 1878-1879, Mar-Dec 1883; SCL 1865-1883, mfm 1865-1883.*

NEWBERRY HERALD AND NEWS   weekly, semi-weekly--created Aug 28, 1884 by merger of the Newberry Herald and the Newberry News. Aug 28, 1884 = vol 20, no 35, T. F. Greneker, R. H. Greneker, Sr., and George B. Cromer (editors), T. F. Greneker (proprietor). Paper became semi-weekly on Jan 5, 1897 and beginning Oct 20, 1903 issued as the Herald and News. Elbert H. Aull and William P. Houseal also associated with paper. *Files: Citizen News [Johnston] 1896-1903; Newberry CL mfm (1884-1885) 25, 1886-1894; SCL orig & mfm (1884-1885) 25, Jan 1886-Oct 1903.*

NEWBERRY NEWS   weekly, Democrat--established 1878, merged with the Newberry Herald Aug 28, 1884, continued by the Newberry Herald and News. Jun 6, 1879 = vol 2, no 23, M. L. Bonham, Jr., and L. W. Simkins (editors). John A. Chapman, R. H. Greneker, Jr., and William P. Houseal also associated with paper. *Files: SCL Jun 6, 1879, Apr 1, 1881, Aug 25, 1882.*

NEWBERRY OBSERVER   weekly, semi-weekly, Democrat--established 1883, became semi-weekly c. 1900, in Mar 1901 changed name to Observer, and in Jul 1928 became the Newberry Observer once more. Merged with the Newberry Daily Herald (successor to the Herald and News) in Oct 1937, continued by the Newberry Observer and Herald & News. Oct 28, 1886 = vol 4, no 43, W. H. Wallace (editor), W. H. Wallace and J. H. M. Kinard (proprietors). R. H. Greneker, Jr., William P. Houseal, A. H. Count, J. W. Earhardt, and J. W. Earhardt, Jr., also associated with paper. *Files: Newberry College mfm 1886-1937; Newberry Observer and Herald & News mfm 1889-1937; SCL (1886-1887) 13, ((1930-1935)) 230, mfm ((1886-1898)) 520, ((1932-1935)) 155.*

NEWBERRY OBSERVER AND HERALD & NEWS   semi-weekly, tri-weekly--created Oct 1937 by the merger of the Newberry Observer and the Newberry Daily Herald (successor to the Herald and News), became tri-weekly Mar 30, 1981. First joint issue Oct 12, 1937 = vol 55, no 82, J. W. Earhardt, Jr. (editor and publisher). Ollie Moye and Ben Morris also associated with paper. *Files: Newberry College, Newberry Observer and Herald & News, and SCL mfm 1937 + .*

NEWBERRY SENTINEL   weekly--established 1849, ceased c. 1855. Sep 1, 1852 = vol 3, no 32, James H. Giles (editor and publisher). Dec 21, 1853 = vol 4, no 17, James Crosson and Thomas P. Slider (editors and proprietors). According to Ellen, this paper was sold to the News Mirror in Mar 1855. *Files: SCL Sep 1, 1852, Dec 21, 1853, Oct 11, Nov 15, 1854.*

NEWBERRY WEEKLY HERALD   weekly--continues Weekly Herald on Jul 12, 1865, continued by the Newberry Herald on Aug 23, 1865. Jul 12, 1865 = vol 1, no 29, Thomas F. and R. H. Greneker (publishers). *Files: SCL orig & mfm Jul 12-Aug 23, 1865.*

NEWS MIRROR   weekly, tri-weekly--according to Ellen, created Feb 9, 1855 by Joseph S. Reid, a new name for the Newberrian (see). In Mar 1855 Reid bought the Newberry Sentinel and the following year changed the name of the News Mirror to the Tri-Weekly Mirror. The Marion Star (Dec 29, 1857) noted that the Newberry Mirror had suspended operations. This paper was succeeded by the Conservatist in Feb 1858. *NFK*

OBSERVER   title of the Newberry Observer from 1901 to 1928, see the Newberry Observer.

PROGRESSIVE AGE   weekly--established c. 1873 by Thomas P. Slider, reportedly co-founder of the Rising Sun. Cited by Rowell 1873 thru 1876. Rowell 1873 and 1874: Thomas P. Slider (editor and publisher). Rowell 1875 and 1876: Thomas P. Slider (editor), R. H. Greneker (publisher). *NFK*

RISING SUN   weekly--established 1856, ceased c. Apr 1865. Suspended operations at times during the Civil War. Mar 3, 1858 = vol 3, no 1, Thomas P. Slider and T. F. Greneker (editors and proprietors). Mar 10, 1865 = vol 3, no 22, T. F. and R. H. Greneker (editors and publishers). According to Ellen, the Rising Sun was founded by Slider and James M. Crosson, the same men who produced the Newberry Sentinel. The Grenekers, who established the Tri-Weekly Herald on Mar 21, 1865, briefly continued the Rising Sun as the Sun (see). *Files: SCL ((1858-1865)) 100, mfm Mar 9, 1859-Mar 7, 1860.*

SUN   weekly--continues Rising Sun c. Apr 1865, but soon ceased. Apr 12, 1865 = vol 3, no 25, T. F. and R. H. Greneker (editors and proprietors). The Grenekers apparently produced the Sun for a brief time as a weekly edition of their Tri-Weekly Herald. *Files: SCL Apr 12, 1865.*

SUN   weekly, Independent Democrat--established 1937, ceased 1972. Oct 22, 1937 = vol 1, no 1, O. F. Armfield (editor and publisher). O. F. Armfield, Jr., also associated with paper. Last issue was Dec 28, 1972 = vol 36, no 31. *Files: Sun Publishing Company [Newberry] 1937-1972.*

TRI-WEEKLY HERALD   tri-weekly--established Mar 1865, became the Weekly Herald on Jun 7, 1865. Mar 21, 1865 = vol 1, no 1, Thomas F. and R. H. Greneker (publishers). Paper was successor to Rising Sun and Sun. *Files: SCL orig & mfm Mar 21-May 31, 1865.*

TRI-WEEKLY MIRROR   see News Mirror.

VOICE OF THE PEOPLE   weekly, prohibition--established 1894, moved to Prosperity c. 1900. Cited in Newberry by Ayer 1896 thru 1900: E. V. Capers (editor), Reform Publishing Company. *NFK*

WEEKLY HERALD   weekly--continues Tri-Weekly Herald on Jun 7, 1865, continued by the Newberry Weekly Herald on Jul 12, 1865. Jun 7, 1865 = vol 1, no 24 (no personnel listed). *Files: SCL orig & mfm Jun 7-Jul 5, 1865.*

PEAK

PEAK NEWS   weekly--established 1888, ceased c. 1890. Ayer 1889: J. D. O'Bryant (editor), J. W. Todd (publisher). Ayer 1890: W. P. Summers (editor and publisher). Not listed by Ayer in 1891. Sep 20, 1889 = vol 2, no 10. The name of H. C. Bailey appears at top of editorial column, but his role is unclear. Published by the Peak News Company. *Files: SCL Sep 20, 1889.*

PROSPERITY

EAGLE EYE   weekly--established 1901, ceased c. 1903. Jan 15, 1902 = vol 1, no 38, W. P. Blanton (editor and proprietor). Cited once in Ayer (1903) as the "Hawk's Eye," J. S. Abercrombie (editor and publisher). *Files: SCL Jan 15, 1902.*

LUTHERAN VISITOR   weekly, religious--established 1868 in Columbia, subsequently moved to Prosperity and Newberry. Cited by Rowell and Ayer in Prosperity 1879 thru 1882, J. Hawkins (editor), W. J. Duffie (publisher). See Lutheran Visitor [Newberry].

NEWS   weekly--continues Prosperity Advertiser c. 1898, ceased c. 1899. News cited once by Ayer (1899): J. W. Blanton (editor), Barre and Blanton (publishers). According to the Newberry Observer (Jan 26, 1899), J. W. and W. P. Blanton had retired from the News and Mrs. L. E. Beard was now editor. *NFK*

PRESS AND REPORTER   weekly--established 1885 as the Reporter, soon issued as the Press and Reporter, and c. 1897 continued by the Prosperity Advertiser. Oct 23, 1895 = vol 11, no 2, E. O. Counts (editor), A. H. Kohn (associate editor). Cited by Ayer 1886 thru 1896. Ayer 1886-1893/4: F. V. Capers (editor and publisher). Ayer 1895: Whites and Kibler (editors and publishers). Ayer 1896: E. O. Counts (editor and publisher). *Files: SCL Jun 26, Oct 23-Nov 6, 1895.*

PROSPERITY ADVERTISER   weekly, Democrat--continues the Press and Reporter c. 1897, continued by the News c. 1898. Nov 24, 1897 = vol 13, no 7, D. H. Witherspoon (editor). Cited by Ayer 1897 and 1898: D. H. Witherspoon (editor and publisher). *Files: SCL Nov 24, 1897.*

PROSPERITY CITIZEN   weekly--established c. 1967 by W. C. Armfield (editor and publisher), ceased c. 1972. Printed in Whitmire by the Whitmire News. Cited by Southern Bell media directory, 1967-1972. *Files: W. C. Armfield [Whitmire] ((1965-1972)).*

REPORTER   see Press and Reporter.

VOICE OF THE PEOPLE   weekly, prohibition--established in Newberry in 1894, moved to Prosperity c. 1900, ceased c. 1901. Cited once by Ayer (1901) in Prosperity: A. E. P. Bedenbaugh (editor), Reform Publishing Company. *NFK*

WHITMIRE

GAZETTE   weekly, Democrat--established 1915, ceased c. 1918. Cited by Ayer 1917 and 1918. Ayer 1917: T. M. Workman (editor), J. F. Cromer (publisher). Ayer 1918: J. F. Cromer (editor and publisher). Not cited by Ayer in 1919. Cromer also was publishing a Gazette in Cross Hill c. 1918. *NFK*

WHITMIRE NEWS   weekly, independent--established in 1934, ceased c. 1936. Feb 1, 1934 = vol 1, no 1, Mrs. W. W. Lewis (editor), Armfield Brothers (publishers). Not cited by Ayer. *Files: SCL mfm (1934-1935) 90.*

WHITMIRE NEWS   weekly, independent--established in 1949. Jun 7, 1951 = vol 2, no 49, Ann E. Lewis (editor and publisher). W. C. Armfield, Kitcy Johnson, Donny Wilder, and Jo Lane Maness also associated with paper. Cited by Ayer 1959 thru 1978. *Files: SCL ((1949-1952)) 135, ((1984- +)), mfm ((1949-1952)) 135; Whitmire News 1980 + ; Whitmire Memorial Library ((1958 +)).*

OCONEE COUNTY

Created by the Constitution of 1868, which also transformed thirty older "districts" into "counties," Oconee County formerly was part of what had been Pickens District. Its name is derived from an Indian word "Uk-oo-na," meaning "the water eyes of the hills" or "the place of springs."

SENECA

ADVERTISER   weekly, Democrat--established 1878, ceased c. 1879. Rowell 1879: J. H. Carlisle (editor and publisher). Not cited by Ayer 1880. *NFK*

FARM AND FACTORY   weekly, semi-weekly, Democrat--"established April 11, 1903" appears on the masthead of a 1922 issue, became the Seneca Journal c. 1930, continuing the number sequence begun in 1903. Cited by Ayer 1907 thru 1930. Ayer 1907: H. L. and R. R. Phillips (publishers). John L. McWhorter and J. M. Phillips also associated with paper. Merged briefly c. 1908 with an earlier Seneca Journal. Apr 5, 1922 = 18th year, no 52. According to the Seneca Journal and Tugaloo Tribune (Aug 8, 1973), John H. Phillips founded Farm and Factory, which later was published by his two sons, Hugh and Ray. *Files: SCL Apr 5, 12, 1922.*

FARM AND FACTORY-JOURNAL   weekly, Democrat--created by merger c. 1908 of Farm and Factory and the Seneca Journal (founded in 1906). Cited once by Ayer (1909): J. M. Phillips (editor), H. L. and R. R. Phillips (publishers). In 1910 Farm and Factory resumed former title. *NFK*

JOURNAL/TRIBUNE   see Journal and Tribune.

JOURNAL AND TRIBUNE   weekly, semi-weekly, tri-weekly, independent--created Sep 26, 1952 by merger of Seneca Journal and Tugaloo Tribune [Westminster]. Sep 26, 1952 = 50th year, no 24, J. A. Gallimore (publisher). Cited by Ayer 1953 + . In addition to Gallimore, Neil Hercules, Dick Reavis, Paul League, Martha Navy, and Jim Dorris associated with paper. Title varies. At times in late 1960s issued as Journal and Tribune...and Farm and Factory (sub-title). From c. 1970-Oct 1985 bore masthead title of Seneca Journal and Tugaloo Tribune. Since Oct 1985 issued as Journal/Tribune. Publication schedule weekly from 1952 to c. 1970, semi-weekly from c. 1970 to present, except c. 1976 when issued tri-weekly for a brief time. In Nov 1986 added word "Weekender" to masthead of Fri edition and began new number system. *Files: Journal/Tribune 1952 + ; SCL (1962-1968) 5, ((1984 +)).*

MESSENGER   weekly, independent--established 1954, moved business office to Clemson [Pickens County] in 1959, though still published in Seneca. See Messenger [Clemson].

NEW CAROLINIAN   weekly, Democrat--established 1897, ceased c. 1898. Cited once by Ayer (1898): J. Ed. Mangum (editor), E. M. Coleman (publisher). Apr 14, 1897 = vol 1, no 4. Mangum also sold all types of insurance and Singer sewing machines. *Files: SCL Apr 14, 1897.*

OCONEE NEWS   weekly, Democrat--established 1891 in Walhalla. According to Ayer, this paper was published in Seneca 1900-1902, then returned to Walhalla once more. Ayer 1900: E. E. Verner (editor), Oconee News Publishing Company. Ayer 1901: D. A. Smith, Jr. (editor), Oconee News Publishing Company. Ayer 1902: J. R. Earle of Walhalla (editor and publisher). See the Oconee News [Walhalla].

SENECA FREE PRESS   weekly, Democrat--established 1883, ceased c. 1889. Cited by Ayer 1884 thru 1889. Founder not known, but J. C. Carey of the Seneca Free Press became a member of the SC Press Association in 1885. Will T. Webb and James W. Livingston also associated with paper. Dec 13, 1889 = vol 7, no 4, whole no 315, J. J. Neville and L. F. Smith (editors). Seneca Journal and Tugaloo Tribune (Aug 8, 1973) quotes from an issue of Aug 10, 1888. *Files: Frances S. Holleman (author of Seneca, South Carolina: Centennial 1873-1973) has Dec 13, 1889.*

SENECA JOURNAL   weekly--established 1881, ceased c. 1882. Cited by Ayer 1882, no pertinent details given, but an ad identifies William P. Calhoun as editor. Aug 19, 1881: William M. Warlick (editor), no vol or issue no. *Files: University of North Carolina Aug 19, 1881. Apparently no files in SC.*

SENECA JOURNAL   weekly, Democrat--established 1906, merged with Farm and Factory c. 1908, continued by Farm and Factory-Journal. Cited once by Ayer (1908): H. L. Boggs (editor), Seneca Publishing Company. *NFK*

SENECA JOURNAL   weekly--continues Farm and Factory, name changed c. 1930, merged with Tugaloo Tribune in 1952, continued by the Journal and Tribune. Cited by Ayer 1931 thru 1952. Ayer 1931: Arthur L. Cox (editor and publisher). R. R. Phillips, Tuck Lucas, L. F. Brabham, Mr. and Mrs. Kenneth Richardson, Ben Payne, and J. A. Gallimore also associated with paper. Jun 11, 1930 = 27th year, no 10. According to this issue, Cox assumed control a few weeks earlier, having purchased Farm and Factory from R. R. Phillips. It is unclear just when title was changed to Seneca Journal. *Files: Journal/Tribune ((1930, 1941-1942)), 1943-1952; SCL Jun 11, 18, 1930, May 9-Jun 6, 1952.*

SENECA JOURNAL AND TUGALOO TRIBUNE   see Journal and Tribune.

SHOPPING GUIDE   weekly, semi-weekly--established 1977. Jun 23, 1985 = vol 9, no 5, Denise Vickery (general manager). Published by the Anderson Independent-Mail. *Files: Shopping Guide retains a one-year file.*

WALHALLA

KEOWEE COURIER   weekly--established in Pickens in 1849, moved to Walhalla on Feb 28, 1868 = vol 3, no 21, J. H. Foy (editor), Robert Young & Company (publisher). Paper was suspended during much of the Civil War and new number system started in Sep 1865. D. A. Smith, R. T. Jaynes, J. W. Shelor, J. A. Steck, T. B. Shelor, F. A. H. Schroder, W. C. Hughes, Mrs. J. A. Steck, Jack H. Brewster, R. R. Phillips, F. W. Smith, Lewis F. Brabham, R. F. Powell, Charles S. Collins, Aston Hetster, L. Abner Hall, J. A. Gallimore, and Jack L. Hunt also associated with paper in Walhalla. *Files: Greenville CL Feb 7, 1884; Keowee Courier ((1888-1929)), 1930 + ; Oconee CL 1977 + ; SCL 1976 + ; Clemson, Oconee CL, and SCL mfm ((1868-1871)) 125, 1872-1885, (1886) 35, 1887-1890, (1891-1893) 34, 1898-1919, Apr 1920-1926, (1927) 43, 1928-Dec 1930, ((1931-1936)) 190, 1937-Jul 1976. For pre-1868 files see the Keowee Courier [Pickens]. Note: Oconee CL has an extensive name index to all of its mfm holdings of this paper.*

OCONEE NEWS   weekly, Democrat--established 1891. Published in Walhalla 1891-1900, in Seneca 1900-1902, then back in Walhalla from 1903 until c. 1911, when ceased. Ayer 1892: N. W. Macauley (editor), Oconee News Company. J. R. Earle and W. B. Loehr also associated with this paper in Walhalla. Last cited by Ayer in 1911. May 14, 1896 = vol 6, no 16, J. R. Earle (editor). *Files: SCL May 14, 1896.*

REACH: THE OCONEE SHOPPER   semi-monthly--established 1980. Jun 15, 1981 = vol 1, no 19, published jointly by the Keowee Courier and the Westminster News. *Files: Keowee Courier and Westminster News ((1980 +)).*

WALHALLA BANNER   weekly--established 1857, ceased c. 1860. According to Ellen, this paper was founded by F. N. Garvin & Company on May 16, 1857. Jul 27, 1859 = vol 3, no 7, Warren R. Marshall (editor), A. Bryce & Son (proprietors), C. C. Terrey (publisher). *Files: Duke Jul 27, 1859. Apparently no files in SC.*

WESTMINSTER

BANNER   weekly--established 1889, ceased c. 1892. Cited by Ayer 1889 thru 1892. Ayer 1889: Will T. Webb (editor and publisher). *NFK*

REACH: THE OCONEE SHOPPER   see Reach: The Oconee Shopper [Walhalla].

SUN   weekly, Democrat--established 1908, ceased c. 1909. Cited once by Ayer (1909): W. B. Loehr (editor and publisher). *NFK*

TIMES   weekly--established 1900, ceased c. 1904. Cited by Ayer 1902 thru 1904. Ayer 1902: John M. Findley (editor and publisher). Ayer 1903: J. H. Renny (editor), Southern Publishing Company. Ayer 1904: R. C. Mecklin (editor), Southern Publishing Company. *NFK*

TUGALOO TRIBUNE   weekly, Democrat--established 1909, merged with the <u>Seneca Journal</u> in 1952, continued by the <u>Journal and Tribune</u>. Cited by Ayer 1910 thru 1952. Aug 24, 1909 = vol 1, no 6, Gaillard and Gossett (editors and proprietors). Dec 5, 1911 = vol 3, no 21, A. L. Gossett (editor and proprietor). Jul 29, 1913, A. L. Gossett (editor and proprietor), Witherspoon and Flack (publishers). W. C. Felder also associated with paper. *Files: SCL (1909-1942) 20.*

WESTMINSTER NEWS   weekly, independent--established 1953. Ayer 1954: Jack L. Hunt (editor and publisher). Frank W. Hix, L. Abner Hall, and James G. Brown also associated with paper. Mar 7, 1973 = vol 20, no 51. Cited by Ayer 1954 thru 1979. *Files: SCL Jun 1, 1983; <u>Westminster News</u> ((1953-1962)), 1963 + .*

WESTMINSTER REVIEW   weekly c. 1911. A. L. Gossett, then editor and publisher of the <u>Tugaloo Tribune</u>, represented the <u>Westminster Review</u> at the SC Press Association meeting in 1911. <u>Westminster Review</u> not cited by Ayer. Paper ceased c. 1911 ? *NFK*

ORANGEBURG COUNTY

Orangeburgh District, now Orangeburg County, was one of seven judicial districts created in 1769. It assumed the name of its principal settlement, which honors Prince William IV of Orange, husband of Anne, daughter of King George II of England. The original name of that community, "Edisto," was changed to Orangeburgh by Swiss settlers who arrived there in 1735.

BOWMAN

LOW COUNTRY GAZETTE   weekly c. 1959.   Cited in State Chamber of Commerce literature, H. R. DeWitt (editor and publisher). Not listed by Ayer. *NFK*

BRANCHVILLE

BANNER   weekly, Democrat--established 1884, ceased c. 1886. Cited by Ayer 1885 and 1886. No personnel named. *NFK*

BRANCHVILLE ENTERPRISE   weekly, Democrat--established 1927, ceased c. 1935. Cited by Ayer 1928 thru 1935: J. A. Latimer (editor and publisher). Jan 18, 1928 = vol 1, no 18. Jun 20, 1930 issue lists E. E. Crowson (editor and publisher). *Files: SCL orig & mfm Jan 18, May 2, 1928, Jun 20, 1930.*

BRANCHVILLE JOURNAL   weekly, Democrat--established 1907, ceased c. 1913. Dec 1, 1909 = vol 3, no 25, Mrs. Estella Smoak Herndon (editor). Cited by Ayer 1908 thru 1913. Ayer 1908: C. A. Graves (editor and publisher). Edgar H. Rawl and Steedman Weatherbee also associated with paper. *Files: SCL orig & mfm Dec 1, 1909, Jan 12, 26, Feb 2, 1910, Nov 16, 1911.*

BUDGET   weekly--established 1894, ceased c. 1896. Cited by Ayer (1896): M. S. Connor (editor and publisher). May have become the Edisto Eagle. *NFK*

EDISTO EAGLE   weekly--established 1895, ceased c. 1897. Cited once by Ayer (1897): M. S. Connor (editor and publisher). May be new name for the Budget. *NFK*

HERALD   weekly--established 1913, ceased c. 1915. Cited once by Ayer (1915): C. C. Bailey (editor and publisher). *NFK*

PROGRESSIVE CHURCH RECORD   semi-monthly, Methodist, black publication--established 1913, ceased c. 1915. Cited once by Ayer (1915): Rev. and Mrs. C. E. Minor (editors), C. E. Minor and Company (publisher). *NFK*

SPECTATOR   weekly, Democrat--established 1887, moved to St. Matthews c. 1888, later published in Orangeburg and Harlin City, ceased c. 1891. Mar 17, 1887 = vol 1, no 1, H. S. Cunningham (editor and publisher). Cited once by Ayer in Branchville (1887). See also Spectator [Orangeburg]. *Files: SCL mfm Mar 17, 24, 1887.*

TRIBUNE   weekly--probably established 1914, ceased c. 1918. Cited only once by Ayer (1918): Hugh Long (editor and publisher). Ayer says founded 1904, may mean 1914, thus making the Tribune successor to the Herald. *NFK*

CORDOVA

SOUTHERN HEADLIGHT   weekly, Republican, black publication (?)--established 1907, ceased c. 1912. Cited by Ayer 1909 thru 1912: J. J. Bowks (editor and publisher). *NFK*

HARLIN CITY

SPECTATOR   see Spectator [Branchville and Orangeburg].

HOLLY HILL

BERKELEY NEWS   weekly, Democrat--established 1900, ceased c. 1904. Cited by Ayer 1901 and 1902: Will K. Jones (editor and publisher). Ayer 1903 and 1904: R. A. Grant (editor and publisher). *NFK*

HOLLY HILL OBSERVER   weekly--established 1972. Oct 19, 1972 = vol 1, no 42, David Michael Walters (editor), William M. Owens (publisher). Lee Hendren and Bert Rickenbacker also associated with paper. *Files: Holly Hill Observer (1972-Jul 1973), Aug 1973 + ; SCL ((1984 +)).*

SANTEE NEWS   weekly--established 1930, ceased c. 1930. Sep 11, 1930 = vol 1, no 1, Santee Publishing Company. No personnel cited. Not listed by Ayer. *Files: SCL Sep 11, 1930.*

NORTH

COURIER   weekly--established 1912, ceased c. 1914. Cited by Ayer 1913 and 1914: Will Walton (editor and publisher). *NFK*

NORTH TRADE JOURNAL   weekly--established 1957. Cited by Ayer 1970 + . Jan 21, 1965 = vol 8, no 3. This issue lists the Merchants Association of North as publisher. Paper printed by Kilgus Printing Company [Bamberg]. *Files: Advertizer-Herald [Bamberg] 1965 + ; Lexington CL 1981 + .*

STAR   weekly, Independent Democrat--established 1917, ceased c. 1918. Cited once by Ayer (1918): W. S. Stokes (editor), Stokes and Stokes (publisher). *NFK*

ORANGEBURG

BLACK FUTURE   bi-monthly c. 1981-1983. See View South News.

BLACK VOICE   weekly, black publication--published in Columbia by Redfern II, JuJu Publications, for the Orangeburg area. See Black News [Columbia].

CAROLINA TIMES   weekly, Republican--established 1865, ceased c. 1867. A prospectus concerning this paper, signed by W. W. Legare and T. C. Andrews, was printed in the Charleston Daily News (Sep 8, 1865). Oct 17, 1866 = vol 1, no 51, T. K. Legare (editor), C. H. Hall (publisher), W. W. Legare (proprietor). By Sep 1867 consisted of only a single sheet. *Files: SCL (Oct 17, 1866-Sep 18, 1867) 45.*

COTTON PLANT   monthly, semi-monthly, agricultural--established in Marion in 1883, published in various communities throughout the state, in Orangeburg c. 1890-1891. Oct 4, 1890 = vol 7, no 50, J. William Stokes (editor and publisher). See Cotton Plant [Greenville and Marion].

EDISTO CLARION   weekly c. 1854-1855. According to a statement in the Lexington Telegraph (May 31, 1855), P. H. Lacey proposed to launch the Edisto Clarion in Orangeburg in Oct 1854. This paper, if it appeared in 1854-1855, may have become the Southron. *NFK*

EDISTO CLARION   weekly, independent--established 1877 as the Tax-Payer, became the Edisto Clarion on Jun 28, 1878 (vol 1, no 38), continuing the number sequence of Tax-Payer. Thad C. Andrews was editor, T. C. Andrews and Son, publishers. Paper continued by the Orangeburg Democrat on Jan 3, 1879. In addition to Andrews, H. G. Sheridan, Stiles E. Mellichamp, and James L. Sims also associated with Edisto Clarion. *Files: SCL (1878) 15.*

ENTERPRISE   weekly, semi-weekly--established 1890 as the Enterprise and Alliance Monitor, became the Enterprise on Nov 12, 1892, ceased c. 1895. Nov 12, 1892 = vol 3, no 27, R. Lewis Berry and C. L. Howell (publishers and proprietors). B. F. Keller, Fred Wannamaker, and B. W. Palmer also associated with paper. Cited by Ayer 1893 thru 1895. Began semi-weekly, became weekly on Jul 22, 1893. *Files: SCL (1892-1894) 60.*

ENTERPRISE AND ALLIANCE MONITOR   weekly, Farmers' Alliance--established 1890, continued by the Enterprise on Nov 12, 1892. May 21, 1890 = vol 1, no 2, Fred Wannamaker (editor), R. Lewis Berry and C. L. Howell (publishers and proprietors). Cited by Ayer 1890 thru 1892. *Files: SCL (1890-1892) 50.*

FIELD   daily except Sun--established 1921, ceased c. 1923. Cited once by Ayer (1923): Arthur Fields (editor and publisher). *NFK*

FREE CITIZEN   weekly, Republican--established 1874, ceased c. 1876. Cited by Rowell 1875 and 1876. Mar 6, 1875 = vol 1, no 30, E. A. Webster (editor), A. Webster (publisher). E. A. Webster was a lawyer and a trial justice. Alonzo Webster, former chaplain of the State Senate and president of Claflin College, was instrumental in the formation of SC State College. In 1875 he was secretary of that institution. *Files: SCL (1875) 17.*

GOSPEL BANNER   semi-monthly, Methodist, black publication--established in St. Matthews in 1890, moved to Orangeburg c. 1892, ceased c. 1892. Cited by Ayer 1892 in Orangeburg: L. A. McCasland (editor and publisher). *NFK*

HERALD   weekly, bi-monthly, black publication--established in Anderson in 1957, ceased ? Not cited by Ayer. Some issues (1968-1971) bear dual datelines--Anderson and Orangeburg. Feb 6, 1968 = vol 10, no 4, Davis Lee (editor and publisher). *Files: SCL Feb 6, 1968, Oct 25, 1970, May 7, 1971.*

METHODIST MESSENGER   semi-monthly, weekly--established as a semi-monthly in Charleston in 1881, moved to Orangeburg c. 1886, issued weekly until ceased c. 1888. Cited by Ayer in Orangeburg 1886 thru 1888: A. Webster (editor), Methodist Messenger Association (publisher). Mar 16, 1887 = vol 6, no 18. *Files: SCL Mar 16, 1887.*

ORANGEBURG DEMOCRAT   weekly--established Jan 3, 1879 (vol 1, no 1), H. G. Sheridan and James L. Sims (proprietors), formerly the Edisto Clarion. Merged with the Orangeburg Times on Sep 29, 1881 to create the Times and Democrat. *Files: SCL 1879-1880; Clemson, Orangeburg CL, SCL, and Times and Democrat mfm Feb 17-Sep 22, 1881.*

ORANGEBURG EVENING NEWS   daily except Sun, Democrat--established 1904, ceased c. 1917. Sep 28, 1904 = vol 1, no 1, R. Lewis Berry and Company (editor and publisher). Cited by Ayer 1905 thru 1917. *Files: SCL Sep 1904-Sep 1912, Sep 3, 1914.*

ORANGEBURG NEWS   weekly--established 1867, merged with the Orangeburg Times in 1875 to create the Orangeburg News and Times. Mar 9, 1867 = vol 1, no 3, Samuel Dibble (editor), Charles H. Hall (publisher). Began as a Democrat paper, then turned Republican. Thad C. Andrews, Malcolm I. Browning, J. Felder Meyers, and A. B. Knowlton also associated with paper. *Files: SCL Mar 1867-Apr 1870, Dec 1870-Mar 1875.*

ORANGEBURG NEWS   weekly, Democrat--established 1931, merged with the Orangeburg Observer c. 1934 to create the Orangeburg Observer and Orangeburg News. Cited once by Ayer (1934): C. H. Trotti (editor and publisher). *NFK*

ORANGEBURG NEWS AND TIMES   weekly--created Mar 20, 1875 by merger of the Orangeburg News and the Orangeburg Times, continuing the number sequence of the Orangeburg News. Mar 20, 1875 = vol 9, no 5, Thad C. Andrews (editor), Orangeburg News Company (publisher). On Sep 29, 1877 reverted to former name of Orangeburg Times and in Sep 1881 merged with the Orangeburg Democrat to create the Times and Democrat. In addition to Andrews, J. Felder Meyers also was associated with this paper. *Files: SCL Mar 20, 1875-Nov 18, 1876, Jan 6-Sep 22, 1877; Orangeburg CL, SCL, and Times and Democrat mfm Apr 7, 1877.*

ORANGEBURG OBSERVER   weekly--established c. 1931, merged with the Orangeburg News c. 1934 to create the Orangeburg Observer and Orangeburg News. Not cited by Ayer. Founding date of 1931 (noted by Ayer when referring to merged papers) may apply to the Orangeburg News, not the Orangeburg Observer. *NFK*

ORANGEBURG OBSERVER AND ORANGEBURG NEWS   weekly, semi-weekly--created by merger of the Orangeburg Observer and the Orangeburg News c. 1934, ceased c. 1949. Cited by Ayer 1935 thru 1949. Ayer 1935: J. P. Gramling (editor), Observer Publishing Company. L. L. McLean, W. B. Wiggins, F. B. Best, Joe Mulieri, and A. B. Clayton also associated with paper. SCL has special 200th anniversary issue [Orangeburg] published in 1935 (vol 5), but no month or day cited. *Files: SCL (1935) 1.*

ORANGEBURG SUN   weekly, semi-weekly, Independent Democrat--continues the Patriot c. 1908, ceased c. 1933. Cited by Ayer 1909 thru 1933. Ayer 1909: Fred Wannamaker (editor and publisher). C. C. Berry, H. H. Wannamaker, and Hugo S. Sims also associated with paper. Jan 14, 1925 = vol 6, no 33, new series, Orangeburg Sun Company (publisher). *Files: Kansas Historical Society Jan 14, 1925. Apparently no files in SC.*

ORANGEBURG TIMES   weekly, Democrat--established 1872, merged with the Orangeburg News on Mar 20, 1875 to create the Orangeburg News and Times, which once more became the Orangeburg Times on Sep 29, 1877 and merged with the Orangeburg Democrat on Sep 29, 1881 to create the Times and Democrat. Feb 14, 1872 = vol 1, no 1, J. S. Heyward (editor), F. P. Beard (associate editor), Heyward and Beard (publishers). Beard soon withdrew and on Jan 30, 1873 Heyward sold the paper to the Orangeburg Times Company, which hired a series of editor-managers: Kirk Robinson, Stephen B. Fowle, F. W. Whitehead, and Stiles R. Mellichamp. *Files: SCL ((Feb 1872-Mar 1875, Sep 1877-Sep 1881)) 340; Clemson, Orangeburg CL, SCL, and Times and Democrat mfm Aug 15, 1879.*

PATRIOT   weekly, Farmers' Alliance--established 1894, continued by the Orangeburg Sun c. 1908. Jul 4, 1895 = vol 2, no 3, James T. Parks (editor). W. O. Tatum, H. H. Brunson, J. H. Funderburg, and A. A. Brantley also associated with paper. *Files: SCL Jul 4, 1895.*

PEOPLE'S RECORDER   weekly, Republican, black publication--established in Barnwell as the Recorder in 1893, published in Columbia by 1896, moved to Orangeburg May 1, 1903, moved back to Columbia c. 1921. Cited by Ayer in Orangeburg 1904 thru 1920. Jun 30, 1903 = vol 10, no 40, A. Boston Lindsay (business manager), C. F. Holmes (editor and publisher). R. E. Richardson also associated with paper. See also People's Recorder [Columbia]. *Files: SCL Jun 20, 1903, Sep 11, 1909.*

PLAIN SPEAKER   weekly, black publication--established 1888, ceased c. 1892. Cited by Ayer 1889 thru 1892. J. H. Fordham listed as manager in 1889, Plain Speaker Publishing Company. E. C. and J. A. Brown also associated with paper. *NFK*

SOUTHEAST ADVOCATE   bi-weekly, Methodist--established c. 1875, ceased c. 1875. During 1874-1875, A. Webster (publisher of the Free Citizen) announced plans to issue the Southeast Advocate. In Nov 1875 the "prospectus" concerning this publication disappears from the Free Citizen; however, Webster quotes editorially from the "S. E. Advocate," indicating some issues may have appeared. Rowell 1875-1876 cites the South-Eastern Advocate [Charleston], A. Webster (editor). *NFK*

SOUTHERN CHRISTIAN ADVOCATE   weekly, Methodist--established in Charleston in 1837, published in various places, including Orangeburg 1901 and 1902. Jan 3, 1901 = vol 64, no 29, John O. Willson (editor), R. Lewis Berry & Company (publisher). Produced by Berry for the Methodist Episcopal Church, South. Paper moved to Spartanburg in Jan 1903. See Southern Christian Advocate [Columbia].

SOUTHRON   weekly--established 1855, ceased c. 1860. May have been successor to the Edisto Clarion. The Edisto Clarion of 1878 indicates it had a predecessor by that name that became the Southron. Apr 30, 1856 = vol 1, no 31, H. D. Kennedy & Company (publisher). According to the Marion Star (Sep 2, 1856), the Southron was for sale. The Daily Columbia Times (Jan 16, 1857) noted that the Southron was being edited by T. B. Logan & Brother. Apparently the paper then suspended operations for about two and one-half years or at some point began a new number sequence. Mar 9, 1859 = vol 1, no 51, A. G. Salley (editor and publisher). Thad C. Andrews was associated with Salley in 1860. *Files: SCL (1856-1860) 15.*

SPECTATOR   weekly--established in Branchville in 1887, published in St. Matthews in 1888, in Orangeburg during 1889 and 1890, and in Harlin City in 1891. Mar 12, 1889 = vol 3, no 1, H. S. Cunningham (editor and publisher). Ceased c. 1891. See also Spectator [Branchville]. *Files: SCL Mar 12, 1889.*

TAX-PAYER   weekly, independent--issued daily during court week, established 1877, became the Edisto Clarion as of Jun 28, 1878. Oct 12, 1877 = vol 1, no 3, James S. Heyward (editor and proprietor). *Files: SCL Oct 12, 1877-Jun 21, 1878.*

TEMPERANCE ADVOCATE   weekly--established in Columbia in 1870, published briefly in Orangeburg when F. P. Beard (editor and publisher of the Temperance Advocate) was associated with the Orangeburg Times. Paper moved to Camden in 1873. Cited by Rowell in Orangeburg in 1872. See Temperance Advocate [Columbia].

TIMES AND DEMOCRAT   weekly, semi-weekly, tri-weekly, daily--created Sep 29, 1881 (vol 10, no 32) by merger of the Orangeburg Times and the Orangeburg Democrat. J. L. Sims and S. R. Mellichamp were the original editors and publishers of the Times and Democrat. Hugo, Henry, and Edward H. Sims and Dean B. Livingston also associated with paper. Began as a weekly, became semi-weekly in Jan 1908, tri-weekly in Jan 1909, and daily in Sep 1919. *Files: SCL (1891-1973) 35; Claflin mfm 1938 + ; SC State College mfm 1953 + ; Winthrop mfm 1956-1983; Orangeburg CL, SCL, and Times and Democrat mfm ((Sep 1881-1884)) 160, 1885-1890, 1892-1905, ((1906-1911)) 230, 1912-1916, 1918-1921, 1923, Jul 1925-May 1927, 1928-1932, 1934 + . Note: Clemson has similar mfm holdings except files cease in 1974.*

VIEW SOUTH   see View South News.

VIEW SOUTH NEWS   weekly, black publication--established c. 1979. Began as a monthly magazine (Vue South) published in Orangeburg c. 1964-1973. In 1979 became View South, a bi-monthly magazine published in Charlotte, N. C., and from 1981 to 1983 issued in Orangeburg as Black Future. Became weekly View South News in 1983. Sep 14-20, 1983 = vol 5, no 12, Cecil J. Williams (editor and publisher), Williams Associates, Inc. Ceased c. 1985 ? *Files: SC State College (1983-1984) 25.*

WEEKLY DISPATCH   weekly, Democrat--established 1894, ceased c. 1896. Nov 17, 1894 = vol 1, no 1, R. Lewis Berry and C. L. Howell (publishers). Cited once by Ayer (1896): C. L. Howell (editor and publisher). *Files: SCL Nov 17, 1894-Aug 21, 1895.*

SANTEE

LAKE MARION JOURNAL   weekly--established 1985. Jul 17, 1985 = vol 1, no 4, Don Woods (editor), Joe Dillon (publisher). A subsidiary of the Regency Holding Company. *Files: Lake Marion Journal 1985 + .*

SPRINGFIELD

EDISTO CITIZEN   weekly, independent--established 1948, ceased c. 1952. Cited by Ayer 1950 thru 1952. Ayer 1950: George Imri (editor), J. L. and F. M. Aull (publishers). Naomi Imri listed as editor in 1952. *NFK*

EDISTO MESSENGER   bi-monthly--established Jun 7, 1961, ceased Aug 18, 1961. Jun 7, 1961 = vol 1, no 1. Robert A. Pierce cited as editor and publisher in issue # 4. Only six issues published. *Files: SCL Jun 7-Aug 18, 1961.*

PICKENS COUNTY

Created in 1826 when old Pendleton District was divided into Anderson and Pickens districts, the latter--now Pickens County--honors General Andrew Pickens (1739-1817) of Revolutionary War fame.

CALHOUN

HIGHLAND SENTINEL   weekly--established Sep 1840, moved to Anderson Jan 7, 1842. Sep 4, 1840 = vol 1, no 1, J. P. Reed (editor and proprietor). Ceased publication in Oct 1843 when paper was sold to James L. Orr, who then founded the Anderson Gazette. *Files: Anderson CL, Clemson, and SCL mfm ((Sep 1840-Oct 1843)) 150.*

CENTRAL

PICKENS COUNTY MESSENGER   weekly--first appears in Ayer 1913 as founded in 1881, P. W. Smith (editor and publisher). Basis of 1881 date unknown, although it may relate to the Easley Messenger of the 1880s. Cited by Ayer 1913 thru 1923. Published as an edition of the Liberty Gazette (1915-1921) and the Greer Citizen (1922-1923). *NFK*

POPULACE   semi-monthly--established 1889, ceased c. 1890. Cited once by Ayer (1890): Populace Printing Company (editor and publisher). *NFK*

CLEMSON

CLEMSON COMMENTATOR   semi-weekly--established Jun 6, 1938, ceased Jul 22, 1938. Jun 6, 1938 = vol 1, no 1, Earl Mazo (editor). Author Ben Robertson served as political columnist for paper. *Files: Clemson orig & mfm Jun 6-Jul 22, 1938.*

MESSENGER   weekly, independent--established in Seneca in 1954, moved business office to Clemson in 1959, although continues to be published in Seneca. Cited by Ayer 1956 + . Jan 8, 1959 = vol 5, no 18, Paul League (editor and publisher). Bob Herndon and J. A. Gallimore also associated with paper. In Nov 1986 Messenger added word "Weekender" to masthead and began new number system. *Files: Clemson 1954 + ; Journal/Tribune [Seneca] 1959 + ; Pickens CL 1978 + ; SCL ((1985 +)).*

EASLEY

AQUARIAN TIMES   weekly, irregular--"underground" mimeographed publication of the early 1970s. Issue at the University of Kansas has no date, no vol number, or issue data. Aquarian Times published at 331 Forest Acres, Easley. *Files: University of Kansas [Lawrence] copy c. 1970. Apparently no files in SC.*

CAROLINA TIMES   weekly--established 1924, ceased c. 1925. Cited once by Ayer (1925): Walter Hester (editor). Apr 18, 1924 = vol 1, no 4, Walter Hester (editor and manager). *Files: SCL Apr 18-May 9, 1924.*

DEMOCRAT   weekly, Democrat--established 1891, ceased c. 1895. Cited by Ayer 1891 thru 1895. Ayer 1891: D. F. Bradley (editor), Bradley and Hester (publishers). J. R. Gossett and C. T. Martin also associated with paper. *NFK*

EASLEY MESSENGER   weekly, Democrat--established 1883, ceased in 1891 when purchased by People's Journal [Pickens]. Oct 12, 1883 = vol 1, no 1, A. W. Hudgens and J. R. Hagood (editors), Hudgens, Hagood & Company (proprietor). Cited by Ayer 1884 thru 1890. T. W. Condon, T. K. Hudgens, J. R. Pritchard, and H. E. Russell also associated with paper. *Files: SCL (1885-1887) 11; Clemson, Pickens CL, and SCL mfm Oct 1883-Oct 1884.*

EASLEY MESSENGER   weekly--established 1895, ceased c. 1896. Cited once by Ayer (1896): A. W. Hudgens (editor and publisher). Obvious attempt to revive earlier publication by the same name. *NFK*

EASLEY PROGRESS   weekly--established 1902. Jul 23, 1902 = vol 1, no 1, D. F. Bradley (editor), Easley Publishing Company (proprietor). C. T. Martin, W. O. Hester, Sr., W. O. Hester, Jr., Julian Hiott, W. D. Spearman, Gary Hiott, Whitseth Hiott, Ray Phillips, Tup Lucas, Arthur L. Cox, L. M. Garrison, J. D. Wyatt, Harold Rogers, William Davey, William J. Ragsdale, Carnis B. Davis, and Jerry D. Vickery also associated with paper. *Files: Easley Progress mfm Jul 1902-1906, 1921 + ; Pickens CL 1937-1960, mfm Jul 1902-1906, 1921 + ; SCL ((1912-1968)) 315, mfm Jul 1902-1906, 1921 + .*

HOMEMAKER   weekly--established 1982 by the Easley Progress. Mar 16, 1982 = vol 1, no 1. *Files: Easley Progress, Pickens CL, and SCL mfm 1982 + .*

SOUTH CAROLINIAN   weekly--established May 18, 1964, only one issue published. May 18, 1964 = vol 1, no 1, Brent Breedin (editor and publisher). Projected supplement for South Carolina weeklies on federal government affairs. *Files: SCL May 18, 1964.*

LIBERTY

BEACON   weekly--established 1897, ceased c. 1898. Cited once by Ayer (1898): J. E. Kinch (publisher). *NFK*

GAZETTE   weekly, Democrat--established 1914, ceased c. 1923. Cited by Ayer 1915 thru 1923: P. W. Smith (editor and publisher). See also the Pickens County Messenger [Central]. *NFK*

MONITOR   weekly--established 1959. Ayer 1962: Joe C. Marett (editor and publisher). Jan 2, 1974 = vol 15, no 46, David Phillips (editor), Marion C. Owens (publisher). William D. Lewis also associated with paper. *Files: Monitor 1974 + ; Pickens CL 1978 + .*

NEWS   weekly, Democrat--established 1910, ceased c. 1912. Cited by Ayer 1911 and 1912: News Publishing Company. No personnel listed. *NFK*

NEWS   weekly, Democrat--established 1924, ceased c. 1926. Cited once by Ayer (1926): L. N. Roy (editor), Julian M. Hiott (publisher). *NFK*

NEWS   weekly--established 1929, ceased c. 1933. Cited by Ayer 1930 thru 1933: P. W. Smith (editor and publisher). *NFK*

PICKENS

KEOWEE COURIER   weekly--established 1849, moved to Walhalla in Feb 1868. May 18, 1849 = vol 1, no 1, W. H. Trimmier (publisher), J. W. Norris, Jr., and E. M. Keith (editors). Paper was suspended c. 1862-1864, and new numbering system implemented after the Civil War. First Walhalla issue Feb 28, 1868 = vol 3, no 21, J. H. Foy (editor), Robert Young & Company (publisher). Foy had just taken over editorial duties from Whitner Symmes, who quit when paper left Pickens but subsequently rejoined staff. Others associated with the Keowee Courier (1849-1868) include W. K. Easley, Robert A. Thompson, and W. H. Holcombe. *Files: Clemson May 1849-May 1851; SCL ((1854-1866)) 280; Clemson, Oconee CL, and SCL mfm May 1849-May 1851, Apr 1857-Jun 1860, (Aug 1860-Dec 1865) 61, 1866-Feb 1868. See also the Keowee Courier [Walhalla]. Note: Oconee CL has an estensive name index to all of its mfm holdings.*

NORTHWEST SENTINEL   weekly--established 1980 by Pickens Sentinel for communities in northwestern Greenville County. Apr 30, 1980 = vol 1, no 1, Bill Williams (editor), Ben Bagwell and Jerry Alexander (publishers). Published in Travelers Rest since 1983. See also Northwest Sentinel [Travelers Rest]. *Files: Northwest Sentinel 1984 + ; Pickens Sentinel Apr 30, 1980.*

PEOPLE'S JOURNAL   weekly, Farmers' Alliance--established 1891, merged with Pickens Sentinel in 1903 to create the Sentinel-Journal. Mar 12, 1891 = vol 1 (no number), T. C. Robinson (editor and manager), Farmers' Publishing Company. This issue notes that the People's Journal had purchased the Easley Messenger (founded in 1883). *Files: SCL mfm ((1891-1903)) 430.*

PICKENS SENTINEL   weekly--established 1871, merged with People's Journal in 1903 to create the Sentinel-Journal, resumed original name of Pickens Sentinel in Oct 1911. Nov 25, 1875 = vol 5, no 13, D. F. Bradley (editor and proprietor). Cited by Rowell 1872: J. R. Holcombe & Company (editor and publisher). J. E. and J. P. Boggs, J. L. O. Thompson, G. E. Robinson, Homer A. Richey, Gary Hiott, Sr., W. L. Matheny, F. V. Clayton, Mrs. Gary Hiott, Gary Hiott, Jr., Ben Bagwell, and Jerry Alexander also associated with paper. *Files: Pickens CL 1937-1960, 1977 + ; Pickens*

Sentinel 1940 + ; Pickens CL and SCL mfm ((1875-1888)) 420, Jan 1890-Sep 1894, Apr-Dec 1903, ((1905-1909)) 240, 1911-1918, Mar 1921-Dec 1924, 1925 + . Note: Clemson has similar mfm holdings that begin in 1875 and cease in Sep 1933.

SENTINEL-JOURNAL weekly--created by merger of People's Journal and Pickens Sentinel in 1903. J. L. O. Thompson was editor at the time of the merger. Pickens Sentinel resumed original name on Oct 12, 1911. See Pickens Sentinel.

RICHLAND COUNTY

Organized in 1799 from part of old Kershaw District, Richland District, now Richland County, presumably was named for "Richland," a plantation owned by Colonel Thomas Taylor, or for the rich soil found along rivers in that region.

CAMP JACKSON   see Fort Jackson

COLUMBIA

AMERICAN LUTHERAN SURVEY   weekly, monthly, religious--established Oct 1914, ceased Jun 1928. Oct 26, 1914 = vol 1, no 1, Walter Harlowe Greever, George Taylor Rugh, and Walter E. Schutte (editors). Note: Could be classified as a periodical. *Files: Lutheran Theological Southern Seminary Oct 1914-Jun 1928.*

BAPTIST COURIER   weekly, religious--continues Working Christian Sep 20, 1877 = vol 1, no 1 (new series), vol 9, no 37 (old series), whole no 416, C. M. McJunkin (editor and proprietor). James A. Hoyt, editor of the Columbia Register, purchased the Baptist Courier in Sep 1878 and moved paper to Greenville in Mar 1879. See Baptist Courier [Greenville].

BEE   weekly, Republican, black publication--established 1907 in Camden as the Camden Bee, moved to Columbia c. 1911, ceased c. 1912. Cited in Columbia once by Ayer (1912): C. C. Clarkson (editor), Camden Bee Publishing Company. *NFK*

BLACK NEWS   weekly, black publication--continues Black on News c. 1977. Jun 20, 1979 = vol 3, no 3, Redfern II (publisher). Issued by JuJu Publishing Company with seven different mastheads: Black News [Columbia], Black Times [Charleston], Black Sun [Florence], Black Star [Greenville], Black Voice [Orangeburg], Black Views [Rock Hill], and Black Post [Sumter]. Cited by Ayer 1983 + . *Files: Black News ((1984 +)); Morris ((1982 +)); Winthrop Nov 26, 1977; SCL ((1979 +)).*

BLACK ON NEWS   irregular, monthly, bi-monthly, weekly, black publication--established Sep 1972, continued by Black News c. 1977. Redfern II (editor), Black On Nation (publisher). No vol-issue data. Not cited by Ayer. *Files: SCL (1974-1976) 50; Winthrop (1973-1977) 26.*

BUSINESS MIRROR   weekly c. 1985--David M. White (editor and publisher), ceased c. 1985. *NFK*

BUSINESS NEWSPAPER   weekly--established 1978, ceased c. 1979. Mar 13, 1978 = vol 1, no 1, Ron Dunn (publisher). Not cited by Ayer. *Files: SCL (Mar-Oct 1978) 12.*

CAROLINA AFRO-WEEKLY   weekly, black publication--established 1969, ceased c. 1974. Nov 3, 1972 = vol 4, no 5, James A. Whetstone (editor), Carolina Afro-Publishing Company. Mazie B. Ferguson also associated with paper. *Files: SCL (Sep 1973-Mar 1974) 17; Winthrop Nov 3, 1972.*

CAROLINA BULLETIN   weekly, tri-weekly, daily--established Jan 1859 by C. K. and J. E. Britton. According to Ellen, paper ceased in Apr 1859 and moved to Charlotte, N. C., where it became the Daily Bulletin. An ad in the Columbia city directory (1859) indicates office was at 146 Richardson Street. *NFK*

CAROLINA FREE PRESS   weekly--established Oct 1923, ceased c. 1924. Oct 25, 1923 = vol 1, no 1. Richard J. Person listed as editor in Dec 15, 1923 issue. Not cited by Ayer. *Files: SCL Oct 25, Nov 3-17, Dec 15, 22, 1923.*

CAROLINA FREE PRESS   weekly, independent--established 1930, ceased c. 1940. Jan 31, 1930 = vol 1, no 1, Ben E. Adams (president), Carolina Publishing Company Cited by Ayer 1932 thru 1940. Also issued as the Free Press with "Carolina" in small letters on masthead. *Files: SCL mfm Jan 31, 1930-Jun 21, 1940.*

CAROLINA PLANTER   weekly, agricultural--established Jan 1840, ceased Jan 12, 1841 when subscribers transferred to Ruffin's Farmers' Register in Virginia. Feb 19, 1840 = vol 1, no 6, R. W. Gibbes (editor), A. S. Johnston (publisher). *Files: SCL (1840-1841) 30.*

CAROLINA TELEGRAPH   weekly--established 1816, ceased c. 1817. Dec 13, 1816 = vol 1, no 49, David P. Hillhouse (publisher). William Cline also associated with paper. *Files: SCL orig & mfm Dec 13, 1816, Jan 3, 1817.*

CHRISTIAN NEIGHBOR   weekly, Methodist--established 1868, ceased c. 1901. Apr 2, 1868 = vol 1, no 1, Sidi H. Browne (editor and proprietor), John A. Elkins (publisher). W. W. Deane also associated with paper. Cited by Rowell and Ayer 1869 thru 1901. *Files: SCL Apr 1868-1885, (1886-1901) 60; Wofford 1868-1900.*

CHRISTIAN SOLDIER   monthly, black publication--established 1898, ceased c. 1900. May 1899 = vol 1, no 10, Richard Carroll (editor). Vehicle to promote work of Reverend Carroll, leading black clergyman of early 20th century. *Files: SCL May 1899.*

CHURCH HERALD   semi-monthly, Episcopal--established in Spartanburg in 1881, moved to Columbia c. 1884, ceased c. 1884. Cited once in Columbia by Ayer (1884). Mar 1, 1884 = vol 4, no 3, Frank Hallam (editor). See also Church Herald [Spartanburg]. *Files: SCL Mar 1, 1884.*

CITIZEN   monthly, irregular--established 1983, ceased c. 1984. Dec 1983 = vol 1, no 1, Jerry Mills (editor and publisher). Publication created to serve Rosewood, Shandon, and Five Points neighborhoods. *Files: SCL (1983-1984) 2.*

CLEAV/AGE   monthly, underground publication--established Sep 1967, ceased ? Sep 1967 = vol 1, no 1, Paul Bloon (editor). *Files: University of Connecticut Sep 1967. Apparently no files in SC.*

COASTAL TIMES   weekly, black publication--established 1983, maintained offices in Summerville, Columbia, and Charleston c. 1983-1984. See Coastal Times [Charleston].

COLUMBIA ADVERTISER   weekly--established 1867, ceased c. 1868. Jan 18, 1868 = vol 1, no 8, "published at the Columbia Job Office of J. L. Kirkwood." *Files: SCL Jan 18, 1868.*

COLUMBIA BANNER   weekly--continues Palmetto-State Banner (established in 1846), which was acquired in 1852 by Dr. Robert Wilson Gibbes, who changed name of paper to Columbia Banner. In Apr 1853 paper merged with the South Carolinian and subsequently was issued as the weekly edition of that daily. Ceased c. 1863. Feb 15, 1853 = vol 7, no 33, R. W. Gibbes (state printer). W. B. Johnston and R. Gaillard also associated with paper. See also Portfolio. *Files: Clemson Aug 5, 1857; SCL (1853-1863) 21.*

COLUMBIA BEACON   weekly c. 1879-1880. According to North, this paper was established in 1879 and ceased in Jan 1880. Not cited by Rowell and Ayer. *NFK*

COLUMBIA COURIER   weekly, black publication--established 1986, James E. Bridgett, Jr. (editor and publisher), New Dimensions Publishers. No issue-vol data given. Ceased c. 1986. *NFK*

COLUMBIA DAILY COMMERCIAL HERALD   daily--established c. 1847, but soon ceased. Apparently an ill-fated attempt by I. C. Morgan (editor and publisher of the Palmetto-State Banner) to launch a daily paper, the first in SC outside of Charleston. *NFK*

COLUMBIA DAILY PHOENIX   daily--continues the Columbia Phoenix on May 15, 1865, continued by the Daily Phoenix on Jul 31, 1865. May 15, 1865 = vol 1, no 39, Julian A. Selby (editor and publisher). The Columbia Phoenix, established as a tri-weekly, soon became a daily. Selby also issued a tri-weekly edition and a weekly publication. See the Tri-Weekly Phoenix and the Weekly Gleaner. *Files: SCL orig & mfm May 15-Jul 31, 1865.*

COLUMBIA DAILY RECORD   daily--continues the Palmetto Yeoman on Jul 20, 1885, succeeded by the Columbia Journal in 1893. Sep 7, 1885 = vol 5, no 43, H. N. Emlyn & Company (publisher), "successor to the Palmetto Yeoman." Paper also issued as the Daily Record and the Columbia Record. *Files: Greenville CL Jan 11, 1888; SCL Jul 1885-Jul 1886, ((1886-1891)) 100, mfm Oct 1885-May 1886, (1887) 8.*

COLUMBIA DAILY REGISTER   see Columbia Register.

COLUMBIA DAILY SUN   daily--established 1873, ceased c. 1873. Aug 19, 1873 = vol 1, no 13, A. C. Moore (editor). Moore, a local attorney, evidently launched this paper as an anti-Daily Phoenix vehicle. Not cited by Rowell. *Files: SCL Aug 19-Sep 4, 1873.*

COLUMBIA DAILY UNION   daily, Republican--continues Daily Union c. Jan 1872. Jan 3, 1872 = vol 2, no 4, whole no 350, L. Cass Carpenter (editor and proprietor). On May 22, 1873 paper merged with the Daily Evening Herald to create the Daily Union-Herald; however, early in 1874 Carpenter was publishing the Columbia Daily Union once more. Feb 17, 1874 = vol 5, no 21, whole no 790, L. Cass Carpenter (editor and proprietor). Erastus W. Everson also was listed as editor at times. On Jun 1, 1874 paper announced it would cease daily and issue only semi-weekly and weekly editions. Continued by the Columbia Semi-Weekly Union and the Weekly Union. *Files: SCL (1872-1874) 60.*

COLUMBIA FREE PRESS AND HIVE   weekly--established Feb 5, 1831 = vol 1, no 1, A[bner] Landrum (publisher). Paper formerly the Edgefield Hive [Pottersville], continued by the Columbia Hive on Feb 4, 1832. *Files: SCL mfm Feb 5, 1831-Jan 28, 1832.*

COLUMBIA GAZETTE   semi-weekly c. 1791. According to Brigham, Robert Haswell, who died late in 1791, provided the General Assembly with 250 copies of the Columbia Gazette during the session held that year. *NFK*

COLUMBIA GAZETTE   weekly--established in 1794, continued by the State Gazette c. Jan 1795. Jan 28, 1794 = vol 1, no 1, although a preliminary issue was published on Jan 14, 1794 by William P. Young and Daniel Faust. Twelve issues and supplements are available in Readex Microprint # 1887. *Files: SCL May 13, Dec 9, 1794; USC mp (Jan 14-Dec 9, 1794) 12.*

COLUMBIA HIVE   weekly--continues the Columbia Free Press and Hive on Feb 4, 1832 = vol 2, no 1, A[bner] Landrum (publisher). Paper ceased c. 1837. *Files: Clemson Dec 22, 1832, Mar 16, 1833; SCL Feb 4, 1832-Jan 26, 1833, (1833-1836) 6.*

COLUMBIA INQUIRER   semi-weekly--established 1932, ceased c. 1932. Feb 3, 1932 = vol 1, no 2, David H. Rembert (editor), John Van Cronkhite (publisher). Paper issued on Sun and Wed. Not cited by Ayer. *Files: SCL Feb 3-14, 1932.*

COLUMBIA JOURNAL   daily, Independent Democrat--established 1893, ceased c. 1895. Apr 6, 1893 = vol 1, no 56 (no personnel listed). According to the State, this afternoon paper was purchased by W. W. Ball in Feb 1894, and the State notes on Dec 23, 1894 that it had suspended operations. Larry W. Boyd also associated with paper. By Oct 1895 its facilities were owned by the Evening News. Ayer cites the Columbia Journal once (1895), indicating it was a successor to the Palmetto Yeoman (established 1879) and the Columbia Daily Record. *Files: SCL (Apr 1893-Dec 1894) 75.*

COLUMBIA MONITOR weekly, religious, black publication--established in Columbia in 1883, moved to Bennettsville c. 1885 and issued as the South Carolina Monitor. Sep 7, 1883 = vol 1, no 2, C. W. McColl (editor and proprietor). Ayer ad 1884: "a lively family newspaper, devoted to the interests of the Africo-American People." *Files: New York Historical Society Sep 7, 1883. Apparently no SC files.*

COLUMBIA PHOENIX tri-weekly, daily--established as a tri-weekly by Julian A. Selby on Mar 21, 1865 (vol 1, no 1). Soon became daily and on May 15, 1865 continued by the Columbia Daily Phoenix. *Files: CLS Mar 21, 23, 28, Apr 1, 18, May 4, 5, 1865; SCL orig & mfm Mar 21-May 13, 1865.*

COLUMBIA RECORD see the Columbia Daily Record (1885-1893).

COLUMBIA RECORD daily--continues the Daily Record on Apr 4, 1913 = vol 16, no 294, James H. Moore (editor), Walter B. Sullivan (publisher). William Banks, R. Charlton Wright, Fitz Hugh McMaster, George A. Buchanan, S. L. Latimer, Jr., H. F. Cauthen, John A. Montgomery, William A. Collins, Ambrose G. Hampton, Thomas N. McLean, and Ben R. Morris also associated with the Columbia Record. Paper purchased by the State in 1945. *Files: Clemson mfm 1925-1939, 1941-1945; Columbia Record, Richland CL, and SCL mfm Apr 1913-1939, 1941 + . Note: Richland CL has index, Nov 1973 + .*

COLUMBIA REGISTER daily--established 1875, ceased c. 1898. Jul 28, 1875 = vol 1, no 1, C. P. Pelham apparently founding editor. H. N. Emlyn, O. F. Howell, W. B. McDaniel, C. C. Tutt, F. H. Marks, Edwin Forde, Charles A. Calvo, Jr., J. W. R. Pope, Thomas Addison, and John S. Reynolds also associated with paper, which published weekly and tri-weekly editions throughout much of its career. See the Weekly Register and the Tri-Weekly Register. Paper also issued as Columbia Daily Register and Daily Register; however, Columbia Register continues as running head on interior pages and as heading for editorial column. *Files: Greenville CL (1888-1897) 6; Spartanburg Methodist College mfm 1875-1887; SCL orig & mfm Jul 1875-Dec 1898.*

COLUMBIA SEMI-WEEKLY UNION semi-weekly, Republican--continues Columbia Daily Union Jun 1874, ceased c. 1876. Sep 21, 1874 = vol 4, no 47, whole no 911, L. C. Carpenter (editor and proprietor). Cited only once by Rowell (1875). Paper, which also issued a weekly edition, probably ceased sometime before 1877 when Carpenter was fined and imprisoned for forgery. *Files: SCL Sep 21, 1874.*

COLUMBIA SUBURBAN NEWS weekly--established in 1953 at 608 1/2 Harden Street in Five Points, Felicia Sisk (editor). This community paper, listed in Columbia city directories in 1954 and 1955, was continued by the West Columbia-Cayce Journal [Lexington County] in 1955. Paper may also have been issued as Columbia's Suburban News. *NFK*

COLUMBIA TELESCOPE   weekly--established 1815, continued by the Columbia Telescope, and Southern Political and Literary Register c. 1821. Jan 23, 1816 = vol 1, no 6, Thomas W. Lorrain (publisher). William Cline and John B. Hines also associated with paper. Occasionally issued as the Telescope. *Files: Camden Archives Apr 25, 1816; SCL orig & mfm (1816-1820) 60.*

COLUMBIA TELESCOPE   weekly, semi-weekly during legislative sessions--continues Columbia Telescope, and South Carolina State Journal c. 1828, ceased c. 1839. Jan 2, 1829 = vol 15, no 1, David W. Sims (publisher). A. S. Johnston also associated with paper. *Files: Clemson Mar 16, 1833; SCL orig & mfm 1829, ((1831-1839)) 100.*

COLUMBIA TELESCOPE, AND SOUTH CAROLINA STATE JOURNAL   weekly--continues South Carolina State Journal, and Columbia Telescope c. 1824, continued by the Columbia Telescope c. 1828. May 29, 1824 = vol 9, no 21, [James A.] Black and [D. E.] Sweeney (publishers). New owners apparently reversed title. Charles A. Bullard and David Sims also associated with paper. *Files: SCL orig & mfm (1824-1825) 6, 1826-1827.*

COLUMBIA TELESCOPE, AND SOUTHERN POLITICAL AND LITERARY REGISTER   weekly--continues Columbia Telescope c. 1821, continued by South Carolina State Journal, and Columbia Telescope c. 1822. Jun 12, 1821 = vol 6, no 26 (new series), William Cline (printer). *Files: SCL orig & mfm Jun 12, 1821.*

COLUMBIA WEEKLY REGISTER   see Weekly Register.

COMMERCIAL TRANSCRIPT   see Transcript.

CONFEDERATE BAPTIST   weekly--established Oct 1862, ceased c. Jan 1865. Oct 1, 1862 = vol 1, no 1, J. L. Reynolds and J. M. C. Breaker (editors), S. W. Bookhart and A. K. Durham (proprietors). By 1865 a subscription cost $10 for 6 weeks, "strictly in advance." *Files: CLS Apr 27, 1864; SCL (1862-1864) 26, mfm Oct 1862-Jan 1865.*

COTTON PLANT   monthly, semi-monthly, agricultural, Grange, Farmers' Alliance--established in Marion in 1883. Published in Greenville 1887-1890, Orangeburg 1891, Columbia 1892-1896, Spartanburg 1897, Laurens 1898, Greenville 1889-1904. Jan 14, 1893 = vol 10, no 25, J. W. Bowden (editor and publisher). Paper then official organ of the SC State Farmers' Alliance. See Cotton Plant [Marion and Greenville].

DAILY ADVERTISER   daily, Republican--according to Woody, published by the Daily Republican c. Sep 1871, soon ceased . *NFK*

DAILY AMERICAN PATRIOT   daily, tri-weekly--established 1866, ceased c. 1866. Jul 10, 1866 = vol 1, no 34, J. E. Britton (editor and proprietor). *Files: SCL Jul 10, 1866.*

DAILY CAROLINA TIMES   daily--established c. 1853, ceased c. 1860. Dec 31, 1855 = vol 3, no 486, Edward H. Britton & Company (publisher). According to King, Britton revived Columbia's Southern Chronicle in 1847 and then worked in Winnsboro for the Fairfield Herald & Register until 1853. John G. Bowman and T. S. Piggott also associated with the Daily Carolina Times, which issued weekly and tri-weekly editions throughout its career. See Weekly Carolina Times and Tri-Weekly Carolina Times. *Files: Sumter County Museum-Archives (1856) 6; SCL (1855) 3, Jan-Jun 1856, (1856-1858) 8.*

DAILY CHRONICLE   daily c. 1867, soon ceased. Oct 5, 1867 = vol 1, no 17, Chronicle Publishing Company. Anonymous editor proposed to issue a tri-weekly edition, too. *Files: SCL (1867) 6.*

DAILY EVENING HERALD   daily, Republican--established Jan 1873, merged with the Columbia Daily Union in May 1873, continued by the Daily Union-Herald. Also published weekly edition. Jan 27, 1873 = vol 1, no 18, L. C. Northrop (editor), E. W. Everson (associate editor), T. C. Andrews (business manager), Andrews, Northrop & Company (publisher). *Files: SCL Jan 27, Apr 22, May 14, 1873.*

DAILY GUARDIAN   see Daily Southern Guardian.

DAILY INDEX   daily, court news for business community--established 1913, ceased c. 1916. Jan 2, 1915 = vol 2, no 205 (no editor or publisher named). Cited once by Ayer (1916). *Files: SCL Jan 2-Sep 25, 1915.*

DAILY PHOENIX   daily--established 1865, ceased c. 1879. Continues Columbia Daily Phoenix on Jul 31, 1865 = vol 1, no 104, Julian A. Selby (editor and publisher). Selby also issued tri-weekly edition and a weekly publication. See Tri-Weekly Phoenix and Weekly Gleaner. Cited by Rowell 1869 thru 1878. Robert Morgan also associated with paper. According to the Columbia Register (Dec 16, 1875), its owners had purchased the Daily Phoenix. In 1878, Henry S. Farley, editor of the Daily Phoenix, also was publishing the tri-weekly Straight-Out Democrat. *Files: Clemson Dec 1, 1866; SCL Jul 1865-Jul 1875, (1876-1878) 3, mfm Jul-Dec 1865, Jan 1868-Apr 1870.*

DAILY RECORD   see Columbia Daily Record (1885-1893).

DAILY RECORD   daily--established 1897, continued by the Columbia Record Apr 4, 1913. May 28, 1897 = vol 1, no 29, George R. Koester (manager). Paul M. Brice, H. A. Whitman, and James A. Hoyt also associated with paper. *Files: Columbia Record and Richland CL mfm Jan 1909-Apr 1912, Jul 1912-Apr 1913; SCL ((1897-1910)) 300, mfm (1898-1905) 23, Jan 1909-Apr 1912, Jul 1912-Apr 1913.*

DAILY REGISTER   see <u>Columbia Register</u>.

DAILY REPUBLICAN   daily--established Aug 14, 1868, continued by the <u>South Carolina Republican</u> [Charleston] in Oct 1868. Aug 14, 1868 = vol 1, no 1, J. W. Denny (printer). According to Woody, paper launched as a weekly, but soon became daily. *Files: Boston Athenaeum (1868) 6. Apparently no SC files.*

DAILY SOUTH CAROLINIAN   daily--established 1849, ceased c. 1867. Dec 18, 1849 = vol 1, no 55, Johnston and Cavis (publishers). Also issued weekly and tri-weekly editions to 1865. See <u>South-Carolinian</u>, <u>Weekly South Carolinian</u>, <u>Columbia Banner</u>, <u>Portfolio</u>, and <u>Tri-Weekly South Carolinian</u>. Mar 14, 1865 issue published in Charlotte, N. C., issues of Apr 29-30, 1865 in Chester. Dr. Robert W. Gibbes, Henry Timrod, and F. G. De Fontaine also associated with paper, which was issued in Charleston 1866-1867. See <u>Daily South Carolinian</u> [Charleston]. *Files: CLS Sep 29, 1858, May 30, 1863, Aug 6, 17, Nov 10, 1864, mfm (1861-1862) 25; SCL (1849-1851) 16, 1852-1856, ((1857-1867)) 300, mfm ((1851-1865)) 500.*

DAILY SOUTH CAROLINIAN   daily--established Jan 1872 by John P. Thomas, continued in Mar 1872 by the <u>South Carolinian</u>. Feb 11, 1872 = vol 1, no 16, John P. Thomas (editor). Also issued tri-weekly edition. *Files: SCL Feb 11, 1872.*

DAILY SOUTHERN GUARDIAN   daily, tri-weekly, weekly--established 1857, ceased 1865. Dec 11, 1858 = vol 2, no 217, Charles P. Pelham (publisher). Motto: "The South--Equality or Independence." Issued at times during the Civil War as the <u>Daily Guardian</u>. Whenever paper scarce, a column or two was deleted from pages and title shortened accordingly. See also the <u>Tri-Weekly Southern Guardian</u> and the <u>Weekly Southern Guardian</u>. Tri-weekly edition (Jul 31, 1858) says paper founded by E. H. Britton (state printer). Ad in Columbia city directory (1859) indicates office was at 177 Richardson Street. *Files: CLS Apr 15, 1861, Apr 23, 24, 1863, Nov 8, 1864; SCL ((1858-1865)) 350, mfm ((1862-1865)) 160.*

DAILY SOUTHERN GUARDIAN   daily, tri-weekly, weekly--established 1869, ceased c. 1870. Mar 13, 1870 = vol 1, no 40, Charles P. Pelham (editor), William H. McCaw and Company (publisher). Cited once by Rowell (1870). An unsuccessful attempt to revive earlier paper by same name. *Files: SCL Mar 13, Apr 6, May 10, 1870.*

DAILY SOUTHERN LIGHT   daily, tri-weekly--established 1857, ceased c, 1857. Oct 9, 1857 = vol 1, no 30, Edwin M. Broughton (publisher). With this issue Broughton dissolved partnership with Thomas H. Walsh. *Files: SCL Oct 9, 1857.*

DAILY TELEGRAPH   daily, tri-weekly--established 1847, ceased Jul 1851. Oct 19, 1847 = vol 1, no 2, Edward Sill and John Stubs (publishers). W. B. Carlisle and Edwin De Leon also associated with paper. According to Ellen, <u>Daily Telegraph</u> merged with the <u>South Carolinian</u> on Jul 9, 1851. <u>Note</u>: SCL has seven fragmentary issues of tri-weekly edition, see Telegraph. Daily files listed here. *Files: SCL Oct 19, 1847-Dec 6, 1849, ((1850-1851)) 250.*

DAILY UNION   daily, Republican--according to Woody, founded Nov 15, 1870 and originally published by the Carolina Printing Company. May 9, 1871 = vol 1, no 148, L. Cass Carpenter (editor), official paper of the state and Richland and Lexington counties. Continued by the Columbia Daily Union in Jan 1872. *Files: SCL May 9-13, 1871.*

DAILY UNION-HERALD   daily, Republican--created May 1873 by merger of the Columbia Daily Union and the Daily Evening Herald. Oct 4, 1873 = vol 5, no 122, whole no 891, T. C. Andrews (business manager), Andrews, Northrop & Company (publisher). By Jan 1874 paper also issuing the Weekly Union-Herald. Published as the Union-Herald 1876-1877, ceased c. 1877. Cited by Rowell 1874 thru 1877. J. G. Thompson also associated with paper. *Files: SCL (1873-1877) 13.*

EAGLE   semi-weekly--established 1882, ceased c. 1882. Jul 15, 1882 = vol 1, no 5, Eagle Publishing Company. Not cited by Ayer. *Files: SCL Jul 15, 22, 29, 1882.*

EAU CLAIRE POST   weekly c. 1954-1955. Cited in Columbia city directory (1955), Anderson P. Neeley (editor and publisher). *NFK*

EVENING NEWS   daily, Democrat--established 1895, ceased c. 1897. Jan 24, 1895 = vol 1, no 1. J. H. Rice listed as editor-in-chief on Jan 28, 1895. P. L. Melton and J. B. Barnett also associated with paper. Cited once by Ayer (1897). Evening News reportedly purchased plant used by the Columbia Journal. *Files: SCL Jan 24-Oct 4, 1895, (1895-1896) 5.*

FIVE POINTS NEWS   weekly--established 1941, ceased c. 1941. Feb 21, 1941 = vol 1, no 1, J. P. Gramling (editor), Five Points Publishing Company. Not cited by Ayer. Paper listed only once in Columbia city directory (1941). *Files: SCL Feb 21-Oct 31, 1941.*

FREE PRESS   see Carolina Free Press (established 1930).

GOSPEL TEMPERANCE UNION   monthly--established 1896, ceased c. 1896. Not cited by Ayer. May 1896 = vol 1, no 2, Gospel Temperance Union of South Carolina (publisher). *Files: SCL May 1896.*

HORIZON   semi-monthly--established 1982, ceased c. 1983. Sep 23, 1982 = vol 1, no 1, William M. Kneece (editor), Horizon Newspaper Company. *Files: SCL (1982-1983) 5.*

ILLUSTRATED FAMILY FRIEND   weekly--established 1851, ceased ? Apr 2, 1853 = vol 2, no 18, Steuart Adair Godman (publisher). *Files: Winthrop Apr 2, 1853.*

LABOR ADVOCATE   weekly, labor--established Aug 1919, continued by the Trade Review Oct 1919. Aug 1, 1919 = vol 1, no 1, issued by Charles S. Henry and Edward C. DuPre. Not cited by Ayer. *Files: SCL Aug-Oct 1919.*

LIGHT   weekly, Republican, black publication--established 1907, ceased c. 1915. Cited by Ayer 1909 thru 1915: C. G. Garrett (editor), Farmers' Union Sun Company and Light Publishing Company (publishers). *NFK*

LIGHT   weekly, black publication--established 1916, ceased c. 1928. Cited by Ayer 1922 thru 1927: C. G. Garrett (editor), Light Publishing Company. Jun 6, 1925 = vol 7, no 1, C. G. Garrett (editor), 2210 Lady Street. Joel H. Jackson also associated with paper. *Files: SCL Jun 6, Aug 22, 1925, Mar 27, 1926, Apr 7, 1928.*

LIGHTHOUSE AND INFORMER   weekly, independent, black publication--created c. 1941 by merger of the Charleston Lighthouse and the People's Informer [Sumter]. Ceased in 1954. Feb 6, 1944 = vol 7, no 33, John H. McCray (editor and publisher). Cited by Ayer 1947 thru 1955. Paper sometimes issued with dual dateline: Columbia and Charleston. See also Lighthouse and Informer [Charleston]. *Files: SCL Feb 6, 1944.*

LUTHERAN AND VISITOR   weekly, religious--created 1868 by merger of the Lutheran Visitor (published in Staunton, Va., 1866-1868) and the Southern Lutheran (published in Charleston and Columbia, 1861-1865?). Continued by the Lutheran Visitor on Aug 12, 1869. Apr 1, 1869 = vol 1, no 34 (new series), vol 3, no 40 (old series), [A. R.] Rude and [J. I.] Miller (editors), Duffie and Chapman (publishers). *Files: Lutheran Theological Southern Seminary mfm 1868-1869; Newberry College orig & mfm 1868-1869; SCL Apr 1, 1869.*

LUTHERAN CHURCH VISITOR   weekly, religious--established Sep 1904, ceased Apr 1919. SCL classifies as newspaper and periodical. Sep 15, 1904 = vol 1, no 1, W. H. Greever (editor-in-chief), official organ of the United Synod of the South. *Files: Lutheran Theological Southern Seminary 1904-1919; Newberry College mfm 1907-1910; SCL orig & mfm 1904-1919.*

LUTHERAN VISITOR   weekly, religious--continues Lutheran and Visitor Aug 1869, ceased 1904. Sep 22, 1869 = vol 2, no 6 (new series), vol 4, no 58 (old series), A. R. Rude, Columbia, and J. I. Miller, Staunton, Va. (editors and publishers). Published in Prosperity and Newberry c. 1892-1904. Paper also may have been issued briefly in Charleston c. 1875-1876. See Lutheran Visitor [Charleston]. *Files: Lutheran Theological Southern Seminary mfm 1869-1904; Newberry College 1869-1904, mfm 1869-1874; SCL (1869) 1, (1887-1899) 75.*

NEW BANNER   irregular, Libertarian--established 1972, ceased c. 1973. Feb 4, 1972 = vol 1, no 1, J. Michael Oliver (managing editor). W. Robert Black also associated with paper. See Underground Newspaper Collection at USC, reels 109 and 137. *Files: USC mfm (1972-1973) 11.*

NEW ERA   weekly--established 1855, ceased c. 1856. According to Ellen, a "Know Nothing" paper published by J. M. Curtis & Company. Jan 4, 1856 is issue no 8. *Files: SCL Jan 4, 1856 (fragment).*

NORTHEASTERN OBSERVER   weekly--established Aug 1971 to serve the region of Dentsville, Forest Acres, and Eau Claire, ceased c. 1971. Aug 26, 1971 = vol 1, no 1, Hugh B. Braddock (editor and publisher). *Files: SCL Aug 26-Sep 22, 1971.*

OSCEOLA   fortnightly, weekly--established May 1972, ceased Jun 1978. May 23, 1972 = vol 1, no 1, Randal Ashley, Mike Forth, John Norton, Tom Priddy, Mike Smith, and Jim Walser (senior editors), Parallex Media Projects, Inc. (publisher). Issued fortnightly May-Nov 1972, then suspended to Jul 1973 when became weekly. Index (1972-1974) available at SCL. *Files: Greenville CL (1973-1978) 38; SCL May 1972-Jun 1978.*

PACIFIC PILOT   weekly c. 1937-1938--publication produced for employees of Pacific Mills, Kern Powell (editor), Carolina Printing Company (publisher). Paper listed once in Columbia city directory (1938). It succeeded a monthly journal of the 1920s, the Spinner, and was, in turn, succeeded in 1943 by yet another monthly, Pacific Truths. *NFK*

PALMETTO GLEANER   weekly, Methodist, black publication--established 1890, ceased c. 1892. Cited by Ayer 1890 thru 1892: C. P. Nelson (editor). *NFK*

PALMETTO LEADER   weekly, black publication--established 1925, ceased c. 1961. Jan 10, 1925 = vol 1, no 1, N. J. Frederick (editor), Palmetto Leader Publishing Company. George H. Hampton, Zack J. Weston, and Arthur W. Aiken also associated with paper. Cited by Ayer 1927 thru 1961. *Files: SCL mfm 1925-1928, 1930-1932, (1933-1934) 3, 1935-1941, 1943, (1944-1957) 50.*

PALMETTO NEWS   weekly c. 1947-1948. Cited in 1948 Columbia city directory, office at 1310 Assembly Street. *NFK*

PALMETTO POST   weekly, black publication--established 1970, ceased c. 1971. Jan 8, 1971 = vol 1, no 19, John W. Goodwin (general manager), Central Printing & Publishing Company. Not cited by Ayer. *Files: SCL (1970-1971) 44; Winthrop Jul 1, 1971.*

PALMETTO POST   weekly, black publication--established Dec 1984. Jan 17, 1985 = vol 1, no 2, Nathaniel Abraham, Jr. (publisher). *Files: Palmetto Post and SCL ((1984 +)).*

PALMETTO-STATE BANNER   weekly--established 1846. Sep 8, 1846 = vol 1, no 1, I. C. Morgan (publisher); however, this was a "trial" issue and publication actually began on Nov 3, 1846. Motto: "Truth is mighty and will prevail." Dr. Robert Wilson Gibbes acquired paper in 1852 and subsequently changed name to Columbia Banner (see).

That paper was absorbed by the South Carolinian in Apr 1853. Alexander Carroll, T. F. Greneker, and John G. Bowman also associated with the Palmetto-State Banner. Circa 1852 paper issuing daily and tri-weekly editions, but no copies known to exist. All issues listed here are weekly. *Files: SCL (1846-1852) 50.*

PALMETTO TIMES   weekly, black publication--established Sep 1962, ceased c. 1964. Sep 20, 1962 = vol 1, no 1, E. Cedric Hart (publisher). Not cited by Ayer. *Files: SCL (1962-1964) 41.*

PALMETTO TIMES   weekly, irregular--established 1983, ceased c. 1983. May 11, 1983 = vol 1, no 1, Harvey William Burgess (editor and publisher). Not cited by Ayer. *Files: SCL May 11, Jun 1, 1983.*

PALMETTO YEOMAN   daily, weekly, Independent Democrat--daily edition established 1879, weekly edition 1881, continued by the Columbia Daily Record on Jul 20, 1885. Dec 18, 1879 = vol 1, no 103, C. M. McJunkin (editor and proprietor). Cited by Ayer 1881 thru 1885. Files listed here are daily; no weekly copies are known to exist. *Files: SCL (1879-1885) 60.*

PEOPLE'S RECORDER   weekly, Republican, black publication--established as the Recorder or Barnwell Recorder in Barnwell in 1893, published in Columbia c. 1896 to 1903 as the People's Recorder, sometimes with dual dateline: Columbia and Union. Motto: "Published for the Elevation of Our Race, and is [sic] an Exponent of Republican Principles." Columbia office was at 1115 Taylor Street in 1900. Paper moved to Orangeburg on May 1, 1903 and returned to Columbia c. 1921. Merged with the Southern Indicator [Columbia] c. 1925. Continued by the Recorder-Indicator. Mar 19, 1898 = vol 7, no 27, C. F. Holmes and S. H. Nix (editors and publishers). See also the People's Recorder [Orangeburg]. *Files: SCL Mar 19, 1898, Dec 21, 1901, mfm Jan 13, 27, 1900.*

PORTFOLIO   weekly--established Jun 1861, ceased c. 1865. Issued by Daily South Carolinian and may have supplanted that paper's weekly edition, the Columbia Banner, at times. Feb 24, 1864 = vol 16, no 25, F. G. De Fontaine & Company (publisher). According to Duke checklist, DuBose's Review received the first issue of Portfolio in Jun-Jul 1861. *Files: SCL Feb 24, 1864, Jan 25, 1865 (photostat).*

PUBLIC DEFENDER   weekly--established 1921, ceased c. 1922. Not cited by Ayer or listed in Columbia city directories. Oct 8, 1921 = vol 1, no 7, H. A. I. Rosenberg (editor and publisher). Paper had office at 4 Kirkland Building. *Files: SCL Oct 8, Nov 19, 1921.*

RECORD   fortnightly, Baptist, black publication--established in 1895, ceased in 1896 and was succeeded by the South Carolina Standard. Cited once by Ayer (1897): A. C. Osborn, D. D. and J. R. Wilson (editors), W. F. White (publisher). *NFK*

RECORDER-INDICATOR   weekly, Republican, black publication--created c. 1925 by merger of the People's Recorder [Columbia and Orangeburg] and the Southern Indicator [Columbia]. Ceased c. 1931. Jan 9, 1926 = vol 27, no 59, R. A. Roach (editor-in-chief), Recorder-Indicator Publishing Company. Cited by Ayer 1927 thru 1931. *Files: SCL (1926) 6.*

REFORM SIGNAL   weekly, Greenback, c. 1882-1883. According to the Charleston News and Courier (Feb 23, 1883), the offices of the Reform Signal burned in Dec 1882, and in Feb 1883 publisher J. Hendrix McLane was trying to re-establish his paper in Winnsboro. Not cited by Ayer. *NFK*

REPORTER   weekly, Democrat--established 1910, ceased c. 1919. Paper bears dual dateline: Edgewold and Columbia. Jan 29, 1910 = vol 1, no 1, John T. Duncan (editor and proprietor). Cited by Ayer 1911 thru 1919. *Files: SCL ((1910-1912)) 122.*

RICHLAND NORTHEAST   weekly, independent--established in 1976 by J. Kenneth Webb. Feb 13, 1985 = vol 10, no 7, Jennifer Nicholson (editor), Harvey Moss (publisher). Helen Rudick and Alanna Ritchie also associated with paper, which sometimes was issued as Richland Northeast Weekly. Cited by Ayer 1982 +. *Files: Richland Northeast 1982 +.*

RICHLAND NORTHEAST WEEKLY   see Richland Northeast.

ST. ANDREWS NEWS   weekly--established in 1968, ceased in 1985. Also issued as the St. Andrews Newsweekly. May 15, 1975 = vol 7, no 36. *Files: Lexington CL 1975-1985; SCL ((1975-1985)) 200.*

ST. ANDREWS NEWSWEEKLY   see St. Andrews News.

SOLDIER   monthly, religious--established 1892, ceased c. 1895. Jan 15, 1894 = vol 3, no 4, L. L. Pickett (editor and proprietor). Motto: "Endure Hardness as a Good Soldier of Jesus Christ." Largely a vehicle for the promotion of books by Reverend Pickett and his friends. *Files: SCL (1894-1895) 5.*

SOUTH CAROLINA BAPTIST   weekly (?) , black publication--established 1918, ceased c. 1920. According to sesquicentennial history of Columbia (1936), paper was edited by J. C. White, who at that time was editor and publisher of the Southern Indicator. *NFK*

SOUTH CAROLINA GAZETTE   weekly--established in Mar 1792, ceased c. Sep 1793. Jul 10, 1792 = vol 1, no 18, Daniel Constable (publisher). Seventeen issues available in Readex Microprint # 1888. *Files: USC mp (Jul 1792-Sep 1793) 17.*

SOUTH CAROLINA GAZETTE   weekly, Democrat--established in 1925, moved to Aiken in 1930 and merged with the Aiken Standard, continued by the Aiken Standard and South Carolina Gazette. Jan 13, 1925 = vol 1, no 1, Walter E. Duncan (editor and publisher). *Files: Clemson Aug 29, 1928; SCL Jan 13, 1925-Sep 3, 1930.*

SOUTH-CAROLINA GAZETTE, AND COLUMBIAN ADVERTISER
weekly, semi-weekly during legislative sessions--continues the South-Carolina State Gazette, and General Advertiser on Nov 29, 1799. Circa Jan 1801 paper continued by the South-Carolina State Gazette, and Columbian Advertiser. According to Brigham, Harvard had several issues in the 1930s. *Files: Harvard (1799-1800) 7. Apparently no SC files.*

SOUTH CAROLINA HERALD   weekly, Baptist, black publication--established 1907, ceased c. 1912. Cited by Ayer 1910 thru 1912: E. A. P. Cheek and Associates (publisher). *NFK*

SOUTH CAROLINA LABOR NEWS   weekly c. 1944-1945. Cited once in Columbia city directory (1945), Ted I. White (editor and publisher), office at 1111 Hampton Street. *NFK*

SOUTH CAROLINA METHODIST ADVOCATE   weekly, Methodist-- continues the Southern Christian Advocate on Nov 25, 1948, continued by the South Carolina United Methodist Advocate on Dec 12, 1968. Nov 25, 1948 = vol 112, no 47, John L. Sandlin (editor and manager). SCL classifies this publication as a periodical. *Files: SCL and Wofford 1948-1968.*

SOUTH CAROLINA MONITOR   see Columbia Monitor.

SOUTH CAROLINA REPUBLICAN   weekly--continues weekly South Carolina Republican [Charleston], which became the Daily Republican shortly before weekly edition moved to Columbia in Sep 1869. Columbia edition ceased in Dec 1870. Feb 5, 1870 = vol 2, no 18, issued by the Republican Printing Press. Cited once by Rowell (1870): Morris and Fox (editors and publishers). *Files: SCL (1870) 7.*

SOUTH CAROLINA STANDARD   fortnightly, Baptist, black publication-- established 1896, ceased c. 1905. Cited by Ayer 1898 thru 1905: A. C. Osborn, D. D. Wilson, and J. R. Wilson (editors and publishers). Paper issued at Benedict College. *NFK*

SOUTH-CAROLINA STATE GAZETTE AND COLUMBIA ADVERTISER
weekly, semi-weekly during legislative sessions ? --continues the South-Carolina State Gazette, and Columbian Advertiser c. 1820. Oct 1, 1822 = vol 28, no 1625, Daniel Faust (state printer). Merged with the Southern Times in Jul 1830, continued by the Southern Times & State Gazette. *Files: orig & mfm Oct 1, 1822, Jan 1827-Dec 1828.*

SOUTH-CAROLINA STATE GAZETTE, AND COLUMBIAN ADVER- TISER   weekly, semi-weekly during legislative sessions--continues South-Carolina Gazette, and Columbian Advertiser c. Jan 1801, continued by the State Gazette, and

Columbian Advertiser in 1816. Apr 24, 1801 = vol 8, no 414, D. and J. J. Faust (state printers). *Files: CLS Dec 10, 1802; SCL orig & mfm (1801-1816) 50.*

SOUTH-CAROLINA STATE GAZETTE, AND COLUMBIAN ADVER-TISER weekly, semi-weekly during legislative sessions ? --continues the State Gazette, and Columbian Advertiser c. 1818, continued by the South-Carolina State Gazette and Columbia Advertiser c. 1820. Oct 13, 1818 = vol 24, no 1403, Daniel Faust (state printer). *Files: SCL orig & mfm Oct 13, 1818.*

SOUTH-CAROLINA STATE GAZETTE, AND GENERAL ADVERTISER weekly, semi-weekly during legislative sessions--continues State Gazette c. Jun 1795, continued by the South-Carolina Gazette, and Columbian Advertiser on Nov 29, 1799. Jun 5, 1795 = vol 2, no 80, William P. Young and Daniel Faust (publishers). According to Brigham, Harvard and the Philadelphia Library Company had copies of paper in the 1930s. *Files: Harvard (1795-1799) 75; Philadelphia Library Company (1795-1796) 20. Apparently no SC files.*

SOUTH CAROLINA STATE JOURNAL, AND COLUMBIA TELESCOPE weekly--continues the Columbia Telescope, and Southern Political and Literary Messenger c. 1822, continued by the Columbia Telescope, and South Carolina State Journal c. 1824. Jul 9, 1822 = vol 7, no 25, William Cline (publisher). Apparently Cline changed title to reflect new status as state printer. *Files: SCL orig & mfm Jul 9, 1822.*

SOUTH-CAROLINA TEMPERANCE ADVOCATE weekly--established 1839, issued as the South Carolina Temperance Advocate and Register of Agricultural and General Literature after Jul 1841. Sep 12, 1839 = vol 1, no 10, Julius J. DuBose (editor), I. C. Morgan (publisher). John G. Bowman and Edwin Heriot also associated with paper, which moved to Charleston in 1852 and then to Camden in 1853 where it was issued once more as the South-Carolina Temperance Advocate. See also the South-Carolina Temperance Advocate [Camden]. *Files: Darlington County Historical Commission Oct 5, 1848; Newberry College Jul 1839-Dec 1847; SCL (1839-1851) 75, mfm (1840-1852) 75.*

SOUTH-CAROLINA TEMPERANCE ADVOCATE AND REGISTER OF AGRICULTURAL AND GENERAL LITERATURE see the South-Carolina Temperance Advocate [Columbia and Camden].

SOUTH CAROLINA UNITED METHODIST ADVOCATE weekly, Methodist--continues the South Carolina Methodist Advocate on Dec 12, 1968 = vol 132, no 48, A. McKay Brabham (editor). SCL classifies as periodical. Note: The word "Advocate" now featured as the name of this publication. *Files: SCL and Wofford 1968 + .*

SOUTH CAROLINA WEEKLY   weekly--established Jan 1948, ceased Jul 1948. Feb 13, 1948 = vol 1, no 7, Joe Mulieri (editor), South Carolina Weekly, Inc. (publisher). *Files: SCL (1948) 15.*

SOUTH-CAROLINIAN   weekly, semi-weekly during legislative sessions--established in 1838. Sep 28, 1838 = vol 1, no 3, A. H. and W. F. Pemberton (publishers). Paper added tri-weekly and daily editions in 1849 and after that date was continued by various publications. See the Weekly South Carolinian, Tri-Weekly South Carolinian, Daily South Carolinian, Columbia Banner, and Portfolio. *Files: SCL ((1838-1849)) 210, mfm ((1838-1849)) 165.*

SOUTH CAROLINIAN   daily, tri-weekly--attempt to revive old Daily South Carolinian in Jan 1872, ceased in Jun 1873. Mar 6, 1872 = vol 1, no 36, John P. Thomas and Thomas J. LaMotte (publishers). W. G. McGaw also associated with paper. Cited by Rowell in 1872 and 1873. *Files: SCL Mar 6, Jun 20, 1872, Nov 6, 1872-May 31, 1873.*

SOUTHEAST FARM PRESS   weekly, agricultural--established 1974, ceased c. 1976. Cited by Ayer 1975 and 1976: Harris H. Barnes, Jr. (editor), William S. McNamee (publisher). *NFK*

SOUTHERN CHRISTIAN ADVOCATE   weekly, Methodist--established in Charleston in 1837, continued by the South Carolina Methodist Advocate on Nov 25, 1948. Jun 24, 1837 = vol 1, no 1, William Capers (editor). James S. Burges, E. H. Myers, W. M. Wightman, T. O. Summers, F. M. Kennedy, W. D. Kirkland, John O. Willson, Charles A. Calvo, Jr., William C. Kirkland, R. E. Stackhouse, E. O. Watson, R. O. Lawton, John Marvin Rast, D. D. Peele, and John L. Sandlin also associated with this paper. Originally published by the South Carolina-Georgia Conference of the Methodist Episcopal Church, this paper moved to Augusta in 1862 and was published there until 1865, in Macon 1866 to Jun 1878, then returning to Charleston until Dec 1886. Since that time it has been published in the following locations: Columbia 1887-1894, Greenville 1895-1898, Columbia 1899-1900, Orangeburg 1901-1902, Spartanburg 1903-Sep 1912, Greenville Sep 1912-1914, Anderson 1915-1918, Columbia 1919-1948. Began as a newspaper but gradually developed a periodical format. SCL classifies as both newspaper and periodical. *Files: CLS Oct 25, 1884; Greenville CL (1888-1889) 23; Newberry College 1838-1847; SCL 1837-1948, mfm 1837-1900, 1903-1905; Wofford 1837-1902, 1906-1948, mfm 1837-1900, 1903-1905.*

SOUTHERN CHRISTIAN HERALD   weekly, Presbyterian--established 1834, moved to Cheraw on Apr 3, 1836, ceased c. 1838. Mar 18, 1834 = vol 1, no 1, R. S. Gladney (editor), Samuel Weir (publisher). M. McLean and G. H. Taylor also associated with paper. *Files: Newberry College Mar 26, 1835-Mar 24, 1837; SCL Mar 18, 1834-Mar 19, 1835, (1836-1838) 50, mfm Mar 30, 1836-Mar 24, 1837.*

SOUTHERN CHRONICLE   weekly--established Jul 1840, ceased c. 1848. Jul 9, 1840 = vol 1, no 1, Samuel Weir and H. Raiford (publishers). *Files: Newberry College* *orig & mfm Jul 7, 1841-Jun 16, 1847; SCL Jul 1840-Dec 1842, (1844-1847) 30, mfm Jul 7, 1841-Jun 16, 1847.*

SOUTHERN HERALD AND WORKING MAN   irregular--established c. 1873, ceased c. 1878--issued "periodically" from Columbia, Gaffney, and New York to promote immigration.   Feb 13, 1878 = vol 4, no 5, [Tilman R.] Gaines & Yingling (proprietors). *Files: SCL Feb 13, 1878.*

SOUTHERN INDICATOR   weekly, Republican, black publication--established 1903, merged with the People's Recorder c. 1925, continued by the Recorder-Indicator. Feb 15, 1913 = vol 8, no 18, N. J. Frederick (editor), Industrial Printing Company (publisher). Cited by Ayer 1916 thru 1926. J. C. White also associated with paper. *Files: SCL (1913-1924) 13, mfm (1921-1923) 14.*

SOUTHERN LUTHERAN   weekly, religious--established in Charleston in 1861, moved to Columbia in 1863, ceased c. 1865. Oct 4, 1863 = vol 3, no 108, N. Aldrich (editor), J[ohn] Bachman (assistant editor). A. R. Rude, who also was associated with paper, helped form the Lutheran and Visitor in 1868. See also the Southern Lutheran [Charleston]. *Files: SCL (1864-1865) 2, mfm (1863-1864) 14.*

SOUTHERN PLOUGHMAN   semi-monthly, Independent Republican, black publication--established 1906, ceased c. 1915. Cited by Ayer 1911 thru 1915: Richard Carroll (editor and publisher). According to Columbia city directories, office at 1013 Washington Street. *NFK*

SOUTHERN PRESBYTERIAN   weekly--established c. 1850 in Milledgeville, Ga., moved to Charleston in 1852, to Columbia in 1861, and to Clinton in 1893. Frequently confused with the Southern Presbyterian Review, a quarterly published from 1847 to 1885. Paper reorganized with new number sequence in 1861 and again after a brief suspension in 1865. Apr 19, 1862 = vol 2, no 24 (new series), A. A. Porter (editor), A. A. Porter & Company (publisher). Dec 28, 1865 = vol 1, no 1 (new series), James Woodrow & Company (publisher). According to Rowell (1873), Woodrow claimed a "larger circulation than any other daily or weekly published in the State." Rowell (1875): "No medical or doubtful advertisement accepted." Paper moved to Clinton in Apr 1893. Ceased c. 1908 when absorbed by the Presbyterian of the South. Elam Sharpe, W. S. Bean, J. Ferdinand and W. S. Jacobs also associated with paper. Some depositories classify as a periodical. See also the Southern Presbyterian [Charleston and Clinton]. *Files: Greenville CL Jul 12, 1866; SCL ((1860-1902)) 850, mfm (1895-1902) 16; Sumter County Museum-Archives (1886-1893) 3.*

SOUTHERN SUN   weekly, Republican, black publication--established 1902, ceased c. 1909.   Feb 24, 1906 = vol 5, no 15, Green Jackson and C. G. Garrett (editors), Southern Sun Publishing Company. Cited by Ayer 1903 thru 1909. According to Columbia city directory (1904-1905), office at 909 1/2 Washington Street. *Files: SCL mfm Feb 24, 1906.*

SOUTHERN TIMES   semi-weekly--established Jan 29, 1830, merged with the South-Carolina State Gazette and Columbia Advertiser Jul 8, 1830, continued by the Southern Times & State Gazette. Jan 29, 1830 = vol 1, no 1, [S. J.] M'Morris and [J. T.] Wilson (publishers). Paper also issued weekly edition. *Files: SCL orig & mfm Jan-Jul 1830.*

SOUTHERN TIMES AND SOUTH CAROLINA STATE GAZETTE weekly--continues the Southern Times and State Gazette c. Mar 1832, continued by the Southern Times and State Gazette c. Nov 1832. May 25, 1832 = vol 3, no 21, John Ramsay Davis (editor), S. J. M'Morris (proprietor). *Files: SCL orig & mfm May 25, 1832.*

SOUTHERN TIMES & STATE GAZETTE   semi-weekly and weekly--created by merger of the Southern Times and the South-Carolina State Gazette and Columbia Advertiser on Jul 8, 1830 = vol 1, no 46, S. J. M'Morris (publisher). Paper ceased semi-weekly edition in Apr 1831 and subsequently changed title of weekly edition to the Southern Times and State Gazette. Early in 1832 paper was continued by the Southern Times and the South Carolina State Gazette. *Files: SCL orig & mfm Jul 1830-May 1831, Oct 8, 1831.*

SOUTHERN TIMES & STATE GAZETTE. FOR THE COUNTRY weekly edition of the Southern Times & State Gazette--established Jul 1830, ceased Apr 1831. Jul 8, 1830 = vol 1, no 46, S. J. M'Morris (publisher). The semi-weekly Southern Times & State Gazette became a weekly in Apr 1831. *Files: SCL orig & mfm Jul 8, 1830.*

SOUTHERN TIMES AND STATE GAZETTE   weekly--continued Southern Times and South Carolina State Gazette c. Nov 1832, ceased c. 1838. Nov 16, 1832 = vol 3, no 46, C. W. Miller and E. F. Braithwaite (publishers). Samuel Weir and S. Donnelly also associated with paper. Masthead motto: "There is not in this wide world a safe depository of Liberty, but the hearts of Patriots, so enlightened as to be able to judge of correct legislation, and so patient and disinterested as to practice self-denial and self-government for the good of all." *Files: Clemson Mar 22, May 3, 1833, Apr 29, 1836; Newberry College Jul 10, 1835-Dec 29, 1837; SCL orig & mfm ((1832-1838)) 150.*

STANDARD   weekly, religious, black publication--established 1919, ceased c. 1927. Aug 6, 1920 = vol 1, no 42, Lee A. Logan (manager and editor). Official organ of the AME Church. Cited by Ayer 1922 thru 1927. *Files: SCL Aug 6, 1920.*

STAR-REPORTER   weekly, independent--established 1963. May 7, 1964 = vol 1, no 29, Harold C. Booker, Jr. (editor and publisher). Cited by Ayer 1966 + . *Files: SCL May 7, 1964, ((1970 +)); Star-Reporter 1963 + .*

STATE   daily, semi-weekly--established 1891. Feb 18, 1891 = vol 1, no 1, N. G. Gonzales (editor and manager), State Publishing Company. Semi-weekly ceased c. 1920, although until the late 1930s one could subscribe to two issues per week (copies of the Tue/Fri editions), sometimes supplemented by special farm news. A printed index [1892-1901, 1903-1911] has been microfilmed and is available at numerous depositories. Richland CL maintains a comprehensive index, Nov 1973 +. Many libraries have random and commemorative issues of the State among their holdings. William E. Gonzales, McDavid Horton, S. L. Latimer, Jr., H. F. Cauthen, W. D. Workman, Jr., W. E. Rone, Jr., Ambrose G. Hampton, Ben R. Morris, and Thomas N. McLean also associated with paper. State (a morning paper) acquired the Columbia Record (evening) in 1945. See S. L. Latimer, Jr., The Story of "The State" (1891-1969) and the Gonzales Brothers (Columbia, 1970). *Files: Darlington County Historical Commission 1921-1930; Clemson, Florence CL, Francis Marion, Richland CL, SCL, SC State Library, State, USC-Aiken, USC-Coastal, and Winthrop mfm 1891 + ; Benedict mfm 1965 + ; Claflin mfm 1963 + ; Columbia College mfm 1891-1916, 1920, 1929, 1937-1946, 1950-1953, 1971 + ; Converse mfm 1969 + ; Furman mfm 1891-1951; Greenville CL mfm 1967-1977; Lexington CL mfm 1965 + ; Newberry College mfm 1975 + ; SC State College mfm 1947-1966; Spartanburg CL mfm 1960 + ; Spartanburg Methodist College mfm 1973-1979; Voorhees mfm 1969-1972.*

STATE GAZETTE   weekly--continues the Columbia Gazette c. Jan 1795, continued by the South-Carolina State Gazette, and General Advertiser c. Jun 1795. Jan 23, 1795 = vol 2, no 4, William P. Young and Daniel Faust (publishers). According to Brigham, Harvard had copies in the 1930s. *Files: Harvard Jan 23, Feb 6, 27, 1795. Apparently no SC files:*

STATE GAZETTE, AND COLUMBIAN ADVERTISER   weekly, semi-weekly during legislative sessions (?)--continues South-Carolina State Gazette, and Columbian Advertiser in 1816, continued by the South-Carolina State Gazette, and Columbian Advertiser c. 1818. Aug 5, 1817 = vol 23, no 1333, Daniel & J. J. Faust (state printers). *Files: SCL orig & mfm Aug 5, 1817.*

STATES-RIGHTS REPUBLICAN   tri-weekly, daily--established Jul 1850, ceased 1852. According to Ellen, became an evening daily on Mar 1, 1851 and suspended operations soon after Jun 1852. Prospectus in Charleston Sun (Nov 9, 1850) lists I. C. Morgan (publisher), assisted by Alexander Carroll. John G. Bowman also associated with paper. *Files: SCL Jul 1, 1850, Apr 21, 1851, May 24, 1852 (all fragments).*

STRAIGHT-OUT DEMOCRAT   tri-weekly--established by the Daily Phoenix in 1878, probably for Wade Hampton's reelection campaign, ceased c. 1879. Sep 9, 1878 = vol 1, no 70, Henry S. Farley (editor), J. A. Selby (publisher). Cited by Rowell in 1879. SCL has a Jun 28, 1878 issue of the Daily Phoenix (vol 16, no 44) with subtitle "A Democratic Straight-Out" and this motto: "Let our just censure attend the true event." *Files: Sumter County Museum-Archives Sep 9, 1878.*

SUNDAY SUN   weekly--established 1876, ceased c. 1876. Not cited by Rowell. May 4, 1876 = vol 1, no 6, W. H. Jackson & Company (publisher). *Files: SCL May 14, 1876.*

TELEGRAPH   tri-weekly--established 1847, ceased Jul 9, 1851, when merged with the South Carolinian. Also issued a daily edition. See the Daily Telegraph. Dec 30, 1847 issue published by Edward Sill and John Stubs (no vol or issue data). *Files: SCL (1847-1851) 7.*

TELESCOPE   see the Columbia Telescope c. 1815.

TEMPERANCE ADVOCATE   weekly--established in Columbia in 1870, published briefly in Orangeburg (1872), then in Camden and Columbia, ceased c. 1876. Cited by Rowell 1871 thru 1876. May 20, 1873 = vol 3, no 27, Frank P. Beard (editor and proprietor). John A. Elkins, C. M. McJunkin, and W. H. Tutt also associated with paper. *Files: SCL (1873-1874) 4.*

TEMPERANCE BANNER   weekly--established 1876, ceased c. 1876. Aug 25, 1876 = vol 1, no 2, W. S. Teague (editor and proprietor). Published at the offices of the Columbia Register. Not cited by Rowell. *Files: SCL Aug 25, 1876.*

TEMPERANCE WORKER   semi-monthly--established 1883, published in Sumter 1885-1887, ceased c. 1887. Cited by Ayer in Columbia in 1884. Ad indicates Rev. A. Coke Smith was then editor-in-chief. See also Temperance Worker [Sumter]. *Files: SCL (1883-1887) 30.*

TRADE REVIEW   weekly, labor--continues Labor Advocate Oct 1919, ceased c. 1920. Oct 17, 1919 = vol 1, no 12, issued by Charles S. Henry and Edward C. DuPre. Not cited by Ayer. *Files: SCL (Oct 1919-Apr 1920) 18.*

TRANSCRIPT   daily, tri-weekly--established in 1851, ceased in 1851. According to Greenville's Southern Patriot (Apr 25, 1851), this paper was to be published by A. A. Haight and C. M. Broughton, with S. Olin Tolley as editor. SCL issues (often one sheet with no masthead) have no vol-issue date and indicate paper also may have appeared as the Commercial Transcript. Motto: "Southern Rights and a Southern Confederation." C. C. Somer also associated with paper. Difficult to determine whether SCL copies are daily or tri-weekly. *Files: SCL (1851) 7.*

TRI-WEEKLY CAROLINA TIMES   tri-weekly--established 1854, ceased c. 1860. Sep 19, 1857 = vol 5, no 969, Edward H. Britton & Company (publishers). At that time, Britton also was issuing daily and weekly editions of this paper. See Daily Carolina Times and Weekly Carolina Times. *Files: SCL (1855-1858) 8.*

TRI-WEEKLY CAROLINIAN   see Tri-Weekly South Carolinian.

TRI-WEEKLY CHRONICLE   tri-weekly--established 1867, ceased c. 1867. May be the tri-weekly edition of a short-lived daily or weekly. No essential data available in issues at SCL. *Files: SCL Oct 15, 17, 1867.*

TRI-WEEKLY PHOENIX   tri-weekly--established as the Columbia Phoenix (tri-weekly) by Julian A. Selby. Mar 21, 1865 = vol 1, no 1. Paper soon became daily, but Selby continued to publish tri-weekly edition, subsequently issued as the Tri-Weekly Phoenix. The tri-weekly edition probably ceased in Dec 1875 when the Columbia Register purchased the Daily Phoenix. *Files: SCL (1866-1871) 13.*

TRI-WEEKLY REGISTER   tri-weekly--established 1876, ceased c. 1886. Apr 7, 1877 = vol 2, no 31, C. P. Pelham (editor), Register Publishing Company. The Columbia Register, a daily paper established in 1875, added weekly and tri-weekly editions in 1876 and continued the latter for about a decade. See also the Columbia Register. *Files: SCL (1877-1883) 4.*

TRI-WEEKLY SOUTH CAROLINIAN   tri-weekly--continues semi-weekly edition of South-Carolinian in 1849, ceased in 1865. Apr 10, 1849 = vol 11, no 30, Johnston and Cavis (publishers). Also appears as the Tri-Weekly Carolinian. Paper continued to issue weekly edition and added daily edition in 1849. See the South-Carolinian, Weekly South Carolinian, Portfolio, and Daily South Carolinian. *Files: CLS Aug 19, 1851; SCL (1849-1856) 80, mfm ((Apr 1849-Mar 1851)) 250, ((Jan 1864-Feb 1865)) 110.*

TRI-WEEKLY SOUTHERN GUARDIAN   tri-weekly--established 1857, ceased 1865. Jul 31, 1858 = vol 1, no 51, E. H. Britton (printer to the House, SC legislature), "Official Journal of Columbia." Charles P. Pelham also associated with paper. See Daily Southern Guardian and Weekly Southern Guardian. *Files: SCL ((1858-1864)) 100.*

UFO   irregular, underground paper c. 1960s. Cited by Robert J. Glessing in the Underground Press in America (1970). *NFK*

UNION-HERALD   see the Daily Union-Herald.

VENTURE   monthly, black publication--established 1978, ceased c. 1979. Nov 1978 = vol 1, no 1, Robert "Paki" Wilson (editor and publisher). *Files: SCL Nov 1978-Mar 1979.*

VIDETTE   weekly--established 1905, ceased c. 1906. Cited once by Ayer (1906): W. T. Crews and W. C. Irby, Jr. (editors and publishers). *NFK*

WATCHMAN   weekly, black publication--established c. 1902, ceased c. 1905. Not cited by Ayer. According to the Columbia city directory (1903), paper issued at 1542 Main Street, J. R. Wilson (manager). Wilson also was associated with the South Carolina Standard, published at Benedict College. The following year, William Howard was editing the Watchman at 1115 Taylor Street. *NFK*

WAY OF FAITH   weekly, religious--established 1890, ceased c. 1931. Aug 8, 1894 = vol 5, no 6, John A. Porter (editor and publisher). J. M. Pike, T. C. Ligon, L. B.

Haynes, John Paul, and the Oliver Gospel Mission associated with paper. Cited by Ayer 1893/4 thru 1931. *Files: SCL (1894, 1898) 4, mfm (Jul 1895-Oct 1897) 50.*

WEEKLY CAROLINA TIMES weekly--established Jan 1855 as weekly edition of the Daily Carolina Times, ceased c. 1860. Jan 11, 1855 = vol 1, no 1, Edward H. Britton & Company (publisher). At that time, Britton also was producing tri-weekly and daily editions. See the Tri-Weekly Carolina Times and the Daily Carolina Times. *Files: SCL Jan 11, Oct 4, 1855, Feb 14, 1856 (all fragments).*

WEEKLY GLEANER, A HOME COMPANION weekly--established 1866, ceased c. 1872. May 27, 1868 = vol 3, no 6, Julian A. Selby (editor and proprietor). Published by the Daily Phoenix; however, this was a separate publication, not simply a weekly edition of that paper. *Files: SCL May 27, 1868, Aug 1869-Nov 1871.*

WEEKLY REGISTER weekly--established 1876, ceased c. 1898. Weekly edition of the Columbia Register. Issued as the Columbia Weekly Register in the 1890s. Oct 13, 1880 = vol 5, no 12. According to Rowell (1879), paper was being published by Calvo, Patton & Company. In addition to Charles A. Calvo, Jr., C. P. Pelham, James A. Hoyt, J. W. R. Pope, and Thomas Hamilton associated with this weekly. *Files: SCL Oct 13, 1880, Jul 22, 1890, Jun 28, 1892.*

WEEKLY SOUTH CAROLINIAN weekly--established 1838, but number system revised after tri-weekly and daily editions added in 1849. May 26, 1853 = vol 4, no 41, Johnston and Cavis (publishers). Continued by the Columbia Banner c. 1853. See also the South-Carolinian and Portfolio. *Files: SCL May 26, 1853.*

WEEKLY SOUTHERN GUARDIAN weekly--established 1857, ceased 1865. Oct 24, 1861 = vol 4, no 22, Charles P. Pelham (state printer). See also the Daily Southern Guardian and the Tri-Weekly Southern Guardian. *Files: SCL (1861-1862) 4.*

WEEKLY UNION weekly c. 1874. Issued by L. Cass Carpenter, editor and proprietor of the Columbia Semi-Weekly Union. *NFK*

WEEKLY UNION-HERALD weekly edition of the Daily Union-Herald c. 1874-1876. *NFK*

WORKING CHRISTIAN weekly, Baptist--established in York in 1869, published in Charleston 1870-1871, and in Columbia as of Oct 19, 1871 = vol 3, no 40, whole no 116, Tilman R. Gaines and William A. Gaines (proprietors). C. M. McJunkin also associated with this paper. Continued by the Baptist Courier on Sep 20, 1877. Note: Files of the Working Christian often cataloged as the "Baptist Courier." *Files: Furman mfm 1869-1877; SCL (1869-1877) 4, mfm 1869-1877.*

WORKING MAN weekly, semi-monthly--established 1873, ceased c. 1875. Jan 5, 1873 = vol 1, no 13, Tilman R. Gaines (editor and proprietor). Motto: "Labor is Capital; Honesty is the best Policy; Knowledge is Power." Cited by Rowell 1873 thru

1875. Manuscript at SCL indicates Gaines was associated with the Palmetto State Immigration Agency in Columbia. *Files: SCL Jun 5, 1873.*

FORT JACKSON

CLICK semi-monthly--established Oct 1918, ceased c. Dec 1918. Oct 5, 1918 = vol 1, no 1, Sgt. Gregory T. Dillon (managing editor), Sgt. Raymond D. Miller (publisher). Official organ of the enlisted men of Camp Jackson--"Covers the Camp like Khaki." Note: Library of Congress has mfm Oct-Dec 1918. *Files: SCL Oct 5, 1918.*

DIAMOND DUST weekly c. 1920-1921. Paper printed briefly by the University of South Carolina Press for personnel at Camp Jackson. May 28, 1921 = vol 1, no 36. *Files: SCL May 28, 1921.*

DIAMOND DUST weekly c. 1947. Published by Arrow Advertising Company for personnel at Fort Jackson. Oct 24, 1947 = vol 1, no 2. *Files: SCL Oct 24, 1947.*

FORT JACKSON JOURNAL weekly--established 1944 for military personnel, ceased c. 1960. Mar 1, 1946 = vol 3, no 8. Number sequence varies. *Files: Fort Jackson Museum 1953-1960; SCL Mar 1-22, 1946, Jul 29, 1955.*

FORT JACKSON LEADER see Leader.

JACKSONIAN weekly--continues Trench and Camp Feb 14, 1919, ceased c. Aug 1919. Feb 14, 1919 = vol 1, no 1, F. L. Poindexter (editor and manager), State (printer). *Files: Fort Jackson Museum Feb 14-Jul 4, 1919; SCL Feb 28, Aug 8, 1919.*

LEADER bi-weekly, weekly--established Jun 1962 as the Fort Jackson Leader, but subsequently changed name to Leader and became weekly. Jun 14, 1962 = vol 1, no 1. *Files: Fort Jackson Library 1983 + ; Fort Jackson Museum 1962-1982; SCL (1967-1970) 4, 1975.*

MONATSBLATTER monthly (?) German POW publication c. 1945. *NFK*

SHORT TIMES monthly, anti-Vietnam War--established c. 1968, ceased ? Mar 1969 = no 3, "Published by GI's for GI's." University of Connecticut has Apr 1, 1971 (vol 4, no 3). Copies also available at Northwestern University. USC has mfm copy in Underground Collection, reel 40. *Files: USC mfm Mar 1969.*

TRENCH AND CAMP weekly, sponsored by the YMCA and produced by major dailies located near WWI army camps--established Oct 1917, ceased c. Feb 1919. Oct 8, 1917 = vol 1, no 1, John Langdon Weber (camp editor), State (publisher). Will W. Nelson was also associated with the Camp Jackson edition. Paper succeeded locally by the Jacksonian in Feb 1919. *Files: Fort Jackson Museum Oct 8, 1917-Sep 29, 1918; SCL (1917-1918) 3.*

HOPKINS

LOWER RICHLAND CHRONICLE   weekly--established 1978, ceased c. 1979.
Jul 28, 1978 = vol 1, no 9, William F. Medlin (editor and publisher). *Files: SCL
(1978) 5*

SALUDA COUNTY

Carved out of Edgefield County during the constitutional convention of 1895, this new creation at first was called "Butler County," but it soon assumed its now familiar name. "Saluda," an Indian word, has been variously defined as meaning "corn," "river of corn," or "leaping waters."

MOUNT WILLING

SALUDA ADVOCATE   weekly, Democrat--established in 1895, this paper moved to Saluda between Mar 1897 and Jan 1898. Mar 4, 1896 = vol 1, no 19, C. B. Bates and R. J. Fuller (editors and publishers). Publication ceased in Dec 1900 but paper continued as the Batesburg Advocate. See Saluda Advocate [Saluda] and Batesburg Advocate [Batesburg]. *Files: SCL (1896-1897) 55.*

TICKET   weekly--established Oct 1895, ceased Nov 1895. Oct 31, 1895 = vol 1, no 1, C. I. Morgan (editor and manager). This short-lived paper contained one page of Delmar news edited by W. H. Hare of that community. *Files: SCL Oct 31-Nov 26, 1895.*

SALUDA

Saluda newspapers now being microfilmed at SCL. When completed, reels will be deposited at the Saluda County Library, Saluda County Historical Society, and SCL.

SALUDA ADVOCATE   weekly, Democrat--established in Mount Willing in 1895, this paper moved to Saluda c. 1897 and to Batesburg in Jan 1901 where it became the Batesburg Advocate. First available issue for 1898 (Jan 26) was published in Saluda, Richard J. Fuller (editor). J. M. Paget and Eugene E. Able also were associated with paper. Although neither paper comments on move from Saluda to Batesburg, the Ridge Spring correspondent notes on Jan 23, 1901 that "We are glad to have the privilege to still claim the Advocate as our paper." *Files: SCL 1898-1900.*

SALUDA COUNTY SENTINEL   weekly, independent--established in 1946, this paper merged with the Saluda Standard on Oct 4, 1973 to create the Saluda Standard-Sentinel. Jul 25, 1947 = vol 1, no 34 (no personnel listed). S. K. Able (cited by Ayer 1947 as publisher) presumably founded the paper. E. D. Johnson and Martin Keeler also were associated with the Saluda County Sentinel. *Files: Saluda CL 1966-1973; SCL Jul 25, Aug 1, 8 (fragment), 1947.*

SALUDA SENTINEL   weekly, Silver Democrat--established 1895, ceased Jan 14, 1903. Oct 31, 1895 = vol 1, no 1, B. F. Sampler (editor), E. H. Aull (publisher). During first year this paper bears various datelines: Dennys, Newberry, and Red Bank [Saluda]. Plant burned in Mar 1902. Editor C. T. Terrell, who had been associated with the Edgefield County Monitor [Johnston], announced on Jan 14, 1903 that he was closing the Saluda Sentinel and would return to the Edgefield County Monitor. A. B. Cargile and W. R. and H. S. Cunningham also were associated with the Saluda Sentinel. *Files: SCL ((1895-1903)) 235.*

SALUDA STANDARD   weekly--established 1902, merged with the Saluda County Sentinel on Oct 4, 1973, continued by the Saluda Standard-Sentinel. Sep 3, 1902 = vol 1, no 1, A. B. Cargile (editor and publisher). F. Earle Bradham, W. Grady Hazel, Lewis A. Clem, E. H. Porter, Ira B. Armfield, and L. B. Eargle also associated with paper. *Files: SCL (1902) 15, Jan 1903-Aug 1935, (1940-1954) 8. Note: Early issues at SCL were received by W. H. Hare of Delmar, who briefly edited a page of Delmar news published in the Ticket [Mount Willing].*

SALUDA STANDARD-SENTINEL   weekly, independent--created Oct 4, 1973 by merger of the Saluda Standard and the Saluda County Sentinel. Oct 4, 1973 = vol 23, no 39, L. B. Eargle (editor), Martin M. Keeler (publisher). Ralph Shealy also associated with paper. *Files: Saluda CL 1973 + ; SCL ((1984 +)).*

TIMES   weekly, Democrat--established 1905, ceased c. 1906. Only cited once by Ayer (1906): Barnard B. Evans (publisher). *NFK*

SPARTANBURG COUNTY

Created in 1798 when old Ninety Six District was divided into five parts, Spartanburg District (now Spartanburg County) was named for a local milita unit, the Spartan Regiment. This contingent, formed in 1776, played a prominent role in the war for independence.

BOILING SPRINGS

STAR NEWS   weekly--established 1979 by Landrum Leader. Paper purchased by Gene McKown in 1980 and continued by the Star Tribune. *NFK*

STAR TRIBUNE   weekly--continues Star News in 1980. Oct 16, 1985 = vol 6, no 42, Lee Oxenrider (editor), Star Publishing Company. Jud Caldwell also associated with paper. *Files: Star Tribune ((1987 +)).*

CAMP CROFT

BAT.   bi-weekly, military news, c. 1942-1943. *Files: Wisconsin Historical Society mfm Apr 3-May 29, 1943. Apparently no files in SC.*

DIE BRUCKE   semi-monthly, German--published by German POWs, continues Die Insel on Nov 15, 1945 = no 16, Franz Friese and Hanns Peters (editors). Ceased c. Mar 1946. See Arndt, German Language Press of the Americas for details. *Files: Library of Congress orig & mfm Nov 15, 1945-Jan 15, 1946. Apparently no files in SC.*

DIE INSEL   semi-monthly, German--established by German POWs in Apr 1945, continued by Die Brucke on Nov 15, 1945. May 15, 1945 = no 4, Hans Dreiner and M. Schleckwerder (editors). See Arndt, German Language Press of the America for details. *Files: Library of Congress orig & mfm May 15-Nov 1, 1945. Apparently no files in SC.*

SPARTAN   irregular, weekly, military news--established May 1943, became weekly Jul 6, 1943, ceased Dec 6, 1945. Published by US Army personnel. Dec 6, 1945 = vol 3, no 32. *Files: SCL Dec 6, 1945.*

CHESNEE

CHESNEE GUIDE   weekly--established by Gene McKown in Nov 1970. Paper continued by the Chesnee Tribune in 1971. *NFK*

CHESNEE TRIBUNE   weekly--continues Chesnee Guide in 1971. Oct 16, 1985 = vol 14, no 42, Jean Wells (editor), Gene McKown (publisher). Shirley Jones also associated with paper. *Files: Chesnee Tribune ((1972 +)).*

CLIFTON

CLIFTON CHRONICLE   weekly, Democrat--continues <u>Clifton World</u> c. 1908, ceased c. 1931. Jun 1, 1912 = vol 16, no 16, R. L. Humphries (business manager), Ed. H. DeCamp (proprietor). Cited by Ayer 1909 thru 1931. Published in Converse after 1912. *Files: SCL Jun 1, 1912, Aug 29, 1914.*

CLIFTON WORLD   weekly, semi-monthly--established in 1897 as weekly, issued semi-monthly 1899-1903, then weekly again, continued by <u>Clifton Chronicle</u> c. 1908. Cited by Ayer 1898 thru 1908. Ayer 1898: J. H. Sloan and ----- Elmore (editors and publishers). Samuel T. Reid and J. R. Smith also associated with paper. *NFK*

ENTERPRISE   weekly, Democrat--established 1894, ceased c. 1895. Cited once by Ayer (1895): T. B. Mangum (editor and publisher). *NFK*

INDUSTRIAL NEWS   weekly, independent--established 1901, ceased c. 1902. Cited once by Ayer (1902): J. P. Babbington (editor and publisher). *NFK*

CONVERSE

CLIFTON CHRONICLE   see <u>Clifton Chronicle</u> [Clifton].

COWPENS

COWPENS BATTLE AXE   weekly--established 1888, ceased c. 1891. Cited by Ayer 1889 thru 1891: John N. Vinson (editor and publisher). *NFK*

COWPENS-PACOLET GUIDE   weekly--established by Gene McKown in Nov 1970, continued by <u>Cowpens-Pacolet Tribune</u> in 1971. *NFK*

COWPENS-PACOLET TRIBUNE   weekly--continues <u>Cowpens-Pacolet Guide</u> in 1971. Oct 16, 1985 = vol 14, no 42, Gene McKown (publisher). Jean Wells also associated with paper. *Files: <u>Cowpens-Pacolet Tribune</u> ((1985 +)).*

CROSS ANCHOR

CAROLINA PROGRESSIONIST   weekly c. 1859. Prospectus dated Mar 12, 1859 in the Narissa Clayton Papers at SCL indicates that Joel H. Clayton (editor) and Dr. Dixon L. Davis (associate editor and proprietor) planned to begin publication about May 1, 1859. *NFK*

GUIDE POST   monthly c. 1956-1957. According to the Greenville News (Jan 17, 1957), Ed. E. and Frances H. Watson were publishing the Guide Post in Cross Anchor. *NFK*

TRI-COUNTY NEWS   monthly c. 1957. According to the Greenville News (Jan 17, 1957), Ed. E. and Frances H. Watson planned to launch the Tri-County News in Feb 1957 to serve residents of Spartanburg, Laurens, and Union counties. *NFK*

INMAN

INMAN PRESS   weekly, Democrat--established 1911, ceased c. 1912. Cited once by Ayer (1912), no personnel listed. *NFK*

INMAN TIMES   weekly--established in 1920 by Charles Byrd Smith. Jun 18, 1965 = vol 46, no 5, Mrs. P. E. Bell (editor), Robert P. Watson (publisher). Cited by Ayer 1928 + . A. M. Cudd, Louise C. Smith, W. B. Henderson, Hilda Morrow, and Milton C. Smith also associated with paper. Now published by Woodruff News. *Files: SCL ((1984 +)), mfm Jun 1965-Dec 1966; Woodruff News ((1921-1966)), 1967 + .*

LANDRUM

LANDRUM GAZETTE   weekly, Democrat--established 1908, ceased c. 1909. Cited once by Ayer (1909): J. G. Landrum (editor), Gazette Publishing Company. *NFK*

LANDRUM LEADER   weekly, independent--established 1955, continued by News Leader c. 1976. Ayer 1957: J. W. Lawrence (editor and publisher). Cited by Ayer 1957 thru 1975. Dorris H. and John F. Lawrence also associated with paper. *Files: News Leader 1955-1976.*

LANDRUM MIRROR   weekly c. 1898--published as part of Tryon (N. C.) Bee, ceased c. 1899. Cited once by Ayer (1898): George F. Morton (editor and publisher). *NFK*

NEWS LEADER   weekly--continues Landrum Leader c. 1976. Oct 28, 1976 = vol 22, no 39, John F. Lawrence (editor), John W. Lawrence, Sr. (editor emeritus). *Files: News Leader 1976 + ; SCL Oct 28, 1976, ((1984 +)).*

PACOLET

COWPENS-PACOLET GUIDE   see Cowpens.

COWPENS-PACOLET TRIBUNE   see Cowpens.

SPARTANBURG

BAPTIST ADVOCATE   weekly, black publication--established 1895, ceased c. 1897. Cited by Ayer 1896 and 1897: G. F. Miller and W. P. Jones (editors). *NFK*

CAROLINA CITIZEN   weekly--established 1922, continued by Sun and Carolina Citizen (daily except Sun) in 1924. Jun 21, 1923 = vol 1, no 32, A. M. Carpenter (editor), Citizens Publishing Company. Cited once by Ayer (1924). *Files: SCL Jun 21, 1923.*

CAROLINA NEW ERA   weekly, Republican--continues Spartanburg Republican in Dec 1871, ceased c. 1874. Cited by Rowell 1872 thru 1874. Rowell 1872-1873: Dr. Jarvan Bryant (editor), A. W. Cummings (business manager). Rowell 1874: J. P. F. Camp (editor), C. J. Lockwood (business manager). *NFK*

CAROLINA SPARTAN   weekly--continues Spartan c. 1853, continued by Spartan c. 1896. Mar 31, 1853 = vol 10, no 7, P. M. Wallace (editor and proprietor)..."Devoted to Southern Rights, Politics, Agriculture and Miscellany." William H. Trimmier, A. T. Cavis, H. L. Farley, and Charles Petty also associated with paper. *Files: Greenville CL May 12, 1880; SCL (1861-1892) 20; Clemson, Furman, and Winthrop mfm Jan 14, 1858-Dec 8, 1864; Cherokee CL, Converse, Greenville CL, Lander, SCL, Spartanburg Methodist College, Spartanburg Herald-Journal, and Wofford mfm Jun 9, 1853-Dec 8, 1864, Feb 8, 1866-Dec 1876, Jan 8, 1879-Dec 1893. Note: SCL also has mfm Apr 18, May 16, 1894.*

CAROLINA SPARTAN   weekly--continues Spartan c. 1898-1900. Merged with Journal on May 28, 1913, continued by Journal and Carolina Spartan (daily). Mar 21, 1900 = vol 57, no 12, Charles Petty (editor and proprietor). E. J. Lide also associated with paper. *Files: SCL (1900-1905) 6, mfm Oct 9, 1901, Apr 30, 1902.*

CAROLINA STATE NEWS   weekly--established 1931, ceased c. 1934. Cited by Ayer 1933 and 1934: Virgil V. Evans (editor and publisher). *NFK*

CHURCH HERALD   semi-monthly, monthly, Episcopal--established in 1881 as semi-monthly, issued monthly in 1883, moved to Columbia c. 1884. Cited by Ayer in Spartanburg 1881 thru 1883. Feb 1, 1881 = vol 1, no 1, J. D. McCollough (editor). See also Church Herald [Columbia]. *Files: SCL Feb 1, Aug 15, 1881, mfm Feb 1, Aug 15, 1881, Jun 1883.*

COTTON PLANT   monthly, semi-monthly, agricultural--established in Marion in 1883. Published in various places, including Spartanburg in 1897. See Cotton Plant [Marion and Greenville].

DAILY HERALD   title of Spartanburg Herald c. 1904. See Spartanburg Herald.

EVENING STAR   daily except Sun--established in 1898 as daily edition of <u>Piedmont Headlight</u> (weekly), ceased c. 1900. Not cited by Ayer. Jan 2, 1899 = vol 1, no 60. Note: According to this issue, <u>Piedmont Headlight</u> was being published semi-weekly (Tue-Fri), although always reported by Ayer as weekly. *Files: SCL mfm Jan 2, 3, 1899.*

EVENING TELEGRAM   daily except Sun, Democrat--established 1899, ceased c. 1900. Cited once by Ayer (1900): Evening Telegram Company (editor and publisher). *NFK*

FREE LANCE   weekly, Democrat--established 1899, continued in 1901 as weekly edition of the <u>Spartanburg Journal</u>, ceased c. 1919. Cited by Ayer 1900 thru 1920. Ayer 1900: T. B. Thackston (editor and publisher). Jul 18, 1902 = vol 4, no 9, Charles H. Henry (editor), Spartanburg Journal Company (publisher). Charles Petty also associated with paper. *Files: SCL and Spartanburg CL Jul 18, 1902-May 5, 1905.*

GREEN STREET MESSENGER   weekly--established 1907, ceased c. 1912. Cited by Ayer 1908 thru 1912. Ayer 1908: W. M. Whiteside (editor), E. B. Atkinson (publisher). *NFK*

JOURNAL   daily--continues <u>Spartanburg Journal</u> c. 1906, merged with <u>Carolina Spartan</u> on May 28, 1913, continued by <u>Journal and Carolina Spartan</u>. Jan 3, 1908 = vol 7, whole no 2304, Charles H. Henry (editor). <u>Journal</u> continued to issue <u>Free Lance</u> as Fri weekly and by 1912 also published a semi-weekly edition. *Files: SCL, Spartanburg CL, <u>Spartanburg Herald-Journal</u>, and Wofford mfm Jan-Jun 1908, 1909, Jul 1912-May 27, 1913.*

JOURNAL AND CAROLINA SPARTAN   daily--created by merger of <u>Journal</u> and <u>Carolina Spartan</u> on May 28, 1913, continued by <u>Spartanburg Journal and Carolina Spartan</u> on Jan 5, 1920. According to issue of May 28, 1913 (no vol-issue data), paper was continuing weekly and semi-weekly editions; however, mastheads indicate semi-weekly ceased within a year and weekly in Jan 1919. Editorial of May 28, 1913 reveals that <u>Journal</u> purchased <u>Carolina Spartan</u> in 1911. Charles P. Clavert, Charles Petty, Harold C. Booker, and Watson Bell associated with paper, 1913-1920. *Files: SCL Jul 1913-Jun 1914, Nov 5, 1914, Jan-Jun 1915; SCL, Spartanburg CL, <u>Spartanburg Herald-Journal</u>, and Wofford mfm May 1913-1915, Jul 1916-Jan 1920.*

LINK   weekly, black publication--established 1902, ceased c. 1906. Cited by Ayer 1904 thru 1906. Ayer 1904: J. H. Manley (editor), Link Publishing Company. *NFK*

NEGRO INDEX   weekly, black publication--established 1916, ceased c. 1922. Cited by Ayer 1917 thru 1922. Ayer 1917: E. W. Bowen (editor), Negro Journal Company. *NFK*

ORPHANS' FRIEND ·   weekly--established 1873, continued by <u>Spartanburg Herald</u> c. 1875. Cited by Rowell 1874 and 1875. Feb 28, 1874 = vol 1, no 20, R. C. Oliver (editor), Carolina Orphan Home (publisher). According to the Temperance Advocate (Oct 9, 1873), the Carolina Orphan Home bought the press of Columbia's South Carolinian in order to teach the printing trade to orphans. *Files: SCL mfm Feb 28, 1874.*

PAPER   fortnightly, weekly--established Jul 1984 as fortnightly, became weekly Sep 19, 1984. Clifford L. Gray (editor), Greenville News-Piedmont (publisher). *Files: Greenville News-Piedmont 1984 + ; Paper 1984 + .*

PIEDMONT HEADLIGHT   weekly, semi-weekly, Democrat--established 1892, continued by Truth in 1901, resumed former title c. 1902, ceased c. 1905. Jun 14, 1895 = vol 3, no 25, T. L. Gantt (editor), People's Journal Publishing Company. Cited by Ayer 1893/4 thru 1901, 1903 thru 1905 as weekly; however, may have been semi-weekly c. 1899. In addition to Gantt, T. B. Thackston, William M. Jones, J. L. Stoppelbein, J. T. Harris, J. C. Garlington, Zack McGee, and G. H. Waddell associated with paper. See also Evening Star (daily) c. 1898-1900. *Files: SCL Sep 1, 1893, mfm (1895-1898) 12.*

PIEDMONT INDICATOR   weekly, Republican, black publication--established 1896, ceased c. 1904. Cited by Ayer 1897 thru 1904. Ayer 1897: Charles H. Jones (editor), Laban Morgan (publisher). *NFK*

REVIEW   weekly--established 1929, ceased c. 1931. Dec 12, 1929 = vol 1, no 43, J. L. Brooks (editor), T. D. Toler (associate editor and publisher). Cited once by Ayer (1931): T. D. Toler (editor), Economy Printing Company. Paper had dual dateline: Spartanburg and Union. *Files: SCL Dec 12, 1929.*

SEMI-WEEKLY HERALD   semi-weekly--established c. 1897 by Spartanburg Herald (daily), ceased c. 1902 when semi-weekly reverted to weekly status. Issue of Aug 6, 1897 indicates J. C. Garlington (editor), no vol-issue data provided. *Files: SCL mfm Aug 6, 1897.*

SOUTHERN CHRISTIAN ADVOCATE   weekly, Methodist--founded in Charleston in 1837, published in various communities, including Spartanburg 1903-1912. See Southern Christian Advocate [Columbia].

SOUTHERN INDICATOR   weekly, Republican, black publication--established 1908, ceased c. 1921. Cited by Ayer 1910 thru 1921: Laban Morgan (editor and publisher). Morgan also published the Piedmont Indicator 1896-1904. *NFK*

SOUTHERN METHODIST   weekly, Methodist--established 1875, ceased c. 1876. Cited once by Rowell (1876): William Baker (editor), Southern Tract Association for the Promotion of Holiness (publisher). *NFK*

SOUTHERN REPORTER   weekly, black publication--established 1900, ceased c. 1903. Cited by Ayer 1902 and 1903: I. E. Lowery (editor), Southern Reporter Publishing Company. *NFK*

SPARTAN   weekly--established 1843, continued by the Carolina Spartan c. 1853. Dec 22, 1843 = vol 1, no 1, Z. D. Cottrell and T. O. P. Vernon (editors and proprietors), T. Wilson (publisher). P. M. Wallace and J. Wofford Tucker also associated with paper. *Files: Cherokee CL, Converse, Greenville CL, Lander, Spartanburg Methodist College, Spartanburg Herald-Journal, and Wofford mfm Feb 27, 1849-Dec 25, 1851; SCL mfm Jul 17, Aug 14, 28, Sep 25, 1844, Feb 6, 27, 1849-Dec 25, 1851.*

SPARTAN   weekly--continues Carolina Spartan c. 1896, continued by Carolina Spartan c. 1898-1900. Jan 8, 1896 = vol 52, no 51, Charles Petty (editor and proprietor). *Files: SCL mfm Jan 8, 1896, Sep 22, 1897, Feb 16, 1898.*

SPARTAN WEEKLY   weekly--established in 1964 by B. D. Daily (editor and publisher), continued by Spartan Weekly & Chesnee-Cowpens News. *NFK*

SPARTAN WEEKLY & CHESNEE-COWPENS NEWS   weekly--continues Spartan Weekly c. 1967. Oct 17, 1985 = vol 21, no 38, B. D. Dailey (editor and publisher). *Files: Spartan Weekly & Chesnee-Cowpens News ((1980 +)).*

SPARTANBURG ADVANCE   weekly, black publication--established 1894, ceased c. 1897. Cited by Ayer 1896 and 1897: P. G. Hammett and R. M. Alexander (editors), Advance Publishing Company. *NFK*

SPARTANBURG DAILY HERALD   title of Spartanburg Herald at times c. 1890-1894. See Spartanburg Herald.

SPARTANBURG EXPRESS   weekly--established 1854, ceased c. 1866. Jan 8, 1857 = vol 3, no 34, T. Stobo Farrow (editor and proprietor). Apr 4, 1866 = vol 1, no 9, new series. John H. Evins, A. S. Douglas, Warren Dupre, and T. A. Hayden & Company also associated with paper. *Files: Cherokee CL and Wofford mfm (1857) 20; SCL mfm ((1857-1866)) 125.*

SPARTANBURG GAZETTE   weekly--established 1869 as Democrat paper, continued by Spartanburg Republican c. 1870. Sep 2, 1869 = vol 1, no 18, Samuel T. Poinier (proprietor). *Files: SCL mfm Sep 2, Oct 21, 27, 1869.*

SPARTANBURG GUIDE   weekly--variant name of Textile Tribune c. 1970. See Spartanburg Guide & Textile Tribune, Textile Tribune, and Spartanburg Tribune.

SPARTANBURG GUIDE & TEXTILE TRIBUNE   weekly--continues Spartanburg Guide and Textile Tribune c. 1970, continued by the Spartanburg Tribune c. 1971. Dec 22, 1971 = vol ? , no 52. *Files: Spartanburg Tribune Dec 21, 1971.*

SPARTANBURG HERALD   weekly, daily--continues Orphans' Friend c. 1875, merged with Spartanburg Journal and Carolina Spartan in 1982, continued by Spartanburg Herald-Journal. Mar 2, 1875 = vol 3, no 2, T. Stobo Farrow, Robert J. Daniel, and H. Bascome Browne (proprietors). Issued weekly to Sep 1890 when daily began. Sep 17,

1890 = vol 1, no 1, William M. Jones and J. C. Garlington (editors). Continued weekly edition 1890-1897, 1902-1921. Published semi-weekly edition c. 1897-1902. See Spartanburg Weekly Herald and Semi-Weekly Herald. Title varies. Paper also issued as Daily Herald c. 1904 and as Spartanburg Daily Herald c. 1890-1894. J. T. Harris, Zack McGhee, John S. Reynolds, P. H. Fike, A. B. Riley, H. L. Watson, Charles O. Hearon, James F. Crook, T. A. Smith, Glen Long, Phil Buckheit, Fred D. Moffitt, and Hubert Hendrix also associated with paper. *Files: Greenville CL Jul 5, 1905; SCL Mar 2, 1875-Feb 25, 1880, (1886-1904) 30, 1906, Aug 17, 1910, May 30, 1916, (1926-1928) 60, Jan 1941-Jan 1943; Converse mfm 1969-1975; SCL, Spartanburg CL and Spartanburg Herald-Journal mfm Mar 2, 1875-Feb 25, 1880, 1907-1915, Jul-Dec 1916, Jul 1917-1946, Apr-Jun 1947, 1948-1982; Spartanburg Methodist College mfm 1971-1979; Union CL mfm Sep 1893-Feb 1904, Jan 1906-Jun 1920; Wofford mfm 1908-1915, Jul-Dec 1916, Jul 1917-1946, Apr-Jun 1947, 1948-1982. Note: Spartanburg CL has index 1978-1982.*

SPARTANBURG HERALD-JOURNAL   daily--created by merger of Spartanburg Herald and Spartanburg Journal and Carolina Spartan on Oct 1, 1982 = vol 52, no 83, Rudy Rivers (editor). Papers under common ownership since 1913 and for many years had been printing a joint Sun edition. *Files: SCL, Spartanburg CL, Spartanburg Herald-Journal, and Wofford mfm 1982 + . Note: Spartanburg CL has index 1982 + .*

SPARTANBURG JOURNAL   weekly c. 1843. According to WPA history of Spartanburg County, the first issue of the Spartan (Dec 22, 1843) states that the "Spartanburg Journal is dead." This history indicates that Asa Muir was editor and publisher of that weekly. *NFK*

SPARTANBURG JOURNAL   daily--established Sep 3, 1900 as daily edition of the Free Lance (weekly), continued by Journal c. 1906. May 9, 1902 = vol 3, no 211, Charles H. Henry (editor), Spartanburg Journal Company. Charles Petty also associated with paper. *Files: SCL orig & mfm Sep 6, 1906, mfm May 9, 1902, Sep 1902-Jul 1905; Spartanburg CL, Spartanburg Herald-Journal, and Wofford mfm Sep 1902-Jul 1905.*

SPARTANBURG JOURNAL AND CAROLINA SPARTAN   daily--continues Journal and Carolina Spartan on Jan 5, 1920 (no vol-issue data), J. C. Hemphill (editor). Paper merged with Spartanburg Herald in 1982, continued by Spartanburg Herald-Journal. P. H. Fike, T. A. Smith, Rudy Rivers, and Fred D. Moffitt also associated with paper. *Files: Converse mfm 1969-1975; SCL, Spartanburg CL, Spartanburg Herald-Journal, and Wofford mfm 1920-1933, Apr 1934-1940, 1950-1982.*

SPARTANBURG METRO   weekly c. 1981-1982, Robert L. Stoddard, Jr. (editor and publisher). Cited in Southern Bell media directory, 1981-1982. *NFK*

SPARTANBURG NEWS   weekly--established 1931, ceased c. 1935. Cited once by Ayer (1935): Walter C. Bentz (editor), Bentz Publishing Company. *NFK*

SPARTANBURG REPUBLICAN   weekly--continues Spartanburg Gazette c. 1870, continued by the Carolina New Era in Dec 1871. Jan 25, 1871 = vol 1, no 35, Samuel T. Poinier (proprietor). Cited once by Rowell (1871): Samuel T. Poinier (editor and publisher). *Files: SCL mfm Jan 25, 1871.*

SPARTANBURG SENTINEL   semi-weekly--established 1874, ceased c. 1875. Cited once by Rowell (1875): Frank M. Browne (editor and publisher). *NFK*

SPARTANBURG TRIBUNE   weekly--continues Textile Tribune in Nov 1971. Dec 22, 1971 = vol 1, no 29, issued as supplement to the Chesnee Guide, Cowpens-Pacolet Guide, Spartanburg Guide, and Blacksburg Times & Cherokee Report. Oct 23, 1985 = vol 60, no 43, Jean Wells (editor), Gene McKown (publisher). *Files: Spartanburg Tribune ((1971 +)).*

SPARTANBURG WEEKLY HERALD   weekly--variant edition of Spartanburg Herald, established in 1873 as Orphans' Friend. Spartanburg Herald began daily edition in 1890, continuing weekly until c. 1921, except 1897-1902 when issued a semi-weekly paper. Jan 17, 1905 (no vol-issue data), P. H. Fike and A. B. Riley (editors). *Files: SCL, Spartanburg CL, and Spartanburg Herald-Journal mfm 1905-1907.*

SUN AND CAROLINA CITIZEN   daily--created in 1924 when Carolina Citizen (weekly) expanded to Sun and Carolina Citizen (daily except Sun), ceased c. 1925. Aug 21, 1924 = vol 1, no 135, A. M. Carpenter (editor), J. T. Fain (business manager). J. O. Hull also associated with paper. Cited once by Ayer (1925). *Files: SCL mfm (1924-1925) 14 fragmentary issues.*

TEXTILE TRIBUNE   weekly--established Nov 1926 as a strike-breaking medium by Robert DeYoung. Cited by Ayer 1929 thru 1971. Ayer 1929: R. L. DeYoung (editor and publisher). James W. Tompson, Vernon R. Foster, William C. Band, Valley Simmonds, and James Hodge also associated with Textile Tribune. Paper purchased by Gene McKown from Hodge in Nov 1969 and continued by the Spartanburg Tribune. In the early 1970s McKown issued a common Tribune section for papers he owned in Spartanburg, Chesnee, Cowpens-Pacolet, and Blacksburg [Cherokee County], but that supplement subsequently was merged with individual publications. *NFK*

TRUTH   weekly, Democrat--title of Piedmont Headlight c. 1902, continues Piedmont Headlight, continued by Piedmont Headlight. Cited by Ayer 1902: J. L. Stoppelbein (editor), Truth Publishing Company. *NFK*

UNA

NEWS REVIEW   weekly, pro-labor--established 1929, ceased 1971. May 1, 1936 = vol 7, no 19, J. L. Brooks (editor). *Files: SCL May 1936-Nov 1945, Feb-Dec 1946, ((1947-1949)) 100, Jan 1950-Dec 1971.*

WOODRUFF

WOODRUFF NEWS   weekly--established 1888, ceased c. 1889. Cited once by Ayer (1889): J. R. Zuberbuhler (publisher). *NFK*

WOODRUFF NEWS   weekly, Democrat--established 1916, ceased c. 1928. Cited by Ayer 1917 thru 1928. Ayer 1917: Samuel T. Creech (editor), Woodruff Publishing Company. J. T. White, E. M. Grissette, J. O. Hull, and P. W. Smith also associated with paper. *NFK*

WOODRUFF NEWS   weekly--established 1950. Cited by Ayer 1952 + . Ayer 1953: Charles E. Smith (editor and publisher). Oct 17, 1985 = vol 36, no 25, Milton C. Smith (editor and publisher). *Files: SCL ((1984 +)); Woodruff News 1960 + , mfm 1950-1959.*

WOODRUFF NEWS AND HERALD   weekly--continues Woodruff Times c. 1910, ceased c. 1911. Cited by Ayer 1910 and 1911: Archie Willis (editor and publisher). *NFK*

WOODRUFF NEWS AND REVIEW   weekly--established 1901, continued by Woodruff Times c. 1909. Cited by Ayer 1903 thru 1909. Ayer 1903: R. H. Sweeney (editor and publisher). *NFK*

WOODRUFF RECORD   weekly, independent--established 1911, ceased c. 1916. Cited by Ayer 1912 thru 1916. Ayer 1912: N. C. Remsen (editor), Record Publishing Company. A. H. Lyon also associated with paper. *NFK*

WOODRUFF TIMES   weekly--continues Woodruff News and Review c. 1909, continued by Woodruff News and Herald c. 1910. Cited once by Ayer (1909): B. E. Holcombe (editor), Public Utility Corporation (publisher). *NFK*

WOODRUFF TIMES   weekly c. 1923-1924. Greer Citizen briefly published an edition entitled the Woodruff Times. Cited by Ayer 1923 and 1924. Ayer 1923: P. W. Smith (editor and publisher); Ayer 1924: W. G. Hamel (editor). *NFK*

WOODRUFF TIMES   weekly, Democrat--established 1948, ceased c. 1952. Cited by Ayer 1950 thru 1952: E. A. Burch (editor and publisher). *NFK*

SUMTER COUNTY

Sumter District, now Sumter County, was formed in 1798 when old Camden District was divided into five parts. The name honors the "Gamecock" of the Revolutionary War, General Thomas Sumter (1734?-1832), who lived at Stateburg.

MAYESVILLE

SOUTHLAND HERALD monthly, black publication, Republican--established 1909, ceased c. 1916. Cited by Ayer 1911 thru 1916: W. M. Boley (editor), Lowery Institute (publisher). *NFK*

SHAW AIR FORCE BASE

FLIGHT LINE weekly--base newspaper, 1942-1943. Jan 29, 1942 = vol 1, no 1, continued by Shaw Field News c. Jan 1943. *Files: Shaw Air Force Base 1942-1943.*

JET GAZETTE weekly--base newspaper, 1949-1956. Jan 28, 1949 (first issue) = vol 6, no 2. Formerly Shaw Field News, continued by Recon Record Jan 1957. *Files: Shaw Air Force Base Jan-Jul 1949, Jan 1951-Dec 1956.*

RECON weekly--base newspaper, Mar 1975-Sep 1981. Mar 20, 1975 (first issue) = vol 27, no 10. Formerly Recon Record, issued as Recon Mar 20, 1975-Sep 24, 1981. Succeeded by Spirit in Oct 1981. *Files: Shaw Air Force Base Mar 20, 1975-Sep 24, 1981.*

RECON RECORD weekly--base newspaper, Jan 1957-Mar 1975. May 18, 1958 = vol 15, no 18. Formerly Jet Gazette, continued by Recon Mar 20, 1975. *Files: Shaw Air Force Base Jan 1957-Mar 1975; SCL May 18, 1958, May 17, 1959, Oct 3, 1974.*

SHAW FIELD NEWS weekly--base newspaper, Jan 1943-Dec 1948. Formerly Flight Line, continued by Jet Gazette Jan 1949. *Files: Shaw Air Force Base Jan 1943-Dec 1948.*

SPIRIT weekly--base newspaper, succeeds Recon in Oct 1981. Oct 1, 1981 = vol 1, no 1, new number sequence. *Files: Shaw Air Force Base Oct 1981 + ; Wisconsin Historical Society mfm Oct 1981 + .*

STATEBURG

CLAREMONT GAZETTE weekly c. 1786. Published briefly in effort to promote Stateburg as the state capital. Charleston Morning Post (Nov 7, 1786) notes that a copy has been forwarded to that city by Rev. Richard Furman. See Brigham for details. *NFK*

SUMTER

BANNER OF FREEDOM   single issue (Apr 10, 1865) printed on one side only by "Printers of the 25th Ohio Vet. Vol. Infantry" on the presses of the Sumter Watchman. Sheet bears this statement: "Owing to 'circumstances over which we have no control,' this number of our paper makes its appearance at Sumter instead of Manning. We hope our readers will excuse us for migrating. It seems to be the rule of adoption by publishers in the corn-fed-eracy to 'ske-daddle' from one place to another, and our General will not allow us to be an exception." Note: Concerning local newspapers, see Thomas McAlpin Stubbs, "The Fourth Estate of Sumter, South Carolina," SC Historical Magazine (Oct 1953), pp. 185-200, and Anne King Gregorie, History of Sumter County, pp. 452-461. *Files: SCL and Sumter County Museum-Archives Apr 10, 1865.*

BLACK POST   weekly, black publication--published in Columbia by Redfern II, JuJu Publications, for Sumter area. See Black News [Columbia].

BLACK RIVER WATCHMAN   weekly--established 1850, merged with Sumter Banner Jun 13, 1855, continued by the Sumter Watchman. Apr 27, 1850 = vol 1, no 1, T. B. Fraser, J. W. Ervin (editors), A. A. Gilbert, John F. DeLorme (publishers). H. L. Darr, L. L. Fraser, Jr., John R. Haynesworth, and John S. Richardson, Jr., also associated with paper. *Files: SCL ((1850-1855)) 250.*

DAILY ITEM   see Sumter Daily Item.

DEFENDER   weekly, black publication, Republican--established 1903, merged with the Pee Dee Watchman [Timmonsville] in 1913, continued by the Pee Dee Watchman and Defender [Timmonsville]. Feb 3, 1910 = vol 7, no 16, W. T. Andrews (editor), Defender Publishing Company. Cited by Ayer 1907 thru 1920. Printed by Sumter Herald. *Files: Sumter County Museum-Archives Feb 3, 1910.*

EVENING NEWS   daily except Sun--established May 1895, ceased Jun 1896. May 20, 1895 = vol 1, no 1, E. F. Miller, J. H. Darr, J. B. Miller (editors), Evening News Company. Printed by Freeman. *Files: Sumter County Museum-Archives May 20, 1895.*

EVENING NEWS   daily except Sun, Democrat--established Dec 1904, ceased c. 1905. Dec 1, 1904 = vol 1, no 1, B. F. Haynesworth (president), Freeman Publishing Company. Ayer 1906 cites as a semi-weekly. *Files: SCL (Dec 1904-Sep 1905) 18; Sumter County Museum-Archives Dec 1, 21, 1904.*

FREEMAN   weekly, semi-weekly, Democrat--established 1891, ceased c. 1906. Cited by Ayer 1892 thru 1906. Apr 21, 1891 = vol 1, no 1, John J. Dargan and Edwin F. Miller (editors and proprietors). Weekly until c. 1904 when Evening News launched, then became semi-weekly. Hugh C. Haynesworth also associated with paper. *Files:*

SCL (1891-1904) 35; Sumter County Museum-Archives Dec 13, 1892, Feb 21, 1896, May 27, 1898.

ITEM   masthead title of <u>Sumter Daily Item</u> (see) after Aug 2, 1987.

JOURNAL OF PROGRESS   weekly, black publication, independent--established 1894, ceased c. 1896. Cited once by Ayer (1896): C. C. Scott (editor and publisher). Produced at plant of <u>Sumter Herald</u>. *NFK*

PEOPLE'S INFORMER   weekly, black publication--established 1936, merged with the <u>Charleston Lighthouse</u> c. 1941 to form the <u>Lighthouse and Informer</u>, published in Columbia. Mar 24, 1939 = vol 2, no 50, E. A. Parker (editor and publisher). Not cited by Ayer. *Files: SCL (1939-1940) 5.*

PROSPECTOR   weekly--established 1905, ceased c. 1909. Cited by Ayer 1908 and 1909: William C. Ivy (editor and publisher). Listed in the <u>Handbook of South Carolina</u> (1907) as the "Sumter Prospector." *NFK*

SAMARITAN HERALD   weekly, daily except Sun, black publication--established 1909, merged with <u>Voice of Job</u> in 1942, continued by the <u>Samaritan Herald and the Voice of Job</u>. Issued weekly except c. 1940-1941 when daily. Cited by Ayer 1920-1930, 1940-1942. Aug 8, 1923 = vol 11, no 6, J. McKenzie Harrison (editor and publisher). *Files: SCL Aug 8, 1923, Apr 14, 1938, Apr 27, Dec 14, 1939; Sumter County Museum-Archives Apr 8, 1937.*

SAMARITAN HERALD AND THE VOICE OF JOB   weekly--continues the <u>Samaritan Herald</u> and the <u>Voice of Job</u> c. 1942, ceased c. 1950. Dec 13, 1945 = vol 3, no 15, Mrs. M. B. Pogue (editor). This issue states that the <u>Samaritan Herald</u> was established Oct 21, 1909 and combined with <u>Voice of Job</u> on Apr 1, 1942. According to issue of Dec 1, 1948, "published weekly except when there are 5 Thursdays in a month." Cited by Ayer 1943 thru 1950. A. R. Howard and J. C. Highe also associated with paper. *Files: SCL Dec 13, 1945, Jan 1, 1948.*

SEMI-WEEKLY WATCHMAN   semi-weekly--title of Tue-Fri edition of <u>Sumter Watchman</u> Oct-Dec 1863, continues <u>Tri-Weekly Watchman</u>. Oct 27, 1863 = vol 3, no 656, J. J. Fleming (editor), Gilbert and Darr (publishers). This edition ceased in Dec 1863, weekly continued. During these weeks publishers offered "entire outfit" of the <u>Horry Dispatch</u> for sale. *Files: SCL (1863) 9.*

SOUTH CAROLINA TOBACCONIST   weekly, tobacco trade--established 1896, ceased c. 1897. Cited once by Ayer (1897): N. G. Osteen (editor and publisher). Feb 25, 1896 = vol 1, no 1, N. G. Osteen (publisher), H. G. Osteen (managing editor). *Files: Sumter County Museum-Archives Feb 25, 1896.*

SOUTHERN WHIG   weekly, anti-nullification--established 1832, merged with the <u>Camden Journal</u> in 1834 to form the <u>Camden Journal and Southern Whig</u>. Jan 26, 1832

= vol 1, no 1, M. D. Richardson (editor and proprietor). William Haynesworth and James Henley Thornwell also associated with paper. *Files: SCL (1832-1834) 40.*

SPIRIT OF THE TIMES   weekly, Democrat--established 1881, moved to Manning in 1884 and became the Manning Times. Cited by Ayer 1882 thru 1885. Ayer ad (1884) lists W. J. Beard (editor and proprietor), William C. Ivy (publisher). Apr 19, 1883 = vol 3, no 4, W. C. Ivy (business manager), W. J. Beard (proprietor). *Files: New York Historical Society Apr 19, 1883. Apparently no files in SC.*

SUMTER ADVANCE   weekly--established 1881, continued by the Sumter Herald Oct 7, 1892. Cited by Ayer 1882 thru 1891. Aug 28, 1882 = vol 2, no 5, H. L. Darr and P. E. Parmelee (publishers). *Files: Greenville CL Aug 24, 1889; SCL (1882-1892) 40; Sumter County Museum-Archives Aug 24, 1889.*

SUMTER BANNER   weekly--established 1846, merged with the Black River Watchman Jun 13, 1855, continued by the Sumter Watchman. Nov 6, 1846 = vol 1, no 1, William J. Francis (publisher). Francis M. Adams, M. M. Noah, Jr., Richard M. Dyson, J. R. Logan, James S. G. Richardson, W. F. Haynesworth, John T. Green, and John Smith Richardson also associated with paper. *Files: SCL ((1846-1855)) 340, mfm Jun 30, 1847; Sumter County Museum-Archives Apr 7, May 5, 19, 1847.*

SUMTER-CLARENDON NEWS   weekly--established Aug 28, 1980, ceased c. Nov 1980. Not cited by Ayer. Published by the Sumter News primarily for Clarendon County. Since the Sumter News altered its title slightly on Nov 6, 1980, becoming the Sumter News (for Sumter and Clarendon Counties), it appears that this subsidiary weekly ceased at that time. Sep 18, 1980 = vol 1, no 4, Ray Hamilton (president). *Files: Lee Hendren [Holly Hill] Sep 18, 1980.*

SUMTER DAILY ITEM   daily--established 1894. Oct 15, 1894 = vol 1, no 1, Hubert G. Osteen (publisher and proprietor). Issued as Daily Item from Oct 1894 to sometime between Aug 1897 and May 1898 when became the Sumter Daily Item (Mon-Sat). Paper added Sun edition on Aug 2, 1987 (no vol-issue data) and shortened masthead title to the Item. Hubert D. and Hubert D. Osteen, Jr., also associated with paper. *Files: Clemson mfm Oct 1960 + ; SCL ((1894-1960)) 6,000, mfm Oct 1960 + ; Sumter County Museum-Archives ((1894-1976)) 100; Sumter Daily Item ((1922 +)), mfm Oct 1960 + . Note: SCL orig files are virtually complete 1936-1960.*

SUMTER DISPATCH   weekly--established 1860, purchased by the Sumter Watchman in 1861 and moved to Conway where continued as the Horry Dispatch (1861-1863). Jan 26, 1860 = vol 1, no 2, T. Waties Dinkins (editor), Francis & DeLorme (publishers). *Files: Sumter County Museum-Archives Jan 26, Jul 4, 1860.*

SUMTER DISTRICT REPORTER   monthly, South Carolina Conference of Methodist Episcopal Church, South--established 1883, ceased c. 1886. Not cited by Ayer. Feb 1885 = vol 3, no 1, A. J. Stokes (editor), N. G. Osteen (publisher). *Files: SCL Feb 1885-Jan 1886.*

SUMTER GAZETTE   weekly c. 1845--revival of the Sumter Gazette, and Constitutional Advocate of the early 1830s, soon ceased. George W. Hopkins (editor and proprietor), about 24 issues printed. Apr 9, 1845 = no 1, no vol number. *Files: SCL Apr 9 (xerox copy), Jul 23, 1845; Sumter County Museum-Archives Apr 9, Jul 23, 1845.*

SUMTER GAZETTE, AND CONSTITUTIONAL ADVOCATE   weekly, pro-nullification--established 1829, ceased c. 1833. Sep 24, 1831 = vol 3, no 3, J. Hardman (publisher). According to Anne King Gregorie, History of Sumter County, this paper was founded by James S. Bowen. Hardman (pseud) presumably was local lawyer John Hemphill. *Files: Clemson Mar 16, Apr 20, 1833; SCL Sep 24, 1831.*

SUMTER HERALD   weekly, semi-weekly--established in 1881 as the Sumter Advance, became the Sumter Herald on Oct 7, 1892 (vol 21, no 1...printing error, should be vol 12) and on Oct 14, 1892 began new number sequence: vol 1, no 1, S. A. Nettles (editor and proprietor). Ceased publication in 1952. Cited by Ayer 1893/4 thru 1953. Issued semi-weekly 1935-1939. In addition to Nettles, A. Wilkes Knight, John M. Knight, Furman Knight, Arthur Knight, F. Jenkins Knight, and R. S. Churchill also associated with paper. *Files: SCL ((1892-1944)) 500, mfm 1896-1949; Sumter County Museum-Archives (1896-1952) 25.*

SUMTER MIRROR   monthly--published by the Sumter Advance Jan-Dec 1882, Mary M. Darr (editor). Not cited by Ayer. *Files: SCL Jan-Dec 1882 (xerox and photostat copies); Sumter County Museum-Archives Jan-Mar 1882.*

SUMTER NEWS   weekly--established 1866, became the True Southron Aug 14, 1873. Jun 1, 1866 = vol 1, no 1, H. L. Darr (proprietor), F. J. Moses, Jr. (editor). N. G. Osteen and William G. Kennedy also associated with paper. *Files: SCL Jun 1, 1866-Aug 7, 1873; Sumter County Museum-Archives Jun 1, 1866-May 23, 1867.*

SUMTER NEWS   weekly--established in 1967 by Ray Hamilton and Mike Karvelas, ceased c. 1981. Feb 22, 1967 = vol 1, no 49, Mike Karvelas (news editor), Ray Hamilton (general manager), Sumter News Publishing Company. Not cited by Ayer. *Files: SCL Jan 1972-Jun 1981; Sumter County Museum-Archives (1967-1976) 50.*

SUMTER PROSPECTOR   see Prospector.

SUMTER WATCHMAN   weekly--created Jun 13, 1855 by merger of the Black River Watchman and the Sumter Banner. On Aug 2, 1881 merged with the True Southron, continued by the Watchman and Southron. Jun 13, 1855 = vol 6, no 7, A. A. Gilbert and J. S. Richardson, Jr. (publishers). Jan 1860 began tri-weekly edition and then issued semi-weekly edition Oct-Dec 1863. See Tri-Weekly Watchman and Semi-Weekly Watchman. John R. Haynesworth, L. L. Fraser, Jr., H. L. Darr, T. E. Flowers, T. E. Gilbert, J. J. Dargan, M. H. McLaurin, and J. J. Fleming also associated with paper.

Files: SCL Jun 1855-1858, (1859-Jan 1865) 60, Sep 1865-Jun 1876, (Jul 1876-Jul 1881) 50, mfm 1870-1871; Sumter County Museum-Archives (1860-1874) 10.

TEMPERANCE WORKER   semi-monthly--established in Columbia in 1883, published in Sumter 1885-1887, ceased c. 1887.   Jan 19, 1885 = vol 2, no 20, H. F. Chreitzberg (editor), N. G. Osteen (publisher). Cited by Ayer in Sumter 1885 thru 1887. Sep-Dec 1887 issues bear dual dateline [Sumter and Chester] after Chreitzberg moved to Chester. J. S. Mattison also associated with paper. See Temperance Worker [Columbia].

TRI-WEEKLY WATCHMAN   tri-weekly--Sumter Watchman (weekly) launched tri-weekly edition on Jun 23, 1860 = vol 1, no 62, Gilbert and Darr (publishers). Paper became semi-weekly in Oct 1863. Weekly edition continued to appear during these years. *Files: SCL (1860-1863) 70; Sumter County Museum-Archives (1861-1863) 30.*

TRUE SOUTHRON   weekly--established 1866 as the Sumter News, became the True Southron Aug 14, 1873, and merged with the Sumter Watchman Aug 2, 1881 to form the Watchman and Southron. Aug 14, 1873 = vol 8, no 11, Darr and Osteen (proprietors). John J. Dargan, Charles H. Moise, D. B. Anderson, and W. D. Blanding also associated with paper. *Files: SCL Aug 14, 1873-Jul 26, 1881; Sumter County Museum-Archives May 13, Jul 22, Aug 5, 1879.*

VINDICATOR   weekly, black publication c. 1883. According to Behling, this paper was edited by Samuel J. Lee. Not cited by Ayer. *NFK*

VOICE OF JOB   weekly c. 1938-1942. Presumably issued by Rev. H. B. Brown of Job's Temple. See the Samaritan Herald and the Voice of Job. *NFK*

WATCHMAN AND SOUTHRON   weekly, semi-weekly--created in 1881 by merger of the Sumter Watchman and the True Southron, absorbed by the Sumter Daily Item in Jan 1930. Aug 2, 1881 = vol 1, no 1, new series, N. G. Osteen (business manager), Julius A. Mood and D. B. Anderson (editors). Became semi-weekly Feb 20, 1909. H. G. Osteen also associated with paper. *Files: Greenville CL (1888-1889) 11; SCL Aug 1881-1890, 1892-Sep 1918, (1919-1929) 20; Sumter County Museum-Archives (1879-1930) 25.*

WEDGEFIELD

MESSENGER OF THE DAY   weekly, black publication, Republican--established 1909, ceased c. 1910. Cited once by Ayer (1910): C. C. Clark (editor and publisher). *NFK*

UNION COUNTY

Formed in 1798 when old Pinckney District was split into two parts--York and Union districts--the latter, now Union County, takes its name from a "union" church once used by several denominations. That structure, built in 1765 in the Brown's Creek area, was about four miles from the present city of Union on what later became the Pinckneyville Road.

SANTUCK

SANTUCK SUN   monthly--established in 1889, ceased c. 1891. Cited by Ayer 1890 and 1891: Charles R. Willeford (editor and publisher). *NFK*

UNION

BAPTIST PRESS   weekly--established in Lake City in 1897 as the South Carolina Baptist, this publication soon moved to Greenwood. It became the Baptist Press in 1905, moved to Union the following year, and merged with the Baptist Courier [Greenville] in 1907. Nov 14, 1906 = vol 10, no 46 (old series), vol 2, no 15 (new series), Victor L. Masters and Lewis M. Rice (editors and proprietors). See also Baptist Press [Greenwood]. *Files: SCL (Nov 1906-Mar 1907) 8.*

NEW ERA   semi-weekly--established 1897, ceased c. 1898. Sep 28, 1897 = vol 1, no 43, J. T. Gantt (editor and publisher). Cited once by Ayer (1898). *Files: SCL Sep 28, 1897.*

PEOPLE'S RECORDER   weekly, black publication, Republican--established in Barnwell as the Recorder or Barnwell Recorder in 1893, moved to Columbia c. 1896. Jan 13, 1900 issue bears dual dateline: Columbia and Union. Two weeks later paper cites only Columbia but boasts of branch offices in Union, Orangeburg, Laurens, Greenville, and Greenwood..."Published for the Elevation of Our Race, and is [sic] an Exponent of Republican Principles." See People's Recorder [Columbia].

PROGRESS   weekly, semi-weekly--established 1900, continued by the Union Progress on Nov 26, 1924. Paper began as a weekly, was issued semi-weekly from Apr 6, 1906 to Jan 2, 1912, then became weekly again. Appears as the Union Progress Nov-Dec 1924 and plans were announced to become daily. Feb 21, 1900 = vol 1, no 2, D. J. Carter (editor), Allan Nicholson (publisher). L. M. Rice and Walter W. Colton also associated with paper. *Files: SCL and Union CL mfm (1900) 40, 1901-Nov 19, 1924.*

REVIEW   weekly--established 1929, ceased c. 1931. Cited once by Ayer (1931): T. D. Toler (editor), Economy Printing Company. Dec 12, 1929 = vol 1, no 43, J. L. Brooks (editor), T. D. Toler (associate editor and publisher). Review also had a Spartanburg office and dual dateline: Union and Spartanburg. See Review [Spartanburg].

STAR weekly. black publication, Republican--established 1897, ceased c. 1898. Cited once by Ayer (1898): P. G. Hammett (editor), Perry C. White (publisher). *NFK*

TIMES-ADVERTIZER weekly--established 1982. Published by Union Daily Times. Aug 15, 1985 = vol 3, no 33. *Files: Union Daily Times 1982 + .*

UNION COUNTY NEWS weekly--established 1966. Jul 20, 1966 = vol 1, no 1, W. H. Whitehead (editor and publisher). J. M. McHugh also associated with paper. Not listed in Ayer. *Files: SCL May 6, 1970, ((1987 +)); Union County News 1966 + .*

UNION DAILY TIMES daily except Sun--created by name change in 1918, continues Union Times. Began daily except Sun and Thu schedule with new number system on Oct 15, 1917, while still issuing Thu weekly paper with old number system. L. M. Rice was editor of both editions, which appeared as the Union Times with subheads: "weekly edition" and "daily edition." In 1918 weekly ceased, and paper became daily except Sun and changed masthead to Union Daily Times. In addition to Rice, William Rice Feaster, Dorothy S. Feaster, and Donald E. Wilder have been associated with paper. *Files: Union Daily Times 1940 + ; SCL (1930-1975) 15; SCL, Union CL, and Union Daily Times mfm 1917-1984; USC-Union mfm ((1918-1936)).*

UNION PROGRESS weekly--created by name change Nov 26, 1924, formerly Progress, continued by the Union Weekly Progress on Jan 7, 1925. Nov 26, 1924 = vol 25, no 22, H. V. Sturdivant (editor and publisher). *Files: SCL and Union CL mfm Nov 26-Dec 31, 1924.*

UNION STANDARD weekly, black publication--established 1906, ceased ? Aug 20, 1906 = vol 1, no 9, J. C. White (editor), G. H. Herndon (president). Motto: "Lift Up the Standard of the People." Not cited by Ayer. *Files: Clemson Aug 20, 1906.*

UNION TIMES weekly--created by name change on Sep 7, 1894 = vol 25, no 36, Josiah Crudup (editor and publisher). Continues Weekly Union Times, continued by Union Daily Times in 1918. M. W. Culp, James E. Hunter, R. L. McNally, W. E. Cook, L. G. Young, John R. Mathis, and Lewis M. Rice also associated with paper. *Files: SCl (1914-1917) 16; SCL, Union CL, and Union Daily Times ((1894-1917)) 800; USC-Union mfm ((1899-1917)) 625.*

UNION WEEKLY PROGRESS weekly--continues Union Progress in 1925. Jan 7, 1925 = vol 1, no 1, H. V. Sturdivant (editor and publisher). Sturdivant announced plans to become a daily publication, but there is no evidence that happened. Cited by Ayer 1925 thru 1931 as Progress with Allan Nicholson as editor and publisher. The appearance of the Review in 1929 indicates that the Union Weekly Progress probably ceased before that date. *Files: SCL and Union CL mfm Jan-Jun 11, 1925.*

UNIONVILLE JOURNAL weekly--established 1851, continued by Unionville Times in Jan 1859. May 31, 1851 = vol 1, no 1, B. F. Arthur (editor), Robert A. McKnight (publisher). *Files: Clemson Jul 4, 1851, Sep 5, 1856, Sep 3, 1858; SCL mfm May*

1851-May 1852, (1852-1858) 8; Union CL (1851-1852) 50; Union County Museum May 1851-May 1852.

UNIONVILLE TIMES   weekly--according to Ellen, this paper was created in Jan 1859 by name change, continues the Unionville Journal, ceased c. 1868. In Jan 1859, W. H. Wallace and Charles E. Boyd were the editors, R. A. McKnight and W. H. Wallace, the publishers. Nov 25, 1859 = vol 1, no 46, P. M. Wallace (editor), Benjamin Wallace (publisher). Editorial column heading: "The Constitution as our fathers gave it, or separate independence." Jul 19, 1867 = vol 2, no 15, Robert A. McKnight (editor and publisher). *Files: Clemson Mar 18, 1859; SCL mfm (1859-1868) 6, some of these papers are fragments.*

WEEKLY UNION TIMES   weekly--established in 1869, successor to the Unionville Times continuing 1866 founding date (new series), but with a new number sequence. According to Rowell (1870): R. W. Shand (editor and publisher). Apr 4, 1873 = vol 4, no 14, new series, R. M. Stokes (editor). Continued by the Union Times on Sep 7, 1894. In addition to Shand and Stokes, Josiah Crudup also was associated with this paper. *Files: SCL, Union CL, and Union Daily Times mfm ((1873-1894)) 350.*

WILLIAMSBURG COUNTY

Separated from Georgetown District in 1802, Williamsburgh District, now Williamsburg County, assumed the name of Williamsburgh Township. That community, created in the early 1700s, probably was named for Prince William IV of Orange, the son-in-law of King George II of England, the same man honored by Orangeburg County.

CADES

ENTERPRISE   weekly--established in 1914, ceased c. 1915. Cited once by Ayer (1915): H. H. Brown (editor), Enterprise Publishing Company. *NFK*

HEMINGWAY

HEMINGWAY JOURNAL   weekly--established in 1940, ceased c. 1940. Not listed in Ayer. This paper began as a supplement to the <u>Myrtle Beach News</u> on Apr 11, 1940 = vol 1, no 1, Mrs. K. E. Creel (editor), C. L. Phillips (publisher). But one week later Paul Barrett was listed as editor, with Mrs. Creel, society editor. *Files: SCL Apr 11-May 24, Jun 7, 21, Jul 12, 1940.*

PRESS AND BANNER   weekly, Independent Democrat--established 1919, ceased c. 1921. Cited by Ayer 1920 and 1921: E. N. Beard (editor), Beard Publishing Company. *NFK*

TRI-COUNTY TRIBUNE   weekly, independent--established 1949, ceased c. 1959. Cited by Ayer 1950 thru 1959. Ayer 1950: Ray T. Martin (editor), H. E. Carraway and J. W. Richards (publishers). Others associated with this paper include Mrs. John B. Dukes, J. J. Hinds, Jr., J. J. Hinds, Sr., J. D. Brown, Jr., and two Timmonsville publishers, A. A. Hennon and James O. Howle. *Files: SCL and Georgetown CL mfm Aug 5, 1949-Jul 25, 1952.*

WEEKLY OBSERVER   weekly--established 1973. Aug 30, 1973 = vol 1, no 1, Greg Smith (editor), Community Newspapers, Inc. Bill McGowan, Carolyn and Edward Sweatt, Brian Huckabee, and Robert Thompson also associated with paper. *Files: SCL ((1984 +)); <u>Weekly Observer</u> 1973 + .*

JOHNSONVILLE

PROGRESS   weekly, Democrat--established 1915, ceased c. 1918. Cited by Ayer 1917 and 1918: P. B. Lockwood (editor), S. O. Eaddy (publisher). *NFK*

KINGSTREE

ALLIANCE LADDER   weekly, Democrat--established 1892, ceased c. 1894. Published in Florence as the Florence Reflector and in Conway as the Horry Monitor. Listed once in Ayer (1893/4): T. C. Willoughby (editor and publisher). *NFK*

COUNTY RECORD   weekly--established 1885, ceased in 1975 when purchased by the News [Kingstree]. Feb 17, 1885 = vol 1, no 1, R. C. Logan (editor and proprietor). Others associated with the County Record include W. E. Cook, P. A. Alsbrook, Louis J. Bristow, C. W. Wolfe, W. F. Tolley, R. K. Wallace, L. H. Cromer, Jr., Myrtle A. Cromer, Vaughn Alsbrook, and Fred R. Sheheen. *Files: SCL (1898-1931) 33, Jan 1932-Apr 1936, Apr 1937-Jun 1975, mfm Feb 17, 1885, Aug 23, 1906; Williamsburg County Civil Defense Office 1938-1950; Williamsburg CL ((1943-1975)).*

KINGSTREE NEWS   weekly--established 1972, continues as the News after Jul 5, 1973. May 18, 1972 = vol 1, no 1, Charles A. Martin (editor and publisher). *Files: News May 1972-Jun 1973.*

KINGSTREE STAR   weekly--established 1856, merged with the Williamsburg Herald c. 1884, continued by the Williamsburg Star and Herald. Oct 11, 1860 = vol 4, no 46, R. C. Logan and D. E. McCreight (editors). After being suspended for nearly a decade, the paper was revived by Logan in 1869. Feb 1, 1871 = vol 2, no 34, new series. Logan was editor and proprietor until 1874; then, according to Rowell, Samuel W. Maurice became editor and publisher, followed by James S. Heyward in 1879. The Star was not cited by Ayer 1881 thru 1884, but Ayer 1885 lists the Williamsburg Star and Herald as founded in 1881 (the year the Williamsburg Herald began). *Files: SCL Mar 31, 1859, Nov 18, 1874, mfm (1860-1874) 9.*

NEWS   weekly--established May 1972 as the Kingstree News, continued by the News Jul 5, 1973 = vol 2, no 8, Jerry R. Sanders (editor and publisher). Cathy Greene, Ken Elkins, William Dupre, Bob Gorman, Vickey D. Nexsen, and Robert L. Stoddard, Jr., also associated with paper. The News absorbed the County Record in Jun 1975. *Files: News Jul 1973 + ; SCL Oct 1973 + ; Williamsburg CL ((1975 +)).*

GOSPEL BUGLE   weekly, evangelical c. 1893. Cited in Remington's Newspaper Annual (1893). No details given. *NFK*

WEEKLY MAIL   weekly, Democrat--established 1901, ceased c. 1907. Cited by Ayer 1903 thru 1907: Phillip H. Stoll (editor), Stoll Brothers (publishers). Jun 23, 1904 = vol 4, no 49. *Files: SCL mfm Jun 23, 1904 (fragment).*

WILLIAMSBURG-FLORENCE JOURNAL   weekly--established Jun 1986, continues News & Shopper [Myrtle Beach]. See News & Shopper [Myrtle Beach] and the Myrtle Beach Journal.

WILLIAMSBURG HERALD   weekly, Democrat--established 1881, merged with Kingstree Star c. 1884, continued by the Williamsburg Star and Herald. Aug 31, 1882 = vol 2, no 31, H. S. Cunningham (editor and proprietor). *Files: SCL Aug 31, 1882, mfm Feb 22, 1883.*

WILLIAMSBURG HERALD   weekly, Democrat--established 1916, ceased c. 1920. Cited by Ayer 1917 thru 1920: F. Earle Bradham (editor and publisher). *NFK*

WILLIAMSBURG REPUBLICAN   weekly, Republican, black publication-- established 1873, ceased c. 1877. Jun 4, 1874 = vol 1, no 43. According to Woody, paper edited by black lawyer S. A. Swails and published by the Kingstree Printing Company. Others associated with the Williamsburg Republican include Louis Jacobs and M. J. Hirsch, both county officials. *Files: SCL Jun 4, 1874.*

WILLIAMSBURG STAR AND HERALD   weekly, Democrat--created c. 1884 by the merger of the Kingstree Star and the Williamsburg Herald, ceased c. 1888. Cited by Ayer 1885 thru 1888. Ayer 1885 cites founding date of 1881 (that of the Williamsburg Herald), but later annuals list the founding date of the Kingstree Star. Ayer 1887: E. G. Chandler (editor and publisher). Ayer 1888: M. B. Lucas (editor and publisher). *NFK*

WILLIAMSBURG TIMES   weekly, independent--established 1955, ceased c. 1958. Cited by Ayer 1955 thru 1958: Mrs. F. S. Herbert (editor). A. A. Hennon of Timmonsville was publisher in 1956; James O. Howle of Timmonsville, in 1957-1958. *NFK*

YORK COUNTY

York District, now York County, was created in 1798 when old Pinckney District was divided into two parts: York and Union. Originally called "New Acquisition," it was named by settlers from York, Pennsylvania, which, in turn, had been named for York, England.

CLOVER

CLOVER HERALD   weekly--established 1928. Cited by Ayer 1929 + . Ayer 1929: H. S. Gault (editor), Clover Herald & Printing Company. Jun 19, 1930 = vol 2, no 28 (no personnel cited). Albert C. Sweat, O. Frank Thornton, Mrs. Charles Drumheller, James H. Owen, and Mike Faulkenberry also associated with paper. *Files: Clover Herald 1928 + , mfm 1964, 1965, 1970; SCL Jun 19, 1930, mfm 1963, 1965-1966; Yorkville Enquirer 1984 + , mfm 1963, 1966-1969, 1971.*

CLOVER JOURNAL   weekly--established 1923 (?), ceased c. 1928. Cited once by Ayer (1928) as published by U. R. Murphy of Mount Holly, N. C., in conjunction with the Belmont Appeal and the Gaston County Appeal. Founding date of 1923 may refer to the North Carolina papers, not the Clover Journal. *NFK*

CLOVER MESSENGER   weekly--established 1917, continued by the Palmetto Post c. 1919. Cited by Ayer 1918 and 1919. Ayer 1918: H. J. Gasque (editor), H. J. Gasque and C. W. Wallace (publishers). Ayer 1919: W. A. Westmoreland and Son (editors and publishers). *NFK*

CLOVER REVIEW   weekly--established 1901, ceased c. 1902. Cited once by Ayer (1902): Lewis B. Gwin Company (publisher). *NFK*

PALMETTO POST   weekly, independent--continues Clover Messenger c. 1919, ceased c. 1926. Cited by Ayer 1920 thru 1926: W. A. Westmoreland and Son (editors and publishers). *NFK*

FORT MILL

CATAWBIAN   weekly--established 1892, ceased c. 1893. Not cited by Ayer. Jul 16, 1892 = vol 1, no 11, W. R. Bradford (publisher). *Files: SCL Jul 16, 1892 (fragment), Jan 25, 1893.*

CLARION   weekly--continues Weekly News c. 1889, ceased c. 1890. Cited by Ayer 1889 and 1890: J. S. Drakeford (editor and publisher). Fragments indicate that 1889 was vol 3. Drakeford disclosed plans on Apr 25, 1889 to start a new paper, but the Clarion was published at least to Dec 1889. *Files: SCL Apr 25, Dec 11, 1889 (fragments).*

FORT MILL NEWS   weekly--established 1890, continued by Fort Mill Times in 1892. Cited once by Ayer (1891): W. B. Ardrey (editor and publisher). Sep 2, 1891 = vol 1, no 47, W. B. Ardrey (editor and proprietor). *Files: SCL Apr 29, 1891 (fragment); Fort Mill Library, SCL, Winthrop, and York CL mfm Sep 2, 1891, Jun 15, 1892.*

FORT MILL TIMES   weekly--continues Fort Mill News in 1892. Cited by Ayer 1895 + . Ayer 1895: W. B. Ardrey (editor and publisher). May 8, 1897 = vol 4, no ? (paper torn), no personnel cited. J. E. McManaway, H. H. and J. E. Smith, B. W. and W. R. Bradford, W. R. Bradford, Jr., Julian Starr, Jr., Jerry P. McGuire, Fred R. Sheheen, and Linda T. O'Hara also associated with paper. *Files: Fort Mill Library 1985 + , mfm May 8, 1897, Mar 1900-1980; Fort Mill Times 1979 + ; SCL ((1914-1984)) 100, mfm May 8, 1897, Mar 1900-1980; Winthrop mfm 1909-1920; York CL mfm May 8, 1897, Mar 1900-1980.*

WEEKLY NEWS   weekly--established 1887, continued by Clarion c. 1889. Jul 13, 1887 = vol 1, no 2, J. S. Drakeford (editor and proprietor). Cited by Ayer 1887 and 1888 as the "News." *Files: Fort Mill Library, SCL, Winthrop, and York CL mfm Jul 13, 1887.*

HICKORY GROVE

SUN   weekly, Democrat--established 1899, ceased c. 1902. Cited by Ayer 1900 thru 1902: J. B. Martin (publisher). *NFK*

LAKE WYLIE

LAKE WYLIE MAGAZINE   monthly--established 1984, Leonard Short (editor), Lake Publishing Company. Despite title, paper describes itself as "an informative and fun newspaper for Lake Wylie communities." *Files: Lake Wylie Magazine 1984 + .*

MC ELWEESVILLE

REPUBLICAN WHIG DEMOCRAT   weekly, pro-nullification--established 1841, ceased ? May 8, 1841 = vol 1, no 4, Jonathan McElwee, Jr., and Patrick Carey (editors and publishers). Note: McElweesville was located on the Landsford Road, seventeen miles from Yorkville and twenty miles from Lancaster. *Files: Library of Congress May 8, 1841. Apparently no files in SC.*

RIVER HILLS

RIVER HILLS PRESS   monthly--established 1976 for the River Hills community, Trina Nochisaki (editor and publisher). *Files: River Hills Press 1976 + .*

ROCK HILL

BLACK VIEWS   weekly, black publication--published in Columbia by Redfern II, JuJu Publications, for the Rock Hill area. See Black News [Columbia]. Also issued as Rock Hill Community Black Views and News. *Files: Winthrop Jun 3, 1979.*

CATAWBA INDEX   weekly--continues Daily Sun in Feb 1897. Feb 5, 1897 = vol 1, no 5, J. H. Evans (publisher). Not cited by Ayer. Ceased c. 1897. *Files: Herald and York CL mfm Feb-Apr 1897.*

DAILY SUN   daily c. 1897--continued by the Catawba Index. According to the Weekly Sun (Jan 7, 1897), the Daily Sun was being issued in Rock Hill. Not cited by Ayer. *NFK*

EVENING HERALD   daily--continues Rock Hill Herald in Dec 1911, continued by the Herald Jan 11, 1986. Jan 1, 1912 = vol 1, no 26, J. T. Fain (editor), Herald Publishing Company. According to Ayer, paper continued to issue a semi-weekly edition (Tue-Thu) until 1915. In addition to Fain, A. W. Huckle, Talbot Patrick, and Wayne T. Patrick associated with paper. *Files: Clemson mfm Jan-Apr, Sep 1912-1974; Herald, SCL, and York CL mfm Jan-Apr, Sep 1912-1986; Winthrop mfm 1928-1986.*

FRIENDSHIP BANNER   weekly, Baptist, black publication--established 1903, ceased c. 1922. Cited by Ayer 1903 thru 1922: M. P. Hall (editor and publisher). *NFK*

HAMPTON HERALD   weekly, Democrat--established 1876, continued by Rock Hill Herald c. 1877. Cited by Rowell and Ayer 1877 thru 1881 as the Hampton Herald: J. M. Ivey & Company (editor and publisher). Name presumably chosen during the Wade Hampton campaign of 1876 and soon changed to Rock Hill Herald. *NFK*

HERALD   daily--continues Evening Herald Jan 11, 1986 (no vol or issue no), Russell H. Rein (executive editor), Wayne T. Patrick (publisher). Name change result of decision to issue Sun edition beginning Mar 2, 1986. Terry C. Plumb and Roger Soude also associated with paper. *Files: Herald, SCL, Winthrop, and York CL mfm 1986 + .*

INDIAN LAND CHRONICLE   weekly--continues the York District Chronicle of Yorkville c. 1859, ceased ? Jan 21, 1859 = vol 3, no 7, Thomas J. Eccles (publisher). *Files: SCL and Winthrop Jan 21, 1859; York CL mfm Jan 21, 1859.*

JOURNAL   semi-weekly--established 1901, continued by the Record in Feb 1904. Jun 5, 1901 = vol 1, no 2, G. W. and J. M. Charlotte (editors), Journal Publishing Company. J. K. Owens also associated with paper. *Files: Herald, SCL, and York CL mfm Jun 5, 1901-Jan 26, 1904.*

LANTERN   weekly--established 1872, ceased c. 1874. Cited by Rowell 1872 thru 1874. Rowell 1872: Johnstone Jones (editor and publisher). Rowell 1873: Gaston Jones (publisher). Rowell 1874: J. M. Watson (editor and publisher). *NFK*

RECORD   semi-weekly, tri-weekly, daily--continues Journal Feb 2, 1904, ceased c. 1930. Feb 2, 1904 = vol 3, no 71, P. L. Garnes (editor and manager). C. K. Schwrar also associated with paper. Cited by Ayer 1905 thru 1930. Issued briefly as a tri-weekly, Sep 13-Dec 13, 1904. Became daily in May 1930 and ceased soon after. *Files: Clemson, Herald, and SCL mfm 1904-1930; York CL mfm 1904-1913, 1915-1917, 1920-1921, Jan-Jun 1923.*

ROCK HILL CHRONICLE   weekly--established c. 1968, ceased c. 1968. Published for about six months by John Carriker. *NFK*

ROCK HILL COMMUNITY BLACK VIEWS AND NEWS   see Black Views.

ROCK HILL GRANGE   weekly--established 1874, ceased c. 1876. Cited by Rowell 1875 and 1876: T. C. Robertson (editor), J. M. Watson (publisher). *NFK*

ROCK HILL HERALD   weekly, semi-weekly--continues Hampton Herald c. 1877, continued by Evening Herald in Dec 1911. Jan 8, 1880 = vol 3, no 24, R. McLure (editor), J. M. Ivey & Company (publisher). J. J. Hull and J. Otis Hull also associated with paper. Issued weekly to Mar 15, 1893, then became semi-weekly. *Files: Clemson, Herald, SCL, and York CL mfm 1880-1911.*

ROCK HILL MESSENGER   weekly, Republican, black publication--established 1896, ceased c. 1921. Cited by Ayer 1897 thru 1921. Jan 26, 1900 = vol 5, no 3, C. P. T. White (editor and manager). *Files: SCL mfm Jan 26, 1900.*

ROCK HILL POST   weekly--established 1949, ceased c. 1951. Dec 16, 1949 = vol 1, no 1, Carl T. Hallman (editor), Rock Hill Post, Inc. *Files: Winthrop mfm Dec 16, 1949-Oct 19, 1951.*

ROCK HILL TIMES   weekly--established in 1970 by W. R. Bradford, Jr. Published in Rock Hill until 1985 when paper moved to Pineville, N. C. Feb 3, 1977 = vol 8, no 5, Willette Dewsnap-Gault (editor), Times Publishing Company. Harper Gault and A. B. Dark also associated with paper. *Files: Rock Hill Times 1984 + ; Winthrop mfm Feb 3, 1977-Dec 28, 1978.*

SOUTHERN LABOR JOURNAL   weekly, union publication c. 1900. Cited once by Ayer (1901): Levy Deas (editor), Trades Union (publisher). No founding date given. Ceased c. 1902. *NFK*

YORK OBSERVER   semi-weekly, tri-weekly--established Apr 12, 1981, one of six regional inserts published by the Charlotte (N. C.) Observer. Began as semi-weekly, soon issued tri-weekly. No volume or issue data, Peter Pipinsky (editor). *Files: Charlotte Observer mfm 1981 + ; York CL 1984 + ; York Observer 1981 + .*

WEEKLY SUN   weekly--established 1897, continued by the Catawba Index after one month of publication in Feb 1897. Jan 1, 1897 = vol 1, no 1, James H. Evans (editor), Rock Hill Printing Company. Not cited by Ayer. Jan 7, 1897 issue notes that these papers were being published in York County: Daily Sun, Weekly Sun, Rock Hill Herald, Rock Hill Messenger, Fort Mill Times, Yorkville Enquirer, and Yorkville Yeoman. *Files: Herald, SCL, and Winthrop mfm Jan 1-29, 1897.*

YORK

ENCYCLOPEDIA   weekly--established in 1825, ceased c. 1826. Oct 22, 1825 = vol 1, no 3, James McKee and Josiah Harris (editors), printed at the Pioneer office by P. Carey, More periodical than newspaper, this publication does contain some local news. *Files: SCL and York CL mfm (1825-1826) 40.*

FARMER'S MISCELLANY   weekly--established 1844, had become Yorkville Miscellany by 1851. Jun 15, 1846 = vol 3, no 19, J. E. Grist (publisher). *Files: Duke Jun 15, 1846. Apparently no files in SC.*

JOURNAL OF THE TIMES   weekly--established 1835, ceased c. 1837 ? Oct 28, 1835 = vol 1, no 25, John E. Grist (publisher). *Files: SCL Oct 28, 1835, Jan 28, Feb 4, 18, 1837.*

NEW ERA   weekly--according to the York News (Jun 7, 1916), the New Era was established Nov 4, 1904 and ceased in Jul 1907. Cited by Ayer 1905 thru 1907: E. G. Sandifer (editor and publisher). Jul 5, 1907 = vol 3, no 35, E. G. Sandifer (editor and publisher). *Files: SCL Jul 5, 1907.*

PEOPLE'S ADVOCATE   weekly c. 1825-1828. Dec 4, 1828 = vol 4, no 6, printed by Alexander H. Dismukes for Beatty and Harris. James McKee and Xerxes H. Cushman also associated with paper. *Files: Rutgers Dec 4, 1828. Apparently no files in SC.*

PINCKNEY WHIG   weekly--established 1833, ceased c. 1834 ? Aug 16, 1833 = vol 1, no 6, N. M. Foulkes (proprietor). *Files: York CL mfm Aug 16, Dec 6, 1833.*

PIONEER   weekly--continues Pioneer and Yorkville Advertiser Feb 1824, continued by the Pioneer and Commercial Register in Apr 1826. Feb 28, 1824 = vol 1, no 29, P. Carey (publisher). *Files: SCL orig & mfm Feb 28-Jul 31, 1824; York CL mfm Feb 28-Jul 31, 1824.*

PIONEER AND COMMERCIAL REGISTER   weekly--continues Pioneer in Apr 1826, continued by Pioneer and South Carolina Whig in Jul 1829. Apr 1, 1826 = vol 3, no 137, P. Carey (publisher). *Files: SCL Apr 1, 1826 (fragment).*

PIONEER AND SOUTH-CAROLINA WHIG   weekly--continues <u>Pioneer and Commercial Register</u> Jul 1829. Jul 4, 1829 = vol 1, no 1 (new series). Paper ceased c. 1831. *Files: Library of Congress (1829-1831) 12. Apparently no SC files.*

PIONEER AND YORKVILLE ADVERTISER   weekly--continues <u>Pioneer and Yorkville Weekly Advertiser</u> Oct 4, 1823, continued by <u>Pioneer</u> Feb 28, 1824. Oct 4, 1823 = vol 1, no 8, P. Carey (publisher). *Files: SCL orig & mfm Oct 4, 1823-Feb 21, 1824; York CL mfm Oct 4, 1823-Feb 21, 1824.*

PIONEER AND YORKVILLE WEEKLY ADVERTISER   weekly--established Aug 16, 1823, continued by the <u>Pioneer and Yorkville Advertiser</u> Oct 4, 1823. Aug 16, 1823 = vol 1, no 1, P. Carey (publisher). *Files: SCL orig & mfm Aug 16-Sep 27, 1823; York CL mfm Aug 16-Sep 27, 1823.*

REMEDY   weekly--established 1851, ceased in Nov 1854 when sold, succeeded by the <u>Yorkville Citizen</u>. Sep 20, 1851 = vol 1, no 1, Thomas J. Eccles (editor and publisher). J. Felix Walker and H. Judge Moore also associated with paper. *Files: SCL (1851-1854) 15, mfm Jan 7, Oct 12, 1853; York CL mfm Jan 7, Oct 12, 1853.*

WORKING CHRISTIAN   weekly, Baptist--established 1869, moved to Charleston in May 1870 and to Columbia in Oct 1871, continued by the <u>Baptist Courier</u> in Sep 1877. Jul 1, 1869 = vol 1, no 1, Tilman R. Gaines (proprietor), Lewis M. Grist (publisher). See <u>Working Christian</u> [Columbia] and <u>Baptist Courier</u> [Greenville].

YORK DISTRICT CHRONICLE   weekly--established in Aug 1856 by Thomas J. Eccles, absorbed the <u>Yorkville Citizen</u> in Nov 1856, moved to Rock Hill c. 1859 and published as the <u>Indian Land Chronicle</u>. Apr 16, 1858 = vol 2, no 24, Thomas J. Eccles (publisher). *Files: Duke Apr 16, 1858. Apparently no files in SC.*

YORK ENTERPRISE   weekly--established 1888, ceased c. 1893. Dec 12, 1888 = vol 1, no 1, W. L. McDonald (editor), York Publishing Company. Cited by Ayer 1889 thru 1892. E. M. Law also associated with paper. *Files: SCL Dec 12, 1888-Dec 4, 1889.*

YORK NEWS   semi-weekly--established 1913, ceased c. 1918. Cited by Ayer 1914 thru 1918. Ayer 1914: W. A. Fair (editor), York Publishing Company. Jun 7, 1916 = vol 3, no 52, Watson Bull (editor). Published as the "York Daily News" Jun 7-9, 1916 for a SC Press Association meeting held in York. *Files: SCL (1916-1917) 7.*

YORKVILLE CITIZEN   weekly--created Nov 1854 by merger of the <u>Yorkville Miscellany</u> and the <u>Remedy</u>, absorbed by the <u>York District Chronicle</u> in Nov 1856. Mar 3, 1855 = vol 1, no 14, W. Rice (editor and publisher). On Oct 13, 1855 (vol 1, no 46) editors Wilson Rice and William B. McCreight contemplated becoming a tri-weekly, but apparently never did. *Files: SCL Mar 3, Oct 13, 1855, Feb 8, 1856.*

YORKVILLE COMPILER   weekly--established 1840, ceased c. 1841. Jun 8, 1840 = vol 1, no 2, John E. Grist (publisher). *Files: SCL orig & mfm Jun 8, 1840-May 21, 1841; York CL mfm Jun 8, 1840-May 21, 1841.*

YORKVILLE ENQUIRER   weekly, semi-weekly--established 1855 as weekly, issued semi-weekly May 7-24, 1861, then weekly to Mar 27, 1895, semi-weekly to c. 1942, then weekly once more. Apr 5, 1855 = vol 1, no 13, Lewis M. Grist (publisher), John L. Miller and Samuel W. Melton (editors and proprietors). W. D., A. M., and James D. Grist, Lucretia M. Shirley, Fred D. Shirley, O. N. Burgess, Gene Graham, and James H. Owen also associated with paper. *Files: Cherokee CL mfm 1856-1866; Chester CL mfm 1858-1869, (1870-1871) 76, 1872-1875; Clemson mfm 1856-1869, (1870-1871) 76, 1872-1889; Furman mfm 1856-1866; Herald [Rock Hill] mfm 1925-1928; SCL (1855) 1, 1890-1915, 1918-1919, 1921-1925, ((1930-1942)) 465, (1943-1961) 3, Nov 1984 + , mfm (1855) 18, 1856-1869, (1870-1871) 76, 1872-1889, 1918, 1925-1928, 1963-1970; Spartanburg Methodist College mfm 1856-1869, (1870-1871) 76, 1872-1889, 1925-1928; Winthrop 1931, 1933-1935, mfm 1858-1867; York CL mfm (1855) 18, 1856-1869, (1870-1871) 76, 1872-1889, (1891-1899) 35, 1918, 1925-1928; Yorkville Enquirer 1984 + , mfm 1963-1971.*

YORKVILLE MISCELLANY   weekly--established in 1844 as the Farmer's Miscellany, by 1851 had become the Yorkville Miscellany. According to Ellen, paper ceased in Nov 1854 when merged with Remedy to create a new publication, the Yorkville Citizen. Jan 22, 1851 = vol 7, no 2, new series, Lewis M. Grist (publisher and proprietor). *Files: SCL and York CL mfm Jan 15, 1851-Jan 25, 1854.*

YORKVILLE NEWS   weekly c. 1878. According to North, paper was established in 1878 and ceased in Sep 1879. Not cited by Rowell. *NFK*

YORKVILLE YEOMAN   weekly, Democrat--established 1893, ceased c. 1903. Cited by Ayer 1893/4 thru 1903. Ayer 1893/4: J. S. Drakeford (editor), Drakeford & Company (publisher). Oct 23, 1896 = vol 4, no 8, J. S. Drakeford (editor), Drakeford & Company (publisher). *Files: SCL Oct 23, 1896, Jul 16, 1897.*

APPENDIX 1

OUT-OF-STATE NEWSPAPER FILES IN SOUTH CAROLINA

The largest collection of out-of-state files is at the Thomas Cooper Library, University of South Carolina, Columbia. It includes the Early State Records Microfilm Project (1,700 reels) compiled by the Library of Congress in cooperation with the University of North Carolina. Among these legislative and administrative records are 53 reels of early newspapers. The Thomas Cooper Library also has 39 boxes of early American newspapers produced by Readex Microprint Corporation and the American Antiquarian Society and 171 reels of underground newspapers (1963-1973) produced by Bell and Howell. Indexes to major current dailies such as the New York Times usually are available wherever files of such newspapers are maintained throughout the state. Benedict College, also in Columbia, has a substantial number of microfilm reels (c. 300) from the Schomberg Collection of the New York Public Library. The focus of this material, which encompasses newspapers, periodicals, and personal papers, is largely black life in the Manhattan area since 1800.

ALABAMA

BIRMINGHAM

DAILY AGE-HERALD *Clemson Oct 20, 1889.*

BIRMINGHAM POST-HERALD *USC mfm Sep 2-30, 1963.*

WIDE-AWAKE *SCL mfm Jan 24, 1900.*

HUNTSVILLE

HUNTSVILLE STAR *SCL mfm Jan 26, 1900.*

MOBILE

MOBILE DAILY REGISTER *Clemson mfm Feb 17, 1859-May 27, 1864. Paper issued as Mobile Advertiser and Register Jun 1861-Jun 1863 and as Mobile Daily Advertiser and Register Jun 1863-Nov 1864.*

MONTGOMERY

ALABAMA JOURNAL *Clemson Mar 16, 23, 1833.*

MONTGOMERY ENTERPRISE   *SCL mfm Jan 26, 1900.*

ARIZONA

FORT WHIPPLE AND PRESCOTT

ARIZONA MINER   *USC mfm Mar 9-Dec 14, 1864.*

MESILLA

MESILLA TIMES   *USC mfm Oct 18, 1860.*

PRESCOTT

ARIZONA MINER   *USC mfm (Jan 10, 1866-Jul 25, 1868) 80.*

DAILY ARIZONA MINER   *USC mfm (Oct 8, 1866-Oct 8, 1867) 47.*

WEEKLY ARIZONA MINER   *USC mfm (Aug 1, 1868-Dec 31, 1870) 75.*

TUBAC

WEEKLY ARIZONIAN   *USC mfm Jun 2, 30, Jul 14, 1859.*

TUSCAN

WEEKLY ARIZONIAN   *USC mfm ((Jun 1859-Apr 1871)) 135.*

ARKANSAS

HELENA

REPORTER   *SCL mfm Feb 1, 1900.*

LITTLE ROCK

AMERICAN GUIDE   *SCL mfm Jan 27, 1900.*

PINE BLUFF

PINE BLUFF WEEKLY HERALD   *SCL mfm Jan 27, 1900.*

CALIFORNIA

LOS ANGELES

LOS ANGELES TIMES   *Anderson CL mfm 1985 + ; Clemson mfm 1981 + ; Furman mfm 1984 + ; Greenville CL mfm 1972 + ; Richland CL mfm 1975-1982; USC mfm 1978 + ; Winthrop mfm 1970 + .*

MONTEREY

CALIFORNIAN   *USC mfm Aug 15, 1846-May 6, 1847.*

SACRAMENTO

PLACER TIMES   *USC mfm Apr 28, 1849-Jun 7, 1850.*

SAN FRANCISCO

ALTA CALIFORNIA   *USC mfm Jan 1-Dec 29, 1849.*

CALIFORNIAN   *USC mfm (May 22, 1847-Nov 11, 1848) 67.*

SAN FRANCISCO CHRONICLE   *USC mfm 1865-1903.*

SAN FRANCISCO EXAMINER   *USC mfm 1865 + .*

WESTERN OUTLOOK   *SCL mfm Jan 27, 1900.*

COLORADO

COLORADO SPRINGS

WESTERN ENTERPRISE   *SCL mfm Jan 6, 1900.*

CANON CITY

CANON TIMES   *USC mfm Dec 22, 1860.*

DENVER

CHERRY CREEK PIONEER   *USC mfm Apr 23, 1859.*

COLORADO STATESMAN   *SCL mfm Jan 27, 1900.*

STATESMAN   *SCL mfm Jan 27, 1900.*

GOLDEN CITY

WESTERN MOUNTAINEER   *USC mfm Dec 7, 1859.*

MOUNTAIN CITY

ROCKY MOUNTAIN GOLD REPORTER AND MOUNTAIN CITY HERALD   *USC mfm (Aug 6-Sep 17, 1859) 8.*

CONNECTICUT

HARTFORD

CONNECTICUT COURANT   *Clemson and USC mp Oct 1764-Dec 1820.*

MIDDLETOWN

MIDDLESEX GAZETTE   *USC mp ((1786-1804)) 135.*

NEW HAVEN

CONNECTICUT GAZETTE   *USC mfm ((Apr 12, 1755-Dec 15, 1759)) 200.*

NEW-HAVEN CHRONICLE   *USC mp Apr 1786-Sep 1787.*

NEW-HAVEN GAZETTE   *USC mp May 1784-Feb 1785.*

NEW-HAVEN GAZETTE, AND THE CONNECTICUT MAGAZINE
USC mp Feb 1786-Jun 1789.

NEW LONDON

CONNECTICUT GAZETTE   *USC mp Jan 1774-Oct 1793, Jan 1794-Dec 1820.*

NEW-LONDON GAZETTE   *USC mp ((Nov 1763-Oct 1773)) 320.*

NEW-LONDON SUMMARY   *USC mp Sep 1758-Sep 1763.*

DELAWARE

WILMINGTON

DELAWARE GAZETTE; OR, THE FAITHFUL CENTINEL   *USC mfm ((Jun 1785-Dec 1790)) 116.*

DISTRICT OF COLUMBIA

GEORGETOWN

COLUMBIAN CHRONICLE   *SCL mfm Mar 13, 1795.*

WASHINGTON

DAILY UNION   *USC mfm May 1845-Apr 1859.*

GLOBE   *USC mfm Dec 1830-Apr 1845.*

HARD TIMES   *USC mfm Oct 1968-Oct 1969.*

IMPARTIAL OBSERVER, AND WASHINGTON ADVERTISER   *SCL mfm Jun 12, Aug 21, Sep 14, 1795.*

MADISONIAN   *USC mfm Aug 1837-Jun 1845.*

NATIONAL INTELLIGENCER   *Camden Archives Feb 26, 1811-Jun 2, 1812; Newberry College Aug 1840-Apr 1842; USC mfm Oct 1800-Dec 1869; Winthrop mp 1800-1820; Wofford mfm Oct 15-Dec 31, 1859.*

NATIONAL REPUBLICAN   *USC mfm Jan-Jun 1885.*

SOUTHERN PRESS   *USC mfm Jun 1850-Aug 1852.*

UNITED STATES TELEGRAPH   *Clemson (1832-1836) 20; USC mfm Feb 1826-Feb 1837. Note: Clemson files contain two "country" editions--Mar 24, Apr 1, 1835.*

UNIVERSAL GAZETTE   *CLS Feb 18, 1814.*

WASHINGTON POST   *Anderson CL mfm 1986 + ; Charleston CL mfm 1972 + ; Clemson mfm 1877 + ; Converse mfm 1969 + ; Furman mfm 1979 + ; Greenville CL mfm 1972 + ; Richland CL mfm 1972-1983; SC State College mfm 1980 + ; USC mfm 1877 + ; USC-Spartanburg mfm 1985 + ; Winthrop mfm 1970 + .*

FLORIDA

JACKSONVILLE

FLORIDA EVANGELIST   *SCL mfm Jan 20, 1900.*

PENSACOLA

FLORIDA SENTINEL   *SCL mfm Jan 26, 1900.*

GEORGIA

ATHENS

HIWASSEAN, & ATHENS GAZETTE   *Clemson Mar 22, 1832.*

SOUTHERN WHIG   *Clemson Oct 1, 1835, Apr 7, May 21, 1836.*

ATLANTA

ATLANTA AGE   *SCL mfm Jan 13, 1900.*

ATLANTA CONSTITUTION   *Benedict mfm 1985 + ; Clemson mfm 1868 + ; College of Charleston mfm 1971 + ; Presbyterian mfm 1868-1876; Richland CL mfm 1977-1982; USC mfm 1868 + ; USC-Salkehatchie mfm 1984 + ; Winthrop mfm 1970 + .*

GATE CITY GUARDIAN   *Cherokee CL, Clemson, and Winthrop mfm Feb 12-Mar 2, 1861.*

SOUTHERN CONFEDERACY   *Cherokee CL, Clemson, Richland CL, and Winthrop mfm Mar 4, 1861-Feb 8, 1865.*

SUNNY SOUTH   *Clemson Jun 12, 1897.*

VOICE OF MISSIONS   *SCL mfm Feb 1, 1900.*

AUGUSTA

AUGUSTA CHRONICLE   *Clemson Aug 24, 1833; USC mfm ((1786-1841)), many gaps and frequent title changes; Winthrop mfm ((1852-1885)).*

AUGUSTA CHRONICLE AND GAZETTE OF THE STATE   *USC mfm ((Apr 11, 1789-May 24, 1794)), files virtually complete.*

AUGUSTA UNION   *SCL mfm Jan 27, 1900.*

DAILY CONSTITUTIONALIST   *Clemson Jan 20, 1871.*

DAILY TRANSCRIPT   *CLS Nov 11, 1865.*

GEORGIA COURIER   *Clemson Oct 19, Nov 31, 1832, Mar 22, Apr 5, 12, Oct 31, 1833. Note: All issues are "country" editions.*

GEORGIA STATE GAZETTE OR INDEPENDENT REGISTER   *USC mfm Oct 1786-Apr 1789.*

WEEKLY STATE RIGHTS' SENTINEL   *Clemson Apr 22, May 20, 1836.*

COLUMBUS

COLUMBUS CHRONICLE   *SCL mfm Jan 27, 1900.*

COLUMBUS ENQUIRER   *Clemson Dec 29, 1832 (fragment).*

MACON

GEORGIA MESSENGER   *Clemson Apr 14, 1836.*

MACON SENTINEL   *SCL mfm Jan 27, 1900.*

MILLEDGEVILLE

GEORGIA JOURNAL   *Clemson Jun 14, 1836.*

SOUTHERN RECORDER   *Clemson Feb 20, 1833, Mar 24, 1835.*

TIMES & STATE RIGHTS' ADVOCATE *Clemson Sep 29, 1835.*

NEW ECHOTA

CHEROKEE PHOENIX *USC mfm ((Feb 21, 1828-May 31, 1834)), virtually complete files in English and Cherokee.*

SAVANNAH

COLUMBIAN MUSEUM & SAVANNAH ADVERTISER *CLS Nov 23, 1798, Jul 1, 1800.*

DAILY MORNING NEWS *CLS Oct 11, 1862.*

GAZETTE OF THE STATE OF GEORGIA *USC mfm Jan 1783-Oct 1788. Index available at SCL.*

GEORGIA GAZETTE *Clemson mfm Apr 1763-1768; USC mfm Apr 1763-May 1770, ((1774-1776)) 100, Oct 1788-Nov 1796, mp Apr 1763-May 1770. Index available at SCL.*

ROYAL GEORGIA GAZETTE *USC mfm (1779-1780) 20, Jan-Dec 1781. Index available at SCL.*

SAVANNAH REPUBLICAN *Clemson mfm 1861-1865.*

SPARTA

STANDARD OF UNION AND FREE TRADE ADVOCATE *Clemson Jan 26, Mar 2, 23, Apr 6, 1833.*

WAYCROSS

GAZETTE AND LAND BULLETIN *SCL mfm Jan 27, 1900.*

ILLINOIS

CHICAGO

CHICAGO DAILY TRIBUNE *Greenville CL mfm 1972-1980; USC mfm 1849 + ; Winthrop mfm 1970 + .*

CHICAGO DEFENDER *USC mfm Apr 1921-Dec 1979.*

CHICAGO WORLD   *SCL mfm Jan 27, 1900.*

KASKASKIA

ILLINOIS HERALD   *USC mfm Dec 13, 1814.*

ILLINOIS INTELLIGENCER   *USC mfm May 27, 1818-May 12, 1819.*

WESTERN INTELLIGENCER   *USC mfm ((May 15, 1816-May 12, 1819)),*
   virtually complete files.

SPRINGFIELD

ILLINOIS JOURNAL   *Clemson Mar 22, 1876.*

INDIANA

VINCENNES

INDIANA GAZETTE   *USC mfm (Aug 7, 1804-Aug 14, 1805) 22.*

WESTERN SUN   *USC mfm Jul 1807-Nov 1809, Jan 1810-Jan 1813, Feb 1813-Sep*
   1815, Dec 1815-Dec 1816.

INDIANAPOLIS

WORLD   *SCL mfm Jan 27, 1900.*

IOWA

DES MOINES

GRANGE VISITOR   *Clemson Jun 25, 1881.*

DUBUQUE

DUBUQUE VISITOR   *USC mfm (May 11, 1836-Jun 16, 1838) 90.*

IOWA NEWS   *USC mfm Jun 3, 1837-Jun 16, 1838.*

KANSAS

PARSONS

PARSON'S WEEKLY BULLETIN   *SCL mfm Jan 26, 1900.*

TOPEKA

PLAINDEALER   *SCL mfm Jan 26, 1900.*

KENTUCKY

CARLISLE

CARLISLE MERCURY   *Winthrop mfm ((1867-1940)).*

FRANKFORT

KENTUCKY STATE JOURNAL   *Winthrop mfm May-Aug 1951.*

LEITCHFIELD

LEITCHFIELD GAZETTE   *Winthrop mfm ((1890-1946)). Files also contain issues of the Leitchfield Courier (1908-1910) and Grayson Gazette (1911).*

LEXINGTON

KENTUCKY GAZETTE   *USC mfm ((Aug 1787-Jul 1791)), files virtually complete.*

KENTUCKY REPORTER   *Winthrop mfm 1808-1821.*

LEXINGTON HERALD   *Winthrop mfm Sep 1966.*

LEXINGTON LEADER   *Winthrop mfm Dec 1965-Sep 1966.*

LEXINGTON STANDARD   *SCL mfm Jan 27, 1900.*

WESTERN MONITOR   *SCL mfm Oct 21, 1814-Nov 29, 1816.*

LOUISVILLE

COURIER-JOURNAL   *USC microcard Feb 15, 1949-Feb 14, 1952; Winthrop mfm May 1972-Dec 1974.*

MADISONVILLE

DAILY HUSTLER   *Winthrop mfm 1909.*

GLENN'S GRAPHIC   *Winthrop mfm ((1900-1902)).*

LOUISIANA

NEW ORLEANS

COURRIER DE LA LOUISIANE   *USC mfm (Apr 1811-Mar 1812) 69.*

LOUISIANA GAZETTE   *USC mfm ((Jul 1804-Jan 1812)).*

MONITEUR DE LA LOUISIANE   *USC mfm Aug 1802-Nov 1803, Jan-Jul 1811, Oct 1811-Mar 1812.*

REPUBLICAN COURIER   *SCL mfm Jan 27, 1900.*

SOUTHERN REPUBLICAN   *SCL mfm Feb 8, 1900.*

TIMES-PICAYUNE   *Clemson mfm Dec 15, 1857-Mar 2, 1866; Greenville CL mfm 1972-1981; USC mfm 1837 + ; Winthrop mfm 1970-1977.*

VIDALIA

CONCORDIA INTELLIGENCER   *USC mfm Aug 12, 1843-Jun 8, 1844.*

MAINE

FALMOUTH

CUMBERLAND GAZETTE   *USC mfm Apr 7-Jul 13, 1786.*

FALMOUTH GAZETTE AND WEEKLY ADVERTISER   *USC mfm Jan 1, 1785-Mar 30, 1786.*

PORTLAND

CUMBERLAND GAZETTE   *USC mfm ((Jul 20, 1786-Dec 26, 1791)).*

EASTERN ARGUS   *Clemson Aug 19, 1812.*

MARYLAND

ANNAPOLIS

MARYLAND GAZETTE   *USC mfm ((1745-1839)), files virtually complete.*

BALTIMORE

AFRO-AMERICAN   *SC State College mfm Dec 1949 + ; Voorhees mfm 1969-1983; Winthrop mfm Mar 30, 1946-Aug 9, 1947.*

BALTIMORE MORNING SUN   *USC mfm Dec 16-31, 1940, Sep 16-30, 1963.*

LUTHERAN OBSERVER   *Newberry College 1831-1833, 1840-1847.*

MARYLAND JOURNAL   *Clemson mfm Aug 20, 1773-Jul 1, 1797.*

NEGRO APPEAL   *SCL mfm Feb 16, 1900.*

EASTON

MARYLAND HERALD, AND EASTERN SHORE INTELLIGENCER
SCL mfm Aug 6, Sep 24, Oct 1-22, 1799.

SILVER SPRING

NATIONAL OBSERVER   *Clemson, USC, and Winthrop mfm 1962-1977; Richland CL mfm 1973-1977.*

MASSACHUSETTS

BOSTON

AMERICAN HERALD   *USC mp Jan 1784-Jun 1788.*

BOSTON ADVANCE   *SCL mfm Feb 17, 1900.*

BOSTON CHRONICLE   *USC mp Oct 1767-Jun 1770.*

BOSTON COURANT   *SCL mfm Jan 6, 1900.*

BOSTON DAILY ADVERTISER   *Clemson mfm Jan 1862-Dec 1865; USC mfm 1836-1844.*

BOSTON EVENING-POST   *USC mp Aug 1735-Apr 1775.*

BOSTON EVENING-POST: AND THE GENERAL ADVERTISER
USC mp Oct 1781-Jan 1784.

BOSTON GAZETTE   *USC mp Dec 1719-Sep 1798.*

BOSTON NEWS-LETTER   *Clemson mfm ((1704-1776)); USC mfm and mp ((1704-1776)). Title varies: Boston News-Letter 1704-1726; Weekly News-Letter 1727-1730; Boston Weekly News-Letter 1730-1757; Boston News-Letter 1757-1762; Boston News-Letter and New-England Chronicle 1762-1763; Massachusetts Gazette. And Boston News-Letter 1763-1768; Boston Weekly News-Letter 1768-1769; Massachusetts Gazette: and the Boston Weekly News-Letter 1769-1776.*

BOSTON NEWS-LETTER AND NEW-ENGLAND CHRONICLE   *see Boston News-Letter.*

BOSTON POST-BOY   *USC mp Apr 1735-Apr 1775.*

BOSTON WEEKLY NEWS-LETTER   *see Boston News-Letter.*

CENSOR   *USC mp Nov 1771-May 1772.*

CHRISTIAN SCIENCE MONITOR   *Clemson mfm 1908 + ; College of Charleston mfm 1922 + ; Converse mfm 1960 + ; Erskine mfm 1960 + ; Francis Marion mfm 1954 + ; Furman mfm 1982 + ; Greenville CL mfm 1981 + ; Morris mfm 1977 + ; Richland CL mfm 1974 + ; USC mfm 1908 + ; Winthrop mfm 1960 + .*

COLUMBIAN CENTINEL   *CLS Dec 5, 1795.*

CONTINENTAL JOURNAL, AND WEEKLY ADVERTISER   *USC mp May 1776-Jun 1787.*

INDEPENDENT CHRONICLE   *USC mp Apr 1776-Dec 1820.*

INDEPENDENT LEDGER, AND THE AMERICAN ADVERTISER   *USC mp Jun 1778-Oct 1786.*

LIBERATOR   *Benedict mfm Jan 1831-Dec 1865.*

MASSACHUSETTS GAZETTE   *Clemson and USC mfm Jul-Oct 1788; USC mp Feb 1786-Nov 1788.*

MASSACHUSETTS GAZETTE. AND BOSTON NEWS-LETTER   *see Boston News-Letter.*

MASSACHUSETTS GAZETTE; AND THE BOSTON WEEKLY NEWS-LETTER   *see Boston News-Letter.*

MASSACHUSETTS SPY   *USC mp Jul 1770-Apr 1775.*

NEW-ENGLAND COURANT   *USC mp Aug 1721-Jun 1726.*

NEW-ENGLAND WEEKLY JOURNAL   *USC mp Oct 1731-Jun 1741.*

POLAR STAR: BOSTON DAILY ADVERTISER   *Furman mfm ((Oct 6, 1796-Jan 1798)).*

WEEKLY NEWS-LETTER   *see Boston News-Letter.*

WEEKLY REHEARSAL   *USC mp Sep 1731-Aug 1735.*

CAMBRIDGE

NEW-ENGLAND CHRONICLE   *USC mp Jun 1775-Apr 1776.*

NEW BEDFORD

NEW BEDFORD GAZETTE   *Clemson Apr 23, 1832.*

NEWBURYPORT

ESSEX JOURNAL   *USC mp Dec 1773-Feb 1777, Jul 1784-Apr 1794.*

PITTSFIELD

PITTSFIELD SUN   *CLS Dec 20, 1832.*

SALEM

ESSEX GAZETTE   *USC mp Aug 1768-Jun 1775.*

SALEM GAZETTE   *USC mp Jan 1781-Feb 1786.*

SALEM GAZETTE   *CLS Sep 20, 1805.* <u>*Note*</u>*: Paper established 1790.*

SPRINGFIELD

SPRINGFIELD REPUBLICAN   *USC mfm 1850, 1852-1853, 1860-1870.*

WORCESTER

AMERICAN HERALD   *USC mp Aug 1788-Oct 1789.*

MASSACHUSETTS SPY   *USC mp May 1775-Mar 1786, Apr 1788-Dec 1820.*

MICHIGAN

DETROIT

DETROIT INFORMER   *SCL mfm Jan 13, 1900.*

MISSISSIPPI

BRANDON

FREE SOUTH   *SCL mfm Jan 20, 1900.*

CLINTON

MISSISSIPPIAN   *Clemson Mar 1, 1833.*

FAYETTE

FAYETTE CHRONICLE *Winthrop mfm ((1907-1911)).*

LOUISVILLE

WINSTON COUNTY JOURNAL *Winthrop mfm ((1893-1913)).*

NATCHEZ

MISSISSIPPI HERALD & NATCHEZ GAZETTE *USC mfm (Apr 15, 1806-Jun 10, 1807) 10.*

MISSISSIPPI MESSENGER *USC mfm (Sep 1805-Aug 1808) 85.*

WEEKLY CHRONICLE *USC mfm (Jul 1808-Jul 1810), virtually complete files.*

VICKSBURG

GOLDEN RULE *SCL mfm Jan 27, 1900.*

LIGHT *SCL mfm Jan 18, 1900.*

MISSOURI

KANSAS CITY

KANSAS CITY OBSERVER *SCL mfm Jan 27, 1900.*

KANSAS CITY TIMES *USC mfm Mar-Jun, Sep-Nov 1917.*

MISSOURI MESSENGER *SCL mfm Jan 26, 1900.*

RISING SUN *SCL mfm Jan 27, 1900.*

ST. LOUIS

ST. LOUIS REVEILLE *USC mfm 1844-1850.*

NEBRASKA

BELLEVIEW CITY

NEBRASKA PALLADIUM   *USC mfm (Jul 1854-Apr 1855) 25.*

OMAHA

ENTERPRISE   *SCL mfm Jan 12, 1900.*

PROGRESS   *SCL mfm Jan 26, 1900.*

NEW HAMPSHIRE

MANCHESTER

DEMOCRAT   *CLS Dec 13, 1840.*

PORTSMOUTH

NEW HAMPSHIRE GAZETTE   *Clemson and USC mfm ((1756-1789)); USC mp ((1756-1820)). Title varies.*

NEW JERSEY

BRIDGETON

EAST-JERSEY REPUBLICAN   *Clemson mp May 22-Jul 3, 1816.*

WASHINGTON WHIG   *Clemson mp Jul 24, 1815-Dec 25, 1820.*

BURLINGTON

NEW JERSEY GAZETTE   *Clemson and USC mfm Dec 5, 1777-Mar 4, 1778.*

CHATHAM

NEW-JERSEY JOURNAL   *Clemson mfm Feb 16, 1779-Nov 25, 1783.*

ELIZABETH TOWN

NEW-JERSEY JOURNAL, AND POLITICAL INTELLIGENCER
Clemson mfm May 10, 1786-Feb 27, 1821; USC mfm ((Oct 18, 1786-Apr 20, 1791)). Paper issued as the New-Jersey Journal after Jun 1792.

POLITICAL INTELLIGENCER   *Clemson mfm Apr 20, 1785-May 3, 1786.*

MOUNT PLEASANT

JERSEY CHRONICLE   *Clemson mfm May 2, 1795-Apr 30, 1796.*

NEW BRUNSWICK

GUARDIAN; OR, NEW-BRUNSWICK ADVERTISER   *Clemson mfm Oct 30, 1798-Oct 22, 1801, Sep 1, 1808-Oct 7, 1813.*

POLITICAL INTELLIGENCER   *Clemson mfm Oct 14, 1783-Apr 5, 1785. Paper also published in Elizabeth Town.*

NEWARK

CENTINEL OF FREEDOM   *Clemson mfm Oct 1796-Aug 1826.*

WOODS'S NEWARK GAZETTE   *Clemson mfm 1791-1793.*

PATERSON

BEE AND PATERSON ADVERTISER   *Clemson mfm Jan 23, Mar 26, Jul 2, 1816.*

TRENTON

NEW-JERSEY GAZETTE   *Clemson and USC mfm Mar 1778-Nov 1786.*

NEW-JERSEY STATE GAZETTE   *Clemson mfm Sep 12, 1792-Jan 3, 1797.*

NEW YORK

HUDSON

BALANCE, AND COLUMBIAN REPOSITORY   *CLS May 15, Oct 2, 1804.*

KINGSTON

NEW-YORK JOURNAL, AND THE GENERAL ADVERTISER *Benedict mfm ((1777-1782)). Paper also issued in Poughkeepsie.*

NEW YORK CITY

BROTHER JONATHAN *CLS Jul 4, 1848.*

CHRISTIAN ADVOCATE AND JOURNAL *Wofford 1826-1837, 1883-1896, mfm 1826-1876.*

COLORED AMERICAN *Benedict mfm Mar 1840-Mar 1841.*

DAY BOOK *Benedict mfm Jan 1852-Aug 1861; CLS Nov 28, 1863. Paper also issued as New York Day Book and Evening Day Book.*

FREEDOM'S JOURNAL *Benedict mfm Mar 1827-Dec 1829.*

GREENLEAF'S NEW YORK JOURNAL AND PATRIOTIC REGISTER *Winthrop mfm 1794-1797.*

JOURNAL OF COMMERCE *Clemson mfm 1980 + ; USC mfm 1948-1981.*

LIBERATOR *Benedict mfm Dec 7, 1929-Dec 15, 1932. Files cover vol 1-3 of official organ of the League of Struggle for Negro Rights.*

METHODIST *Wofford Jan-Dec 1872.*

METROPOLITAN RECORD AND NEW YORK VINDICATOR *CLS Dec 16, 1865, Apr 14, 1866.*

MORNING TELEGRAPH *USC mfm Jan 1928-Jan 1933.*

NATIONAL ANTI-SLAVERY STANDARD *Benedict mfm 1840-1871.*

NEGRO WORLD *Benedict mfm Jul 1926-Jun 1933.*

NEW LEADER *USC mfm Jan 19, 1924-Apr 29, 1950.*

NEW YORK AGE *Benedict mfm 1905-1957.*

NEW YORK COMMERCIAL ADVERTISER *Furman mfm (1801-1803) 15.*

NEW YORK DAILY ADVERTISER *Furman mfm (May 1-31, 1802) 15.*

NEW YORK EVANGELIST *CLS (Jan 1830-Oct 1832) 60.*

NEW-YORK EVENING POST *Benedict mfm 1804-1866, 1897-1899; Claflin mfm Jan 1856-Dec 1860; Furman mfm (Nov 16, 1801-Jan 1802) 45; USC mfm May 1-Jun 12, 1929.*

NEW-YORK GAZETTE [WILLIAM BRADFORD'S] *Benedict mfm ((1726-1744)).*

NEW-YORK GAZETTE [WEYMAN'S] *USC mp Feb 1759-Dec 1767.*

NEW-YORK GAZETTE; AND WEEKLY MERCURY *Benedict mfm and USC mp Jan 1768-Nov 1783.*

NEW YORK HERALD *CLS Jan 28, 1859, Apr 15, 1865; USC mfm Aug 1835-Dec 1868.*

NEW YORK HERALD-TRIBUNE *USC mfm Apr 19, 1924-Apr 24, 1966.*

NEW YORK-JOURNAL; OR GENERAL ADVERTISER *USC mp Oct 1766-Aug 1776.*

NEW-YORK MERCURY *Benedict mfm and USC mp Aug 1752-Jan 1768.*

NEW YORK OBSERVER *Clemson Feb 25, Apr 9, 1858.*

NEW YORK TRIBUNE *USC mfm Apr 1841-Mar 1924; Winthrop mfm 1875-1906. Index (mfm) available at USC, 1875-1906.*

NEW YORK SUNDAY MERCURY *Benedict mfm ((1841-1864)).*

NEW YORK TIMES *Baptist College, Citadel, Clemson, Columbia College, Converse, Francis Marion, Furman, Greenville CL, Lander, Newberry College, Presbyterian, Richland CL, USC, USC-Aiken, USC-Coastal, Winthrop, and Wofford mfm 1851 + ; Anderson CL mfm 1970 + ; Benedict mfm 1924 + ; Bob Jones mfm 1914 + ; Charleston CL mfm 1929 + ; Claflin mfm 1963 + ; Coker mfm 1963 + ; College of Charleston mfm 1896 + ; Columbia Bible College mfm 1983 + ; Erskine mfm 1914-1977; Florence CL mfm 1966-1970; Hartsville Library mfm 1973-1974; Limestone mfm 1973 + ; Morris mfm 1967-Feb 1969, 1976 + ; SC State College mfm 1939 + ; SC State Library mfm 1958 + ; Spartanburg CL mfm 1977 + ; Spartanburg Methodist College mfm 1982 + ; USC-Salkehatchie mfm 1970 + ; USC-Spartanburg mfm 1960 + ; .USC-Sumter mfm 1952 + ; USC-Union mfm 1977 + ; Voorhees mfm 1970 + ; York CL mfm 1972-1978.*

NEW-YORK WEEKLY JOURNAL *USC mp Oct 1733-Mar 1751.*

NEW YORK WEEKLY TRIBUNE *Coker 1861-1863; USC mfm 1841-1854.*

NOVYI MIR: EZHEDNEVNAIA RABOCHAIA GAZETA *USC mfm* *(1916-1917) [see Menshevik Collection, reels 61-63].*

PM *USC mfm Jun 18, 1940-Jun 22, 1948.*

PORTER'S SPIRIT OF THE TIMES *USC mfm Jul 10-Aug 7, 1858.*

PROTESTANT VINDICATOR *Newberry College Jul 1835-Jun 1838. Paper also issued as the American Protestant Vindicator.*

RIVINGTON'S NEW-YORK GAZETTE. *Benedict and Clemson mfm ((1773-1783)); USC mp Apr 1773-Nov 1775, 1777-1783. Frequent title changes. Also issued as Rivington's New-York Gazetteer, Royal Gazette, and Rivington's New-York Royal Gazette.*

SPANISH REVOLUTION *USC [reprint] Aug 19, 1936-May 1, 1938.*

STANDARD [HENRY GEORGE] *USC mfm Jan 8, 1887-Aug 31, 1892.*

SUN *Benedict mfm Oct 1859-Feb 1867; USC mfm Nov 1889-Dec 1903. Note: USC files include both morning and evening editions.*

VILLAGE VOICE *College of Charleston mfm 1981 + ; USC and Winthrop mfm 1955 + .*

WALL STREET JOURNAL *Anderson CL mfm 1986 + ; Baptist College mfm 1966 + ; Charleston CL mfm 1958 + ; Clemson, USC, and USC-Aiken mfm Jul 1889-Dec 1891, Jul 1892 + ; College of Charleston mfm 1958 + ; Converse mfm 1968 + ; Florence CL mfm 1972 + ; Francis Marion mfm 1958 + ; Furman mfm 1975 + ; Greenville CL mfm 1958 + ; Newberry College mfm 1975 + ; Richland CL mfm 1973 + ; SC State College mfm 1979-1984; USC-Coastal mfm 1968 + ; USC-Spartanburg mfm 1960 + ; Winthrop mfm 1925 + .*

WALL STREET TRANSCRIPT *USC mfm Jan 1970-Sep 1981.*

WEEKLY ANGLO-AFRICAN *SCL mfm Jul 23, 1859-Jul 14, 1860.*

WOMEN'S WEAR DAILY *Winthrop mfm 1971 + .*

WORLD *CLS Apr 4, May 6, 1863; Benedict mfm 1861-1866, 1898-1899; USC mfm Dec 15, 1919-Feb 27, 1931.*

NORTH CAROLINA

ASHEVILLE

ASHEVILLE DAILY CITIZEN   *Clemson Sep 21, 1899.*

ASHEVILLE NEWS AND MOUNTAINEER FARMER   *SCL mfm Jul 16, 1869.*

CHARLOTTE

AFRO-AMERICAN PRESBYTERIAN   *SCL mfm Dec 21, 1899.*

CHARLOTTE DEMOCRAT   *Winthrop mfm ((1853-1897)). Paper also issued as the Western Democrat and the Charlotte Home and Democrat.*

CHARLOTTE OBSERVER   *Clemson and USC mfm Mar 1892 + ; Converse mfm 1969-1976; Winthrop mfm 1952 + .*

EDENTON

EDENTON GAZETTE   *USC mfm Nov 19, Dec 11, 1800, Apr 9, 1801.*

EDENTON INTELLIGENCER   *USC mfm Apr 9, Jun 4, 1788.*

ENCYCLOPEDIAN INSTRUCTOR, AND FARMER'S GAZETTE   *USC mfm May 21, 1800.*

NORTH-CAROLINA GAZETTE; OR THE EDENTON INTELLIGENCER   *USC mfm Dec 19, 1787.*

POST-ANGEL, OR UNIVERSAL ENTERTAINMENT   *USC mfm Sep 10, Nov 12, 1800.*

STATE GAZETTE OF NORTH-CAROLINA   *USC mfm (1790-1791) 40.*

FAYETTEVILLE

FAYETTEVILLE GAZETTE   *USC mfm (1789, 1792-1793) 30.*

NORTH-CAROLINA CENTINEL   *USC mfm Jul 25, Aug 8, 15, 29, 1795.*

NORTH-CAROLINA CHRONICLE; OR, FAYETTEVILLE GAZETTE   *USC mfm (Feb 1790-Mar 1791) 35.*

HILLSBOROUGH

NORTH-CAROLINA GAZETTE   *USC mfm Oct 6, 1785, Feb 16, 1786.*

NEW BERN

MARTIN'S NORTH-CAROLINA GAZETTE   *USC mfm Jul 11, Dec 19, 1787.*

NEWBERN GAZETTE   *USC mfm (1798-1804) 12.*

NORTH-CAROLINA GAZETTE   *Clemson and USC mfm ((1751-1759, 1768-1778, 1783-1798)).*

NORTH-CAROLINA MAGAZINE   *USC mfm (Jun 1764-Jan 1765) 28.*

PINEVILLE

PINEVILLE PIONEER   *Winthrop Dec 5, 1979 [vol 1, no 1].*

ROCK HILL TIMES   *Established in Rock Hill, S. C., in 1970, paper moved to Pineville in 1985. See Rock Hill Times in SC section.*

RALEIGH

CAROLINA ERA   *USC mfm Jun 1871-Dec 1876. Paper also issued as the Weekly Era and the Tri-Weekly Era.*

GAZETTE   *SCL mfm (Apr 17, 1897-Feb 19, 1898) 39.*

SENTINEL   *USC mfm Jun 1866-Dec 1871. Paper also issued as the Weekly Sentinel.*

STAR, AND NORTH CAROLINA GAZETTE   *Clemson Jan 18, Feb 15, 1833.*

WEEKLY NORTH CAROLINA STANDARD   *USC mfm Jan 1856-Dec 1870.*

RUTHERFORDTON

CAROLINA GAZETTE   *Clemson Jun 30, 1836.*

NORTH CAROLINA SPECTATOR AND WESTERN ADVERTISER   *Clemson Mar 2, 16, Apr 3, 1833.*

RUTHERFORDTON STAR   *USC mfm May 1866-Apr 1872.*

SALISBURY

NORTH-CAROLINA MERCURY, AND SALISBURY ADVERTISER
USC mfm (1799-1801) 45.

WESTERN CAROLINIAN   *Clemson Dec 24, 1832, Jan 14, Feb 25, Apr 22, 1833.*

WESTERN VINDICATOR   *Clemson Sep 25, 1871.*

YADKIN & CATAWBA JOURNAL   *Clemson Mar 25, Apr 4, 1833.*

WILMINGTON

CAPE-FEAR MERCURY   *USC mfm (1769-1775) 14.*

DAILY JOURNAL   *Clemson mfm Jan 2, 1860-Jul 14, 1866.*

HALL'S WILMINGTON GAZETTE   *USC mfm (1797-1798) 29.*

NORTH-CAROLINA GAZETTE   *USC mfm (1765-1766) 5.*

WILMINGTON CENTINEL, AND GENERAL ADVERTISER   *USC mfm (Jun 1788-Mar 1789) 34.*

WILMINGTON CHRONICLE   *USC mfm (Jul 1795-Mar 1796) 20.*

WILMINGTON GAZETTE   *USC mfm ((1799-1816)).*

WILMINGTON POST   *USC mfm Aug 1867-May 1868, May 1872-Aug 1875.*

OHIO

CINCINNATI

CINCINNATI DAILY COMMERCIAL   *Benedict mfm Apr 1861-Dec 1865.*

CENTINEL OF THE NORTH-WESTERN TERRITORY   *USC mfm (Nov 1793-Jan 1795) 42.*

CLEVELAND

GAZETTE   *SCL mfm Jan 13, Apr 6, 1900, Apr 13, 1901.*

XENIA

OHIO STANDARD AND OBSERVER   *SCL mfm Jan 27, 1900.*

OKLAHOMA

LANGSTON CITY

LANGSTON CITY HERALD   *SCL mfm Jan 27, 1900.*

TAHLEQUAH

CHEROKEE ADVOCATE   *USC mfm Oct 29, 1846, Dec 9, 1847, Jun 5, Aug 14, 1848.*

OREGON

OREGON CITY

OREGON SPECTATOR   *USC mfm Feb 5, 1846-May 30, 1851.*

PENNSYLVANIA

LANCASTER

PENNSYLVANIA PACKET   *Clemson mfm and USC mp Nov 1777-Jun 1778. See also, Pennsylvania Packet [Philadelphia].*

PHILADELPHIA

AMERICAN WEEKLY MERCURY   *USC mp Dec 1719-May 1746.*

CAREY'S DAILY ADVERTISER   *see Daily Advertiser.*

CHRISTIAN BANNER   *SCL mfm Jan 12, 1900.*

CONSTITUTIONAL DIARY AND PHILADELPHIA EVENING ADVERTISER   *Furman mfm (Dec 1799-Jan 1800) 9.*

DAILY ADVERTISER   *Furman mfm Feb-Sep 1797. Paper issued as Carey's Daily Advertiser Jul-Sep 1797.*

DEFENDER   *SCL mfm Jan 27, 1900.*

FREEMAN'S JOURNAL   *Clemson mfm Apr 1781-Jul 1785; USC mp Apr 1781-May 1792.*

LEVEL OF EUROPE AND NORTH AMERICA   *USC mp Oct 1794-Feb 1795.*

NATIONAL GAZETTE   *Clemson mfm and USC mp Oct 1791-Oct 1793.*

NATIONAL GAZETTE AND LITERARY REGISTER   *CLS Nov 15, 1831.*

PENNSYLVANIA CHRONICLE, AND UNIVERSAL ADVERTISER   *USC mp Jan 1767-Feb 1774.*

PENNSYLVANIA EVENING POST   *Clemson mfm Jan 1775-Dec 1779; USC mp Jan 1775-Oct 1784.*

PENNSYLVANIA GAZETTE   *CLS Mar 8, 1775; USC mfm Dec 1728-Oct 1815, [reprint] 1728-1789.*

PENNSYLVANIA LEDGER   *Clemson mfm Jan 28, 1775-May 23, 1778.*

PENNSYLVANIA PACKET   *Clemson mfm and USC mp Oct 1771-Sep 1777, Jul 1778-Dec 1790. Paper issued in Lancaster Nov 1777-Jun 1778.*

PHILADELPHIA MINERVA   *USC mp Feb 1795-Jul 1798.*

PHILADELPHIA RECORD   *USC mfm Aug 3-13, 1883.*

PORCUPINE'S GAZETTE   *CLS Jan 8, 1798.*

POULSON'S AMERICAN DAILY ADVERTISER   *CLS Oct 21, 1800, Clemson Nov 23, 1832.*

PUBLIC LEDGER   *CLS Mar 25, 1836.*

UNITED STATES GAZETTE   *CLS Jul 9, 1827.*

PITTSBURGH

PITTSBURGH COURIER   *Benedict mfm 1923-1961; Claflin mfm 1923 + ; Morris 1980 + ; SC State College mfm 1923-1982; USC mfm 1911-1981; Voorhees mfm*

1923-1981; Winthrop mfm 1931-1932. Paper also issued as the <u>New Pittsburgh Courier</u>.

SCHUYLKILL HAVEN

WEEKLY LEDGER   *CLS Apr 23, 1853-Oct 7, 1854.*

YORK

YORK DEMOCRATIC PRESS   *USC mfm Jun 1839-Dec 1862.*

RHODE ISLAND

NEWPORT

NEWPORT MERCURY   *USC mfm Jan 1763-Apr 1766.*

NEWPORT MERCURY, OR, THE WEEKLY ADVERTISER   *USC mfm (Jan 1758-Dec 1762) 48.*

PROVIDENCE

PROVIDENCE GAZETTE   *USC mp Aug 1762-Oct 1825.*

TENNESSEE

COLUMBIA

WESTERN CHRONICLE   *SCL mfm Nov 17, 1810.*

JACKSON

JACKSON HEADLIGHT   *SCL mfm Jan 27, 1900.*

MEMPHIS

MEMPHIS DAILY APPEAL *Clemson mfm Jul 18, 1857-May 4, 1866.*

NASHVILLE

CHRISTIAN ADVOCATE *Wofford 1890-1906.*

COLORED TENNESSEAN *SCL mfm (1865-1866) 6.*

TEXAS

AUSTIN

FREE MAN'S PRESS *SCL mfm (1868) 7.*

MEXICAN CITIZEN *USC mfm Mar 17, 24, Apr 21, May 26, 1831.*

TEXAS GAZETTE *USC mfm (Sep 1829-Feb 1832) 51.*

BRAZORIA

ADVOCATE OF THE PEOPLE'S RIGHTS *USC mfm Feb 22, 1834.*

CONSTITUTIONAL ADVOCATE AND TEXAS PUBLIC ADVERTISER *USC mfm Sep 5, 1832, Jun 15, 1833.*

TEXAS REPUBLICAN *USC mfm (Jul 1834-Nov 1835) 37.*

CORSICANNA

OIL CITY AFRO-AMERICAN *SCL mfm Jan 27, 1900.*

DALLAS

DALLAS EXPRESS *SCL mfm Jan 13, 1900.*

ITEM *SCL mfm Jan 27, 1900.*

HOUSTON

INDEPENDENT *SCL mfm Jan 27, 1900.*

WESTERN STAR   *SCL mfm Jan 27, 1900.*

NACHITOCHEE

EL MEXICANO   *USC mfm Jun 19, 1813.*

NACOGDOCHES

GACETA DE TEXAS   *USC mfm May 25, 1813.*

SAN FELIPE DE AUSTIN

TELEGRAPH AND TEXAS REGISTER   *USC mfm Oct 10, 1835-Apr 14, 1836.*

WACO

PAUL QUINN WEEKLY   *SCL mfm Jan 27, 1900.*

VERMONT

BENNINGTON

VERMONT GAZETTE   *USC mfm ((Jun 7, 1784-May 24, 1793)), files virtually complete.*

VERMONT GAZETTE, OR FREEMAN'S DEPOSITORY   *USC mfm Jun 5, 1783-May 24, 1784.*

ST. JOHNSBURY

FARMERS HERALD   *USC mfm Jul 1828-Dec 1832.*

WINDSOR

VERMONT JOURNAL, AND THE UNIVERSAL ADVERTISER   *USC mfm Aug 7, 1783-Jul 26, 1785.*

VIRGINIA

FREDERICKSBURG

GENIUS OF LIBERTY   *SCL mfm Nov 13, 1798, May 3, 1799.*

LYNCHBURG

LYNCHBURG DAILY VIRGINIAN   *Clemson mfm Aug 3, 1858-Aug 31, 1866.*

NORFOLK

JOURNAL AND GUIDE   *Voorhees mfm 1969-1982; Winthrop mfm Jul-Dec 1946.*

PETERSBURG

NATIONAL PILOT   *SCL mfm Feb 1, 1900.*

RICHMOND

DAILY DISPATCH   *Clemson mfm Jan 1859-Dec 1866; Wofford mfm Jul 1864-Dec 1865.*

DAILY RICHMOND EXAMINER   *Clemson Mar 2, Jun 16, Sep 27, 1863.*

JEFFERSONIAN AND VIRGINIA TIMES   *Clemson (Apr 1832-Jul 1833) 28.*

RECORD OF NEWS, HISTORY AND LITERATURE   *SCL Jun 18-Dec 10, 1863.*

REFORMER   *SCL mfm Jan 27, 1900.*

RICHMOND ENQUIRER   *Camden Archives Nov 3, 1820-Dec 28, 1821; CLS Mar 27, 1863; Clemson (Oct 1861-Mar 1863) 7; USC mfm May 1804-Jan 1867; Wofford mfm Oct-Dec 1859.*

RICHMOND WHIG   *Clemson Aug 21, 1862, mfm Jan 1, 1860-Jul 31, 1865.*

RICHMOND WHIG & PUBLIC ADVERTISER   *Clemson (Feb 1834-Jun 1835) 19.*

SENTINEL   *Clemson Apr 15, Sep 5, 1863.*

TIMES   *Clemson mfm Sep-Dec 1890.*

TIMES-DISPATCH   *CLS Apr 13, 1908.*

VIRGINIA GAZETTE: AND RICHMOND DAILY ADVERTISER
    Furman mfm (Oct-Dec 1792) 14.

SPRINGFIELD

AIR FORCE TIMES   *Shaw Air Force Base microfiche Jul 28, 1980 + .*

ARMY TIMES   *Fort Jackson 1983 + ; SC State College mfm 1940-1977.*

STAUNTON

LUTHERAN VISITOR   *Newberry College orig & mfm Jan 1866-Jun 1868.*

WILLIAMSBURG

VIRGINIA GAZETTE   *CLS, Clemson, and USC mfm ((1736-1780)).*

WASHINGTON

SEATTLE

SEATTLE REPUBLICAN   *SCL mfm Jan 19, 1900.*

WORLD   *SCL mfm Jan 4, 1899.*

WISCONSIN

MILWAUKEE

EMANCIPATOR   *Benedict mfm May 19-Sep 8, 1877.*

MILWAUKEE JOURNAL   *USC mfm 1884 + .*

MILWAUKEE LEADER   *USC mfm ((Nov 29, 1929-Jan 14, 1939)), files virtually*
    complete.

WYOMING

CHEYENNE

CHEYENNE LEADER   *USC mfm Sep 19, 1867-Sep 19, 1868.*

APPENDIX 2

FOREIGN NEWSPAPER FILES IN SOUTH CAROLINA

Except for a few standard items such as the London Times, most of these collections have been created by individual researchers associated with various colleges and universities throughout the state.

ANTIGUA AND BARBUDA

ST. JOHN'S

WORKER'S VOICE   *Benedict mfm ((1965-1967)).*

ARGENTINA

BUENOS AIRES

LA PRENSA   *USC mfm Jan 1969-Dec 1974.*

BAHAMAS

NASSAU

NASSAU GUARDIAN   *Clemson mfm Jan 1863-Dec 1866.*

BRAZIL

RECIFE

A LUTA   *USC mfm (Jan-Aug 1948).*

O POPULAR   *USC mfm (Aug 28-Nov 27, 1948).*

SAO PAULO

ACAO SOCIALISTA   *USC mfm (Dec 1958-Aug 1960) 8.*

FOHLA SOCIALISTA   *USC mfm Nov 27, 1947.*

O ESTADO DE SAO PAULO   *USC mfm Feb 1966-Apr 1975.*

ORIENTACAO SOCIALISTA   *USC mfm Nov 5, 1946, Mar 1, May 1, Jun 20, 1947.*

REHENSA SOCIALISTA   *USC mfm Jul 1956.*

RIO DE JANEIRO

IMPRENSA POPULAR   *USC mfm Jan 1951-Aug 1958.*

VANGUARDA SOCIALISTA   *USC mfm Sep 1945-Aug 1948.*

BRITISH HONDURAS [Belize]

BELIZE

BELIZE ADVERTISER   *USC mfm Jun 29, 1839-Jan 11, 1840, May 21, 1881-Oct 25, 1884, Dec 25, 1886-Jan 1, 1887, Jul 28, 1888-Apr 27, 1889.*

BELIZE ADVERTISER AND BRITISH HONDURAS GAZETTE   *USC mfm Feb 27, 1887-May 19, 1888.*

BELIZE INDEPENDENT   *USC mfm Oct 11-Dec 27, 1888, Apr 26, 1894-Apr 17, 1896.*

BRITISH HONDURAS COLONIST AND BELIZE ADVERTISER   *USC mfm Jul 20, 1867-Nov 28, 1868.*

CENTRAL AMERICAN TELEGRAPH   *USC mfm Mar 26, Apr 10, 25, May 10, 28, 1873.*

COLONIAL GUARDIAN   *USC mfm Jan 7, 1882-Mar 30, 1907.*

COLONIST   *USC mfm ((Dec 31, 1864-Aug 25, 1866)), files virtually complete.*

COMMERCIAL ADVERTISER   *USC mfm Jul 3-Aug 28, 1867.*

HONDURAS GAZETTE & COMMERCIAL ADVERTISER   *USC mfm Jul 1, 1826-Jun 30, 1827.*

NEW ERA, AND BRITISH HONDURAS CHRONICLE   *USC mfm Feb 11, 1871-Feb 24, 1872.*

TIMES OF CENTRAL AMERICA   *USC mfm ((Aug 31, 1894-Dec 26, 1896)), files virtually complete.*

CAMEROON

VICTORIA

CAMEROON OUTLOOK   *USC ((Aug 1972-Jul 1976)) 500.*

CAMEROON TIMES   *USC Jan 1971-Jun 1973, ((Jul 1973-May 1977)), Jun 1977-Jul 1978.*

NEW CAMEROON   *USC Sep-Dec 1970.*

YAOUNDE

CAMEROON TRIBUNE   [daily, in French]   *USC Jul-Dec 1975, ((Jan-Apr 1976)) 100.*

CAMEROON TRIBUNE   [weekly, in English]   *USC (Oct 1975-Sep 1976) 44.*

L'EFFORT CAMEROUNAIS   *USC Jan 1973-Jan 1975.*

L'UNITE   *USC Jan-Dec 1972, ((Jan 1973-Feb 1980)).*

CHINA

PEKING [Beijing]

JEN MIN JIH PAO [People's Daily]   *USC mfm Jan 1954-Dec 1973.*

KUANG MING JIH PAO [Brilliant Daily]   *USC mfm Jan 1954-Dec 1973.*

SHANGHAI

SHEN PAO   *USC [reprint] 1872-1887.*

CUBA

HAVANA

GRANMA   [English edition] *USC mfm Feb 20, 1966-Dec 1975.*

TIMES OF HAVANA   *USC mfm Feb 4, 1957-Nov 3, 1960.*

ENGLAND

The microfilm files at the Thomas Cooper Library, University of South Carolina, Columbia, include 1207 reels of early English newspapers--the Burney Collection of the British Museum and the Nicholls Collection of the Bodleian Library at Oxford University. A guide to these newspapers, dating from 1603 to 1818, is available at that library.

BATH

BATH JOURNAL   *Winthrop mfm ((1772-1775)).*

BRISTOL

FELIX FARLEY'S BRISTOL JOURNAL   *USC mfm Apr 1752-1800.*

LEEDS

YORKSHIRE POST   *USC mfm Nov 1879-May 1940.*

YORKSHIRE WEEKLY POST   *USC mfm Jan 1883-Dec 1896.*

LONDON

DAILY CHRONICLE   *USC mfm Aug 1-Nov 30, 1918.*

DAILY CITIZEN   *USC mfm Oct 1913-Mar 1915.*

DAILY EXPRESS   *USC mfm Apr 1900-Dec 1974.*

DAILY HERALD   *USC mfm Jan 1911-Sep 1964.*

DAILY NEWS   *USC mfm Sep 2-Dec 31, 1918.*

DAILY TELEGRAPH AND MORNING POST   *USC mfm Jun 1855-1964, 1973-1975, Dec 1978-Nov 1979.*

GAZETTEER AND LONDON DAILY ADVERTISER   *USC mfm Nov 1763-Apr 1764.*

GAZETTEER AND NEW DAILY ADVERTISER   *SCL mfm Apr-May 1768; USC mfm ((Apr 1764-Dec 1787)), files virtually complete.*

LONDON GAZETTE   *Benedict mfm 1774-1784; USC mfm ((Nov 1665-1800)), files virtually complete.*

LLOYD'S EVENING POST   *CLS Jan 30-Sep 1, 1800.*

LONDON CHRONICLE   *CLS Mar 11-13, 1766.*

OBSERVER   *USC mfm Jan 1967-Dec 1975.*

PALL MALL GAZETTE   *USC mfm Feb 1865-1923.*

POOR MAN'S GUARDIAN   *USC [reprint] Jul 1831-Dec 1835.*

ST. JAMES CHRONICLE AND LONDON EVENING POST   *CLS Jan 23, 1812.*

SUNDAY TIMES   *Clemson mfm 1980 + ; USC mfm 1965-1983; USC-Coastal mfm 1859-1875, 1914-1919, 1939-1949, 1973 + ; Winthrop mfm Nov 1822 + .*

TIMES   *Clemson, USC and Winthrop mfm 1785 + ; College of Charleston mfm 1788 + ; Converse mfm 1974, 1981 + ; Francis Marion mfm 1786 + ; Furman mfm 1785-1820; Richland CL mfm 1974-1983; USC-Coastal mfm 1861-1865, 1914-1919, 1939-1949, 1973 + ; Wofford mfm 1785-1890. Note: Paper suspended publication Dec 1978-Nov 1979. Files of the <u>Daily Telegraph</u> for those months are substituted on mfm and included in index.*

WESTMINSTER GAZETTE   *USC mfm Jan 1893-Jan 1928.*

MANCHESTER

MANCHESTER GUARDIAN   *USC mfm May 1821 + .*

MANCHESTER GUARDIAN WEEKLY *Richland CL mfm 1978-1982; USC Jan 1948-Dec 1965, mfm Sep 1919-Dec 1948, Jan 1959-1964, 1966 + ; Winthrop mfm 1959-1980; Wofford mfm 1959-1980.*

MANCHESTER MERCURY *Wofford mfm 1752-1830.*

FRANCE

PARIS

CHICAGO TRIBUNE [Paris edition] *USC mfm Jul 1917-Nov 1934.*

COURRIER EXTRAORDINAIRE; OU LE PREMIER ARRIVE *Winthrop mfm Mar 3, 1790-Aug 11, 1792.*

LE FIGARO *Clemson mfm 1979-1983; USC mfm Jan 1971-Dec 1975.*

GOLOS *USC mfm Sep 1914-Jan 1915.*

LE MONDE *USC mfm Dec 1944 + .*

LE MONDE DIPLOMATIQUE *USC mfm May 1954 + .*

NACHALO *USC mfm Sep 1916-Mar 1917.*

NASHE SLOVO *USC mfm Jan 1915-Sep 1916.*

NOVAIA EPOKA *USC mfm (Apr 5-May 3, 1917) 15.*

NEW YORK HERALD-TRIBUNE [European edition] *USC mfm 1920-Jun 1940.*

GERMANY

BERLIN

DER ANGRIFF *USC mfm Jul 4, 1927-Feb 3, 1932.*

DEUTSCHE KOLONIALZEITUNG *USC mfm 1884-1922.*

FRANKFURT

FRANKFURTER ALLGEMEINE, ZEITUNG FUR DEUTSCHLAND
USC mfm Jun 1953-Jan 1981.

FRANKFURTER ZEITUNG   *USC mfm Jul 24, 1914-Aug 14, 1920.*

HAMBURG

DIE WELT   *USC mfm Jan 1970-Jul 1975.*

DIE ZEIT   *USC mfm Nov 1972 + .*

MUNICH

VOLKISCHER BEOBACHTER   *USC mfm Jan 3, 1920-Nov 9, 1923, Feb 26, 1925-Dec 31, 1933, Jul 1, 1933-Apr 14, 1944.*

IRELAND

DUBLIN

IRISH INDEPENDENT   *USC mfm Dec 1891-Dec 1913, Jan-Sep 1915, Jan 1916-Dec 1976.*

IRISH TIMES   *USC mfm Jan 1916-Dec 1945.*

JAPAN

OSAKA

MAINICHI DAILY NEWS   *Furman mfm 1979.*

TOKYO

JAPAN TIMES AND ADVERTISER   *Winthrop mfm 1941-1982.*

MEXICO

MEXICO CITY

EXCELSIOR   *USC mfm Jan 1965-Dec 1973.*

RHODESIA [Zimbabwe]

SALISBURY [Harare]

AFRICAN WEEKLY   *USC mfm Sep 1952-Jan 24, 1962.*

BANTU MIRROR   *USC mfm Mar 1952-Jan 1962.*

CENTRAL AFRICAN EXAMINER   *USC mfm ((Jun 1957-Dec 1965)), files virtually complete.*

DAILY NEWS   *USC mfm Feb 1962-Aug 1964.*

RUSSIA

The microfilm files at the Thomas Cooper Library, University of South Carolina, Columbia, include 76 reels of Menshevik newspapers, periodicals, pamphlets, and books produced by the Hoover Institution at Stanford University. A guide to these materials is available at that library.

LENINGRAD

VECHERNIAIA ZVEZDA   *USC mfm Feb-May 1918.*

VOLIA NARODA   *USC mfm ((May 7, 1917-May 5, 1918)).*

MOSCOW

IZVESTIIA   *USC mfm Jan 1958-Dec 1980.*

MOSCOW NEWS   [English] *USC mfm Jan 1961-Dec 1985.*

Antiquarian Society, Center for Research Libraries, Kansas State Historical Society, New York Historical Society, New York State Library, Rutgers University, State Historical Society of Wisconsin, and Western Reserve Historical Society.

Watson, Harry L. "Early Newspapers of Abbeville District, 1812-1834," Proceedings, South Carolina Historical Association (1940), pp. 18-35.

Wescott, Mary, and Allene Ramage (Compilers). A Checklist of United States Newspapers (and Weeklies Before 1900) in the General Library [Duke University]. Durham, N. C., 1937.

West, James L. "Early Backwoods Humor in the Greenville Mountaineer, 1826-1840," Mississippi Quarterly (Winter, 1971), pp. 69-82.

Winship, George Parker. "French Newspapers in the United States from 1790 to 1800," Papers of the Bibliographical Society of America XIV (1920), part 2, pp. 82-147.

Woody, Robert H. Republican Newspapers of South Carolina. Charlottesville, Va., 1936.

Zarif, Gladys Echols. "The Development of a Contemporary Black Newspaper: The Charleston Chronicle Newspaper of Charleston, South Carolina." M. A. thesis, University of South Carolina, 1986.

INDEX TO NEWSPAPERS PUBLISHED IN

SOUTH CAROLINA

U P D A T E: microforms received, files revised